The Norton Sampler

Third Edition

W. W. NORTON & COMPANY, INC.
also publishes

THE NORTON ANTHOLOGY OF AMERICAN LITERATURE
edited by Ronald Gottesman et al.

THE NORTON ANTHOLOGY OF ENGLISH LITERATURE
edited by M. H. Abrams et al.

THE NORTON ANTHOLOGY OF MODERN POETRY
edited by Richard Ellmann and Robert O'Clair

THE NORTON ANTHOLOGY OF POETRY
edited by Arthur M. Eastman et al.

THE NORTON ANTHOLOGY OF SHORT FICTION
edited by R. V. Cassill

THE NORTON ANTHOLOGY OF WORLD MASTERPIECES
edited by Maynard Mack et al.

THE NORTON FACSIMILE OF
THE FIRST FOLIO OF SHAKESPEARE
prepared by Charlton Hinman

THE NORTON INTRODUCTION TO LITERATURE
edited by Carl E. Bain, Jerome Beaty, and J. Paul Hunter

THE NORTON READER
edited by Arthur M. Eastman et al.

and the
NORTON CRITICAL EDITIONS

The Norton Sampler

Short Essays
for Composition

Third Edition

Thomas Cooley

The Ohio State University

W · W · NORTON & COMPANY
New York · London

Printed in the United States of America.

Third Edition

Library of Congress Cataloging in Publication Data
Main entry under title:
The Norton Sampler.
    1. College readers.   2. Essays.   3. English
language—Rhetoric.   I. Cooley, Thomas, 1942–
PE1417.N6   1985   808′.0427   84–18912

ISBN 0-393-95412-9

W. W. Norton & Company, Inc., 500 Fifth Avenue,
New York, N.Y. 10110
W. W. Norton & Company Ltd., 37 Great Russell Street,
London WC1B 3NU

   5 6 7 8 9 0

William Allen: "How to Set a World Record" used by permission of the author. The article first appeared in the
   Columbus Dispatch, December 23, 1973.
Isaac Asimov: "What Do you Call a Platypus?" Copyright 1971 by the National Wildlife Federation. Reprinted from
   the March-April issue of *National Wildlife Magazine* with the permission of Dr. Isaac Asimov.
Russell Baker: "A Nice Place to Visit." Copyright 1980 by The New York Times Company. Reprinted by permission.
Afton Blake: "First Word" from *Omni* magazine, August 1983. Copyright 1983 by Omni Publications International,
   Ltd. and reprinted by permission.
Bruce Catton: "Grant and Lee: A Study in Contrasts," from *The American Story*, edited by Earl Schenck Miers.
   Copyright © 1956 by Broadcast Music, Inc. Used by permission of the copyright holder.
Paul Colinvaux: "Japan" from *The Fate of Nations* (New York, Simon & Schuster, Inc., 1980). Copyright © 1980
   by Paul Colinvaux. Reprinted by permission of Simon & Schuster, Inc.
Joan Didion: "On Going Home" from *Slouching towards Bethlehem* (New York, Farrar Straus & Giroux, 1967, 1968).
   Copyright © 1967, 1968 by Joan Didion. Reprinted by permission of Farrar Straus & Giroux, Inc.
Annie Dillard: pages 12–19 from *Holy the Firm*. Copyright © 1977 by Annie Dillard. Reprinted by permission of
   Harper & Row, Publishers, Inc. "How I Wrote the Moth Essay—and Why" and journal selections containing
   earlier versions of "Transfiguration" [editor's title] reprinted by permission of the author and her agent Blanche
   C. Gregory, Inc. Copyright © 1985 by Annie Dillard.
David E. Dubber: "Crossing the Bar on a Fiberglas Pole" courtesy of David E. Dubber.
Loren Eiseley: From "The Angry Winter" in *The Unexpected Universe*, copyright © 1968 by Loren Eiseley.
   Reprinted by permission of Harcourt Brace Jovanovich, Inc.
Ellen Goodman: "The Just-Right Wife" © 1984 The Boston Globe Newspaper Company/Washington Post Writers
   Group. Reprinted with permission.

Contents

Exposition   61

2. Essays That Classify and Divide   63

('Theria' or just 'beasts') are all the other 4,231 known
living species of mammals."

3. Essays That Analyze a Process   97

"Though one would expect innovation from the
undisputed leader in the field of garbage, New York is
forced to dispose of its trash in ways familiar to every
small town in the country. . . ."

"Meanwhile the wasp, having satisfied itself that the victim
is of the right species, moves off a few inches to dig the
spider's grave. . . . Now and again the wasp pops out of the
hole to make sure that the spider is still there."

"My own gift—broom balancing—was developed in my
back yard when I was a child. When I remembered the
unusual ability, I immediately wrote the editors of the
Guinness book in London. . . ."

"Spit should be blown, not ptuied weakly with the lips,
which often results in dribble. Spitting should convey
forcefulness of purpose, concentration, pride. Spit down,
not in the direction of others. Spit in the glove and on
the fingers, especially after making a real knucklehead
play. . . ."

4. Essays That Analyze Cause and Effect 137

"But not everybody is aware that high cost and easy comfort
are merely two of the effects of the vast cooling of America.
In fact, air conditioning has substantially altered the
country's character and folkways."

"High school permanently damaged my self-esteem. I
learned what it meant to be impotent; what is meant to
be invisible. None of this improved my character, spurred
my ambition, or gave me a deeper understanding of life."

"In Iran, I was an American citizen and considered myself
an American, even though my father was Iranian. I loved
baseball and apple pie and knew the words to the
'Star-Spangled Banner.' . . . I did not realize my life
would be affected until I read that bumper sticker in the
high school parking lot which read, 'Piss on Iran.' "

"Then the United States did two things for Japan. They
placed an embargo on the sale of oil needed to sustain
Japanese armies, and they put all American warships into one
handy disposable package in a harbor in Hawaii."

5. Essays That Define 169

"Imagine, if you will, a time warp that could put you face
to face with a medieval Christian serf."

"People feel safer behind some kind of physical barrier. If
a social situation is in any way threatening, then there is
an immediate urge to set up such a barricade."

Contents

Persuasion and Argumentation

9. Essays That Appeal to Reason

10. Essays That Appeal to Emotion and Ethics   335

Essays for Further Reading

"*I have been assured by a very knowing American of my
acquaintance in London, that a young healthy child well
nursed is at a year old a most delicious, nourishing, and
wholesome food, whether stewed, roasted, baked, or
boiled. . . .*"

"*I felt the same damp moss covering the worms in the bait
can, and saw the dragonfly alight on the tip of my rod. . . .
It was the arrival of this fly that convinced me beyond any
doubt that everything was as it always had been, that the
years were a mirage and that there had been no years.*"

"*Political language—and with variations this is true of all
political parties, from Conservatives to Anarchists—is
designed to make lies sound truthful and murder respectable,
and to give an appearance of solidity to pure wind. One can
not change this all in a moment, but one can at least change
one's own habits. . . .*"

"*The question of whether or not you could go home again
was a very real part of the sentimental and largely literary
baggage with which we left home in the fifties; I suspect that
it is irrelevant to the children born of the fragmentation
after World War II.*"

Preface

When the second edition of the *Sampler* appeared a few years ago, the editor's *Preface* remarked that revisions were "extensive." With the third edition, I have a deeper understanding of that word. The new essays are here: about a dozen of them, including one of the prizewinners from a national student competition. As always, my first concern has been to find well-written essays that illustrate standard rhetorical strategies and that appeal to students with diverse backgrounds and interests. As always, the essays, new and returning, are published without omissions.

The main revisions, intended to keep the *Sampler* abreast of innovations in the classroom and the journals, however, have to do with the writing *process*. In preparing the new edition, I contacted most of the writers whose work appears in the following pages and asked them how they did it. A surprisingly large number, including E. B. White, Russell Baker, Isaac Asimov, Ellen Goodman, and Annie Dillard, generously responded, and their comments are here.

At first, Annie Dillard, Pulitzer Prize-winning poet and essayist, consented to an interview on the process of writing "Transfiguration," the most admired essay by a living writer in the collection, according to questionnaires returned by teachers who use the book. To the editor's delight, she then agreed to write a full-scale essay instead. Based on the author's journals, notes, and earlier drafts of her essay on the death of a moth, this original work appears in an introductory section new to the third edition, "The Writing Process."

Subsequent chapters incorporate the wealth of information supplied by other writers who graciously responded to the editor's appeal. In addition to the essays and study questions of previous editions, you will now find at the end of each chapter a section called "Writers on the Writing Process." In interviews, letters, notes, and miniessays, the writers themselves explain how specific pieces in the collection were composed and, in general, how and why they write.

It was Edgar Allan Poe who said that a long poem does not exist. As editor of these readings for composition, I have kept in mind the unity of effect that Poe taught us to value. Most of the essays in this collection, therefore, are only two to four pages long, and even the longest can be easily read at a single sitting.

It is misleading to talk about unity, however, when one is dealing with a fragment. How do we tell our students about beginnings, middles, and ends or about an author's shapely rhetoric when the shape is actually an editor's? (I have found that even "classics" such as Alexander Petrunkevitch's "The Spider and the Wasp" are routinely reprinted with amputations.) It is the rhetoric of the short piece that our students are learning in beginning composition classes, and such pieces have their own unique rules of order. Thus I have taken pains to gather *complete* essays or, in a few cases (indicated in the headnotes), *complete* chapters of books.

The organization of the *Sampler* remains essentially the same, though it represents but one way of proceeding, hardly the only way. The new introductory chapter exposes the student to the writing process as a whole. The rest of the book is organized by the traditional modes of discourse. Narration comes first because these are personal narratives and many teachers like to begin a course by having students write about their own experience.

The next six chapters, the bulk of the book, illustrate strategies of exposition and can be taken up in any order, though here the plan has been to build from the simple (as I perceive it) to the more complex. For example: Chapter 5 ("Essays That Define") presents extended definitions that draw upon the techniques of classification and analysis discussed earlier.

Description is treated in a single chapter (Chapter 8) because this mode is seldom isolated from the others in practice; the teacher who requires more examples will find them throughout the collection. Chapters 9 and 10 are devoted to persuasion and argumentation, and they observe the classical division of persuasion into *logos, pathos,* and *ethos* (although I have not burdened the student with these terms). Some teachers will want to start here.

The questions after each selection are intended to help students understand what they are reading and especially to aid them in analyzing standard rhetorical strategies and techniques. The comparative questions—which invite students to make connections between essays—are an innovation; and so is the inclusion of student essays in full parity with those of the professionals. The "Essays for Further Reading" are more complicated, and generally longer, than the rest; but they too have been selected from a wide range of subjects.

Many people have had a hand in this third edition of the *Sampler,* and the editor wishes to thank them here: Barry Wade, Theresa Reid, Lucienne Thys, and Victoria Thys have devoted many hours to this book. The following colleagues, students, and friends at Ohio State have also been most helpful: William Allen, Richard D. Altick, Daniel R. Barnes, Toni Bates, Morris Beja, Phillip Carroll, Ellen Carter, Edward P. J. Corbett, David O. Frantz, Paul Fullmer, John B. Gabel, Kim Gainer, Sara Garnes, Susan Helgeson, Frank O'Hare, Barbara Rigney, Arnold Shapiro, Frances Shapiro, Charles Wheeler, and Christian K. Zacher.

For the criticism and encouragement that guided me in the initial stages of writing, I wish to thank the following at other places: Judith Barnet, Cape Cod Community College; Richard Benston, Bakersfield College; Harry Brent, Rutgers University—Camden College of Arts and Sciences; Lois Bueler, Winona State University; Larry Carver, the University of Texas at Austin; John Cope, Western State College of Colorado; Charles B. Dodson, University of North Carolina at Wilmington; Betty Flowers, the University of Texas at Austin; Ramsey Fowler, Memphis State University; Barbara Goff, Rutgers University—Cook College; David Goslee, the University of Tennessee; William Gracie, Miami University; Joan Hartman, the College of Staten Island; Robert W. Hill, Clemson University; John Huxhold, Meramec Community College; Bernetta Jackson, Washington University; H. Gerald Joiner, Clayton Junior College; Russ Larson, Eastern Michigan University; Kristin Lauer, Fordham University; James MacKillop, Onondaga Community College; Catharine McCue, Framingham State College; John Mellon, University of Illinois at Chicago Circle; Tom Miles, West

Virginia University; Robin Mitchell, Marquette University; James Murphy, California State University—Hayward; Elizabeth Penfield, University of New Orleans; Richard Poulsen, Brigham Young University; Kenn Sherwood Roe, Shasta College; Charles Schuster, the University of Iowa; Jayana Sheth, Baruch College; Susan Shreve, George Mason University; Lynne Shuster, Erie Community College; Donald Smith, University of New Haven; Tori Haring Smith, University of Illinois at Urbana-Champaign; Craig Snow, the University of Arizona; William Tucker, the University of North Carolina at Greensboro; John L. Vifian, Central Washington State College; and J. Peter Williams, County College of Morris.

Introduction

Suppose that you went on a strenuous camping trip in the mountains, while all your friends decided to relax at the seashore. Suppose, also, that you got bored after two days without company and that you composed a letter inviting your best friend to forsake the surf and join you on the rocks. Your letter might contain the following elements:

— the story of your time on the road, your arrival in camp, and the events of the first two days, including an account of the skunk that got into your provisions;
— directions for getting there and a list of equipment, food, and clothes to bring;
— a description of your campsite, the yellow tent, the beautiful blue valley in the distance, and the crystal lake nearby;
— all the reasons why your friend should join you and why the mountains are preferable to the shore.

The four parts of your letter would conform to the four traditional MODES [1] (or "means") of writing: NARRATION, EXPOSITION, DESCRIPTION, and PERSUASION. The first part would be in the narrative mode. Narration is writing that tells a story; it records events, actions, adventures. It tells, in short, what happened. The part of your letter that gives directions is exposition. This is informative writing, or writing that explains. In this book, exposition receives more attention than the other modes because it is the one you are likely to use most often in the years to come. Examinations, term papers, insurance claims, job and graduate school applications, sales reports, almost every scrap of practical

---

[1] Terms printed in all capitals are defined in the Glossary.

prose you write over a lifetime, including your last will and testament, will demand expository skills.

The third part of your letter, of course, is description. This is the mode that captures how a person, thing, place, or idea looks, feels, sounds, or otherwise impresses the senses or the mind. The last part of your letter, the part designed to convince your friend to join you, is in the persuasive mode. Persuasion is writing that seeks assent, conveys advice, or moves the reader to action. In a sense, all writing is persuasion because the writer must convince the reader that what he or she says deserves to be heeded.

As our hypothetical letter to a friend suggests, the four modes of writing seldom appear in "pure" states. An accomplished writer is not likely to say, "Well I shall produce an expository definition today." The mode (or means) that a writer chooses will vary with his or her purpose (as in our letter). A writer may set out to define something and end up describing it or telling the story of its invention. Writers often mix the modes in actual practice, and you will find more than one essay in this collection that could be placed under a different heading.

Nevertheless, a single mode often dominates the others in any given essay. Furthermore, composing themes that largely narrate, explain, describe, or persuade is a valuable exercise toward learning to write well; and so is concentrating on a single strategy within a mode. A good piece of exposition, for example, may follow several methods of development; but before learning to combine, say, PROCESS ANALYSIS with DEFINITION it is useful to study each of these strategies independently. Therefore, the modes and strategies of writing have been separated in this book.

The narrative mode is exemplified in Chapter 1 ("Essays in the First Person Singular"). The next six chapters (2–7) give examples of the common strategies of exposition: CLASSIFICATION, PROCESS ANALYSIS, CAUSE AND EFFECT, DEFINITION, COMPARISON AND CONTRAST, METAPHOR AND ANALOGY. Chapter 8 ("Essays That Appeal to the Senses") is a collection of descriptive writing. Chapter 9 ("Essays That Appeal to Reason") and Chapter 10 ("Essays That Appeal to Emotion and Ethics") present examples of the different strategies of persuasion. At the end of the book you will find a collection of "Essays for Further Reading."

No one expects you to imitate word for word these highly finished productions of professional writers (though you may well emulate some of the student writing included here). But you can analyze standard rhetorical devices and techniques and so learn to use them in your own writing.

By RHETORIC, as the term will be applied in these pages, we mean "the art of using language effectively"—both in writing and in reading. A skilled writer is usually a skilled reader, in fact. The patterns of words on the written page (and of the sounds those words stand for) lodge themselves in the reader's head. When the writer puts pen to paper, therefore, he or she has a store of patterns to impose upon his or her own black marks. A writer learns some patterns of language by hearing them used orally. But others—such as the printed alphabet—can only be learned by reading.

The purpose of this collection of readings, then, is that set forth by Mark Twain in "The Art of Authorship." Attempting to analyze his own methods of composition, Twain found that "whenever we read a sentence and like it, we unconsciously store it away in our model-chamber; and it goes with a myriad of its fellows to the building, brick, by brick, of the eventual edifice which we call our style. And let us guess that whenever we run across other forms—bricks—whose color, or some other defect, offends us, we unconsciously reject these, and so one never finds them in our edifice."

This is a book of prose forms. Each essay offers proven rhetorical designs that you can store away in your "model-chamber," ready at hand whenever you have a verbal edifice to construct. Such a collection provides this further advantage over reading at random: the defective bricks have already been discarded for you.

The Writing Process

WRITING is a little like baking bread. Before you can serve it, you must go through a busy process of sifting and blending. In the chapters to follow, you will get a taste of both the baking and the loaf. Essays by professional and student writers are accompanied in this collection by study questions asking you to probe their work. Many of these questions, you will notice, are about the finished product of the writer's labor, but many others address the process behind it. You will also find comments on the writing process by the writers themselves as they respond to inquiries from the editor about their methods.

Many professional writers learn the art of authorship as Mark Twain did—"unconsciously." Some writers, however, especially if they are also teachers of writing, can speak of their methods with a clarity that lifts the veil for us. One of these is the poet and essayist Annie Dillard, winner of the Pulitzer Prize for her prose narrative Pilgrim at Tinker Creek.

Referring to essays you will encounter later in this book, Dillard writes: "Richard Selzer's 'The Discus Thrower' evokes about as much feeling as any essay you can find, but it never describes any feeling whatever. The same is true for the famous ending of E. B. White's 'Once More to the Lake'; he creates a sense of mortality without mentioning it. [E. B. White comments on that famous ending in "Essays for Further Reading."] Hemingway, I believe, taught us all this particular form of excellence; it distinguishes modern writing. All readers are sophisticated enough to grasp it—but not all writers are conscious enough to have noticed it: don't describe emotions!"

Evoking feelings instead of describing them is a key strategy in Dillard's own "Transfiguration," an essay about the writer's calling reprinted in the following pages. In an effort to "de-

5

mystify" (her word) the writing process for you, Annie Dillard has written a new essay explaining how she composed it. Going back to the author's notebooks and earliest recollections of the death of a moth, this new essay about writing traces the composition of the earlier piece from its inception through revisions made after it had already appeared in print.

Once you have read "Transfiguration," but before you go on to "How I Wrote the Moth Essay—and Why," take a look at the questions in between. Typical of the study questions following all the essays in this collection, they will help you to understand the work Dillard is analyzing. Then turn to the author's comments on the process of writing it. Later, if you want more examples of essays built upon METAPHOR and ANALOGY,[1] you can read Chapter 7. Or, for an essay that treats the same natural object in a different light, you might try Virginia Woolf's classic, "The Death of the Moth," in Chapter 8.

[1] Terms printed in all capitals are defined in the Glossary.

Annie Dillard

Transfiguration

Annie Dillard was born in Pittsburgh in 1945. She attended private school there and, later, Hollins College in Roanoke, Virginia, from which she received a master's degree in English literature in 1968. She lived in the Roanoke Valley from 1965 to 1975, when she moved to Puget Sound. In 1979, she returned to the East Coast, where she now lives with husband Gary Clevidence and baby Rosie in Connecticut and on Cape Cod. Dillard has written a book of poems, Tickets for a Prayer Wheel (1974); a prose narrative, Pilgrim at Tinker Creek (1974), which won a Pulitzer Prize; a short prose narrative, Holy the Firm (1982), from which "Transfiguration" (editor's title) is taken; a book of literary theory, Living by Fiction (1982); and a collection of narrative essays, Teaching a Stone to Talk (1982); and recently Encounters with Chinese Writers. "Transfiguration" originally appeared in a somewhat different version in Harper's under the title "The Death of a Moth."

I live on northern Puget Sound, in Washington State, alone.   1
I have a gold cat, who sleeps on my legs, named Small. In the morning I joke to her blank face, Do you remember last night? Do you remember? I throw her out before breakfast, so I can eat.

There is a spider, too, in the bathroom, with whom I keep   2
a sort of company. Her little outfit always reminds me of a certain moth I helped to kill. The spider herself is of uncertain lineage, bulbous at the abdomen and drab. Her six-inch mess of a web works, works somehow, works miraculously, to keep her alive and me amazed. The web itself is in a corner behind the toilet, connecting tile wall to tile wall and floor, in a place where there is, I would have thought, scant traffic. Yet under the web are sixteen or so corpses she has tossed to the floor.

The corpses appear to be mostly sow bugs, those little   3

armadillo creatures who live to travel flat out in houses, and die round. There is also a new shred of earwig, three old spider skins crinkled and clenched, and two moth bodies, wingless and huge and empty, moth bodies I drop to my knees to see.

Today the earwig shines darkly and gleams, what there is of   4 him: a dorsal curve of thorax and abdomen, and a smooth pair of cerci [1] by which I knew his name. Next week, if the other bodies are any indication, he will be shrunken and gray, webbed to the floor with dust. The sow bugs beside him are hollow and empty of color, fragile, a breath away from brittle fluff. The spider skins lie on their sides, translucent and ragged, their legs drying in knots. And the moths, the empty moths, stagger against each other, headless, in a confusion of arching strips of chitin like peeling varnish, like a jumble of buttresses for cathedral domes, like nothing resembling moths, so that I should hesitate to call them moths, except that I have had some experience with the figure Moth reduced to a nub.

Two summers ago I was camping alone in the Blue Ridge   5 Mountains in Virginia. I had hauled myself and gear up there to read, among other things, James Ramsey Ullman's *The Day on Fire*, a novel about Rimbaud that had made me want to be a writer when I was sixteen; [2] I was hoping it would do it again. So I read, lost, every day sitting under a tree by my tent, while warblers swung in the leaves overhead and bristle worms trailed their inches over the twiggy dirt at my feet; and I read every night by candlelight, while barred owls called in the forest and pale moths massed round my head in the clearing, where my light made a ring.

Moths kept flying into the candle. They would hiss and recoil,   6 lost upside down in the shadows among my cooking pans. Or they would singe their wings and fall, and their hot wings, as if melted, would stick to the first thing they touched—a pan, a lid, a spoon— so that the snagged moths could flutter only in tiny arcs, unable to struggle free. These I could release by a quick flip with a stick; in the morning I would find my cooking stuff gilded with torn flecks

[1] Plural of *cercus*, posterior "feeler" of an insect.
[2] French poet Arthur Rimbaud (1854–1891) himself began writing at age sixteen and produced his major work before he was twenty. Ullman's novel was published in 1958.

of moth wings, triangles of shiny dust here and there on the aluminum. So I read, and boiled water, and replenished candles, and read on.

One night a moth flew into the candle, was caught, burnt dry, [7] and held. I must have been staring at the candle, or maybe I looked up when a shadow crossed my page; at any rate, I saw it all. A golden female moth, a biggish one with a two-inch wingspan, flapped into the fire, dropped her abdomen into the wet wax, stuck, flamed, frazzled and fried in a second. Her moving wings ignited like tissue paper, enlarging the circle of light in the clearing and creating out of the darkness the sudden blue sleeves of my sweater, the green leaves of jewelweed by my side, the ragged red trunk of a pine. At once the light contracted again and the moth's wings vanished in a fine, foul smoke. At the same time her six legs clawed, curled, blackened, and ceased, disappearing utterly. And her head jerked in spasms, making a spattering noise; her antennae crisped and burned away and her heaving mouth parts crackled like pistol fire. When it was all over, her head was, so far as I could determine, gone, gone the long way of her wings and legs. Had she been new, or old? Had she mated and laid her eggs, had she done her work? All that was left was the glowing horn shell of her abdomen and thorax—a fraying, partially collapsed gold tube jammed upright in the candle's round pool.

And then this moth-essence, this spectacular skeleton, began to [8] act as a wick. She kept burning. The wax rose in the moth's body from her soaking abdomen to her thorax to the jagged hole where her head should be, and widened into flame, a saffron-yellow flame that robed her to the ground like any immolating monk. That candle had two wicks, two flames of identical height, side by side. The moth's head was fire. She burned for two hours, until I blew her out.

She burned for two hours without changing, without bending [9] or leaning—only glowing within, like a building fire glimpsed through silhouetted walls, like a hollow saint, like a flame-faced virgin gone to God, while I read by her light, kindled, while Rimbaud in Paris burnt out his brains in a thousand poems, while night pooled wetly at my feet.

And that is why I believe those hollow crisps on the bathroom [10] floor are moths. I think I know moths, and fragments of moths, and chips and tatters of utterly empty moths, in any state. How many of you, I asked the people in my class, which of you want to give your lives and be writers? I was trembling from coffee, or cigarettes, or the closeness of faces all around me. (Is this what we live for? I thought; is this the only final beauty: the color of any skin in any light, and living, human eyes?) All hands rose to the question. (You, Nick? Will you? Margaret? Randy? Why do I want them to mean it?) And then I tried to tell them what the choice must mean: you can't be anything else. You must go at your life with a broadax. . . . They had no idea what I was saying. (I have two hands, don't I? And all this energy, for as long as I can remember. I'll do it in the evenings, after skiing, or on the way home from the bank, or after the children are asleep. . . .) They thought I was raving again. It's just as well.

I have three candles here on the table which I disentangle from   11
the plants and light when visitors come. Small usually avoids them, although once she came too close and her tail caught fire; I rubbed it out before she noticed. The flames move light over everyone's skin, draw light to the surface of the faces of my friends. When the people leave I never blow the candles out, and after I'm asleep they flame and burn.

QUESTIONS

Understanding

1. What is the most important ANALOGY in Dillard's essay? What is she comparing to what?

2. What is Dillard referring to in paragraph 10 when she says, "I'll do it in the evening, after skiing, or on the way home from the bank . . ."?

3. At what cost does Dillard seem to think the writer does her (or his) work?

4. When Dillard draws an analogy between the moth and an "immolating monk" (par. 8) or a "flame-faced virgin" (par. 9), she gets beyond the realm of merely natural phenomena. Into what?

5. What is "miraculous" about the spider's web in paragraph 2? Of

all nature as Dillard sees it? What miracle does she celebrate throughout the essay?

6. Why does Dillard refer to the corpses of the moths beneath the spider web in her bathroom?

7. What kind of beauty does Dillard have in mind when she refers to "the color of any skin in any light, and living, human eyes" (par. 10)?

8. What is the significance of the book Dillard is reading when the moth burns?

Strategies and Structure

1. When did you first realize that Dillard's essay draws an extended analogy between the writer and the moth? How does she introduce the comparison without saying flatly, "The writer is like . . ."?

2. How does Dillard's main analogy help to explain the kind of beauty the writer seeks? Her (or his) dedication to her art?

3. How does Dillard's main analogy convey her own sense of awe and wonder at the sacredness of the writer's calling?

4. What analogy is Dillard drawing in the line, "You must go at your life with a broadax . . ." (par. 10)?

5. What is the effect of Dillard's calling the moth "she" instead of "it"? Of Dillard's wondering whether the moth has finished her earthly work (par. 7)?

6. How effective do you find the specific details of the DESCRIPTION in paragraph 3? Explain your answer.

7. How does Dillard give the impression of seeing her world intently, as if through a magnifying glass?

8. In paragraph 9, moth and candle seem almost to be holding the night at bay. How does Dillard create this impression? How does she get across to us the sudden flare of the moth as it first hits the flame?

9. Dillard's analogies are developed through a personal NARRATIVE of the sort exemplified in Chapter 1. Which parts of her narrative are set in the present (the time at which she writes)? Where is she located physically in the present time?

10. In what *two* places is the past action of Dillard's narrative located? When does she return to the present?

11. How does Dillard achieve a welcome comic relief in paragraph 11?

Words and Figures of Speech

1. What is the effect of Dillard's including "like a jumble of buttresses for cathedral domes" in the list of SIMILES at the end of paragraph 4?
2. Look up *transfiguration* in your dictionary. What does it mean in religious terms? How does it apply to Dillard's essay?
3. Why do you think Dillard uses such technical terms as *thorax*, *cerci*, and *chitin* (par. 4)?
4. How effective do you find the phrase "scant traffic" in paragraph 2? What is the effect of the word *raving* in paragraph 10?
5. Why does Dillard capitalize *Moth* in paragraph 4?
6. Consult your dictionary as necessary for the following words: *lineage* (par. 2), *bulbous* (2), *dorsal* (4), *thorax* (4), *translucent* (4), *chitin* (4), *buttresses* (4), *gilded* (6), *replenished* (6), *essence* (8), *immolating* (8).

Comparing

1. Which of the insects described in Lewis Thomas's "On Societies as Organisms" (Chapter 7) most closely resembles Dillard's burning moth?
2. In a sense, Dillard's account of the death of a moth and Virginia Woolf's account of the same phenomenon (Chapter 8) come to opposite conclusions. What are those conclusions? Explain the contrast.

Annie Dillard

How I Wrote the Moth Essay—and Why

Annie Dillard's essay on the death of a moth, reprinted in the preceding pages, is the kind of work that makes the reader itch to interrogate the absent author. Or burn, in this case. If only we could go to the source for an authoritative answer to a fundamental question: How was it done? In particular, the editor wanted to know from the author: When did you first think of comparing the writer to a burning moth? You mention Rimbaud and the moths, but when and how did it occur to you to put the two together? How did you come to the idea of writing as burning, a consuming and purifying act? Do you still define writing and the writer that way? How much revising did you do in this essay? In the book from which it is taken? Could you describe any struggle you recall with particular words, phrases, or images? What kind of audience did you have in mind? Why did you write the piece? Why do you write? What advice would you give to beginners? Annie Dillard's generous reply to these and many other questions about the process of composing the essay you have just read was "How I Wrote the Moth Essay—and Why," an essay on an essay. It appears here for the first time in print.

It was November 1975. I was living alone, as described, on an island in Puget Sound, near the Canadian border. I was thirty years old. I thought about myself a lot (for someone thirty years old), because I couldn't figure out what I was doing there. What was my life about? Why was I living alone, when I am gregarious? Would I ever meet someone, or should I reconcile myself to all this solitude? I disliked celibacy; I dreaded childlessness. I couldn't even think of anything to write. I was examining every event for possible meaning.

I was then in full flight from success, from the recent fuss over a book of prose I'd published the previous year called *Pilgrim at Tinker Creek*. There were offers from editors, publishers, and Hollywood and network producers. They tempted me with world travel, film and TV work, big bucks. I was there to turn from literary and commercial success and to rededicate myself to art and to God. That's how I justified my loneliness to myself. It was a feeble justification and I knew it, because you certainly don't need to live alone either to write or to pray. Actually I was there because I had picked the place from an atlas, and I was alone because I hadn't yet met my husband.

My reading and teaching fed my thoughts. I was reading Simone Weil, *First and Last Notebooks*. Simone Weil was a twentieth-century French intellectual, born Jewish, who wrote some of the most interesting Christian theology I've ever read. She was brilliant, but a little nuts; her doctrines were harsh. "Literally," she wrote, "it is total purity or death." This sort of fanaticism attracted and appalled me. Weil had deliberately starved herself to death to call attention to the plight of French workers. I was taking extensive notes on Weil.

In the classroom I was teaching poetry writing, exhorting myself (in the guise of exhorting my students), and convincing myself by my own rhetoric: commit yourself to a useless art! In art alone is meaning! In sacrifice alone is meaning! These, then, were issues for me at that time: dedication, purity, sacrifice.

Early that November morning I noticed the hollow insects on the bathroom floor. I got down on my hands and knees to examine them and recognized some as empty moth bodies. I recognized them, of course, only because I'd seen an empty moth body already—two years before, when I'd camped alone and had watched a flying moth get stuck in a candle and burn.

Walking back to my desk, where I had been answering letters, I realized that the burning moth was a dandy visual focus for all my recent thoughts about an empty, dedicated life. Perhaps I'd try to write a short narrative about it.

I went to my pile of journals, hoping I'd taken some nice,

specific notes about the moth in the candle. What I found disappointed me at first: that night I'd written a long description of owl sounds, and only an annoyed aside about bugs flying into the candle. But the next night, after pages of self-indulgent drivel, I'd written a fuller description, a description of the moth which got stuck in candle wax.

The journal entry had some details I could use (bristleworms on the ground, burnt moths' wings sticking to pans), some phrases (her body acted as a wick, the candle had 2 flames, the moth burned until I blew it out), and, especially, some verbs (hiss, recoil, stick, spatter, jerked, crackled).

Even in the journals, the moth was female. (From childhood reading I'd learned to distinguish moths by sex.) And, there in the journal, was a crucial detail: on that camping trip, I'd been reading about Rimbaud. Arthur Rimbaud—the French symbolist poet, a romantic, hotheaded figure who attracted me enormously when I was sixteen—had been young and self-destructive. When *he* was sixteen, he ran away from home to Paris, led a dissolute life, shot his male lover (the poet Verlaine), drank absinthe which damaged his brain, deranged his senses with drunkenness and sleeplessness, and wrote mad vivid poetry which altered the course of Western literature. When he was in his twenties, he turned his back to the Western world and vanished into Abyssinia as a gunrunner.

With my old journal beside me, I took up my current journal and scribbled and doodled my way through an account of my present life and the remembered moth. It went extraordinarily well; it was not typical. It seemed very much "given" given, I think, because I'd asked, because I'd been looking so hard and so long for connections, meanings. The connections were all there, and seemed solid enough: I saw a moth burnt and on fire; I was reading Rimbaud hoping to rededicate myself to writing (this one bald statement of motive was unavoidable); I live alone. So the writer is like the moth, and like a religious contemplative: emptying himself so he can be a channel for his work. Of course you can reinforce connections with language: the bathroom moths are like a jumble of buttresses for cathedral domes; the female moth is like an immolating monk, like a hollow saint, a flame-

Jan B.

Kindling

Two summers ago I was camping alone in the Blue Ridge mountains in Virginia. I had hauled myself and gear up there to read, among other things, James Ramsey Ullman's The Day on Fire, a novel that had made me want to be a writer when I was sixteen; I was hoping it would do it again. So I read every day sitting under a tree by my tent, pausing to eat four or five times and walk once or twice, and I read every night while warblers swung in the leaves overhead and bristleworms trailed their inches over the twiggy dirt at my side, and I read every night by candlelight, while the barred owls called in the forest and pale moths massed in the clearing. I read, made a ring.

Moths kept flying into the candle. They would hiss and recoil, lost upside down in the shadows among my cooking pans. Or they would singe their wings and fall, and their hot wings would stick, as if melted, to whatever they touched, a pan, a lid, a spoon, so that the snagged moths could struggle only in tiny arcs, unable to flutter free. These I could release by a quick flip with a stick; in the morning I would find my cooking stuff embossed with torn flecks of moth wings, little triangles of shiny dust here and there on the aluminum. So I read, and boiled water, and replenished candles, and read on. was caught, burned dry, and held burning.

One night one female moth flew into the candle, sizzled, dropped her abdomen into the wet wax, stuck, flamed and fried in a second. Her wings burnt right off and disappeared in a thin, foul smoke; her legs spattered and curled, her head crackled and jerked (like small arms fire)

I must have been staring at the candle, or maybe I looked up when a shadow crossed my page; at any rate, I saw it all.

faced virgin gone to God; Rimbaud burnt out his brains with poetry while night pooled wetly at my feet.

I liked the piece enough to rewrite it. I took out a couple of paragraphs—one about why I didn't have a dog, another that ran on about the bathroom spider. This is the kind of absurdity you fall into when you write about anything, let alone about yourself. You're so pleased and grateful to be writing at all, especially at the beginning, that you babble. Often you don't know where the work is going, so you can't tell what's irrelevant.

It doesn't hurt much to babble in a first draft, so long as you have the sense to cut out irrelevancies later. If you are used to analyzing texts, you will be able to formulate a clear statement of what your draft turned out to be about. Then you make a list of what you've already written, paragraph by paragraph, and see what doesn't fit and cut it out. (All this requires is nerves of steel and lots of coffee.) Most of the time you'll have to add to the beginning, ensuring that it gives a fair idea of what the point might be, or at least what is about to happen. (Suspense is for mystery writers. The most inept writing has an inadvertent element of suspense: the reader constantly asks himself, where on earth is this going?) Usually I cnd up throwing away the beginning: the first part of a poem, the first few pages of an essay, the first scene of a story, even the first few chapters of a book. It's not holy writ. The paragraphs and sentences are tesserae—tiles for a mosaic. Just because you have a bunch of tiles in your lap doesn't mean your mosaic will be better if you use them all. In this atypical case, however, there were very few extraneous passages. The focus was tight, probably because I'd been so single-minded before I wrotc it.

I added stuff, too, to strengthen and clarify the point. I added some speculation about the burning moth: had she mated and laid her eggs, had she done her work? Near the end I added a passage about writing class: which of you want to give your lives and become writers?

Ultimately I sent it to *Harper's* magazine, which published it.

"With my old journal beside me, I took up my current journal and scribbled and doodled my way through an account of my present life and the remembered moth." Page from the first draft of "Transfiguration."

29

in there were quickly, too.

The rip on thigh seam is 10" long. Oh, dear jeans.

Last night moths kept flying into the candle. They would hiss & spatter & recoil, lost upside down & flopping in the shadows among the pans on the table. Or — and this happened often, & again tonight — they'd burn their wings, & then their wings would _stick_ to the next thing they'd touch — the edge of a pan, a lid. . . . these I could free with a quick flip with a spoon or something.

Some, of course, burnt badly & couldn't get away. One moth flew in the near candle. Her wings burnt right off, her legs & head crackled and jerked. Her body was stuck upright in the wax; it must have been dry. Moths are dry. Because it acted as a wick; without burning itself, it drew up wax from the pool, and gave off a steady flame for two hours, until I blew ~~the candle~~ it out. That one candle had two flames. Brightened up my whole evening.

I was screaming to them last night. I got upset, & it was in my voice. Wonder what the neighbors thought: no! don't do it! please — no! So tonight I read in the lodge. After the B & O, I read upstairs on the couch.

Talked to Steve, at Cortes w/ KK; talked to Richard twice, at noon, & now.

I don't know what those firm segmented multi-legged invertebrates are, but they're all over the place up here. Bristleworms? They're hard on the outside, chitinous I guess. Anyway. One on the path today was on its side, struggling. A big spider of the harvestman sort, but w/ a big grey body, was all over it doing I know not what, & so was a fly.

The early drafts, and the *Harper's* version, had a different ending, a kind of punch line that was a series of interlocking statements:

> I don't mind living alone. I like eating alone and reading. I don't mind sleeping alone. The only time I mind being alone is when something is funny; then, when I am laughing at something funny, I wish someone were around. Sometimes I think it is pretty funny that I sleep alone.

I took this ending out of the book version, which is the version you have. I took it out because the tone was too snappy, too clever; it reduced everything to celibacy, which was really a side issue; it made the reader forget the moth; and it called too much attention to the narrator. The new ending was milder. It referred back to the main body of the text.

Revising is a breeze if you know what you're doing—if you can look at your text coldly, analytically, manipulatively. Since I've studied texts, I know what I'm doing when I revise. The hard part is devising the wretched thing in the first place. How do you go from nothing to something? How do you face the blank page without fainting dead away?

To start a narrative, you need a batch of things. Not feelings, not opinions, not sentiments, not judgments, not arguments, but specific objects and events: a cat, a spider web, a mess of insect skeletons, a candle, a book about Rimbaud, a burning moth. I try to give the reader a story, or at least a scene (the flimsiest narrative occasion will serve), and something to look at. I try not to hang on the reader's arm and bore him with my life story, my fancy self-indulgent writing, or my opinions. He is my guest; I try to entertain him. Or he'll throw my pages across the room and turn on the television.

I try to say what I mean and not "hide the hidden meaning." "Clarity is the sovereign courtesy of the writer," said J. Henri Fabre, the great French entomologist, "I do my best to achieve it." Actually, it took me about ten years to learn to write clearly. When I was in my twenties, I was more interested in showing off.

What do you do with these things? You juggle them. You toss them around. To begin, you don't need a well defined point. You don't need "something to say"—that will just lead you to reiterat-

First encounter with the flaming moth: a page from Annie Dillard's journal, August–October 1974.

ing clichés. You need bits of the world to toss around. You start anywhere, and join the bits into a pattern by your writing about them. Later you can throw out the ones that don't fit.

I like to start by describing something, by ticking off the five senses. Later I got back to the beginning and locate the reader in time and space. I've found that if I take pains to be precise about *things*, feelings will take care of themselves. If you try to force a reader's feelings through dramatic writing ("writhe," "ecstasy," "scream"), you make a fool of yourself, like someone at a party trying too hard to be liked.

I have piles of materials in my journals—mostly information in the form of notes on my reading, and to a lesser extent, notes on things I'd seen and heard during the day. I began the journals five or six years after college, finding myself highly trained for taking notes and for little else. Now I have thirty-some journal volumes, all indexed. If I want to write about arctic exploration, say, or star chemistry, or monasticism, I can find masses of pertinent data under that topic. And if I browse I can often find images from other fields that may fit into what I'm writing, if only as metaphor or simile. It's terrific having all these materials handy. It saves and makes available all those years of reading. Otherwise, I'd forget everything, and life wouldn't accumulate, but merely pass.

The moth essay I wrote that November day was an "odd" piece—"freighted with heavy-handed symbolism," as I described it to myself just after I wrote it. The reader must be startled to watch this apparently calm, matter-of-fact account of the writer's life and times turn before his eyes into a mess of symbols whose real subject matter is their own relationship. I hoped the reader wouldn't feel he'd been had. I tried to ensure that the actual, historical moth wouldn't vanish into idea, but would stay physically present.

A week after I wrote the first draft I considered making it part of the book (*Holy the Firm*) I had been starting. It seemed to fit the book's themes. (Actually, I spent the next fifteen months fitting the book to its themes.) In order to clarify my thinking I jotted down some notes:

moth in candle:
>   the poet—materials of world, of bare earth at feet, sucked up,
>   transformed, subsumed to spirit, to air, to light
>   the mystic—not through reason
>   but through emptiness
>   the martyr—virgin, sacrifice, death with meaning.

I prefaced these notes with the comical word "Hothead."

It had been sheer good luck that the different aspects of the historical truth fit together so nicely. It had actually been on that particular solo camping trip that I'd read the Rimbaud novel. If it hadn't been, I wouldn't have hesitated to fiddle with the facts. I fiddled with one fact, for sure: I foully slandered my black cat, Small, by saying she was "gold"—to match the book's moth and little blonde burnt girl. I actually had a gold cat at that time, named Kindling. I figured no one would believe it. It was too much. In the book, as in real life, the cat was spayed.

This is the most personal piece I've ever written—the essay itself, and these notes on it. I don't recommend, or even approve, writing personally. It can lead to dreadful writing. The danger is that you'll get lost in the contemplation of your wonderful self. You'll include things for the lousy reason that they actually happened, or that you feel strongly about them; you'll forget to ensure that the *reader* feels anything whatever. You may hold the popular view that art is self-expression, or a way of understanding the self—in which case the artist need do nothing more than babble uncontrolledly about the self and then congratulate himself that, in addition to all his other wonderfully interesting attributes, he is also an artist. I don't (evidently) hold this view. So I think that this moth piece is a risky one to read: it seems to enforce these romantic and giddy notions of art and the artist. But I trust you can keep your heads.

Narration

1

Essays in the
First Person Singular

NARRATION [1] is the story-telling mode of writing; it recounts
actions and events; it answers the question, "What happened?" The essays in this chapter are written in the narrative mode. They are personal narratives in which each
author records experiences from his or her private life.

One reason for beginning with personal narratives is suggested by Henry David Thoreau's famous opening words in
Walden:

In most books, the *I*, or first person, is omitted; in this it will
be retained; that, in respect to egotism, is the main difference.
We commonly do not remember that it is, after all, always the
first person that is speaking. I should not talk so much about
myself if there were anybody else whom I knew as well. . . .
Moreover, I, on my side, require of every writer, first or last, a
simple and sincere account of his own life. . . .

The common feature of these openly autobiographical selections is the controlling presence of a distinct personality—
like yours. You may not think that you know yourself well,
but whom do you know better?

Another reason for beginning with personal narratives is
that essays have always been personal. Our modern word
essay comes from the French essayer, meaning "to try." An
essay is your personal trial or attempt to grapple with a
subject or problem. Yours and nobody else's. Another person addressing the same subject would necessarily speak in
a different voice from a different perspective. Because they

[1] Terms printed in all capitals are defined in the Glossary.

invited readers to listen in (like informal guests in the writer's living room), these modest attempts at self-expression became known as "personal" or "familiar" essays.

Any writer who gives an account of his or her own experiences must understand the difference between events and the telling of events. Think of actions as sounds for a moment—the sounds of a college band playing the national anthem. When the band strikes up "Oh, say can you see," your ear hears trombones, trumpets, and drums all in a single harmonious strain. If you were to look at the written parts of the different instruments in their music-holders, however, you would have to separate them. You might follow a single bar of trombone music, then race over to the trumpet section, then back to the drums. But you would be alternating between parts, as the readers of a book must do when his or her eyes move from left to right and down the printed page. Events in real life often occur simultaneously; in a written narrative, they must be printed in sequence.

The sequence of events in a narrative is called the PLOT; unlike random events in real life, the plot of a narrative must be controlled and directed by the narrator. So must the POINT OF VIEW. Point of view is the vantage from which a narrative is told. It is not a difficult concept to master if you think of the difference between watching a football game in the stadium and watching it on television. The camera controls your point of view on the screen; you see only what the camera focuses upon. In the stands, however, you are free to scan the entire field, to watch the quarterback or the line, to concentrate on the cheerleaders. Your point of view is determined by your eyes alone; your vantage is a high place above the total action.

In narration, point of view is controlled in part by the grammatical PERSON in which an author chooses to write. Many narratives are told "in the third person" or "from the third-person point of view." For example, you might write: "The tornado hit while George was playing cards; he had just drawn a third ace, but when he plunked it down, the table was gone." Here the narrator and George are different persons; the narrator does not say how George felt inside at the crucial moment; the story is told after the fact and from the outside (of George). The essays in this chapter are "first-person" narratives, the point of view you would adopt in an autobiography or an account of your adventures during the first day of your college career. Here the "I" is an actor in each drama, and we see the world of the narrative through the narrator's eyes.

Authors of narrative essays in the first person have great freedom: they may record their personal thoughts on anything that has happened to them. As attested by master essayist E. B. White (whose "Once More to the Lake" appears at the end of this volume), "There is one thing the essayist cannot do, though—he cannot indulge himself in deceit or in concealment, for he will be found out in no time." Modern readers of essays, like Thoreau, require a "simple and sincere account"—the sincerity that comes of personal integrity and the simplicity that comes from discipline. The essayist may wander at will, but may not ramble. He or she may be relaxed, even self-indulgent. But if the reader can not follow along because the essayist writes obscurely or is dishonest, their partnership will be disbanded. And this is what a personal essay amounts to, finally—a friendly partnership between reader and author.

Loren Eiseley

The Angry Winter

Born in Lincoln, Nebraska, in 1907, Loren Eiseley was a distinguished anthropologist and sociologist. After graduate work at
the University of Pennsylvania, he taught there for twelve years
before becoming Franklin Professor of Anthropology and History
of Science in 1961. The recipient of over thirty-five honorary
degrees from universities throughout the U.S. and Canada, he also
taught at the University of Kansas, Oberlin College, Columbia,
Berkeley, and Harvard. Eiseley's major works include The Im-
mense Journey (1957); Darwin's Century (1958); The Firmament
of Time (1960); The Mind as Nature (1962); and The Invisible
Pyramid (1970). The following personal narrative is the complete
Part 1, Chapter 5, of The Unexpected Universe (1969). It recalls
a deep winter's conflict between the author and his dog. The
volume bears the following dedication: "To Wolf, who sleeps
forever with an ice age bone across his heart, the last gift of one
who loved him." Loren Eiseley died in 1977.

A time comes when creatures whose destinies have crossed   1
somewhere in the remote past are forced to appraise each
other as though they were total strangers. I had been huddled
beside the fire one winter night, with the wind prowling outside and shaking the windows. The big shepherd dog on the
hearth before me occasionally glanced up affectionately,
sighed, and slept. I was working, actually, amidst the debris
of a far greater winter. On my desk lay the lance point of ice
age hunters and the heavy leg bone of a fossil bison. No remnants of flesh attached to these relics. The deed lay more than
ten thousand years remote. It was represented here by naked
flint and by bone so mineralized it rang when struck. As I

worked in my little circle of light, I absently laid the bone beside me on the floor. The hour had crept toward midnight. A grating noise, a heavy rasping of big teeth diverted me. I looked down.

The dog had risen. That rock-hard fragment of a vanished beast was in his jaws and he was mouthing it with a fierce intensity I had never seen exhibited by him before.   2

"Wolf," I exclaimed, and stretched out my hand. The dog backed up but did not yield. A low and steady rumbling began to rise in his chest, something out of a long-gone midnight. There was nothing in that bone to taste, but ancient shapes were moving in his mind and determining his utterance. Only fools gave up bones. He was warning me.   3

"Wolf," I chided again.   4

As I advanced, his teeth showed and his mouth wrinkled to strike. The rumbling rose to a direct snarl. His flat head swayed low and wickedly as a reptile's above the floor. I was the most loved object in his universe, but the past was fully alive in him now. Its shadows were whispering in his mind. I knew he was not bluffing. If I made another step he would strike.   5

Yet his eyes were strained and desperate. "Do not," something pleaded in the back of them, some affectionate thing that had followed at my heel all the days of his mortal life, "do not force me. I am what I am—and cannot be otherwise because of the shadows. Do not reach out. You are a man, and my very god. I love you, but do not put out your hand. It is midnight. We are in another time, in the snow."   6

"The *other* time," the steady rumbling continued while I paused, "the other time in the snow, the big, the final, the terrible snow, when the shape of this thing I hold spelled life. I will not give it up. I cannot. The shadows will not permit me. Do not put out your hand."   7

I stood silent, looking into his eyes, and heard his whisper through. Slowly I drew back in understanding. The snarl diminished, ceased. As I retreated, the bone slumped to the floor. He placed a paw upon it, warningly.   8

And were there no shadows in my own mind, I wondered. Had I not for a moment, in the grip of that savage utterance, been about to respond, to hurl myself upon him over an invisible haunch ten thousand years removed? Even to me the shadows had whispered—to me, the scholar in his study.   9

"Wolf," I said, but this time, holding a familiar leash, I spoke 10
from the door indifferently. "A walk in the snow." Instantly from
his eyes that other visitant receded. The bone was left lying. He
came eagerly to my side, accepting the leash and taking it in his
mouth as always.

A blizzard was raging when we went out, but he paid no heed. 11
On his thick fur the driving snow was soon clinging heavily. He
frolicked a little—though usually he was a grave dog—making up
to me for something still receding in his mind. I felt the snow-
flakes fall upon my face, and stood thinking of another time, and
another time still, until I was moving from midnight to midnight
under ever more remote and vaster snows. Wolf came to my side
with a little whimper. It was he who was civilized now. "Come
back to the fire," he nudged gently, "or you will be lost." Automatically I took the leash he offered. He led me safely home and
into the house.

"We have been very far away," I told him solemnly. "I think 12
there is something in us that we had both better try to forget."
Sprawled on the rug, Wolf made no response except to thump his
tail feebly out of courtesy. Already he was mostly asleep and
dreaming. By the movement of his feet I could see he was running
far upon some errand in which I played no part.

Softly I picked up his bone—our bone, rather—and replaced it 13
high on a shelf in my cabinet. As I snapped off the light the white
glow from the window seemed to augment itself and shine with a
deep, glacial blue. As far as I could see, nothing moved in the
long aisles of my neighbor's woods. There was no visible track,
and certainly no sound from the living. The snow continued to
fall steadily, but the wind, and the shadows it had brought, had
vanished.

QUESTIONS

Understanding

1. Who are the "creatures" of Eiseley's first sentence?
2. What "other time" is he talking about in paragraphs 6 and 7?
   Why was the "terrible" snow also "final" (par. 7)?
3. Apparently the dog in Eiseley's narrative is not hungry, because

he goes to sleep easily after playing. Why, then, does he snarl over a fossilized bone that he could not eat even if he wanted to?

4. What is it that both dog and man should try to forget in paragraph 12?

Strategies and Structure

1. The dog's resistance to the man (pars. 5–8) is one of the two principal actions in Eiseley's narrative. What is the other? Where is it narrated?

2. In Eiseley's little drama, setting and lighting effects are very important. What are the chief *places* of his narrative, and how do they serve him? How do the desklamp and the powerful "white glow" of the snow contribute to the real conflict of the drama?

3. Where does that drama actually take place?

4. What is the function of the leash in paragraph 11?

5. How is the man who tells this story different from the man it is told about?

6. As the narrator, Eiseley has the difficult task of portraying the thoughts of an animal. How does he solve this difficulty?

7. Why does Eiseley end by referring to his neighbor's woods and the vanished shadows?

Words and Figures of Speech

1. Why is "Wolf" an appropriate name for the dog in Eiseley's narrative?

2. There are literal shadows on the snow outside the scholar's window, but what are the "shadows" that flit through his mind and the mind of the dog?

3. Why might Eiseley picture himself as "huddled" by the fire while the wind is "prowling" outside (par. 1)? How does this METAPHOR fit in with the rest of the narrative?

4. What are the CONNOTATIONS of "glacial" in paragraph 13? Why do you suppose Eiseley chose this word instead of "diamond" or "ice" blue?

5. He does not use the word, but how might *instinct* be applied in a discussion of Eiseley's narrative?

6. Consult your dictionary for the meanings of any of the following words that are not familiar to you: *destiny* (par. 1), *appraise* (1), *debris* (1), *chide* (4), *visitant* (10), *augment* (13).

Comparing

1. Eiseley's personal narrative tells a story, but it also explains one cause of human (and animal) aggression. When you study CAUSE AND EFFECT essays in Chapter 4, compare Eiseley's analysis of aggressive behavior with Paul Colinvaux's in "Why Japan Bombed Pearl Harbor." Do they confirm or contradict one another?
2. When Eiseley's dog threatens to spring, which does he resemble more closely, the spider or the wasp in Alexander Petrunkevitch's essay on those two creatures in Chapter 3?

Discussion and Writing Topics

1. Tell the story of an occasion on which you almost "lost your head." Recount the events leading up to the incident in such a way as to suggest *why* you acted as you did.
2. It was once thought that criminals were throwbacks to man's animalistic ancestors. What do you think of this explanation for criminal behavior? Do you suppose Eiseley would accept it? Why or why not?
3. What is the "collective unconscious" posited by some modern psychologists?
4. What is a cultural anthropologist? What does he or she study?

David Dubber

Crossing the Bar on a Fiberglas Pole

*David Dubber was a freshman at Indiana University when he
wrote this account of breaking a collegiate pole-vaulting record.
He graduated in 1967 with a B.S. in business, and now lives with
his family in Evansville, Indiana. A professional writer in the
public relations and advertising division of a large pharmaceutical
company, Dubber is working on "an American fictional novel."*

A one hundred foot asphalt runway leads to a metal shoot   1
and metal standards and a crossbar. Behind the shoot rises
a pile of foam rubber scraps. This is the pole vaulting field at
the 1963 S. I. A. C. (Southern Indiana Athletic Conference)
Track and Field Meet. The stands are filled.

The meet is over but the crowd has stayed to watch the   2
finish of the pole-vaulting event. There are two television
cameras trying to squeeze in just one more Double Cola commercial before swinging back to tape the last of the vaulting
event. The crossbar has been raised to thirteen feet, six inches,
nearly a foot higher than the old, long-standing record. It is
my job—it seems my duty since I have kept the crowd—to
gather my strength into one single attempt to propel my body
up and over that crossbar with the aid of my fiberglas pole.
Many times lately I have heard people debating whether or
not the pliable fiberglas pole should be allowed in competition. People say that one has only to "hang on to the thing
and it will throw you to any desired height."

These recollections bring me much bitterness as I stand   3 before my trial. I am developing a fatalistic attitude toward this towering height and wish I had never come out for track, or at least I wish I had never heard of this silly "bending" pole. But it is too late to untwine this tightly woven cord; the crowd is waiting. I completely dismiss distracting thoughts and put all my powers, mental and physical, into this one leap.

Mentally I run through the particulars of the vault. I have   4
counted my steps down to the tape mark on the runway where my left foot is to hit the runway for the last time. I must remember to keep my body loose to conserve strength. I must also remember to strike my left foot on the mark hard enough to give me a four-foot jump on the pole before switching my balance and strength to my hands; otherwise I will not get off the ground. It must be a quick and trained reflex that is well routed in the grooves of my mind.

Now the crowd is dead silent. I count ten as I leave the world—   5
seeing only the runway and crossbar directly ahead, believing only that I will succeed in clearing the bar, hearing only the beating of my own heart. Slowly I begin an easy jog down the runway as the pole I cling to bounces slightly in front of me in a syncopation of my steps. Gradually my speed picks up until my body attains a swift glide. The tip of the pole descends as I approach the shoot. Although my main concern is making good contact between the end of my pole and the shoot, I am also watching the tape marking. After a few years practice, a vaulter learns to compensate for any misjudgment the last few strides before he reaches the shoot. Through some inexplicable mechanism the vaulter's sub-conscious tells his body how much to shorten or lengthen the stride in order to hit the take-off mark. Just as the tip of my pole touches the backstop of the shoot, I push the pole straight forward and with one final bound I smack the pavement with the ball of my left foot and straighten my half bent left leg with a great thrust to give me my height on the pole.

All my weight shifts to my hands, and as the angle of the pole   6
increases toward the vertical, my body climbs to about three-fourths the height of the crossbar. As I come up I throw my head back toward the ground causing my hips to sweep upward until my feet pass through my line of vision and on, one foot further, so that I am now completely upside down. The pole bends suddenly to about four feet from the ground, and my body, remaining

in the inverted position, falls rapidly with it. In my upside down position, all the stress is put on the abdominal area of the body. The tension wrenches the stomach and the intestines. The pole now stops its bend and starts to reflex back up to a straight position, but my body is still falling straight down. At this moment the strain multiplies as my body is brought to an abrupt stop and then starts back in the opposite direction. The inverted position must be maintained. Unbelievable pressure is put on the abdominal area. My hands and fingers clench the pole like wrenches. Just as the deep-sea pole comes alive in the hands of a fisherman when he has hooked a fighting sailfish, this pole strains to pull away from me as it jiggles violently from side to side. I feel I can't hold on any longer. In my fury to keep from losing the pole I wish the people who had said one merely has to "hang on" to the fiberglas pole for the ride could take my place now and try "hanging on" to this monster. I feel the muscle fibers along my stomach straining to the point of popping, and my numb fingers seem to be slipping off the rising pole; but suddenly, my body ceases to resist and rises upward toward the stars.

I am amazed to realize that I am still on the pole. My body [7] writhes slowly to the left, and my feet come up to the crossbar. My body continues turning as the bar passes under my shins, knees, and thighs, and my body stops in a half-twist as the crossbar stands directly under my waist. At this point I lock my arms in a half-bent position, the pole begins its final slight bend. My waist is approximately three feet higher than my hands and well above the crossbar. The slight bend of the pole lowers my body four to six inches. I keep my arms locked in bent position as again the pressure mounts on my tight, quivering stomach muscles. As the pole becomes a straight line, I straighten my arms out keeping my head forward and down, my body arched into a parabola around the crossbar. I stiffen my arms, and the fingertips, tired and pained, become the only things supporting my weight on the pole. I push off with my stiff fingertips, pulling my elbows up, back, and over; I throw my head back as my weak fingers barely clear the bar. I let go of all tension and let my body fall easily, down, and backward—sinking into the soft white mass, seeing only the dark blue sky. Wait! Not only the dark blue sky, but also a crossbar lying across the tops of two standards up there in the heavens, quivering a bit perhaps, but not falling, not in a thousand years. The hundred or so people who have gathered around the pit rush to pick me up as the masses in the stands exhale a roar. I look back at the pole lying over there alone, still, and I know what a marvelous monster it is to ride.

QUESTIONS

Understanding

1. Dubber's job is to clear the bar at a record height. Why is it also his "duty" (par. 2)?
2. As the pole launches him upward, Dubber wishes that critics of the fiberglas pole could take his place. Why? What does he want them to find out?
3. Dubber is writing about a single event and a relatively unfamiliar sport, but what does his narrative suggest about competition in general?

Strategies and Structure

1. Why does Dubber keep referring to the fiberglas pole? Besides narrating the story of how he broke the record, what *argument* is he developing? What is the counterargument of his opponents?
2. What is the effect of the last sentence in paragraph 1? What difference would it have made if Dubber had written instead, "The stands *were* filled"?
3. If the opening paragraphs of this essay create suspense, does the last paragraph continue the suspense or resolve it? Explain your answer.
4. Dubber mentions the crowd at the beginning and end of his narrative. What happens to the crowd in between? Why?
5. To read the last three paragraphs of this essay takes much longer than an actual pole vault. Dubber could not possibly have formulated all these sensations while he broke the record. Does this mean his account is "untrue"? Why or why not?

Words and Figures of Speech

1. PERSONIFICATION is the device of conferring life on inanimate

objects. Where does Dubber use this figure of speech? Why does he use it?

2. When Dubber starts to "leave the world" (par. 5), he is taking off from the physical earth. In what other sense can these words be understood?

3. If you find anything awkward in the following phrases, suggest ways of changing them: "untwine this tightly woven cord" (par. 3); "abdominal area of the body" (6); "marvelous monster" (7).

Comparing

1. In Chapter 3, you will encounter essays that analyze processes. What process is Dubber explaining as he tells his story? When you read Garrison Keillor's "Attitude" (Chapter 3), compare his attitude toward baseball with Dubber's toward his sport.

Discussion and Writing Topics

1. Has any experience in sports—a tournament competition, a particularly smooth dive, a lucky hook shot—made you understand for a moment how a champion athlete feels? Tell the story of that experience. Try to convey its sensations and the glimpse of mastery that it gave you.

2. Narrate your triumph in a board game (like Monopoly or chess) as if it required all the stamina, skill, and split-second timing of a field sport. Be as dramatic as you please.

3. Do you consider competition to be healthy? Why or why not? To what extent is it avoidable in life?

Joyce Maynard

Four Generations

Born in 1953, Joyce Maynard grew up in Durham, New Hampshire, where her father taught at the university. Maynard thus spent her adolescence in the 1960s, only she saw it as a time with no place for youth; at nineteen, while a sophomore at Yale, Maynard published her first book, Looking Backward: A Chronicle of Growing Up Old in the Sixties *(1973). Since then, Maynard has produced the daughter so proudly displayed in "Four Generations" and a novel called* Baby Love *(1981). Published in 1979, the following personal narrative tells the story of another daughter's belated visit to the bedside of a dying grandparent.*

My mother called last week to tell me that my grand-   1
mother is dying. She has refused an operation that would
postpone, but not prevent, her death from pancreatic cancer.
She can't eat, she has been hemorrhaging, and she has severe
jaundice. "I always prided myself on being different," she told
my mother. "Now I *am* different. I'm yellow."

My mother, telling me this news, began to cry. So I became   2
the mother for a moment, reminding her, reasonably, that my
grandmother is eighty-seven, she's had a full life, she has all
her faculties, and no one who knows her could wish that she
live long enough to lose them. Lately my mother has been
finding notes in my grandmother's drawers at the nursing
home, reminding her, "Joyce's husband's name is Steve. Their
daughter is Audrey." In the last few years she hadn't had the
strength to cook or garden, and she's begun to say she's had
enough of living.

My grandmother was born in Russia, in 1892—the oldest   3

daughter in a large and prosperous Jewish family. But the prosperity didn't last. She tells stories of the pogroms and the cossacks who raped her when she was twelve. Soon after that, her family emigrated to Canada, where she met my grandfather.

Their children were the center of their life. The story I loved   4
best, as a child, was of my grandfather opening every box of Cracker Jack in the general store he ran, in search of the particular tin toy my mothed coveted. Though they never had much money, my grandmother saw to it that her daughter had elocution lessons and piano lessons, and assured her that she would go to college.

But while she was at college, my mother met my father, who   5
was blue-eyed and blond-haired and not Jewish. When my father sent love letters to my mother, my grandmother would open and hide them, and when my mother told her parents she was going to marry this man, my grandmother said if that happened, it would kill her.

Not likely, of course. My grandmother is a woman who used to   6
crack Brazil nuts open with her teeth, a woman who once lifted a car off the ground, when there was an accident and it had to be moved. She has been representing her death as imminent ever since I've known her—twenty-five years—and has discussed, at length, the distribution of her possessions and her lamb coat. Every time we said goodbye, after our annual visit to Winnipeg, she'd weep and say she'd never see us again. But in the meantime, while every other relative of her generation, and a good many of the younger ones, has died (nursed usually by her), she has kept making knishes, shopping for bargains, tending the healthiest plants I've ever seen.

After my grandfather died, my grandmother lived, more than   7
ever, through her children. When she came to visit, I would hide my diary. She couldn't understand any desire for privacy. She couldn't bear it if my mother left the house without her.

This possessiveness is what made my mother furious (and then   8
guilt-ridden that she felt that way, when of course she owed so much to her mother). So I harbored the resentment that my mother—the dutiful daughter—would not allow herself. I—who had always performed specially well for my grandmother, danced and sung for her, presented her with kisses and good report cards —stopped writing to her, ceased to visit.

But when I heard that she was dying, I realized I wanted to go to   9
Winnipeg to see her one more time. Mostly to make my mother
happy, I told myself (certain patterns being hard to break). But
also, I was offering up one more particularly fine accomplishment:
my own dark-eyed, dark-skinned, dark-haired daughter, whom my
grandmother had never met.

I put on my daughter's best dress for our visit to Winnipeg, the   10
way the best dresses were always put on me, and I filled my
pockets with animal crackers, in case Audrey started to cry. I
scrubbed her face mercilessly. On the elevator going up to her
room, I realized how much I was sweating.

Grandma was lying flat with an IV tube in her arm and her eyes
shut, but she opened them when I leaned over to kiss her. "It's
Fredelle's daughter, Joyce," I yelled, because she doesn't hear well
anymore, but I could see that no explanation was necessary. "You
came," she said. "You brought the baby."

Audrey is just one, but she has seen enough of the world to   12
know that people in beds are not meant to be so still and yellow,
and she looked frightened. I had never wanted, more, for her to
smile.

Then Grandma waved at her—the same kind of slow, finger-   13
flexing wave a baby makes—and Audrey waved back. I spread her
toys out on my grandmother's bed and sat her down. There she
stayed, most of the afternoon, playing and humming and sipping
on her bottle, taking a nap at one point, leaning against my grandmother's leg. When I cranked her Snoopy guitar, Audrey stood up
on the bed and danced. Grandma wouldn't talk much anymore,
though every once in a while she would say how sorry she was that
she wasn't having a better day. "I'm not always like this," she
said.

Mostly she just watched Audrey. Sometimes Audrey would get   14
off the bed, inspect the get-well cards, totter down the hall. "Where
is she?" Grandma kept asking. "Who's looking after her?" I had
the feeling, even then, that if I'd said, "Audrey's lighting matches,"
Grandma would have shot up to rescue her.

We were flying home that night, and I had dreaded telling her,   15
remembering all those other tearful partings. But in the end, I was
the one who cried. She had said she was ready to die. But as I
leaned over to stroke her forehead, what she said was, "I wish I
had your hair" and "I wish I was well."

On the plane flying home, with Audrey in my arms, I thought   16
about mothers and daughters, and the four generations of the family that I know most intimately. Every one of those mothers loves
and needs her daughter more than her daughter will love or need
her some day, and we are, each of us, the only person on earth
who is quite so consumingly interested in our child.

Sometimes I kiss and hug Audrey so much she starts crying—   17
which is, in effect, what my grandmother was doing to my mother,
all her life. And what makes my mother grieve right now, I think,
is not simply that her mother will die in a day or two, but that,
once her mother dies, there will never again be someone to love
her in quite such an unreserved, unquestioning way. No one else
who believes that, fifty years ago, she could have put Shirley Temple out of a job, no one else who remembers the moment of her
birth. She will only be a mother, then, not a daughter anymore.

Audrey and I have stopped over for a night in Toronto, where   18
my mother lives. Tomorrow she will go to a safe-deposit box at the
bank and take out the receipt for my grandmother's burial plot.
Then she will fly back to Winnipeg, where, for the first time in
anybody's memory, there was waist-high snow on April Fool's
Day. But tonight she is feeding me, as she always does when I
come, and I am eating more than I do anywhere else. I admire the
wedding china (once my grandmother's) that my mother has set
on the table. She says (the way Grandma used to say to her, of the
lamb coat), "Some day it will be yours."

QUESTIONS

Understanding

1. Who are the representatives of the four generations cited in Maynard's title? What do they have in common physically?
2. Why had Maynard stopped writing and visiting her Canadian
   grandmother before the last visit described here? Why does she go
   back to see the dying woman?
3. What does her treatment of Maynard's baby reveal about the
   grandmother? What does Maynard's presenting the baby as a
   proud "accomplishment" (par. 9) reveal about *her*?

4. How does Maynard treat her daughter when they are alone together?
5. With her own daughter, is Maynard breaking the generational pattern that has characterized her family for so long, or is she repeating it? Explain your answer.
6. Who seems to be more concerned with death here, the dying grandmother or the granddaughter? Why do you say so?
7. In Maynard's narrative, how does the grandmother's long-standing attitude toward her children and grandchildren resemble her attitude toward life when she is dying?

Strategies and Structure

1. Roughly how many years does Maynard's narrative span in all? Where does she mention the earliest years?
2. Most of Maynard's narrative tells what happened in the past, though not necessarily the distant past. After comparing the verb TENSES in paragraph 18 with those in paragraph 13, explain whether Maynard's visit to her dying grandmother is an event of the present or the past time of the narrative.
3. What events are taking place in the present time of Maynard's narrative?
4. "Four Generations" is both an account of events over time and a meditation upon their meaning. Point out passages in which Maynard comments directly on the meaning of events. How else does she give her narrative a sense of meditation or reflection?
5. By what carefully selected specific details does Maynard give us a picture of her grandmother in paragraphs 5 and 6? What physical charactcristics and qualities of temperament do these details reveal? How does Maynard begin to characterize her grandmother in the very first paragraph of this essay?
6. By what specific details in paragraphs 13–15 does Maynard reveal the grandmother's state of mind in the presence of death? The granddaughter's?
7. How would you describe the *pace* of Maynard's narration in paragraphs 7–12? How does the length of the paragraphs here compare with that of other paragraphs in the narrative?
8. Why do you think Maynard breaks the text of her essay after paragraphs 3 and 15? Why do you suppose she puts the third paragraph, about her grandmother's distant past, before the break rather than after?

9. What is the effect of ending this narrative by referring to the wedding china (par. 18)?

Words and Figures of Speech

1. In paragraph 9, Maynard presents her daughter to her grandmother as an "accomplishment." Which single word in paragraph 8 names the quality in the grandmother that encourages "accomplishments" in her offspring?
2. What are the CONNOTATIONS of *consumingly* in paragraph 16? How does Maynard's treatment of her own daughter in paragraph 17 justify the use of this strong word?
3. Explain the difference in DENOTATION between *emigrated* (par. 3) and *immigrated*.
4. What is the effect of Maynard's choice of the word "reasonably" in paragraph 2?
5. Why does Maynard refer to "pogroms" in paragraph 3 instead of "persecution" or "discrimination"?
6. Consult your dictionary for any of these words that you don't know: *pancreatic* (par. 1), *hemorrhaging* (par. 1), *jaundice* (par. 1), *cossacks* (par. 3), *coveted* (par. 4), *elocution* (par. 4), *imminent* (par. 6), and *knishes* (par. 6).
7. What is the difference in meaning between *imminent* (par. 6) and *eminent*?

Comparing

1. Compare and contrast Maynard's treatment of the generations and family continuity with Joan Didion's handling of the same theme in "On Going Home" ("Essays for Further Reading").
2. How does Maynard's account of handing down a tradition from mother to daughter *contrast* with E. B. White's account of a father and son in "Once More to the Lake" ("Essays for Further Reading")?

Discussion and Writing Topics

1. Do you think Maynard was justified in not writing or visiting her grandmother when she was well? Why or why not?

2. Write an essay that gives an account of your own last visit with a relative or friend.

3. Write an essay about your family that tells about events and gestures (at a family reunion, perhaps) that show a family resemblance in spirit or behavior across several generations.

Mary E. Mebane

The Back of the Bus

Mary E. Mebane was born in 1933 in the Wildwood community
near Durham, North Carolina, a member of the last generation
of Americans to endure legal segregation in the South. The daughter of a dirt farmer who sold junk to raise cash, she attended North
Carolina College in Durham (graduating summa cum laude) and
later the University of North Carolina at Chapel Hill, where she
took the M.A. and Ph.D. degrees. Now a resident of Milwaukee,
she has taught writing at the University of Wisconsin (Milwaukee campus) and at South Carolina State College. In 1971 on the
Op-Ed page of the New York Times, Mebane described a bus
ride from Durham to Orangeburg, S.C., that "realized for me
the enormousness of the change" in the lives of black Americans
since the Civil Rights Act of 1964, when legal segregation was
overturned. That bus ride was the germ of two autobiographical
volumes, Mary (1981) and Mary Wayfarer (1983). "The Back of
the Bus" (editor's title) is a complete chapter from the earlier
book. The author herself explains how and why she wrote it in an
interview following the study questions on her essay.

Historically, my lifetime is important because I was part
of the last generation born into a world of total legal segregation in the Southern United States. When the Supreme
Court outlawed segregation in the public schools in 1954, I
was twenty-one. When Congress passed the Civil Rights Act
of 1964, permitting blacks free access to public places, I was
thirty-one. The world I was born into had been segregated for
a long time—so long, in fact, that I never met anyone who
had lived during the time when restrictive laws were not in
existence, although some people spoke of parents and others
who had lived during the "free" time. As far as anyone knew,

the laws as they then existed would stand forever. They were meant to—and did—create a world that fixed black people at the bottom of society in all aspects of human life. It was a world without options.

Most Americans have never had to live with terror. I had had to live with it all my life—the psychological terror of segregation, in which there was a special set of laws governing your movements. You violated them at your peril, for you knew that if you broke one of them, knowingly or not, physical terror was just around the corner, in the form of policemen and jails, and in some cases and places white vigilante mobs formed for the exclusive purpose of keeping blacks in line.   2

It was Saturday morning, like any Saturday morning in dozens of Southern towns.   3

The town had a washed look. The street sweepers had been busy since six o'clock. Now, at eight, they were still slowly moving down the streets, white trucks with clouds of water coming from underneath the swelled tubular sides. Unwary motorists sometimes got a windowful of water as a truck passed by. As it moved on, it left in its wake a clear stream running in the gutters or splashed on the wheels of parked cars.   4

Homeowners, bent over industriously in the morning sun, were out pushing lawn mowers. The sun was bright, but it wasn't too hot. It was morning and it was May. Most of the mowers were glad that it was finally getting warm enough to go outside.   5

Traffic was brisk. Country people were coming into town early with their produce; clerks and service workers were getting to the job before the stores opened at ten o'clock. Though the big stores would not be open for another hour or so, the grocery stores, banks, open-air markets, dinettes, were already open and filling with staff and customers.   6

Everybody was moving toward the heart of Durham's downtown, which waited to receive them rather complacently, little knowing that in a decade the shopping centers far from the center of downtown Durham would create a ghost town in the midst of the busiest blocks on Main Street.   7

Some moved by car, and some moved by bus. The more affluent used cars, leaving the buses mainly to the poor, black and white, though there were some businesspeople who avoided the trouble of trying to find a parking place downtown by riding the bus.   8

I didn't mind taking the bus on Saturday. It wasn't so crowded. 9
At night or on Saturday or Sunday was the best time. If there were
plenty of seats, the blacks didn't have to worry about being asked
to move so that a white person could sit down. And the knot of
hatred and fear didn't come into my stomach.

I knew the stop that was the safety point, both going and com- 10
ing. Leaving town, it was the Little Five Points, about five or six
blocks north of the main downtown section. That was the last stop
at which four or five people might get on. After the stop, the driver
could sometimes pass two or three stops without taking on or
letting off a passenger. So the number of seats on the bus usually
remained constant on the trip from town to Braggtown. The nearer
the bus got to the end of the line, the more I relaxed. For if a white
passenger got on near the end of the line, often to catch the return
trip back and avoid having to stand in the sun at the bus stop until
the bus turned around, he or she would usually stand if there were
not seats in the white section, and the driver would say nothing,
knowing that the end of the line was near and that the standee
would get a seat in a few minutes.

On the trip to town, the Mangum Street A&P was the last point 11
at which the driver picked up more passengers than he let off.
These people, though they were just a few blocks from the downtown section, preferred to ride the bus downtown. Those getting on
at the A&P were usually on their way to work at the Duke University Hospital—past the downtown section, through a residential
neighborhood, and then past the university, before they got to
Duke Hospital.

So whether the driver discharged more passengers than he took 12
on near the A&P on Mangum was of great importance. For if he
took on more passengers than got off, it meant that some of the
newcomers would have to stand. And if they were white, the driver
was going to have to ask a black passenger to move so that a white
passenger could sit down. Most of the drivers had a rule of thumb,
though. By custom the seats behind the exit door had become "colored" seats, and no matter how many whites stood up, anyone
sitting behind the exit door knew that he or she wouldn't have to
move.

The disputed seat, though, was the one directly opposite the exit 13
door. It was "no-man's-land." White people sat there, and black
people sat there. It all depended on whose section was fuller. If the

back section was full, the next black passenger who got on sat in the no-man's-land seat; but if the white section filled up, a white person would take the seat. Another thing about the white people: they could sit anywhere they chose, even in the "colored" section. Only the black passengers had to obey segregation laws.

On this Saturday morning Esther and I set out for town for our [14] music lesson. We were going on our weekly big adventure, all the way across town, through the white downtown, then across the railroad tracks, then through the "colored" downtown, a section of run-down dingy shops, through some fading high-class black neighborhoods, past North Carolina College, to Mrs. Shearin's house.

We walked the two miles from Wildwood to the bus line. [15] Though it was a warm day, in the early morning there was dew on the grass and the air still had the night's softness. So we walked along and talked and looked back constantly, hoping someone we knew would stop and pick us up.

I looked back furtively, for in one of the few instances that I [16] remembered my father criticizing me severely, it was for looking back. One day when I was walking from town he had passed in his old truck. I had been looking back and had seen him. "Don't look back," he had said. "People will think that you want them to pick you up." Though he said "people," I knew he meant men—not the men he knew, who lived in the black community, but the black men who were not part of the community, and all of the white men. To be picked up meant that something bad would happen to me. Still, two miles is a long walk and I occasionally joined Esther in looking back to see if anyone we knew was coming.

Esther and I got to the bus and sat on one of the long seats at the [17] back that faced each other. There were three such long seats—one on each side of the bus and a third long seat at the very back that faced the front. I liked to sit on a long seat facing the side because then I didn't have to look at the expressions on the faces of the whites when they put their tokens in and looked at the blacks sitting in the back of the bus. Often I studied my music, looking down and practicing the fingering. I looked up at each stop to see who was getting on and to check on the seating pattern. The seating pattern didn't really bother me that day until the bus started to get unusually full for a Saturday morning. I wondered what was happening, where all these people were coming from. They got on and got on until the white section was almost full and the black section was full.

There was a black man in a blue windbreaker and a gray pork-pie hat sitting in no-man's-land, and my stomach tightened. I wondered what would happen. I had never been on a bus on which a black person was asked to give a seat to a wnite person when there was no other seat empty. Usually, though, I had seen a black person automatically get up and move to an empty seat farther back. But this morning the only empty seat was beside a black person sitting in no-man's-land. [18]

The bus stopped at Little Five Points and one black got off. A young white man was getting on. I tensed. What would happen now? Would the driver ask the black man to get up and move to the empty seat farther back? The white man had a businessman's air about him: suit, shirt, tie, polished brown shoes. He saw the empty seat in the "colored' section and after just a little hesitation went to it, put his briefcase down, and sat with his feet crossed. I relaxed a little when the bus pulled off without the driver saying anything. Evidently he hadn't seen what had happened, or since he was just few stops from Main Street, he figured the mass exodus there would solve all the problems. Still, I was afraid of a scene. [19]

The next stop was an open-air fruit stand just after Little Five Points, and here another white man got on. Where would he sit? The only available seat was beside the black man. Would he stand the few stops to Main Street or would the driver make the black man move? The whole colored section tensed, but nobody said anything. I looked at Esther, who looked apprehensive. I looked at the other men and women, who studiously avoided my eyes and everybody else's as well, as they maintained a steady gaze at a far-distant land. [20]

Just one woman caught my eye; I had noticed her before, and I had been ashamed of her. She was a stringy little black woman. She could have been forty; she could have been fifty. She looked as if she were a hard drinker. Flat black face with tight features. She was dressed with great insouciance in a tight boy's sweater with horizontal lines running across her flat chest. It pulled down over a nondescript skirt. Laced-up shoes, socks, and a head rag completed her outfit. She looked tense. [21]

The white man who had just gotten on the bus walked to the 22
seat in no-man's-land and stood there. He wouldn't sit down, just
stood there. Two adult males, living in the most highly industri-
alized, most technologically advanced nation in the world, a nation
that had devastated two other industrial giants in World War II
and had flirted with taking on China in Korea. Both these men,
either of whom could have fought for the United States in Germany
or Korea, faced each other in mutual rage and hostility. The white
one wanted to sit down, but he was going to exert his authority and
force the black one to get up first. I watched the driver in the
rearview mirror. He was about the same age as the antagonists.
The driver wasn't looking for trouble, either.

"Say there, buddy, how about moving back," the driver said, 23
meanwhile driving his bus just as fast as he could. The whole bus
froze—whites at the front, blacks at the rear. They didn't want to
believe what was happening was really happening.

The seated black man said nothing. The standing white man 24
said nothing.

"Say, buddy, did you hear me? What about moving on back." 25
The driver was scared to death. I could tell that.

"These is the niggers' seats!" the little lady in the strange outfit 26
started screaming. I jumped. I had to shift my attention from the
driver to the frieze of the black man seated and white man standing to the articulate little woman who had joined in the fray.

"The government gave us these seats! These is the niggers' seats." 27
I was startled at her statement and her tone. "The president said
that these are the niggers' seats!" I expected her to start fighting at
any moment.

Evidently the bus driver did, too, because he was driving faster 28
and faster. I believe that he forgot he was driving a bus and
wanted desperately to pull to the side of the street and get out
and run.

"I'm going to take you down to the station, buddy," the driver 29
said.

The white man with the briefcase and the polished brown shoes 30
who had taken a seat in the "colored" section looked as though he
might die of embarrassment at any moment.

As scared and upset as I was, I didn't miss a thing. 31

By that time we had come to the stop before Main Street, and 32 the black passenger rose to get off.

"'You're not getting off, buddy. I'm going to take you down-   33
town.'' The driver kept driving as he talked and seemed to be
trying to get downtown as fast as he could.

"These are the niggers' seats! The government plainly said these   34
are the niggers' seats!'' screamed the little woman in rage.

I was embarrassed at the use of the word "nigger" but I was   35
proud of the lady. I was also proud of the man who wouldn't get
up.

The bus driver was afraid, trying to hold on to his job but   36
plainly not willing to get into a row with the blacks.

The bus seemed to be going a hundred miles an hour and every-   37
body was anxious to get off, though only the lady and the driver
were saying anything.

The black man stood at the exit door; the driver drove right past   38
the A&P stop. I was terrified. I was sure that the bus was going to
the police station to put the black man in jail. The little woman
had her hands on her hips and she never stopped yelling. The bus
driver kept driving as fast as he could.

Then, somewhere in the back of his mind, he decided to forget   39
the whole thing. The next stop was Main Street, and when he got
there, in what seemed to be a flash of lightning, he flung both doors
open wide. He and his black antagonist looked at each other in the
rearview mirror; in a second the windbreaker and porkpie hat were
gone. The little woman was standing, preaching to the whole bus
about the government's gift of these seats to the blacks; the man
with the brown shoes practically fell out of the door in his hurry;
and Esther and I followed the hurrying footsteps.

We walked about three doors down the block, then caught a   40
bus to the black neighborhood. Here we sat on one of the two long
seats facing each other, directly behind the driver. It was the custom. Since this bus had a route from a black neighborhood to the
downtown section and back, passing through no white residential
areas, blacks could sit where they chose. One minute we had been
on a bus in which violence was threatened over a seat near the exit
door; the next minute we were sitting in the very front behind the
driver.

The people who devised this system thought that it was going to   41
last forever.

QUESTIONS

Understanding

1. Why does Mary Mebane claim a national significance for the events of her private life in "The Back of the Bus"?

2. Mebane's essay recalls events that occurred during her youth under "legal segregation." Was it *written* before or after *de*segregation? How do you know?

3. Why did the bus driver of Mebane's essay threaten to drive to the police station? What was his official duty under the segregation code?

4. Why do you suppose the businessman with the briefcase and brown shoes chose to take the separate seat in the back of the bus instead of the place on the bench across from the exit? Was he upholding or violating segregation by doing so?

5. With what emotion in particular did young Mary and her sister react to the confrontation they witnessed that May morning in Durham?

6. Who are the "people" to whom Mebane refers in paragraph 41?

Strategies and Structure

1. The bulk of Mebane's essay is a personal NARRATIVE. Where does the narrative part begin? Where does it end?

2. Mebane interrupts her account of a particular Saturday to supply information of a more general sort in paragraphs 10–13. What is she explaining to the reader, and why is this information necessary?

3. What is young Mary's role throughout the bus ride? In which paragraph is it defined most clearly?

4. Point out several paragraphs or passages that seem to be told from young Mary's POINT OF VIEW. Indicate several others that come from the point of view of the adult author looking back at an event in her youth. Besides time, what is the main difference in their perspectives?

5. What is the effect of Mebane's referring to the black passenger who confronts the bus driver as "the windbreaker and porkpie hat" (par. 39). Point to other examples of such objectifying in her essay. Whose point of view do they help to capture?

6. Why do you think Mebane begins her narrative with the street

sweepers who doused the pavement on the morning of Mary's ride and with the homeowners who dreamily put their yards in order?

7. How does the bus in Mebane's narrative serve to objectify the segregation laws? Why, historically, might a bus have been a likely place for racial segregation to be challenged?

8. How does Mebane use the increasing speed of the Durham bus to confirm what she has to say about the precariousness of the "system" (par. 41)?

9. Mary gets on the bus in paragraph 17. The strangely dressed woman screams out in paragraph 26. Who is the only person on the bus to speak in between? Do you think that the bus young Mary rode was in reality so still? Why might the author exaggerate the silence in an artful retelling of the event?

Words and Figures of Speech

1. Why does the author refer to the seat across from the exit as a "no-man's land" (par. 13)? Where did the term originate?

2. In the terminology of architecture, what is a "frieze" (par. 26)? Why is the METAPHOR appropriate here?

3. Look up *insouciance* (par. 21) in your dictionary. How does the word prepare you for the rebellious behavior of the "stringy" little woman?

4. A word like *insouciance* would not have been in the speaking vocabulary of a girl so young as Mary: it belongs, rather, to the writing vocabulary of the mature author. Pick out other words and phrases in Mebane's essay that young Mary could not have been expected to know.

5. In the interview following these study questions, Mary Mebane says that she composes early drafts of her writing partly in "black dialect." What traces of black or "Southern" speech can you detect in the finished product?

6. Why do you suppose Mebane elected to publish her account largely in what is called Standard Edited English? Why not cast the whole essay in the language of a particular race or region?

7. What are the two possible meanings of *scene* (par. 19)? How might Mebane's essay be said to illustrate both meanings?

8. Which of the many meanings of *articulate* (par. 26) in your dictionary best fits the woman who screams back at the bus driver?

Comparing

1. Deairich Hunter was only a little older than the girl in "The Back of the Bus" when he wrote "Ducks vs. Hard Rocks" (Chapter 2). What do the environments of these two young people have in common? How do their reactions to their surroundings resemble each other? Where do they differ?

2. How does the way "The Back of the Bus" is told resemble the way Ellen Willis speaks in "Memoirs of a Non-Prom Queen" (Chapter 4)?

Discussion and Writing Topics

1. "The Back of the Bus" is more than a personal experience essay. How effective do you find it as a political statement? Explain your answer.

2. Describe a bewildering bus, train, plane, or other trip you made in the past from the standpoint of your present insight and maturity.

3. Spend a few hours in a public bus station observing and (unobtrusively) taking notes. Write an essay on the experience in which you use the physical place to help capture a slice of the social or political life of your town, city, or school.

4. Write about a trip you have repeated, a movie you have seen more than once, a person who has returned into your life, or some other recurring experience. Use the *difference* between the two experiences to illustrate a significant change in yourself or in your world.

Writers on the Writing Process:
*An Interview with Mary Mebane**

EDITOR: How old is the girl in "The Back of the Bus"?   1

MEBANE: I was in the tenth grade—about fifteen or sixteen.   2

EDITOR: The book in which it first appeared was published in   3
1981. When was the essay *written*?

MEBANE: The piece was finished in the summer of 1972. It   4
took that long to find a publisher for the book. I was about
ready to give up.

EDITOR: When did you first get the idea of writing about buses?   5

MEBANE: In 1970. It was August, and I was riding a Trailways   6
bus from Durham, N.C., where I was born, to Orangeburg,
S.C. I'm a great bus rider, have been for years. I recommend
it for anyone who wants to really see the country.

EDITOR: What caused you to write about the experience?   7

MEBANE: The first time I went to Orangeburg was in June   8
1965. My brother drove me down from Durham at night. It
was around two in the morning when we crossed the line
into South Carolina. Riding the bus down in daylight was
unthinkable then, and yet here I was only five years later
crossing the North Carolina line in a public bus. My stomach
tightened slightly. The driver started laying into a black
teenager, something about a ticket. They went back and
forth, back and forth, and then the white driver just stopped
arguing. I smiled to myself and relaxed. And we took the
bus in silence on down to Orangeburg. A decade earlier the
bus driver would have been an enforcer of the segregation
laws like the driver of teenage Mary's bus, and every black
passenger on the bus would have been terrified. That difference between then and now was the germ of two essays I

* Conducted in Milwaukee, Wisconsin, January 30, 1984.

later wrote, the piece in *The Norton Sampler* and an earlier piece that appeared in the *New York Times* in January 1971.

EDITOR: The earlier essay was "The Black and White Bus Lines." When did you compose it?   9

MEBANE: Soon after the bus reached Orangeburg, within a   10 month. It describes bus travel in the present after desegregation. A lot of people read the piece in the *Times*, and I was encouraged to do more.

EDITOR: What was your purpose for writing about young Mary's   11 wild ride in Durham many years ago?

MEBANE: I wanted to show what it was like to live under legal   12 segregation *before* the Civil Rights Act of 1964.

EDITOR: When did your experience as a girl riding a bus first   13 come back to you as the way to show this?

MEBANE: Before the Trailways reached Orangeburg. My mind   14 is constantly linking the past and the present: that's the way I see the world.

EDITOR: Why a bus, why not some other place?   15

MEBANE: The bus was the one place where the segregation laws   16 might be challenged. Not in the bus station because blacks sat in a separate section; not in a white restaurant or restroom because they were off-limits. In a movie house you went in a separate entrance and walked upstairs. The segregation laws were enforced by space. The bus just had a sign: "Whites, please sit from the front. Colored, please sit from the rear." Only on a bus were the two cultures in close proximity in the same space.

EDITOR: So the bus serves in your essay as an enclosed space for   17 the action to take place in, like a stage?

MEBANE: Yes. I often think in play terms when I write. The   18 man in the porkpie hat was the bus driver's antagonist.

EDITOR: Why were the people on the bus so deathly silent be-   19 fore the "articulate" little woman started screaming?

MEBANE: They were all scared to death. The white passengers,   20 too. The man in the brown shoes looked like a businessman, an orderly person from an orderly world. When he walked onto that bus, I think for a second he saw the horror of a society that perpetuated racial segregation. When the bus stopped, everybody scattered like a yardful of chickens.

EDITOR: Why did you mention the truck that washes the street [21] clean on the morning of Mary's ride? Why not launch right into the adventure instead of beginning the account this way?

MEBANE: To me the street washing was a sign of normality [22] and ordinary routine. The reader is about to see an ugly scene. Terror is more terrifying when it strikes innocence.

EDITOR: Is "The Back of the Bus" inspired, then, by your recol- [23] lection of physical terror?

MEBANE: And psychological terror. The police used to meet the [24] bus whenever it pulled into the station. Two in the morning, three in the morning. They didn't have to do anything. They were enforcing segregation by their mere presence. When I heard the teenage boy talk back to the driver of the Orangeburg bus, I started trying to think of other acts of resistance I had seen. I came to recall the man in the porkpie hat because he was the only case of direct resistance I had actually witnessed before desegregation.

EDITOR: Is conflict a good subject, in general, to write about? [25]

MEBANE: Especially if it's resolved. The conflict between the [26] black man and the driver was resolved when the driver decided to forget the whole thing and flung open the door. I can give you an example of an incident that never developed into a conflict situation. When I became old enough to vote I went to register at the Braggtown schoolhouse in Durham county. As I went in the building, I met neighbors of mine coming out. They were black. Inside I stood for some time with the white people going into the principal's office. When I got to the counter, the woman didn't look at me, but she told me everybody had to write his name on a list. Now a number of white people had registered in between, but the name immediately above mine on the list was my neighbor's. It was a segregated list.

EDITOR: Did you ever write about that incident? [27]

MEBANE: I wouldn't be able to write about it effectively be- [28] cause nothing happened. There was only a potential conflict, and so it was never resolved.

EDITOR: Can you give an example of the kind of incident that   29
does make good writing material, like the incident you witnessed as a girl riding the bus in Durham?

MEBANE: I wrote this one up recently, but it hasn't been pub-   30
lished yet. I was walking down Wisconsin [a major street in
Milwaukee] in front of McDonald's one Sunday when this
black woman of about thirty stopped and admired my hat.
She was as sleek and stylish as a fashion model flashing down
the runway. She walked on down the street toward Gimbel's and
the river. I was waiting for the bus. I heard declaiming in the
street, and I looked up. It was the sleek woman. I realized then
that she was deranged. What had happened in her life, I wondered, that a woman who looked to be on top of the world had
been hurt so badly that she was driven crazy? It was the contrast
beween the way she looked and the way she actually was that
made this woman something to write about for me.

EDITOR: I want to ask you a question now about language. You   31
say that the little woman who started screaming on Mary's
bus was dressed with great "insouciance." A word like that
would not have been in young Mary's vocabulary. When did
such words occur to you for reporting her experience?

MEBANE: *Insouciance* is part of my adult writing vocabulary. It   32
got there from reading. I first thought of the way the woman
looked and tried to get the visual image down on paper. The
formal word for how her appearance had affected me came
later, as I was polishing the piece. I compose at the typewriter. It has to be an electric to keep up with my thoughts.
When I have the germ of an essay, I try to recall everything
connected with it. I type, type, type—to get it all down. This
is the fruitcake effect. Put in all the concrete details you can
think of. Later you can take out anything that doesn't fit. I
leave plenty of space between each line and in the margins
for rewriting. Often I begin to write in a mixture of formal,
"literary" language and black idiom. Certain black words and
phrases can cut right to the heart of a situation. They can
turn tragic experiences into humor and make it bearable. At
the start I can sound like Richard Pryor—without the profanity. Then I come back and insert words like *insouciance*.
I love literary language, too, and I am writing for a general

audience. But black readers like my writing, I think, because I can express the pain. What happened to teenage Mary was painful to remember, yet I can bear to retell it because of the man in the porkpie hat. He resisted and won.

EDITOR: So did the "articulate" woman. Is writing a liberating form of articulation for you, too?   33

MEBANE: Absolutely. I didn't start writing until my late thirties, didn't have much success till my forties. Then people read my work and started talking or writing to me about it, and I realized I was articulating many aspects of human experience for us both, reader and writer. I can live when I can write.   34

WRITING TOPICS for Chapter One
Essays in the First Person Singular

1. Write an autobiography in which you give a chronological account of the formative events of your life.

2. Which aspects of college have you found most different from high school? Which have you found especially shocking or liberating? Tell the story of your adjustment to a new environment.

3. Have you had a religious or intellectual experience that has *changed* your life? Try to recapture it.

4. Do you have a special skill or talent (like David Dubber's)? Relate how it has served you in past challenges or emergencies.

5. Recount your reaction to the news of a relative's or close friend's death.

6. Describe your reaction to one of the following: an athletic event; an election or political rally; a meeting with a famous person; an impressive building or natural scene; an accident.

7. Recall a childhood journey that you find unusually memorable. Organize your account around the stages of the journey.

8. From your own perspective, tell the story of a family reunion you have attended. Pay special attention to the oldest family members.

9. How do you expect to act at the tenth anniversary of your high school graduating class? The twentieth? Describe the scene.

Exposition

2
Essays That
Classify and Divide

When we divide a group of similar objects, we separate them from one another. For example, a physiologist divides human beings according to body types: mesomorph (muscular and bony), ectomorph (skinny), and endomorph (soft and fleshy). When we CLASSIFY [1] an object, we place it within a group of similar objects. The zoologist puts a monkey and a man in the order Primates because both mammals have nails and opposable thumbs. A librarian classifies Mark Twain's Adventures of Huckleberry Finn along with Herman Melville's Moby-Dick because both are works of prose fiction by nineteenth-century American authors. Shakespeare's Macbeth would go into a different class, however, because its distinguishing features are different. The technical definition of a class is a group with the same distinguishing features.

The simplest classification systems divide things into those that exhibit a set of distinguishing features and those that do not. A doctor conducting genetic research among identical male twins would divide the human race first into Males and Females; then he would subdivide the Males into Twins and Non-Twins; and finally he would subdivide the Twins into the categories, Identical and Nonidentical.

The doctor's simple system has limited uses, but it resembles even the most complicated systems in one respect. The categories do not overlap. They are mutually exclusive. A classification system is useless if it "cross-ranks" items. Suppose, for example, that we classified all birds according to

[1] Terms printed in all capitals are defined in the Glossary.

the following categories: Flightless, Nocturnal, Flat-billed, Web-Footed. Our system might work well enough for owls (nocturnal), but where would a duck (flat-billed, web-footed) fit? Or a penguin (flightless, web-footed)? A system of classifying birds must have one and only one pigeonhole for pigeons. Otherwise it makes a distinction that does not distinguish, a flaw as serious as failing to make a distinction that really does exist. Our faulty system would not differentiate between a penguin and an ostrich since both are flightless, but a naturalist would see a big difference between the two.

The distinguishing features of a class must set its members apart from those of other classes or subclasses. How the features of a given class are defined, however, will vary with who is doing the classifying and for what purpose. A teacher divides a group of thirty students according to scholarship: types A, B, C, D, and F. A basketball coach would divide the same group of students into forwards, guards, and centers. The director of a student drama group would have an entirely different set of criteria. All three sets are valid for the purposes they are intended to serve. And classification must serve some larger purpose, or it becomes an empty game.

When you write a classification theme, keep your purpose firmly in mind. Are you classifying teachers in order to decide what a good teacher is? To demonstrate that different kinds of teachers can be equally instructive? To explain why some teachers fail? Return often to your reasons and conclusions, for classification is a method of organization that should propose as well as arrange.

The following paragraph from an essay on lightning by Richard Orville goes well beyond merely dividing its subject into three categories:

> There are several types of lightning named according to where the discharge takes place. Among them are intracloud lightning, by far the most common type, in which the flash occurs within the thundercloud; air-discharge lightning, in which the flash occurs between the cloud and the surrounding air; and cloud-to-ground lightning, in which the discharge takes place between the cloud and the ground.

This short paragraph names the types of lightning. But it also suggests a basis for defining all three types ("according to where the discharge takes place"); it defines them on that basis; it tells us that intracloud lightning is the commonest type; and it sets up all that follows.

In the next paragraphs of his essay, Orville explains what causes the three kinds of lightning; how much electrical power they generate; how scientists study them, and where such familiar names as "forked, streak, heat, hot, cold, ribbon, and bead" lightning fit into these categories. After discussing the related topic of thunder, Orville ends by explaining why we need to know as much as possible about his subject. The final sentence of his essay reads: "In the end, we hope that our effort will bring the goal of lightning prediction, and perhaps limited control, within the realm of applied technology."

The author of our example has taken the trouble to study lightning, classify it, and explain his system to us because human life and property may depend upon such efforts in the future. You may not be writing about life-and-death matters, but your theme should explain why a particular system of classification is valid, what we can learn from it, and what good that knowledge can do.

Deairich Hunter
Ducks vs. Hard Rocks

When he wrote "Ducks vs. Hard Rocks," Deairich Hunter was a
high school junior in Wilmington, Delaware, and a columnist
for The Eye, a student news magazine. For four months, Hunter
lived in Brooklyn and attended the predominantly black, inner-
city school he describes in "Ducks vs. Hard Rocks." Hunter was
a duck, one who escaped by returning to his old school in a less
fierce environment. Hunter stayed long enough in the ghetto,
however, to learn the basic categories into which he and his
classmates fell—in New York and other densely urban centers.
This essay by a student is about trying to stay out of the "hard
rocks" category long enough to grow up and still remember.

Although the chaos and viciousness of the Miami riot hap- 1
pened months ago, the chaos and viciousness of daily life for
many inner-city black people goes on and on. It doesn't seem
to matter where you are, though some places are worse than
others. A few months ago I left my school in Wilmington,
Delaware, moved to Brooklyn, New York, and really began to
understand.

After you stay in certain parts of New York for awhile, that 2
chaos and viciousness gets inside of you. You get used to seeing
the younger guys flashing pistols and the older ones shooting
them. It's not unusual to be walking down the street or
through the park and see somebody being beaten or held up.
It's no big deal if someone you know is arrested and beat up
by the cops.

In my four months in Brooklyn I was mugged three times. 3

Although such events may seem extraordinary to you, they 4

are just a part of life in almost any minority neighborhood. It seems like everybody knows how to use some kind of weapon, whether it's a pair of nun-chucks (two round sticks attached by a chain) or an ice pick. As long as it will do the job, you can use it.

In Brooklyn you fall into one of two categories when you start   5 growing up. The names for the categories may be different in other cities, but the categories are the same. First, there's the minority of the minority, the "ducks," or suckers. These are the kids who go to school every day. They even want to go to college. Imagine that! School after high school! They don't smoke cheeb (marijuana) and they get zooted (intoxicated) after only one can of beer. They're wasting their lives waiting for a dream that won't come true.

The ducks are usually the ones getting beat up on by the ma-   6 jority group—the "hard rocks." If you're a real hard rock you have no worries, no cares. Getting high is as easy as breathing. You just rip off some duck. You don't bother going to school; it's not necessary. You just live with your mom until you get a job— that should be any time a job comes looking for you. Why should you bother to go look for it? Even your parents can't find work.

I guess the barrier between the ducks and the hard rocks is the   7 barrier of despair. The ducks still have hope, while the hard rocks are frustrated. They're caught in the deadly, dead-end environment and can't see a way out. Life becomes the fast life—or incredibly boring—and death becomes the death that you see and get used to every day. They don't want to hear any more promises. They believe that's just the white man's way of keeping them under control.

Hard rocks do what they want to do when they want to do it.   8 When a hard rock goes to prison it builds up his reputation. He develops a bravado that's like a long, sad joke. But it's all lies and excuses. It's a hustle to keep ahead of the fact that he's going nowhere.

Actually, there is one more category, but this group is not really   9 looked upon as human. They're the junkies. They all hang to-gether, but they don't actually have any friends. Everybody in the neighborhood knows that a drug addict would cut his own throat if he could get a fix for it. So everybody knows junkies will stab you in the back for a dollar.

A guy often becomes a junkie when he tries to get through the   10
despair barrier and reach the other side alone. Let's say a hard
rock wants to change, to better himself, so he goes back to school.
His friends feel he's deserting them, so they desert him first. The
ducks are scared of him and won't accept him. Now this hard rock
is alone. If he keeps going to school, somebody who is after him
out of spite or revenge will probably catch him and work him over.
The hard rock has no way to get back. His way of life is over; he
loses his friends' respect, becoming more and more of an outcast.
Then he may turn to drugs.

I guess the best way to help the hard rocks is to help the ducks.   11
If the hard rocks see the good guy making it, maybe they will
change. If they see the ducks, the ones who try, succeed, it might
bring them around. The ducks are really the only ones who might
be able to change the situation.

The problem with most ducks is that after years of effort they   12
develop a negative attitude, too. If they succeed, they know they've
got it made. Each one can say he did it by himself and for himself.
No one helped him and he owes nobody anything, so he says, "Let
the hard rocks and the junkies stay where they are"—the old every-
man-for-himself routine.

What the ducks must be made to realize is that it was this same   13
attitude that made the hard rocks so hard. They developed a sense
of kill or be killed, abuse or be abused, take it or get taken.

The hard rocks want revenge. They want revenge because they   14
don't have any hope of changing their situation. Their teachers
don't offer it, their parents have lost theirs, and their grandparents
died with a heartful of hope but nothing to show for it.

Maybe the only people left with hope are the only people who   15
can make a difference—teens like me. We, the ducks, must learn
to care. As a fifteen-year-old, I'm not sure I can handle all that.
Just growing up seems hard enough.

QUESTIONS

Understanding

1. Who or what is Hunter classifying in this essay?
2. What is a "duck" as Hunter defines one? A "hard rock"?

3. What is the third category in Hunter's classification system?
4. On whom does the main hope for the future of all three groups depend, according to Hunter? Why them and not the other groups?
5. To which category does Hunter himself belong?

Strategies and Structure

1. This is an essay in classification, but it also sets forth a "thesis," or proposition supported by persuasive argument. Where does Hunter set forth his thesis? What is it?
2. Why do you think Hunter waits until after he has classified his subject to make his plea instead of doing so beforehand?
3. In what sense is Hunter's essay itself evidence in support of his thesis about the need for caring? In which paragraph does he suggest that the responsibility of saving the others may be too great for even the most compassionate of ducks?
4. The minority that Hunter is classifying would understand his categories but might not appreciate the part of his essay that makes a plea to do away with these very categories. To whom does Hunter address this plea? Who is his intended audience here?
5. "Ducks vs. Hard Rocks" sounds like the title of an essay in comparison and contrast (Chapter 6). Why is this nevertheless an essay in classification rather than comparison?

Words and Figures of Speech

1. What is "bravado" (par. 7)? How is it different from courage?
2. How effective do you find the SIMILE in which Hunter compares the bravado of the hard rocks to "a long, sad joke" (par. 7)?
3. Hunter's use of such SLANG words as *ducks, hard rocks, nun-chucks* (par. 3), *cheeb* (par. 4), and *zooted* (par. 4) shows that he knows the "lingo" of his environment. How does this knowledge of language help establish his authority as our interpreter, despite his tender age? Interpreter of what?
4. Hunter's TONE when he defines ducks (par. 5) is heavily sarcastic. (See SATIRE in the glossary.) Read this paragraph out loud to yourself in the tone of voice you think Hunter intended. By the use of what punctuation mark does the author signal the tone of this passage for us?
5. Why do you suppose the hard rocks call a duck a duck?

Comparing

1. Hunter's essay calls for the triumph of conscious intention (a positive as opposed to a "negative attitude") over "the situation." How do his grounds for hoping to change human behavior resemble Sam Keen's in the next essay, "Face of the Enemy"?

Discussion and Writing Topics

1. Does it matter that Hunter was only fifteen years old when he wrote his essay? Does this knowledge undermine or support his authority here? Would he be more or less compassionate, do you think, if he were much older? If he had stayed in Brooklyn?
2. Are Hunter's categories of inner-city types accurate, in your opinion? Does he leave out any sub-groups you can think of?
3. How would you sub-divide a racial or regional group (Oriental or Indian Americans, inner-city students, rural blacks or whites, "wasps") of whom you have first-hand experience? Write a classification essay about that group.

Sam Keen
Faces of the Enemy

Sam Keen is a free-lance writer, lecturer, and contributing editor to Psychology Today. In An Apology for Wonder (1969), he defended the religious sentiment in modern society. "Faces of the Enemy" is about warfare rather than worship, but it is another study in mass psychology, namely the human tendency to demand and define visible enemies. Recently published in Esquire, Keen's essay is a synopsis of his book scheduled to appear under the same title in 1985.

The world, as always, is debating the issues of war and   1
peace. Conservatives believe safety lies in more arms and increased firepower. Liberals place their trust in disarmament and a nuclear freeze. I suggest we will be saved by neither fire nor ice, that the solutions being offered by the political right and left miss the mark. Our problem lies not in our technology, but in our minds, in our ancient tendency to create our enemies in our own imagination.

Our best hope for avoiding war is to understand the psy-   2
chology of this enmity, the ways in which our mind works to produce our habits of paranoia, projection, and the making of propaganda. How do we create our enemies and turn the world into a killing ground?

We first need to answer some inevitable objections,   3
raised by the advocates of power politics, who say: "You can't psychologize political conflict. You can't solve the problem of war by studying perception. We don't *create* enemies. There are real aggressors—Hitler, Stalin, Qaddafi."

True: There are always political, economic, and territo-   4
rial causes of war. Wars come and go; the images we use to

dehumanize our enemies remain strangely the same. The unchanging projections of the hostile imagination are continually imposed onto changing historical circumstances. Not that the enemy is innocent of these projections—as popular wisdom has it, paranoids sometimes have *real* enemies. Nevertheless, to understand the hostile imagination we need to temporarily ignore the question of guilt and innocence. Our quest is for an understanding of the unchanging images we place on the enemy.

Paranoia is not an occasional individual pathology, but rather it is the human condition. History shows us that, with few exceptions, social cohesion within tribes is maintained by paranoia: when we do not have enemies, we invent them. The group identity of a people depends on division between insiders and outsiders, us and them, the tribe and the enemy.   5

The first meaning of *the enemy is* simply the stranger, the alien. The bond of tribal membership is maintained by projecting hostile and divisive emotions upon the outsider. Paranoia forms the mold from which we create enemies.   6

In the paranoid imagination, *alien* means the same as *evil,* while the tribe itself is defined as good: a single network of malevolent intent stretches over the rest of the world. "They" are out to get "us." All occurrences prove the basic assumption that an outside power is conspiring against the community.   7

In the language of rhetoric, every war is a crusade, a "just" war, a battle between good and evil. Warfare is a ritual in which the sacred blood of our heroes is sacrified to destroy the enemies of God.   8

We like to think that theocracies and holy wars ended with the coming of the Industrial Revolution and the emergence of secular cultures in the West. Yet in World War I the kaiser was pictured as the devil; in World War II both Germany and the U.S. proclaimed *Gott mit uns,* "In God We Trust"; each accused the other of being Christ-killers. Sophisticated politicians may insist that the conflict between the U.S. and the USSR is a matter of pragmatic power politics, but the theological dimensions have not disappeared. President Reagan warns us against "the aggressive impulses of an evil empire" and asks us to "pray for the salvation of all those who live in totalitarian darkness, pray they will discover the joy of knowing God."   9

By picturing the enemy as the enemy of God we convert the [10] guilt associated with murder into pride. A warrior who kills such an enemy strikes a blow for truth and goodness. Remorse isn't necessary. The warrior engaged in righteous battle against the enemies of God may even see himself as a priest, saving his enemy from the grip of evil by killing him.

The enemy not only is a demon but is also a destroyer of [11] culture. If he is human at all, he is brutish, dumb, and cruel, lower on the scale of evolution than The People. To the Greeks he was a barbarian. To the Americans he was, most recently, a "gook" or "slant." To the South African he is a black or "colored."

The barbarian theme was used widely in World War II [12] propaganda by all participants. Nazi anti-semitic tracts contrasted the sunny, healthy Aryan with the inferior, dark, and contaminated races—Jews, Gypsies, Eastern Europeans. American soldiers were pictured as Chicago-style gangsters. Blacks were portrayed as quasi-gorillas despoiling the artistic achievements of European civilization. One poster used in Holland warned the Dutch that their supposed "liberators" were a mélange of KKK, jazz-crazed blacks, convicts, hangmen, and mad bombers. In turn, the U.S. frequently pictured the Germans as a Nazi horde of dark monsters on a mindless rampage.

The image of the barbarian represents a force to be feared: [13] power without intelligence, matter without mind, an enemy that must be conquered by culture. The warrior who defeats the barbarian is a culture hero, keeping the dark powers in abeyance.

Associated with the enemy as barbarian is the image of the [14] enemy as rapist, the destroyer of motherhood.

As rapist, the enemy is lust defiling innocence. He is according to Nazi propaganda the Jew who lurks in the shadows waiting to seduce Aryan girls. Or in the propaganda of the Ku Klux Klan he is the black man with an insatiable lust for white women. In American war posters he is the Jap carrying away the naked Occidental woman.

The portrait of the enemy as rapist, destroyer of the madonna, warns us of danger and awakens our pornographic imagination by reminding us of the enticement of rape. The appeal to sexual adventure is a sine qua non in motivating men to go to war: To the warrior belong the spoils, and chief among the spoils are the enemy's women.

The power of bestial images to degrade is rooted in the neu- 17 rotic structure of the hostile imagination. Karen Horney[1] has shown that neurosis always involves a movement between glorified and degraded images of the self. In warfare we act out a mass neurosis whereby we glorify ourselves as agents of God and project our feelings of degradation and impotence upon the enemy. We are suprahuman; therefore they must be subhuman. By destroying the bestial and contaminated enemy we can gain immortality, escape evil, transcend decay and death.

In the iconography of propaganda, the enemy is the bringer 18 of death. He is Death riding on a bomb, the Grim Reaper cutting down youth in its prime. His face is stripped of flesh, his body a dangling skeleton.

War is an irrational ritual. Generation after generation we 19 sacrifice our substance in a vain effort to kill some essential enemy. Now he wears an American or Soviet face. A moment ago he was a Nazi, a Jew, a Moslem, a Christian, a pagan. But the true face of the enemy, as Saint Paul said, is Death itself.[2] The unconscious power that motivates us to fight for Peace, kill for Life, is the magical assumption that if we can destroy this particular enemy we can defeat Death.

Lying within each of us is the desire for immortality. And 20 because this near-instinctive desire for immortality is balanced by the precariously repressed fear that death might really eradicate all traces of our existence, we will go to any extreme to reassure ourselves. By submitting to the divine ordeal of war, in which we are willing to die or kill the enemy who *is* Death, we affirm our own deathlessness.

It is easy to despair when we look at the human genius for 21 creating enemies in the image of our own disowned vices. When we add our mass paranoia and projection to our constantly progressing weapons technology, it seems we are doomed to destroy ourselves.

[1] Modern Freudian psychologist (1885–1952) known for her innovative theories on the psychology of women.
[2] "The last enemy *that* shall be destroyed *is* death." (1 Corinthians 15:26)

But the persistent archetypal images of the enemy may point in   22
a more hopeful direction. We demean our enemies not because
we are instinctively sadistic, but because it is difficult for us to kill
others whom we recognize as fully human beings. Our natural empathy, our instinct for compassion, is strong: society does what it
must to attempt to overcome the moral imperative that forbids us
from killing.

Even so, the effort is successful only for a minority. In spite of   23
our best propaganda, few men and women will actually try to kill
an enemy. In his book *Men Against Fire,* Brigadier General S. L. A.
Marshall presents the results of his study of American soldiers
under fire during World War II. He discovered that *in combat*
the percentage of men who would fire their rifle at the enemy *even
once* did not rise above 25 percent, and the more usual figure was
15 percent. He further discovered that the fear of killing was every
bit as strong as the fear of dying.

If it is difficult to mold men into killers, we may still hope to   24
transform our efforts from fighting an outward enemy to doing
battle with our own paranoia. Our true war is our struggle against
the antagonistic mind. Our true enemy is our propensity to make
enemies. The highest form of moral courage requires us to look at
ourselves from another perspective, to repent, and to reown our
own shadows. True self-knowledge introduces self-doubt into our
minds. And self-doubt is a healthy counterbalance to the dogmatic,
self-righteous certainty that governs political rhetoric and behavior;
it is, therefore, the beginning of compassion.

QUESTIONS

Understanding

1. According to Sam Keen, the root causes of war and peace are not
   arms and armies but what?
2. Why, in Keen's view, is it essential for us to understand the psychology of hatred?
3. Keen's essay outlines five main ways of imagining our enemies.
   What are they? Which one encompasses all the others?
4. In Keen's view, why has humankind long striven to *invent* enemies where they do not already exist?

3. Sigmund Freud's theory of psychology is founded, in part, upon the ideas of *repression* and *projection*. What do these terms mean to a psychologist and how do they help explain the psychology of hatred set forth in "Faces of the Enemy"?

4. In paragraph 24 Keen advises us that the way to end war and warring is "to reown our own shadows." What is meant by this FIGURE OF SPEECH exactly? How does it fit in with the idea of repression?

5. "The Grim Reaper" in paragraph 18 is, of course, death. What is a reaper and what grim emblem of his office does the hooded skeleton usually carry in this common PERSONIFICATION?

6. What is *iconography* (par. 18)? Not only Death but all the other "faces" we project upon The Enemy are "icons" in a sense. How so?

7. Consult your dictionary for meanings of any of the following words you do not already know: *enmity* (par. 2), *propaganda* (pars. 2, 12, 18), *pathology* (par. 5), *malevolent* (par. 7), *rhetoric* (as applied to argumentation and debate, par. 8), *theocracies* (par. 9), *secular* (par. 9), *pragmatic* (par. 9), *anti-semitic* (par. 12), *quasi* (par. 12), *despoiling* (par. 12), *mélange* (par. 12), *abeyance* (par. 13), *insatiable* (par. 15), *sine qua non* (par. 16), *bestial* (par. 17), *eradicate* (par. 20), *archetypal* (par. 22), *demean* (par. 22), *sadistic* (par. 22), *empathy* (par. 22), *propensity* (par. 24), *dogmatic* par. 24).

Comparing

1. How well does Keen's "them-and-us" theory of human aggression explain the conflict between the U.S. and Japan as analyzed by Paul Colinvaux in "Why Japan Bombed Pearl Harbor" (Chapter 4)?

Discussion and Writing Topics

1. What new "faces" can you add to Keen's gallery of images?

2. Recall several people, strangers or otherwise, who have moved you to anger or aggressive acts. Divide these "enemies" into categories and subcategories, and write an essay entitled, "My Hit List."

3. "Faces of the Enemy" defines warfare as neurosis. To what extent do you agree or disagree that human conflict is basically "sickness"?

4. How do you interpret Keen's paraphrase of Karen Horney's theory of psychology: "that neurosis always involves a movement between glorified and degraded images of the self"? Can you think of any objections or exceptions to this theory of mental illness?

Susan Allen Toth

Cinematypes

A native of Iowa, Susan Allen Toth went to school at Smith College, Berkeley, and the University of Minnesota (Ph.D., 1969). She is now a professor of English at Macalester College in St. Paul, where she teaches and does research in American local-color fiction, women's studies, and geography in literature. She is the author of Blooming: A Small-Town Girlhood *(1981) and a new book,* Ivy Days: Making My Way out East *(1984). "Cinematypes" was first printed in* Harper's *(May, 1980) with the subtitle, "Going to the Movies." It classifies films, but Toth's wistful essay in classification is mainly about other types, one of whom was born in 1940 and has been going to the movies (the same ones) almost ever since. The author describes the composition of "Cinematypes" at the end of this chapter.*

Aaron takes me only to art films. That's what I call them,[1] anyway: strange movies with vague poetic images I don't always understand, long dreamy movies about a distant Technicolor past, even longer black-and-white movies about the general meaninglessness of life. We do not go unless at least one reputable critic has found the cinematography superb. We went to *The Devil's Eye*,[1] and Aaron turned to me in the middle and said, "My God, this is *funny*." I do not think he was pleased.

When Aaron and I go to the movies, we drive our cars[2] separately and meet by the box office. Inside the theater he sits tentatively in his seat, ready to move if he can't see well, poised to leave if the film is disappointing. He leans away from me, careful not to touch the bare flesh of his arm against the bare flesh of mine. Sometimes he leans so far I am afraid he may be touching the woman on his other side. If the movie

[1] 1960 satiric comedy by Swedish director Ingmar Bergman, generally known for the starkness and seriousness of his films.

is very good, he leans forward, too, peering between the heads of the couple in front of us. The light from the screen bounces off his glasses; he gleams with intensity, sitting there on the edge of his seat, watching the screen. Once I tapped him on the arm so I could whisper a comment in his ear. He jumped.

After *Belle de Jour*[2] Aaron said he wanted to ask me if he could stay overnight. "But I can't," he shook his head mournfully before I had a chance to answer, "because I know I never sleep well in strange beds." Then he apologized for asking. "It's just that after a film like that," he said, "I feel the need to assert myself." 3

Pete takes me only to movies that he thinks have redeeming social value. He doesn't call them "films." They tend to be about poverty, war, injustice, political corruption, struggling unions in the 1930s, and the military-industrial complex. Pete doesn't like propaganda movies, though, and he doesn't like to be too depressed, either. We stayed away from *The Sorrow and the Pity*;[3] it would be, he said, just too much. Besides, he assured me, things are never that hopeless. So most of the movies we see are made in Hollywood. Because they are always topical, these movies offer what Pete calls "food for thought." When we saw *Coming Home*, Pete's jaw set so firmly with the first half-hour that I knew we would end up at Poppin' Fresh Pies afterward. 4

When Pete and I go to the movies, we take turns driving so no one owes anyone else anything. We leave the car far from the theater so we don't have to pay for a parking space. If it's raining or snowing, Pete offers to let me off at the door, but I can tell he'll feel better if I go with him while he finds a spot, so we share the walk too. Inside the theater Pete will hold my hand when I get scared if I ask him. He puts my hand firmly on his knee and covers it completely with his own hand. His knee never twitches. After a while, when the scary part is past, he loosens his hand slightly and I know that is a signal to take mine away. He sits companionably close, letting his jacket just touch my sweater, but he does not infringe. He thinks I ought to know he is there if I need him. 5

---

[2] Sensual 1967 movie by Spanish director Luis Buñuel, in which the glamorous actress Catherine Deneuve plays the role of a prostitute.

[3] 1972 documentary by Marcel Ophuls about France during the Nazi occupation. *Coming Home*, below: 1978 film of a wounded Vietnam veteran returning home.

One night, after *The China Syndrome*,[4] I asked Pete if he wouldn't like to stay for a second drink, even though it was past midnight. He thought a while about that, considering my offer from all possible angles, but finally he said no. Relationships today, he said, have a tendency to move too quickly. **6**

Sam likes movies that are entertaining. By that he means movies that Will Jones in the *Minneapolis Tribune* loved and either *Time* or *Newsweek* rather liked; also movies that do not have sappy love stories, are not musicals, do not have subtitles, and will not force him to think. He does not go to movies to think. He liked *California Suite* and *The Seduction of Joe Tynan*,[5] though the plots, he said, could have been zippier. He saw it all coming too far in advance, and that took the fun out. He doesn't like to know what is going to happen. "I just want my brain to be tickled," he says. It is very hard for me to pick out movies for Sam. **7**

When Sam takes me to the movies, he pays for everything. He thinks that's what a man ought to do. But I buy my own popcorn, because he doesn't approve of it; the grease might smear his flannel slacks. Inside the theater, Sam makes himself comfortable. He takes off his jacket, puts one arm around me, and all during the movie he plays with my hand, stroking my palm, beating a small tattoo on my wrist. Although he watches the movie intently, his body operates on instinct. Once I inclined my head and kissed him lightly just behind his ear. He beat a faster tattoo on my wrist, quick and musical, but he didn't look away from the screen. **8**

When Sam takes me home from the movies, he stands outside my door and kisses me long and hard. He would like to come in, he says regretfully, but his steady girlfriend in Duluth wouldn't like it. When the *Tribune* gives a movie four stars, he has to save it to see with her. Otherwise her feelings might be hurt. **9**

I go to some movies by myself. On rainy Sunday afternoons I often sneak into a revival house or a college auditorium for old Technicolor musicals, *Kiss Me Kate, Seven Brides for Seven Brothers, Calamity Jane*, even, once, *The Sound of Music*. Wearing saggy jeans so I can prop my feet on the seat in front, I sit **10**

---

[4] 1979 movie warning against the dangers of nuclear power plants.
[5] Popular 1979 movies, both starring Alan Alda among others.

toward the rear where no one can see me. I eat large handfuls of popcorn with double butter. Once the movie starts, I feel completely at home. Howard Keel and I are old friends; I grin back at him on the screen. I know the sound tracks by heart. Sometimes when I get really carried away I hum along with Kathryn Grayson, remembering how I once thought I would fill out a formal like that. I am rather glad now I never did. Skirts whirl, feet tap, acrobatic young men perform impossible feats, and then the camera dissolves into a dream sequence I know I can comfortably follow. It is not, thank God, Bergman.

If I can't find an old musical, I settle for Hepburn and Tracy, 11 vintage Grant or Gable, on adventurous days Claudette Colbert or James Stewart. Before I buy my ticket I make sure it will all end happily. If necessary, I ask the girl at the box office. I have never seen *Stella Dallas* or *Intermezzo*.[6] Over the years I have developed other peccadilloes: I will, for example, see anything that is redeemed by Thelma Ritter. At the end of *Daddy Long Legs* I wait happily for the scene when Fred Clark, no longer angry, at last pours Thelma a convivial drink. They smile at each other, I smile at them, I feel they are smiling at me. In the movies I go to by myself, the men and women always like each other.

QUESTIONS

Understanding

1. Toth is classifying not movies, but what or whom exactly?
2. Toth names representatives of three types. Which one would you characterize as a protective companion? Which one seems most intense? Which represents the provincial, boy-next-door type?
3. Who represents the fourth type in Toth's classification system? How would you characterize this person?
4. What kind of movie does Toth herself prefer? What does she think of the kinds of movies her male friends take her to?
5. How strong are the personal attachments between Toth and her dates? How do they end differently from the movies she likes to see?

[6] Two 1930s tearjerkers.

6. Why do Toth's friends only take her to the kinds of movies *they* like? What does this habit reveal about them?

Strategies and Structure

1. Toth describes her relationship with Aaron in three paragraphs. The first tells the kind of movie he prefers; the second describes how he behaves toward her when they go to the movies; the third describes "afterwards." To what extent does this pattern hold for the next two "cinematypes" she describes?

2. Toth devotes one paragraph to her kind of movie and a second paragraph to how she behaves when she goes to the movie alone. Why doesn't she include a third paragraph at the end?

3. Toth is sensitive to "signals" (par. 5). What signal do the characters give each other in her favorite movies but not in real life?

4. Who drives when Toth goes or is taken to the movies? How do these details about transportation help characterize her companions and her relationships with them? Point out other similar concrete details (such as the references to popcorn) by which Toth deftly pictures her types.

5. Toth says Pete will hold her hand "when I get scared if I ask him" (par. 5). What role is she playing here? Where else in the essay does she seem to act the same way?

6. Films project images by bathing them in an intense light that seems to flicker as the frames shift. What influence of cinematic technique upon Toth's presentation of her types can you detect in paragraphs 2, 5, and 8?

Words and Figures of Speech

1. With both Aaron and Pete, Toth "goes" to the movies. What verb does she use with Sam? Why the shift?

2. Given the personality she assumes here, why does Toth call what she sees "movies" instead of "films"? What are the differences in the CONNOTATIONS of the two terms?

3. What is an "art" film (par. 1)?

4. What does his use of the CLICHÉ "food for thought" (par. 4) reveal about Pete?

5. "Cinematography" (par. 1) is the technical name for the visual art of film making. How does Toth's use of such terms suggest another image of her besides the one she displays at the movies?

6. Consult your dictionary if you are ill at ease with any of the following: *tentatively* (par. 2), *propaganda* (par. 4), *topical* (par. 4), *companionably* (par. 5), *infringe* (par. 5), *tattoo* (par. 8), *peccadilloes* (par. 11), and *convivial* (par. 11).

Comparing

1. Compare and contrast the personality of the author of "Cinematypes" with that of the author of "Memoirs of a Non-Prom Queen," in Chapter 4. Which one seems more sure of herself, and why do you say so?
2. How do both Toth and Joyce Maynard ("Four Generations," Chapter 1) give the impression of being *detached* from their subjects?

Discussion and Writing Topics

1. Movies, especially those made in Hollywood, are said to appeal to the American public as a form of wish fulfillment, of dreams-come-true. How does Toth's experience at the movies support or go against this observation? Your own experience?
2. In what ways, if any, do you find the "rules" of dates and dating to impose role-playing and "typing" upon the participants?
3. Classify dates you have had by type. Describe each type as vividly as you can by citing specific details, including bits of conversation, that dramatize the relationships. Be as objective or peevishly personal as you like.

Isaac Asimov

What Do You Call a Platypus?

Isaac Asimov was born in Petrovichi, Russia, in 1920, entered the
United States at age three, and became a naturalized citizen in
1928. After attending undergraduate and graduate school at
Columbia (Ph.D. in chemistry, 1948), he began teaching bio-
chemistry at the Boston University School of Medicine. His more
than three hundred books deal with an astounding range of sub-
jects: bio-chemistry, the human body, ecology, mathematics,
physics, astronomy, genetics, history, the Bible, and Shakespeare—
to name only a few. Asimov's first real acclaim came with a short
story, "Nightfall," in 1941; he continues to be best known, per-
haps, for his science fiction, including I, Robot (1950); the
"Foundation" trilogy (1951–53); and The Caves of Steel (1954).
"What Do You Call a Platypus?" is an essay on taxonomy, the
science of classification, that shows both the limitations of that
science and how it can provide new knowledge of the world.
After the study questions, you will find comments by Asimov
himself on the process of writing this essay and his work in
general.

In 1800, a stuffed animal arrived in England from the newly   1
discovered continent of Australia.

The continent had already been the source of plants and   2
animals never seen before—but this one was ridiculous. It was
nearly two feet long, and had a dense coating of hair. It also
had a flat rubbery bill, webbed feet, a broad flat tail, and a
spur on each hind ankle that was clearly intended to secrete
poison. What's more, under the tail was a single opening.

Zoologists stared at the thing in disbelief. Hair like a mam-   3
mal! Bill and feet like an aquatic bird! Poison spurs like a
snake! A single opening in the rear as though it laid eggs!

There was an explosion of anger. The thing was a hoax. Some   4
unfunny jokester in Australia, taking advantage of the distance
and strangeness of the continent, had stitched together parts of
widely different creatures and was intent on making fools of innocent zoologists in England.

Yet the skin seemed to hang together. There were no signs of   5
artificial joining. Was it or was it not a hoax? And if it wasn't a
hoax, was it a mammal with reptilian characteristics, or a reptile
with mammalian characteristics, or was it partly bird, or *what?*

The discussion went on heatedly for decades. Even the name   6
emphasized the ways in which it didn't seem like a mammal
despite its hair. One early name was *Platypus anatinus* which is
Graeco-Latin [1] for "Flat-foot, ducklike." Unfortunately, the term,
platypus, had already been applied to a type of beetle and there
must be no duplication in scientific names. It therefore received
another name, *Ornithorhynchus paradoxus*, which means "Bird-
beak, paradoxical."

Slowly, however, zoologists had to fall into line and admit that   7
the creature was real and not a hoax, however upsetting it might
be to zoological notions. For one thing, there were increasingly
reliable reports from people in Australia who caught glimpses of
the creature alive. The *paradoxus* was dropped and the scientific
name is now *Ornithorhynchus anatinus*.

To the general public, however, it is the "duckbill platypus,"   8
or even just the duckbill, the queerest mammal (assuming it is a
mammal) in the world.

When specimens were received in such condition as to make it   9
possible to study the internal organs, it appeared that the heart
was just like those of mammals and not at all like those of reptiles.
The egg-forming machinery in the female, however, was not at all
like those of mammals, but like those of birds or reptiles. It
seemed really and truly to be an egg-layer.

It wasn't till 1884, however, that the actual eggs laid by a crea-   10
ture with hair were found. Such creatures included not only the
platypus, but another Australian species, the spiny anteater. That
was worth an excited announcement. A group of British scientists
were meeting in Montreal at the time, and the egg-discoverer, W.
H. Caldwell, sent them a cable to announce the finding.

---

[1] Combination of Greek and Latin; many scientific names put Latin endings
on Greek roots.

It wasn't till the twentieth century that the intimate life of the [11] duckbill came to be known. It is an aquatic animal, living in Australian fresh water at a wide variety of temperatures—from tropical streams at sea level to cold lakes at an elevation of a mile.

The duckbill is well adapted to its aquatic life, with its dense [12] fur, its flat tail, and its webbed feet. Its bill has nothing really in common with that of the duck, however. The nostrils are differently located and the platypus bill is different in structure, rubbery rather than duckishly horny. It serves the same function as the duck's bill, however, so it has been shaped similarly by the pressures of natural selection.

The water in which the duckbill lives is invariably muddy at the [13] bottom and it is in this mud that the duckbill roots for its food supply. The bill, ridged with horny plates, is used as a sieve, dredging about sensitively in the mud, filtering out the shrimps, earthworms, tadpoles and other small creatures that serve it as food.

When the time comes for the female platypus to produce [14] young, she builds a special burrow, which she lines with grass and carefully plugs. She then lays two eggs, each about three quarters of an inch in diameter and surrounded by a translucent, horny shell.

These the mother platypus places between her tail and abdo- [15] men and curls up about them. It takes two weeks for the young to hatch out. The new-born duckbills have teeth and very short bills, so that they are much less "birdlike" than the adults. They feed on milk. The mother has no nipples, but milk oozes out of pore openings in the abdomen and the young lick the area and are nourished in this way. As they grow, the bills become larger and the teeth fall out.

Yet despite everything zoologists learned about the duckbills, [16] they never seemed entirely certain as to where to place them in the table of animal classification. On the whole, the decision was made because of hair and milk. In all the world, only mammals have true hair and only mammals produce true milk. The duckbill and spiny anteater have hair and produce milk, so they have been classified as mammals.

Just the same, they are placed in a very special position. All the [17] mammals are divided into two subclasses. In one of these subclasses ("Prototheria" or "first-beasts")are the duckbill and five species of the spiny anteater. In the other ("Theria" or just "beast") are all the other 4,231 known species of mammals.

But all this is the result of judging only living species of mammals. Suppose we could study extinct species as well. Would that help us decide on the place of the platypus? Would it cause us to confirm our decision—or change it? 18

Fossil remnants exist of mammals and reptiles of the far past, but these remnants are almost entirely of bones and teeth. Bones and teeth give us interesting information but they can't tell us everything. 19

For instance, is there any way of telling, from bones and teeth alone, whether an extinct creature is a reptile or a mammal? 20

Well, all living reptiles have legs splayed out so that the upper part above the knee is horizontal (assuming they have legs at all). All mammals, on the other hand, have legs that are vertical all the way down. Again, reptiles have teeth that all look more or less alike, while mammals have teeth that have different shapes, with sharp incisors in front, flat molars in back, and conical incisors and premolars in between. 21

As it happens, there are certain extinct creatures, to which have been given the name "therapsids," which have their leg bones vertical and their teeth differentiated just as in the case of mammals. —And yet they are considered reptiles and not mammals. Why? Because there is another bony difference to be considered. 22

In living mammals, the lower jaw contains a single bone; in reptiles, it is made up of a number of bones. The therapsid lower jaw is made up of seven bones and because of that those creatures are classified as reptiles. And yet in the therapsid lower jaw, the one bone making up the central portion of the lower jaw is by far the largest. The other six bones, three on each side, are crowded into the rear angle of the jaw. 23

There seems no question, then, that if the therapsids are reptiles they are nevertheless well along the pathway towards mammals. 24

But how far along the pathway are they? For instance, did they have hair? It might seem that it would be impossible to tell whether an extinct animal had hair or not just from the bones, but let's see— 25

Hair is an insulating device. It keeps body heat from being lost too rapidly. Reptiles keep their body temperature at about that of the outside environment. They don't have to be concerned over loss of heat and hair would be of no use to them. 26

Mammals, however, maintain their internal temperature at 27

nearly 100° F. regardless of the outside temperature; they are "warm-blooded." This gives them the great advantage of remaining agile and active in cold weather, when the chilled reptile is sluggish. But then the mammal must prevent heat loss by means of a hairy covering. (Birds, which also are warm-blooded, use feathers as an insulating device.)

With that in mind, let's consider the bones. In reptiles, the   28
nostrils open into the mouth just behind the teeth. This means that reptiles can only breathe with their mouths empty. When they are biting or chewing, breathing must stop. This doesn't bother a reptile much, for it can suspend its need for oxygen for considerable periods.

Mammals, however, must use oxygen in their tissues constantly,   29
in order to keep the chemical reactions going that serve to keep their body temperature high. The oxygen supply must not be cut off for more than very short intervals. Consequently mammals have developed a bony palate, a roof to the mouth. When they breathe, air is led above the mouth to the throat. This means they can continue breathing while they bite and chew. It is only when they are actually in the act of swallowing that the breath is cut off and this is only a matter of a couple of seconds at a time.

The later therapsid species had, as it happened, a palate. If they   30
had a palate, it seems a fair deduction that they needed an uninterrupted supply of oxygen that makes it look as though they were warm-blooded. And if they were warm-blooded, then very likely they had hair, too.

The conclusion, drawn from the bones alone, would seem to be   31
that some of the later therapsids had hair, even though, judging by their jawbones, they were still reptiles.

The thought of hairy reptiles is astonishing. But that is only   32
because the accident of evolution seems to have wiped out the intermediate forms. The only therapsids alive seem to be those that have developed *all* the mammalian characteristics, so that we call them mammals. The only reptiles alive are those that developed *none* of the mammalian characteristics.

Those therapsids that developed some but not others seem to   33
be extinct.

Only the duckbill and the spiny anteater remain near the border   34
line. They have developed the hair and the milk and the single-

boned lower jaw and the four-chambered heart, but not the nipples or the ability to bring forth live young.

For all we know, some of the extinct therapsids, while still having their many-boned lower jaw (which is why we call them reptiles instead of mammals), may have developed even beyond the duckbill in other ways. Perhaps some late therapsids had nipples and brought forth living young. We can't tell from the bones alone. 35

If we had a complete record of the therapsids, flesh and blood, as well as teeth and bone, we might decide that the duckbill was on the therapsid side of the line and not on the mammalian side. —Or are there any other pieces of evidence that can be brought into play? 36

An American zoologist, Giles T. MacIntyre, of Queens College, has taken up the matter of the trigeminal nerve, which leads from the jaw muscles to the brain. 37

In all reptiles, without exception, the trigeminal nerve passes through the skull at a point that lies between two of the bones making up the skull. In all mammals that bring forth living young, without exception, the nerve actually passes *through* a particular skull bone. 38

Suppose we ignore all the matter of hair and milk and eggs, and just consider the trigeminal nerve. In the duckbill, does the nerve pass through a bone, or between two bones? It has seemed in the past that the nerve passed through a bone and that put the duckbill on the mammalian side of the dividing line. 39

Not so, says MacIntyre. The study of the trigeminal nerve was made in adult duckbills, where the skull bones are fused together and the boundaries are hard to make out. In young duckbills, the skull bones are more clearly separated and in them it can be seen, MacIntyre says, that the trigeminal nerve goes between two bones. 40

In that case, there is a new respect in which the duckbill falls on the reptilian side of the line and MacIntyre thinks it ought not to be considered a mammal, but as a surviving species of the otherwise long-extinct therapsid line. 41

And so, a hundred seventy years after zoologists began to puzzle out the queer mixture of characteristics that go to make up the duckbill platypus—there is still argument as to what to call it. 42

Is the duckbill platypus a mammal? A reptile? Or just a duckbill platypus? 43

QUESTIONS

Understanding

1. What are the chief distinguishing features of mammals as reported by Asimov? Of reptiles?
2. Which mammalian features does the platypus lack? Which reptilian characteristics does it possess?
3. How does the example of the platypus show the limitations of the zoological CLASSIFICATION system?
4. What new evidence does Asimov cite for reclassifying the platypus? How convincing do you find it? Why?

Strategies and Structure

1. Why do you think Asimov begins his case for reclassifying the platypus by recounting the confused history of how the animal got its name?
2. Why does it matter what we *call* a platypus? For what ultimate purpose is Asimov concerned with the creature's name?
3. Why does Asimov refer to extinct creatures beginning with paragraph 18? What is the function of the therapsids (par. 22) in his line of reasoning?
4. This essay in reclassification ends with three alternatives (par. 43). Why three instead of just two?
5. The logic of paragraph 32 depends upon an unstated assumption about the order of evolution. Which does Asimov assume came first, reptiles or mammals? How does this assumption influence his entire ARGUMENT? Is the assumption valid?

Words and Figures of Speech

1. Why was "paradoxical" (par. 6) an appropriate part of the platypus's name? How does it differ in precise usage from "ambiguous" and "ambivalent"?
2. Asimov refers to the "egg-forming machinery" (par. 9) of the female platypus. How technical is this term? What does it suggest about the audience for whom Asimov intends this essay?
3. What is meant by "the pressures of natural selection" (par. 12)?

4. Asimov's essay is an exercise in "taxonomy," although he does not use the word. What does it mean according to your dictionary?

Comparing

1. Asimov's essay has some features of a logical argument of the sort you will encounter in Chapter 9. What is he attempting to prove or disprove? When you read Richard Restak's "The Other Difference between Boys and Girls" in Chapter 9, compare the kind of evidence used to support his logical argument with the kind used to support Asimov's.

Discussion and Writing Topics

1. What would *you* call a platypus? Why?
2. Explain why a whale is classified as a mammal instead of a fish.
3. A classification system provides a means of arranging information about the known world. Using Asimov's train of thought or some other example, explain how classification systems also help us gain *new* knowledge.

Writers on the Writing Process:
Isaac Asimov and Susan Allen Toth

Recovering the mental processes behind any piece of writing   1
is difficult, even if attempted before the ink dries. The difficulty
is greatly compounded, of course, for the prolific writer working over a period of many years; and no writer in America is
more prolific than Isaac Asimov. When asked to explain how
and why he wrote "What Do You Call a Platypus?" the author
replied: "Your queries have succeeded in embarrassing me, but
to answer your questions is almost impossible. You must understand that I have written, quite literally, 300 books and up to
3,000 shorter pieces. I am continually writing every day all
day."

One among those thousands of shorter pieces whose compo-   2
sition Asimov has recovered, in part, is his best-known science
fiction story, "Nightfall." Asimov got the idea for the story
from two sources available to any writer, not just the writer of
fiction. They are the work of other writers and the suggestions
of friends (including editors and teachers).

The other writer in this case was Ralph Waldo Emerson,   3
who once exclaimed, "If the stars should appear one night in a
thousand years, how would men believe and adore; and preserve for many generations the remembrance of the city of
God." In 1941 Asimov's friend John W. Campbell, then editor
of *Astounding Fiction,* mused over this passage and suggested
that twenty-one-year-old Asimov write about what would happen if the stars appeared to humankind only once in a thousand years.

"It was a crucial moment for me," Asimov recalls *In Mem-*   4
ory Yet Green. He had composed more than thirty stories at
the time, but only three rated "three stars or better on my
old zero-to-five scale." Taking off from his friend's suggestion,

Asimov produced in twenty-one days the work that established him as a major writer of science fiction. (A letter from the author still bears the return address, "Nightfall, Inc.")

Asimov's first published work of nonfiction was a textbook, *Biochemistry and Human Metabolism* (1950). He remembers it as a "distressing failure." A collaboration with two other authors (whose writing styles clashed with Asimov's), the book nevertheless confirmed Asimov in the role he adopts in "What Do You Call a Platypus?" "I'm on fire to explain, and happiest when it's something reasonably intricate which I can make clear step by step."

Where does he get the urge to be an explainer? "It's the easiest way I can clarify things in my own mind." The "reasonably intricate" question that Asimov clarified for himself by the process of writing the "Platypus" essay was whether or not scientists were wrong to classify the duckbill as a mammal. What about the fossil record, the only record left by the platypus's prehistoric ancestors? Might it not show that the platypus had evolved from a reptile? Or even a bird? "What Do You Call a Platypus?" is a working out of this inquiry "step by step" on paper.

In Asimov's case the gap between urge and paper is unusually brief. Asked why many writers revise heavily instead of publishing their first drafts, Asimov protested: "I *do* always print the first words that pop into my head. I don't know how I decide a beginning or an ending or a title. I just sit down and type and that's that." (Asimov has trained himself to type ninety words per minute, and over the last thirty years he has produced an average of a book every month and a half.) He can write quickly without revising, says Asimov, because after so much practice writing "comes as naturally as breathing to me."

Well aware that his method is not for beginning writers, Asimov was reluctant at first to have it reported: "it's not a good thing to tell students." But just as there is more than one way to classify a platypus, there is more than one way to write. Few writers have Asimov's "good fortune at being able to do it without [prior] thought," but many practicing writers discard the old formulas and outlines they were once taught in school. The writing process is as idiosyncratic as the thinking process, and the right way to write is any way that works for the writer.

Although her methods are different, the author of "Cinematypes" writes out of the same motive that urges Asimov to explain: "I write," Toth says, "to give clarity and shape to my own feelings and perceptions of things—sometimes to rid my mental attic of old snapshots and bits of dialogue—and because I love to hear the sounds of words and the rhythm of sentences in my head."

She vividly recalls the feeling that prompted "Cinematypes":   10 "As you might have guessed, I wrote this essay out of sheer frustration one day—shortly after attending a series of movies with three 'real-life' characters much like the ones described in the piece. I remember thinking, 'There *must* be better alternatives!' "

Toth turned her sense of frustration to conscious effect during   11 the writing process. As her intention came clear, she aimed "to show *this is the way it was*." To achieve this aim, she drew directly upon the experience of movie-going, but she was "not above changing details of 'reality' to make the real more real, if you see what I mean. (I'm sure I'd flay alive a student who wrote that last sentence.)" How much she altered the facts in the interests of truth is suggested by the reaction of one of her "types" to his portrait. "One of the models for a character in this essay didn't even recognize himself, which astonished—and delighted—me."

Toth's title for "Cinematypes" was originally "Going to the   12 Movies"; "I think I had the title at the start of the piece," she says, "though I can't quite remember." Toth still likes her original title because "it was laconic, quiet, and left the reader free to draw his/her own conclusions about what the piece was about." Editors at *Harper's*, where "Cinematypes" first appeared, felt, however, that "Going to the Movies" was too "prosaic" and came up with the new title.

Toth is hardly down on editors, though. A trouble spot for her   13 while composing "Cinematypes" was the ending. She labored over it "with lots of sweat, one rejected revision, tinkering with words and sentences, irritation & frustration & just wishing it were over with." Finally, Debbie McGill, whom Toth calls "an acute editor," suggested "an ending not quite as bitter and misanthropic as my first one."

The major revisions in Toth's essay came in the last section,   14 but she revised throughout "substantially." How? "I worked hard on each sentence to shorten, condense, and suggest as much as possible." As she revises, Toth strives "to understate and let the meaning emerge through carefully chosen detail and shadings of tone; I always worry about pounding my reader on the head. Much of the time I'm thinking to myself, 'It's awful, but funny. It's funny but awful.' "

What kind of audience did she have in mind as she composed [15] "Cinematypes"? She wrote it as she usually writes: "for an intelligent, open-minded reader of general education but familiar with books—someone who is not afraid of feelings—and who is alive to the nuances of irony."

And what of the "alternatives" she hoped to find? Are there less [16] obtuse "types" with which to stand before the marquee? "There are," says the former companion of Aaron, Pete, and Sam. "I no longer go to so many movies alone."

WRITING TOPICS for Chapter Two
Essays That Classify and Divide

Write an essay on one of the following subjects that uses classification or division as its organizing principle. Remember that a good classification essay not only assigns members to a class but also gives interesting reasons for the divisions it makes and draws interesting conclusions about its subject:

1. Your teachers in high school or college

2. Blind dates

3. Drugs and drug-abusers

4. Moral codes

5. Fraternities or sororities

6. Neighborhoods, high schools, or churches in your hometown

7. Landlords in the campus area

8. Fast-food restaurants

9. Food in the dining facilities on your campus

10. Attitudes toward getting a college education

11. Cameras, bicycles, or motorcycles

12. Modern families

13. Movies you have seen in the last year

14. Television soap operas

15. Styles of rock, folk, country and western, or classical music

16. Ways of seeing (for the first time) a city, museum, or foreign country

17. Ways of reacting to personal disappointment or tragedy

18. Life-styles among people under thirty

3

Essays That
Analyze a Process

Analysis breaks its object into components. It differs from
CLASSIFICATION [1] *by attending to a particular member of a*
class rather than the class in general. When we classify an
artichoke, for example, we put it in the category of "thistle-
like plants." When we analyze an artichoke, we pull apart
an individual specimen and note that it is made up of layer
upon layer of fibrous green scales. If we analyze the growth
of an artichoke from a seed, we are analyzing a process
(which tends to be in motion) rather than an object (which
tends to be stable). Most how-to-do-it essays analyze pro-
cesses, as do most accounts of how something works (a
typewriter, a city transit system, gravity). The selections in
this chapter are essays in PROCESS ANALYSIS.

In the following analysis, John McPhee tells how orange
juice concentrate is made from fresh oranges:

As the fruit starts to move along a concentrate plant's assembly
line, it is first culled. In what some citrus people remember as
"the old fresh-fruit days," before the Second World War,
about forty per cent of all oranges grown in Florida were
eliminated at packinghouses and dumped in fields. Florida milk
tasted like orangeade. Now, with the exception of split and
rotten fruit, all of Florida's orange crop is used. Moving up a
conveyer belt, oranges are scrubbed with detergent before they
roll on into juicing machines. There are several kinds of juicing
machines, and they are something to see. One is called the
Brown Seven Hundred. Seven hundred oranges a minute go into
it and are split and reamed on the same kind of rosettes that

---

[1] Terms printed in all capitals are defined in the Glossary.

are in the centers of ordinary kitchen reamers. The rinds that come pelting out the bottom are integral halves, just like the rinds of oranges squeezed in a kitchen. Another machine is the Food Machinery Corporation's FMC In-line Extractor. It has a shining row of aluminum teeth. When an orange tumbles in, the upper jaw comes crunching down on it while at the same time the orange is penetrated from below by a perforated steel tube. As the jaws crush the outside, the juice goes through the perforations in the tube and down into the plumbing of the concentrate plant. All in a second, the juice has been removed and the rind has been crushed and shredded beyond recognition.

From either machine, the juice flows on into a thing called the finisher, where seeds, rag, and pulp are removed. The finisher has a big stainless-steel screw that steadily drives the juice through a fine-mesh screen. From the finisher, it flows on into holding tanks. . . .

The first thing to notice about this analysis is that it combines several processes into one. McPhee describes the journey of fresh oranges from the time they enter the conveyor belt until the juice reaches the holding tanks. But because all companies do not use the same machines, he must digress to explain the differences between the Brown Seven Hundred and the In-line Extractor. The discussion returns from its divergent branches in the beginning of the second paragraph, "From either machine. . . ." McPhee picks up the flow so smoothly that we hardly notice any interruption; but, like many accounts of a complex process, his is a composite. The author has reduced the complexities to their elements and takes care of inconsistencies in brief asides to the reader. (The business of extracting "chilled juice" from fresh oranges is so different from making concentrate that McPhee has to describe it in a separate segment of his account.)

One aside in our example, however, has little to do with the process of making orange concentrate. This is the author's reference to the days before World War II when all Florida milk tasted like orangeade. To keep our interest, McPhee is laying out many things at once, including the changing history of Florida's citrus industry. Process analysis often draws upon other strategies of EXPOSITION *and upon the other* MODES OF DISCOURSE. *When McPhee switches from what happened in "the old fresh-fruit days" to what happens "now," he slips into* NARRATION. *Process analysis might even be regarded as a specialized form of narration that tells what happens* from one stage of a process to another. But the ultimate purpose of process analysis is to explain how rather than to tell what. And although process analysis often describes the parts of an operation, it focuses upon their function rather than their appearance (the business of DESCRIPTION).

Perhaps the most important lesson to be learned from McPhee's analysis is that he divides the process of making concentrate into stages: (1) culling, (2) scrubbing, (3) extracting, (4) straining, (5) storing. When you begin an essay in process analysis, make a list of the stages of the operation you are describing or the directions you are giving. Once you have a rough list of stages, make sure that they are separate and distinct. (McPhee does not isolate the movement of oranges up the conveyor belt as a stage because the conveyor is involved in more than one stage of the process of making concentrate.) When you are satisfied that none of the items on your list repeat others and that you have omitted no essential items, you are ready to decide upon the order in which your steps will be presented to the reader.

The usual order of a process analysis is chronological, beginning with the earliest stage of the process and ending with the last or with the finished product. If you are describing a cyclical rather than a linear process, however, you will have to break into the cycle at an arbitrary point, proceed through the cycle, and return to your starting place. For example, you might describe the circulation of the blood by starting as it leaves the heart, tracing it through the arteries and vessels, and concluding as it flows back into the heart. If the order of the process you are describing is controlled by a piece of mechanism, let that mechanism work for you. The first part of McPhee's analysis is organized as much by that conveyor belt as by time. Whatever order you choose, do not digress from it so long that the reader loses the sequence. Sequence is the backbone of process analysis, and it must be flexible yet strong.

Katie Kelly

Garbage

Katie Kelly, a free-lance writer, lives in New York City, but her hometown is Albion (Boone Co.), Nebraska (population: 2010), to which she returns once a year or so. A former contributing editor of Time and an editor and contributor to women's magazines, she is the author of The Wonderful World of Women's Wear Daily (1972) and My Prime Time: Confessions of a T.V. Watcher (1980). The following essay is Kelly's analysis of how New York City processes its enormous flow of garbage. Soon after writing this piece for the Saturday Review, she published a book-length investigation of the same subject, Garbage: The History and Future of Garbage in America (1973).

New Yorkers are a provincial lot. They wear their city's 1 accomplishments like blue ribbons. To anyone who will listen they boast of leading the world in everything from Mafia murders to porno moviehouses. They can also boast that their city produces more garbage than any other city in the world. In fact, it produces more than many countries.

In its 1970–71 garbage season—a boffo season if there ever 2 was one—New York City produced an average of 28,900 tons per day, as against a mere 4,800 tons per day for Los Angeles and a paltry 2,000 tons per day for San Francisco. But it is not only in quantity that New York excels. Fully 20 per cent of the city's garbage consists of quality paper: canceled checks, rough drafts of Broadway hits, executive memos, IBM punch cards, and so on. On Mondays alone seven million pounds of the Sunday *New York Times* are donated to New York garbage cans.

Then there's the packaging. According to the city's flam- 3

boyant environmental protection administrator, Jerome Kretchmer, in the rest of the country packaging accounts for under 20 per
cent of the total garbage; in New York, for 40 per cent. Much of
this whopping total consists of flip tops, snack paks, variety packs,
plastic cases, bottles, tin cans, and other containers. Another big
chunk is aluminum. If the aluminum that New Yorkers throw out
every day were converted into Reynolds Wrap, it would make a
sheet more than 7,500 miles long—roughly the distance from New
York to Samoa.

The remaining 40 per cent of Fun City's garbage consists of   4
such mundane leavings as egg shells, coffee grounds, wilted lettuce
leaves, and pot scrapings, together with such odds and ends as tex-
tile scraps, tires, wood, glass, plastics, etc. (The 73,000 cars abandoned on New York City streets last year constitute a separate class
of garbage. Though some find their way to the dump, most of
these wrecks are bought up by scrap dealers.)

If New York produces more garbage than any other city in the   5
world, it stands to reason that the cost of getting rid of it must be
correspondingly prodigious. It is. Last year the bill for pickup,
processing, and delivery came to $176,246,604. Though one would
expect innovation from the undisputed leader in the field of garbage, New York is forced to dispose of its trash in ways familiar to
every small town in the country: It burns the stuff in incinerators—
about 30 per cent of New York City garbage is incinerated—and/or
buries it in landfills.

The largest of the city's seven incinerators, the Brooklyn incin-   6
erator is a yellow-brick building with high walls, few windows, and
two 200-foot-tall smoke stacks, one of which is equipped with an
electrostatic precipitator to reduce pollution. (Although a cut
above the average in cleanliness, New York's incinerator stacks still
spew thousands of pounds of soot over the city every day.) Garbage trucks parade up to the Brooklyn plant, dumping their loads
into a pit capable of holding 12,500 tons of garbage. A crane
moves back and forth over this pit, periodically clanking down to
gouge out a one-ton bite. The crane then drops the garbage onto
conveyor belts, which in turn feed it into the incinerator ovens.

Measuring thirty by seven by two hundred feet, each of the   7
Brooklyn incinerator's four ovens is capable of burning up ten tons
of garbage an hour at temperatures averaging 1,600° to 1,800° F.
The towering stacks create such an upward draft that, upon look-

ing into one of the iron grates, I felt as if, if I didn't hold on, I would be sucked into that fiery furnace.

After the garbage has been burned, the cooled residue is dumped   8
onto barges, which are towed off by tugboats to one of five landfill sites around the city. The largest of these is the 3,000-acre Fresh Kills site on Staten Island.

Fresh Kills, which daily receives about 11,000 tons of garbage,   9
is a strange place. Much of this former swampland resembles the ash heaps of *The Great Gatsby*.[1] Vast, forlorn, endless. A vision of death. In the foreground, a discarded funeral wreath. A doll with outstretched arms. A man's black sock. A nylon stocking. And, beyond, refrigerators, toilets, bathtubs, stoves.

Yet Fresh Kills is also—in places and in its own way—unexpect-   10
edly beautiful. Thousands of gulls wheel in the air. Banking sharply, they dip down one by one to settle in for a good feast. In areas where the garbage is fresh, there is an overpowering stench, but where it is older, its blanket of earth is covered with grass, bushes, shrubs, trees. Summertime in Fresh Kills is a time of flowers and birdsong. A volunteer vegetable garden flourishes in the landfill. Here, in the world's largest compost heap, the seeds and sprouts of kitchen scraps thrive. Come fall, offices all around New York's City Hall are decorated with gourds and pumpkins harvested at Fresh Kills. In the fall, too, quail and pheasants scurry through Fresh Kills' underbrush, creating a problem for the Department of Sanitation: Hunters try to poach on this municipal game preserve.

"Fresh Kills turns me on," Jerome Kretchmer said a few days   11
after my visit to the site. Recently, he went on, he had taken his seven-year-old daughter's class out to Fresh Kills for a field trip. Even the sight of the barges heading off for the landfill sites excited him: "You can stand on the shore on Monday morning and watch the barges going out. And you know what went on in New York City over the weekend. There are fetuses and dead cats. Packages, boxes, cartons from fancy stores, dress scraps. Wow, man! Whatever went on in the city is going out to Fresh Kills. You can see it all. What we used. What we wasted."

Opened in 1948, Fresh Kills is already almost full to the brim,   12

[1] Novel by F. Scott Fitzgerald published in 1925; it compares modern life to a wasteland of ashes near a Long Island railroad track.

for New York City, like every other city in this country, has more
garbage than it can cope with. The city is, in fact, due to run out
of landfill space—preferably swampland or a sandpit or gulley—in
1985. The solution: Pile it higher. But even here there are limits.
As one city official put it: "We have to leave some room between
the sea gulls and the planes."

"It sure has changed out here," one worker, who has been at   13
Fresh Kills for years, told me. "Why, there used to be fresh natural
springs over there." He gestured out over the hundreds of acres
of garbage. Natural crab beds once flourished in the area. Now
they, too, are gone, buried under tons of garbage.

QUESTIONS

Understanding

1. In what two ways does New York City's garbage differ from that
   of other cities? What about the process of handling that garbage?
   How different is *it*?
2. Why does Fresh Kills "turn on" (par. 11) Administrator Kretchmer? What story does he read in the city's garbage?
3. New York's great garbage dump is a place of death for Kelly
   (par. 9). What other associations does it hold for her? In which
   direction does the last paragraph (13) tip the balance?

Strategies and Structure

1. Kelly divides the process of handling New York's garbage into
   three main stages. If the first is collection, what are the other
   two? Where are they explained?
2. To which stage does Kelly pay least attention? Should she have
   paid more? Why or why not?
3. Abandoned cars are a substantial form of garbage that Kelly leaves
   out of her process analysis. Why does she do so?
4. Point out specific details (for example, the money figures in paragraph 5) by which Kelly establishes her authority as an expert
   in the "field" she is explaining to us.
5. What is the purpose of the last sentence in paragraph 7?

6. What is the role of environmental protectionist Kretchmer in Kelly's essay?

7. How effective do you find the example of the giant aluminum roll in paragraph 3? Explain your answer.

8. What is the effect of including "fetuses" in the list of items in paragraph 11? How interesting do you find most of the "catalogues" of garbage in Kelly's essay?

Words and Figures of Speech

1. "Fresh Kills" may sound like a well-chosen name for a garbage graveyard, but in American place-names "Kill" has nothing to do with death. What geographical meaning does the word have, according to your dictionary?

2. Describe the TONE of Kelly's essay as set by SLANG words like *boffo* (par. 2) and *Fun City* (4).

3. Look up any of the following words you do not already know: *provincial* (par. 1), *paltry* (2), *flamboyant* (3), *mundane* (4), *prodigious* (5), and *innovation* (6).

Comparing

1. What hints of a PERSUASIVE ARGUMENT about ecology can you find in Kelly's PROCESS ANALYSIS? How does the evidence set forth in her essay confirm Paul Colinvaux's "ecological thesis"—that human culture is altered by changes in population and living habits—in "Why Japan Bombed Pearl Harbor" (Chapter 4)?

2. How does Kelly's reporter resemble Susan Allen Toth's female movie-goer in "Cinematypes" (Chapter 2)?

Discussion and Writing Topics

1. How does your hometown or city dispose of its garbage? Of cars abandoned on the streets? Explain either process step by step.

2. Some cities (Cleveland, Ohio, for example) are experimenting with garbage as a source of fuel. Conceive and analyze such an ideal recycling process.

3. Cities in many parts of the U.S. must cope with the problem of snow removal in winter. How well does your town handle the job? What steps are taken after a snowfall? What additional steps would you recommend to the mayor?

4. A town's history may often be read in its refuse. Describe a dump you have visited as the end product of some sequence of human events.

Alexander Petrunkevitch

The Spider and the Wasp

Alexander Petrunkevitch (1875–1964), a native of Russia who came to the United States in his late twenties, was a world-renowned zoologist. After lecturing briefly at Harvard, he taught at Indiana University and then Yale for many years. Author of learned books on insects and a treatise in German on free will, he also translated poems by Byron (into Russian) and Pushkin (from Russian into English). Beginning in 1911, with an index to the species in Central and South America, Petrunkevitch devoted more than fifty years to the study of spiders. (His second book on amber spiders appeared in the year of his death.) "The Spider and the Wasp," which analyzes a natural process of life-out-of death, is a product of that life-long fascination.

To hold its own in the struggle for existence, every species of animal must have a regular source of food, and if it happens to live on other animals, its survival may be very delicately balanced. The hunter cannot exist without the hunted; if the latter should perish from the earth, the former would, too. When the hunted also prey on some of the hunters, the matter may become complicated. 1

This is nowhere better illustrated than in the insect world. Think of the complexity of a situation such as the following: There is a certain wasp, *Pimpla inquisitor*, whose larvae feed on the larvae of the tussock moth. *Pimpla* larvae in turn serve as food for the larvae of a second wasp, and the latter in their turn nourish still a third wasp. What subtle balance between fertility and mortality must exist in the case of each of these four species to prevent the extinction of all of them! 2

An excess of mortality over fertility in a single member of the group would ultimately wipe out all four.

This is not a unique case. The two great orders of insects, Hymenoptera and Diptera, are full of such examples of interrelationship. And the spiders (which are not insects but members of a separate order of arthropods) also are killers and victims of insects.

The picture is complicated by the fact that those species which are carnivorous in the larval stage have to be provided with animal food by a vegetarian mother. The survival of the young depends on the mother's correct choice of a food which she does not eat herself.

In the feeding and safeguarding of their progeny the insects and spiders exhibit some interesting analogies to reasoning and some crass examples of blind instinct. The case I propose to describe here is that of the tarantula spiders and their arch-enemy, the digger wasps of the genus Pepsis. It is a classic example of what looks like intelligence pitted against instinct—a strange situation in which the victim, though fully able to defend itself, submits unwittingly to its destruction.

Most tarantulas live in the Tropics, but several species occur in the temperate zone and a few are common in the southern U.S. Some varieties are large and have powerful fangs with which they can inflict a deep wound. These formidable looking spiders do not, however, attack man; you can hold one in your hand, if you are gentle, without being bitten. Their bite is dangerous only to insects and small mammals such as mice; for a man it is no worse than a hornet's sting.

Tarantulas customarily live in deep cylindrical burrows, from which they emerge at dusk and into which they retire at dawn. Mature males wander about after dark in search of females and occasionally stray into houses. After mating, the male dies in a few weeks, but a female lives much longer and can mate several years in succession. In a Paris museum is a tropical specimen which is said to have been living in captivity for 25 years.

A fertilized female tarantula lays from 200 to 400 eggs at a time; thus it is possible for a single tarantula to produce several thousand young. She takes no care of them beyond weaving a cocoon of silk to enclose the eggs. After they hatch, the young walk away, find convenient places in which to dig their burrows and spend the rest of their lives in solitude. Tarantulas feed mostly on insects and millepedes. Once their appetite is appeased, they digest the food for several days before eating again. Their sight is poor, being limited to sensing a change in the intensity of light and to the perception of moving objects. They apparently have little or no sense of hearing, for a hungry tarantula will pay no attention to a loudly chirping cricket placed in its cage unless the insect happens to touch one of its legs.

But all spiders, and especially hairy ones, have an extremely   9
delicate sense of touch. Laboratory experiments prove that tarantulas can distinguish three types of touch: pressure against the body wall, stroking of the body hair and riffling of certain very fine hairs on the legs called trichobothria. Pressure against the body, by a finger or the end of a pencil, causes the tarantula to move off slowly for a short distance. The touch excites no defensive response unless the approach is from above where the spider can see the motion, in which case it rises on its hind legs, lifts its front legs, opens its fangs and holds this threatening posture as long as the object continues to move. When the motion stops, the spider drops back to the ground, remains quiet for a few seconds and then moves slowly away.

The entire body of a tarantula, especially its legs, is thickly   10
clothed with hair. Some of it is short and woolly, some long and stiff. Touching this body hair produces one of two distinct reactions. When the spider is hungry, it responds with an immediate and swift attack. At the touch of a cricket's antennae the tarantula seizes the insect so swiftly that a motion picture taken at the rate of 64 frames per second shows only the result and not the process of capture. But when the spider is not hungry, the stimulation of its hairs merely causes it to shake the touched limb. An insect can walk under its hairy belly unharmed.

The trichobothria, very fine hairs growing from disklike mem-   11
branes on the legs, were once thought to be the spider's hearing organs, but we now know that they have nothing to do with sound. They are sensitive only to air movement. A light breeze makes them vibrate slowly without disturbing the common hair. When one blows gently on the trichobothria, the tarantula reacts with a quick jerk of its four front legs. If the front and hind legs are stimulated at the same time, the spider makes a sudden jump. This reaction is quite independent of the state of its appetite.

These three tactile responses—to pressure on the body wall, to [12] moving of the common hair and to flexing of the trichobothria— are so different from one another that there is no possibility of confusing them. They serve the tarantula adequately for most of its needs and enable it to avoid most annoyances and dangers. But they fail the spider completely when it meets its deadly enemy, the digger wasp Pepsis.

These solitary wasps are beautiful and formidable creatures. [13] Most species are either a deep shiny blue all over, or deep blue with rusty wings. The largest have a wing span of about four inches. They live on nectar. When excited, they give off a pungent odor—a warning that they are ready to attack. The sting is much worse than that of a bee or common wasp, and the pain and swelling last longer. In the adult stage the wasp lives only a few months. The female produces but a few eggs, one at a time at intervals of two or three days. For each egg the mother must provide one adult tarantula, alive but paralyzed. The tarantula must be of the correct species to nourish the larva. The mother wasp attaches the egg to the paralyzed spider's abdomen. Upon hatching from the egg, the larva is many hundreds of times smaller than its living but helpless victim. It eats no other food and drinks no water. By the time it has finished its single gargantuan meal and become ready for wasphood, nothing remains of the tarantula but its indigestible chitinous skeleton.

The mother wasp goes tarantula-hunting when the egg in her [14] ovary is almost ready to be laid. Flying low over the ground late on a sunny afternoon, the wasp looks for its victim or for the mouth of a tarantula burrow, a round hole edged by a bit of silk. The sex of the spider makes no difference, but the mother is highly discriminating as to species. Each species of Pepsis requires a certain species of tarantula, and the wasp will not attack the wrong species. In a cage with a tarantula which is not its normal prey the wasp avoids the spider, and is usually killed by it in the night.

Yet when a wasp finds the correct species, it is the other way [15] about. To identify the species the wasp apparently must explore the spider with her antennae. The tarantula shows an amazing tolerance to this exploration. The wasp crawls under it and walks over it without evoking any hostile response. The molestation is so great and so persistent that the tarantula often rises on all eight legs, as if it were on stilts. It may stand this way for several minutes. Meanwhile the wasp, having satisfied itself that the victim is of the right species, moves off a few inches to dig the spider's grave. Working vigorously with legs and jaws, it excavates a hole 8 to 10 inches deep with a diameter slightly larger than the spider's girth. Now and again the wasp pops out of the hole to make sure that the spider is still there.

When the grave is finished, the wasp returns to the tarantula   16
to complete her ghastly enterprise. First she feels it all over once more with her antennae. Then her behavior becomes more aggressive. She bends her abdomen, protruding her sting, and searches for the soft membrane at the point where the spider's leg joins its body—the only spot where she can penetrate the horny skeleton. From time to time, as the exasperated spider slowly shifts ground, the wasp turns on her back and slides along with the aid of her wings, trying to get under the tarantula for a shot at the vital spot. During all this maneuvering, which can last for several minutes, the tarantula makes no move to save itself. Finally the wasp corners it against some obstruction and grasps one of its legs in her powerful jaws. Now at last the harassed spider tries a desperate but vain defense. The two contestants roll over and over on the ground. It is a terrifying sight and the outcome is always the same. The wasp finally manages to thrust her sting into the soft spot and holds it there for a few seconds while she pumps in the poison. Almost immediately the tarantula falls paralyzed on its back. Its legs stop twitching; its heart stops beating. Yet it is not dead, as is shown by the fact that if taken from the wasp it can be restored to some sensitivity by being kept in a moist chamber for several months.

After paralyzing the tarantula, the wasp cleans herself by drag-   17
ging her body along the ground and rubbing her feet, sucks the drop of blood oozing from the wound in the spider's abdomen, then grabs a leg of the flabby, helpless animal in her jaws and drags it down to the bottom of the grave. She stays there for many minutes, sometimes for several hours, and what she does all that time in the dark we do not know. Eventually she lays her egg and attaches it to the side of the spider's abdomen with a sticky secretion. Then she emerges, fills the grave with soil carried bit by bit in her jaws, and finally tramples the ground all around to hide any

trace of the grave from prowlers. Then she flies away, leaving her descendant safely started in life.

In all this the behavior of the wasp evidently is qualitatively different from that of the spider. The wasp acts like an intelligent animal. This is not to say that instinct plays no part or that she reasons as man does. But her actions are to the point; they are not automatic and can be modified to fit the situation. We do not know for certain how she identifies the tarantula—probably it is by some olfactory or chemo-tactile sense—but she does it purposefully and does not blindly tackle a wrong species. [18]

On the other hand, the tarantula's behavior shows only confusion. Evidently the wasp's pawing gives it no pleasure, for it tries to move away. That the wasp is not simulating sexual stimulation is certain, because male and female tarantulas react in the same way to its advances. That the spider is not anesthetized by some odorless secretion is easily shown by blowing lightly at the tarantula and making it jump suddenly. What, then, makes the tarantula behave as stupidly as it does? [19]

No clear, simple answer is available. Possibly the stimulation by the wasp's antennae is masked by a heavier pressure on the spider's body, so that it reacts as when prodded by a pencil. But the explanation may be much more complex. Initiative in attack is not in the nature of tarantulas; most species fight only when cornered so that escape is impossible. Their inherited patterns of behavior apparently prompt them to avoid problems rather than attack them. For example, spiders always weave their webs in three dimensions, and when a spider finds that there is insufficient space to attach certain threads in the third dimension, it leaves the place and seeks another, instead of finishing the web in a single plane. This urge to escape seems to arise under all circumstances, in all phases of life and to take the place of reasoning. For a spider to change the pattern of its web is as impossible as for an inexperienced man to build a bridge across a chasm obstructing his way. [20]

In a way the instinctive urge to escape is not only easier but more efficient than reasoning. The tarantula does exactly what is most efficient in all cases except in an encounter with a ruthless and determined attacker dependent for the existence of her own species on killing as many tarantulas as she can lay eggs. Perhaps [21] in this case the spider follows its usual pattern of trying to escape, instead of seizing and killing the wasp, because it is not aware of its danger. In any case, the survival of the tarantula species as a whole is protected by the fact that the spider is much more fertile than the wasp.

QUESTIONS

Understanding

1. In which paragraph does Petrunkevitch announce his main topic? When does he actually begin to discuss it? How do the wasp larvae of paragraph 2 anticipate his main "case"?

2. If the digger wasp's favorite kind of tarantula always loses the deadly struggle between them, why does that species not disappear?

3. What might happen to the digger wasp if it were a more prolific breeder? What delicate natural balance do spider and wasp together illustrate?

4. What opposing kinds of behavior do spider and wasp respectively represent?

5. The first half of paragraph 8 is a miniature process analysis. What process does it analyze?

Strategies and Structure

1. Petrunkevitch begins his process analysis with its end result and then returns to the first step, the wasp's hunt for her prey. What is that end result? In which paragraph is it explained?

2. Point out the six stages—from hunting to burying—into which Petrunkevitch analyzes the wasp's conquest of the spider.

3. Petrunkevitch enlarges the combat between spider and wasp to human scale by calling the wasp "her" and by referring to the wasp as the spider's "arch-enemy" (par. 5). Point out other similar techniques by which he minimizes the difference in scale between our world and the world of the insects.

4. Petrunkevitch's process analysis incorporates elements of the COMPARISON AND CONTRAST essay (Chapter 6). Does his compari-

son alternate point by point between spider and wasp, or does he concentrate on one for a while and then concentrate on the other? Explain your answer by referring to several specific passages.

5. Paragraph 12 is a TRANSITION paragraph. Which sentences look backward? Which look forward?

6. Which sentence in paragraph 19 sets up the remainder of the essay?

7. How does paragraph 4 fit in with the rest of Petrunkevitch's essay?

Words and Figures of Speech

1. Such words as *Hymenoptera, Diptera, arthropods,* and *trichobothria* (pars. 3, 9, 11) show that Petrunkevitch, a distinguished zoologist, was comfortable with the technical vocabulary of science; but this essay is sprinkled with nontechnical terms as well, for example: *wasphood* (par. 13), *pops out of the hole* (15), *shot* (16), *prowlers* (17). Give several other examples of your own.

2. From the range of Petrunkevitch's DICTION, what conclusions can you draw about the make-up of the readership of *Scientific American,* the magazine in which this essay appeared?

3. Consult your dictionary for the exact meanings of any of the following words you cannot define precisely: *subtle* (par. 2), *carnivorous* (4), *progeny* (5), *formidable* (6, 13), *appeased* (8), *tactile* (12), *pungent* (13), *gargantuan* (13), *chitinous* (13), *molestation* (15), *exasperated* (16), *secretion* (17, 19), *qualitatively* (18), *instinct* (5, 18), *olfactory* (18), *simulating* (18), *anesthetized* (19).

Comparing

1. How, according to Petrunkevitch's essay, do insects acquire their distinctive patterns of intelligence and instinct? Does this explanation confirm or deny Loren Eiseley's explanation of how animals acquire theirs in "The Angry Winter" (Chapter 1)?

2. In its treatment of the relationship between the human world and the insect world, how does the scale of Petrunkevitch's essay resemble that of Annie Dillard's "Transfiguration" (reprinted in "The Writing Process")?

Discussion and Writing Topics

1. Describe the process by which an insect or animal that you have observed feeds its young and starts them off in life.
2. Analyze the stages of maturation that bring a human being to adulthood.
3. Develop a parallel between two insects and two people (or types of people) with whom you are familiar.
4. Do you have a pet that has shown signs of true intelligence over and beyond mere instinct? Describe his or her behavior.

William Allen

How to Set a World Record

William Allen teaches creative writing at the Ohio State University. He was born in Dallas, Texas, in 1940 and grew up there, more or less. A graduate of California State University, Long Beach, he studied creative writing at the University of Iowa (M.F.A., 1970). Editor of the Ohio Journal, he has contributed stories and essays to the New York Times, Saturday Review, Antioch Review, Reader's Digest, and other publications. He is the author of Starkweather (1976), the story of a mass-murderer, To Tojo from Billy-Bob Jones (1977), a novel, and a collection of essays entitled The Fire in the Birdbath and Other Disturbances (1985). "How to Set a World Record" explains how even a college bookworm can become a champion, and Allen explains how he wrote the essay in an interview at the end of this chapter.

Absolutely anyone can set a world record. The key to doing   1
something better, longer, faster, or in larger quantity than anyone else is *desire*. Desire fostered by proper attitude.

Before I set my world record, I was a great fan of *The*   2
Guinness Book of World Records and read each new edition from cover to cover. I liked knowing and being able to tell others that the world's chug-a-lug champ consumed 2.58 pints of beer in 10 seconds, that the world's lightest adult person weighed only 13 pounds, that the largest vocabulary for a talking bird was 531 words, spoken by a brown-beaked budgerigar named Sparky. There is, of course, only a fine line between admiration and envy, and for awhile I had been secretly desiring to be in that book myself—to astonish others just as I had been astonished. But it seemed hopeless. How could a nervous college sophomore, an anonymous bookworm, per-

form any of those wonderful feats? The open-throat technique necessary for chug-a-lugging was incomprehensible to my trachea—and I thought my head alone must weigh close to 13 pounds.

One day I realized what was wrong. Why should I want to **break** a record at all? Why not blaze a trail of my own? Now, as you can see, I definitely had desire, but more than that I discovered I had talent. This is where we may differ. You may have no talent at all. If not, you can still go on to set a world record that will be well worth setting. It requires no talent to wear a sock longer than anyone else has ever worn a sock. It requires no talent to wear a nickel taped to your forehead longer than anyone else—it requires desire fostered by proper attitude.

First, though, search long and hard for that hidden talent you may possess. Let me offer one important guideline. Don't follow the beaten path. Look for your own personal gift, the little something that you've always had a knack for, a certain way with. It could conceivably be anything at all—sewing on buttons efficiently, waxing a car fast yet well, or speed-rolling your hair.

My own gift—broom-balancing—was developed in my back yard when I was a child. When I remembered the unusual ability, I immediately wrote the editors of the Guinness book in London.

Dear Sirs:

I have read with enjoyment *The Guinness Book of World Records* and want you to know that I intend to contribute to your next edition.

Thinking back today, I recalled that as a child I had an uncanny talent for balancing a common house broom on the end of my forefinger. Rushing to the kitchen, I found that I have retained this gift over the years. Since almost everyone must have at some time attempted this feat, I think it would be an appropriate addition to your book.

I would like to know exactly what must be done to establish a record—how many witnesses, what sort of timing device, etc. If you will provide me with this information, I will provide you with a broom-balancing record that should astonish your readers and last for years to come.

Sincerely,
William Allen

The reply came the next week.

Dear Mr. Allen:

In order to establish a world record of broom-balancing, we would like to have the confirmation of a newspaper report and an affidavit from one or more witnesses. With regard to the timing device, I think that a good wrist watch with a second hand would prove sufficient for this purpose.

Please let us know the duration of your best effort.

Sincerely,
Andrew Thomas
Assistant Editor

It sounds simple, but a lot of preparation must go into setting a   6
world record. You can't just set it. You must advertise, generate public interest. The purpose of this is to lure in the news media. It's absolutely necessary to have a write-up if your record is going to stick. And, of course, you will want the article for your scrapbook later on. Imagine what would happen if you just went into the bathroom and brushed your teeth for eight hours and then called the newspapers. They would think you were crazy. But if you generated interest beforehand—involved a local drugstore chain, got a name-brand toothpaste to sponsor you—then you wouldn't be crazy at all. You might even come to be something of an authority and make a career out of promoting things to do with teeth.

I took a slightly different tack. I ran an ad in the college news-   7
paper which read, in part: "FREE BEER! FREE BEER! Come one, come all, to Bill Allen's Broom-Balancing Beer Bust! Yes, friends, Bill will attempt to balance a common house broom on his forefinger for at least one hour to establish a world record. The editors of *The Guinness Book of World Records* in London are anxiously awaiting the outcome. The evening will be covered by the press. Ties will not be necessary. Come one, come all, to this historic event!"

May I suggest you find yourself a good manager before you try   8
to set your record. My roommate, Charlie, was mine and he proved to be invaluable. On the big night, he drew with chalk a small circle on the living room floor so I would have a place to stand. He cunningly scattered copies of the Guinness book on the coffee table. He had the good sense to make me wear a coat and tie: "You don't want to go down in history looking like a bum, do you? Of course not. You want to make a good impression."

The ad in the paper paid off, naturally. Over 50 people showed 9
up, filling our apartment and spilling out onto the lawn. Some
left after their two-beer limit, but most remained to see the outcome. There was some problem, though, in holding the group's
interest. For the first 10 minutes or so, they were fine, placing bets,
commenting on my technique. After that, their minds tended to
stray. They began to talk of other matters. One couple had the
nerve to ask if they could put music on and dance in the kitchen.

Charlie handled the situation like a professional. He began to 10
narrate the event, serving as a combination sportscaster and master
of ceremonies. "Ladies and gentlemen, give me your attention
please. We are at mark 15 minutes. At this time, I would like you
to look at Bill's feet. You will notice that they are not moving.
This is an indication of his skill. If you've ever tried broom-balancing yourself, you know that the tendency is to run around the
room in an effort to maintain stability."

Someone said, "He's right. I tried it today and that's exactly 11
what you do."

At the 20-minute mark, Charlie said, "Ladies and gentlemen, I 12
have an announcement. Bill's previous top practice time was 20
minutes. He has just beaten his own record! Anything can happen
from here on in, folks. Pay attention."

You might be wondering about my emotions at this point. I 13
hadn't slept well the night before, and all day I had been a nervous
wreck. I hadn't been able to eat. I had a horrible sinking feeling
every time I thought about what was coming up. But once I
started, I found I wasn't nervous at all. Not a trace of stage fright.
In fact, I blossomed under the attention. I realized this was where
I had belonged all along—in the center. Someone began to strum
a guitar and I foolishly began to bob my broom in time to the
music. "Don't get cocky," my manager warned. "You've got a long
way to go yet."

At mark 30 minutes, Charlie held up his hands for silence. "Lis- 14
ten to this, folks! The halfway point has been passed! We're halfway to history! And I want you people to know that Bill is feeling
good! He's not even sweating! I swear I don't understand how he
does it. How many people can even stand in one place that long?"

I had no clear idea who was in the room, or what they were 15
doing. In order to balance a broom, you have to stare right at the

straw. I'm not sure why this is, but it's certainly the case. You can't look away for even a second. By using peripheral vision, I was able to see a vague sea of heads but it wasn't worth the effort and I gave up. While in this awkward position, I heard the low, sinister voice of a stranger address me: "You know everyone here thinks you're crazy, don't you? I think I'll just step on your feet and see how you like that. You couldn't do anything about it. You wouldn't even know who did it because you can't look down."

"Charlie!" I called. "Come here!"   16

My manager had the situation under control in seconds. After   17
he had hustled the character out the door, he said, "Don't worry, folks. Just a heckler. One in every crowd, I guess."

I must say that Charlie's earlier remark that I was in good shape   18
was a lie—and I was feeling worse by the second. At mark 45 minutes, my neck seemed to have become locked in its upward arch. My legs were trembling and the smaller toes on each foot were without feeling. My forefinger felt like it was supporting a length of lead pipe. But more startling, I think, was the strain on my mind. I felt giddy. Strange that I have this gift, I reflected. I can't even walk around the block without occasionally wobbling off to one side. It suddenly seemed as though all the balance normally spread throughout the human body had somehow converged in my forefinger. Wouldn't it be ironic, I thought dizzily, if I just toppled over? I sniggered, seeing myself flat on my back with the broom still perfectly poised on my finger. Then I began to observe the broomstraw in incredible detail. Each stick seemed huge, like trees . . . logs . . . telephone poles. . . .

"Are you okay?" Charlie asked. I snapped out of it and reported   19
my condition. He turned to the crowd. "Folks! With only ten minutes to go, I would like us to reflect on the enormous physical and mental strain Bill is suffering right before our eyes. It's the price all champions pay, of course, when they go the distance, when they stretch the fibers of their being to the breaking point." His voice became lower, gruffer. "You may as well know. Bill has been hallucinating for some time now. But think of it, folks. While all over this country of ours, people are destroying their minds with dangerous drugs, Bill here is achieving the ends they seek—" his voice rose: he cried, "—with *no chance* of dangerous after-effects!"

Even in my condition, I knew he was going too far. I called him   20
over to loosen my shoelaces and whispered, "Cut the speeches,
okay? Just let them watch for awhile."

The hour mark came amazingly fast after that. There was a loud   22
10-second countdown, then the press's flashbulbs and strobes began going off like starbursts. Everybody began clapping and cheer-
ing. Using my peripheral vision, I saw that the crowd was on its
feet, jumping around. I saw the happy, grinning faces.

I kept balancing. Charlie conferred with me, then yelled,   22
"Folks! Bill is not going to stop! He says he will balance till he
drops! Isn't he something? Take your seats, ladies and gentlemen.
You're witnessing history tonight. Relax and enjoy it." The group
was for seeing me drop, all right, but they didn't want to wait
around all night for it. They became louder and harder to handle.
They wanted more beer. At mark one hour, 15 minutes, I was on
the verge of collapse anyway, so I gave in and tossed the broom in
the air. With a feeble flourish, I caught it with the other hand
and the record was set.

But no world record is *truly* set until someone has tried and   23
failed to break it. After the congratulations, the interviews, the
signing up of witnesses, it was time for everybody else to try. They
didn't have a chance, of course. Most lasted only a pitiful few
seconds, and the two best times were seven and 10 minutes. These
two had talent but lacked the rest of the magic combination.

My record never appeared in *The Guinness Book of World*   24
Records. I'm not sure why. Maybe they thought I should have
gone longer. Maybe the plane carrying the news went down in the
Atlantic. At any rate, they never wrote back and I never bothered
to check on it. I knew by then that it didn't matter. The record
had still been set. I had the write-up—and this alone brought me
all the acclaim I could handle.

You, too, can enjoy the same success. And don't worry if you   25
don't have a talent such as mine. There is a man in Iowa who
collects dirty oil rags. He has over a thousand so far—more than
anyone else in the world. He's not in the Guinness book, either,
but people still stop by almost daily to see his collection and ask
his opinion about this or that. His picture often appears in the
local papers.

All it takes is desire fostered by proper attitude.   26

QUESTIONS

Understanding

1. Allen gives his entire analysis of how to set a record in the single phrase "desire fostered by proper attitude"—which sounds like an advertising slogan. What other process is he actually illustrating?
2. Who is even better at this operation than Allen's broom-balancer? How does he show *his* talent?
3. Why does Allen's broom-balancer continue past "mark one hour"?
4. Does Allen's essay suffer because his record never appeared in the Guinness book? Why or why not?

Strategies and Structure

1. Point out each stage into which Allen analyzes the process of promoting the broom-balancing event.
2. How do the language and TONE of Allen's advertisement in paragraph 7 reflect the language and tone of the essay as a whole?
3. "Desire fostered by proper attitude" makes a distinction without a real difference. How does this redundancy fit in with the general spirit of Allen's essay?
4. Why does Allen quote word for word his correspondence with the Guinness editor instead of just giving an excerpt or a summary?
5. What is the effect of Allen's aside to Charlie in paragraph 20, "Cut the speeches, okay"?
6. What is the effect of the broom-balancer's getting caught up in his own promotion after "mark one hour"? How does Charlie get similarly carried away?
7. Allen's champion did not inquire why his time was never recorded because he already had "all the acclaim I could handle" (par. 24). How is this explanation in keeping with the way Allen has portrayed his character earlier, especially in paragraphs 2 and 13?
8. Allen's comic PROCESS ANALYSIS is helped along by NARRATION. Which parts are in the narrative mode? How do they contribute to the analysis?

9. From whose POINT OF VIEW is the incident in paragraph 15 told? How do you know?

Words and Figures of Speech

1. Why does Allen compare the flash bulbs and strobes to "starbursts" in paragraph 21?
2. The prefix *in* often means "not" (*invalid*, for example); but look up *invaluable* (par. 8) in your dictionary.
3. Why does Allen prefer to call broom-balancing his "gift" rather than his "skill"?

Comparing

1. Compare the tone of Allen's essay with Calvin Trillin's tone in "Literally" (Chapter 7). In which essay is the tone more complicated? How so?
2. In what ways does Allen's broom-balancer resemble the pole-vaulter in David Dubber's "Crossing the Bar on a Fiberglas Pole" (Chapter 1)?

Discussion and Writing Topics

The following is Allen's list of "10 World Records Waiting to Be Set." Make up your own somewhat more serious list (churning, cow milking, chimney sweeping, canoe rowing, for example) and write a PROCESS ANALYSIS explaining how to set a record in one of them:

1. How many pennies can you fit in your mouth?
2. How far can you throw an ostrich feather, standing at ground level with zero wind velocity?
3. How much weight can you gain in one week?
4. How many beers can you pour in before they begin to pour out?
5. How long can you look at yourself in the mirror, with eyelids taped open to avoid blinking?
6. How many pairs of black and navy blue socks can you mate in one hour under artificial light?

7. How many milkweed seeds can you pile up on a plate 10 inches in diameter?

8. How long can you carry a brick?

9. How many *New York Times*es can you eat at one sitting?

10. How many world record possibilities can you think of in 10 minutes?

Garrison Keillor

Attitude

Garrison Keillor as born in Anoka, Minnesota, in 1942. Since the age of eighteen, Keillor has worked in broadcasting, usually for Minnesota Public Radio, and now looms, even without his hat, as "America's tallest radio comedian." Author of humorous essays and stories for the New Yorker, the Los Angeles Times, the Atlantic, and other periodicals, Keillor in 1974 began writing and producing "The Prairie Home Companion." This weekly variety show features regular visits to Keillor's mythical Lake Wobegon "where all the men are good looking, all the women are strong, and all the children are above average." In 1980 Keillor won the Peabody Award for distinguished broadcasting. "Attitude" (originally published in the New Yorker and collected in 1981 in Happy to Be Here) tells how to act like a winner when you are actually losing.

Long ago I passed the point in life when major-league ball-players begin to be younger than yourself. Now all of them are, except for a few aging trigenarians and a couple of quadros who don't get around on the fastball as well as they used to and who sit out the second games of doubleheaders. However, despite my age (thirty-nine), I am still active and have a lot of interests. One of them is slow-pitch softball, a game that lets me go through the motions of baseball without getting beaned or having to run too hard. I play on a pretty casual team, one that drinks beer on the bench and substitutes freely. If a player's wife or girlfriend wants to play, we give her a glove and send her out to right field, no questions asked, and if she lets a pop fly drop six feet in front of her, nobody agonizes over it.

Except me. This year. For the first time in my life, just as I am entering the dark twilight of my slow-pitch career, I find myself taking the game seriously. It isn't the bonehead play that bothers me especially—the pop fly that drops untouched, the slow roller juggled and the ball then heaved ten feet over the first baseman's head and into the next diamond, the routine singles that go through outfielders' legs for doubles and triples with gloves flung after them. No, it isn't our stone-glove fielding or pussyfoot base-running or limp-wristed hitting that gives me fits, though these have put us on the short end of some mighty ridiculous scores this summer. It's our attitude.

Bottom of the ninth, down 18–3, two outs, a man on first   3
and a woman on third, and our third baseman strikes out. *Strikes out!* In slow-pitch, not even your grandmother strikes out, but this guy does, and after his third strike—a wild swing at a ball that bounces on the plate—he topples over in the dirt and lies flat on his back, laughing. *Laughing!*

Same game, earlier. They have the bases loaded. A weak   4
grounder is hit toward our second baseperson. The runners are running. She picks up the ball, and she looks at them. She looks at first, at second, at home. We yell, "Throw it! Throw it!" and she throws it, underhand, at the pitcher, who has turned and run to back up the catcher. The ball rolls across the third-base line and under the bench. Three runs score. The batter, a fatso, chugs into second. The other team hoots and hollers, and what does she do? She shrugs and smiles ("Oh, silly me"); after all, it's only a game. Like the aforementioned strikeout artist, she treats her error as a joke. They have forgiven themselves instantly, which is unforgivable. It is *we* who should forgive them, who can say, "It's all right, it's only a game." They are supposed to throw up their hands and kick the dirt and hang their heads, as if this boner, even if it is their sixteenth of the afternoon—*this* is the one that really and truly breaks their hearts.

That attitude sweetens the game for everyone. The sinner   5
feels sweet remorse. The fatso feels some sense of accomplishment; this is no bunch of rumdums he forced into an error but a team with some class. We, the sinner's teammates, feel momentary anger at her—dumb! dumb play!—but then, seeing her grief, we sympathize with her in our hearts (any one of us might have made that mistake or one worse), and we yell en-

couragement, including the shortstop, who, moments before, dropped an easy throw for a force at second. "That's all right! Come on! We got 'em!" we yell. "Shake it off! These turkeys can't hit!" This makes us all feel good, even though the turkeys now lead us by ten runs. We're getting clobbered, but we have a winning attitude.

Let me say this about attitude: Each player is responsible for his or her own attitude, and to a considerable degree you can *create* a good attitude by doing certain little things on the field. These are certain little things that ballplayers do in the Bigs, and we ought to be doing them in the Slows.   6

1. When going up to bat, don't step right into the batter's box as if it were an elevator. The box is your turf, your stage. Take possession of it slowly and deliberately, starting with a lot of back-bending, knee-stretching, and torso-revolving in the on-deck circle. Then, approaching the box, stop outside it and tap the dirt off your spikes with your bat. You don't have spikes, you have sneakers of course, but the significance of the tapping is the same. Then, upon entering the box, spit on the ground. It's a way of saying, "This here is mine. This is where I get my hits."   7

2. Spit frequently. Spit at all crucial moments. Spit correctly. Spit should be *blown*, not ptuied weakly with the lips, which often results in dribble. Spitting should convey forcefulness of purpose, concentration, pride. Spit down, not in the direction of others. Spit in the glove and on the fingers, especially after making a real knucklehead play; it's a way of saying, "I dropped the ball because my glove was dry."   8

3. At bat and in the field, pick up dirt. Rub dirt in the fingers (especially after spitting on them). Toss dirt, as if testing the wind for velocity and direction. Smooth the dirt. Be involved with dirt. If no dirt is available (e.g., in the outfield), pluck tufts of grass. Fielders should be grooming their areas constantly between plays, flicking away tiny sticks and bits of gravel.   9

4. Take your time. Tie your laces. Confer with your teammates about possible situations that may arise and conceivable options in dealing with them. Extend the game. Three errors on three consecutive plays can be humiliating if the plays occur   10

within the space of a couple of minutes, but if each error is separated from the next by extensive conferences on the mound, lace-tying, glove adjustments, and arguing close calls (if any), the effect on morale is minimized.

5. Talk. Not just an occasional "Let's get a hit now" but [11] continuous rhythmic chatter, a flow of syllables: "Hey babe hey babe c'mon babe good stick now hey babe long tater take him downtown babe . . . hey good eye good eye."

Infield chatter is harder to maintain. Since the slow-pitch [12] pitch is required to be a soft underhand lob, infielders hesitate to say, "Smoke him babe hey low heat hey throw it on the black babe chuck it in there back him up babe no hit no hit." Say it anyway.

6. One final rule, perhaps the most important of all. When [13] your team is up and has made the third out, the batter and the players who were left on base do not come back to the bench for their gloves. *They remain on the field, and their teammates bring their gloves out to them.* This requires some organization and discipline, but it pays off big in morale. It says, "Although we're getting our pants knocked off, still we must conserve our energy."

Imagine that you have bobbled two fly balls in this rout and [14] now you have just tried to stretch a single into a double and have been easily thrown out sliding into second base, where the base runner ahead of you had stopped. It was the third out and a dumb play, and your opponents smirk at you as they run off the field. You are the goat, a lonely and tragic figure sitting in the dirt. You curse yourself, jerking your head sharply forward. You stand up and kick the base. How miserable! How degrading! Your utter shame, though brief, bears silent testimony to the worthiness of your teammates, whom you have let down, and they appreciate it. They call out to you now as they take the field, and as the second baseman runs to his position he says, "Let's get 'em now," and tosses you your glove. Lowering your head, you trot slowly out to right. There you do some deep knee bends. You pick grass. You find a pebble and fling it into foul territory. As the first batter comes to the plate, you check the sun. You get set in your stance, poised to fly. Feet spread, hands on hips, you bend slightly at the waist and spit the expert spit of a veteran ballplayer—a player who has known the agony of defeat but who always bounces back, a player who has lost a stride on the base paths but can still make the big play.

This is *ball*, ladies and gentlemen. This is what it's all about.   15

QUESTIONS

Understanding

1. In the twilight of his softball career, Garrison Keillor has a beef with his defeatist teammates. It's not so much their losing that bothers him as what?
2. According to Coach Keillor, it is unforgivable to forgive yourself for making a blooper on the playing field. Why?
3. How has Keillor himself played in the past? Why do you suppose he has changed?
4. Keillor is explaining in detail how to foster a winning attitude, but who and who alone is responsible for acquiring it?
5. Among his six pointers, which does Keillor stress the most?

Strategies and Structure

1. Keillor introduces the specific subject of his essay in paragraph 2. Identify the sentence that states his topic most directly. Why do you think this author chose to make his topic sentence a short line drive instead of a long looper like the second sentence in paragraph 1?
2. Keillor's pointers for playing authentic ball are offered tongue-in-cheek (glove-in-mouth?). To what extent, nonetheless, do they show an expert familiarity with the customs and rituals of the "Bigs"?
3. "Attitude" tells us how to develop a proper one, but it is also telling us how to participate correctly in an American ritual. An element of ritual since ancient times is incantation. Point to ritualistic patterns of language in Keillor's essay that amount to comic incantations. What other ritualistic elements can you find in his instructions?

4. The purpose of ritual is to convert the profane into the sacred. How does Keillor's treatment of the batter's box in pointer #1 illustrate this intention?

5. What is Keillor's professed attitude toward players who profane the rituals of baseball? How does it color the TONE of his essay?

6. What role does Keillor play in the next-to-last paragraph? To what extent is this section an application of the advice that has gone before?

7. After delivering the longest paragraph in his entire essay, Keillor ends with one of the shortest, a single sentence. Where have similar shifts occurred earlier? Given Keillor's subject, how effective do you find this brief way *out*?

Words and Figures of Speech

1. Why does Keillor refer to himself as a "goat" in paragraph 14? Why not some other animal—a jackass or a turkey, say?

2. *Ptuied* (par 8) is an example of onomatopoeia. So is *dribble* in the same paragraph. What kind of language does this Greek term refer to?

3. How well does the "dark twilight" of paragraph 2 fit in with the author's tone throughout? Point to other examples of comic exaggeration in "Attitude."

4. To what is Keillor opposing "the Slows" in paragraph 6? Where did he get the first term? Where else does he show a tendency to abbreviate and nickname? Who is he imitating with this trait?

5. Why are there no main verbs in the first sentences of Keillor's third and fourth paragraphs? Who does he sound like here?

6. What is the grammatical mood of the one-word sentence, "Talk" (par. 5)? Why this mood and not a straight declarative?

Comparing

1. As an essay in ritual, "Attitude" is the work of an insider. How does this viewpoint compare with that of the speaker in Horace Miner's "Body Ritual among the Nacirema" in Chapter 8?

2. Both Keillor and William Allen ("How to Set a World Record," immediately preceding) are writing about "attitude." Which one takes up, so to speak, where the other leaves off? In what ways do the speakers in the two essays resemble one another? How do they and their methods differ?

Discussion and Writing Topics

1. What specific instructions would you add to Keillor's list?

2. Write an essay in which you explain how to adopt a winning attitude in one of the following sports: croquet, darts, bumper cars, touch football, guts frisbee, fly-fishing, skeet shooting, ping-pong, badminton, horseshoes, or kite flying.

3. Ellen Goodman, author of "The Just-Right Wife" (Chapter 5) and many other essays, has complained that baseball crams five minutes of action into two or three hours of play. Write an essay in which you explain how to make the American pastime a snappier game, one better suited to the demands of home viewing in the electronic age.

Writers on the Writing Process:

An Interview with William Allen[1]

EDITOR: When did the great broom-balancing event described   1
in "How to Set a World Record" take place?

ALLEN: I set my record in the spring of 1967, when I was a   2
senior at California State at Long Beach. To my knowledge
the record holds today.

EDITOR: How did you get to be a champion broom balancer   3
in the first place?

ALLEN: I'm self-taught. As an only child I spent a lot of time   4
in the backyard alone. One day a broom wound up on my
forefinger and stayed an impressive length of time. I never
had to train or practice, though the day I set my record I
did balance a broom for about twenty minutes, just to reassure myself that I still had the touch.

EDITOR: Did you really have the nerve to apply for a place in   5
The Guinness Book of World Records?

ALLEN: I did, of course, submit my record to the Guinness   6
book, but the fellow who wrote back was the one with the
nerve. He wanted me to set it again, only with a tray and a
glass of water on the end of the broom. I refused, pointing
out that it would mar the purity of the act. In the essay, I
chose to simplify things by saying they never wrote back. In
retrospect I can see that their response could have fit nicely
into the piece, but at the time it just seemed to complicate
the story I was trying to tell.

EDITOR: Where did the subject for that story come from? How   7
did you get the notion of balancing a broom in public and
writing about it?

ALLEN: I was a humor writer for our college newspaper. I had my   8

[1] Conducted in Columbus, Ohio, June 1984.

131

own column. I remember it was near the end of the year, and I was desperate for ideas. So I invented an event to have something to write about. How I thought of broom balancing, I will never know. It was just the sort of thing the persona in my column would do. Also there was a push for me to run for student-body president, on a whimsy and joy ticket, and I figured the publicity would help my chances. It did, too, though I backed out of the race anyway when I realized that I didn't want to be a politician.

EDITOR: Your persona, the "anonymous bookworm": how different is he from William Allen? 9

ALLEN: He *is* me, but he is also a fictional self. I read a lot in college, but I wasn't anonymous. I believe most of us are two people—the savvy, confident person we try to project to the world, and the vulnerable, inadequate person who gets loose in our nightmares. I think of my persona as my ingenuous, inferior alter ego. I know I'm more of a realist than he is, but in some ways his innocence makes him more interesting. That's why I use him as a character in my writing. 10

EDITOR: Did you already have him in mind when you wrote your column in the college newspaper? 11

ALLEN: I was beginning to get him then. In the column, I wrote about setting the record more or less in the order it all happened, as a chronicle. Then six years later I decided to write about the event again, as an essay. In the intervening years my alter ego had become more sharply defined. When you write personal essays, as I do, it's important to project a personality that readers can relate to. Before, I had my subject; now I also had my point of view as a writer. 12

EDITOR: What about your roommate Charlie. Did he really behave as you say he did? 13

ALLEN: Charlie is the roommate I never had. He didn't exist at the broom-balancing event, though the sports editor of the college paper did do a countdown with a stopwatch. In a way, I think Charlie is an expression of the other me—the writer who is a kind of circus barker: "Step right up, ladies and gentlemen. . . ." 14

EDITOR: Would you advise beginning writers to think carefully about their audience during the writing process? 15

ALLEN: Only if they want somebody to read what they have to say. [16] It's not important to consider the needs of the reader if you don't mind doing all that work for nothing. Or if you don't mind being misunderstood.

EDITOR: So you had three things in mind when you began to com- [17] pose "How to Set a World Record": a subject, the audience, and your point of view?

ALLEN: That's right. Without a point of view, in the sense of a [18] characteristic way of looking at the world, a writer can't control tone or style.

EDITOR: What is tone in writing? [19]

ALLEN: It comes across in the feeling a reader gets from a piece of [20] writing. In the broadest characterization, we can say that a piece seems humorous or morbid. Mine are usually humorous, I hope. The shades of tone come from the attitude of the writer toward his or her subject matter and toward life in general. The tone of "How to Set a World Record" reflects my usual way of taking the universe seriously. But as a superb essayist, E. B. White, once said, "There's just a hint of a snicker in it."

EDITOR: How is tone *achieved* in writing? [21]

ALLEN: It is the end product of everything that goes into the writ- [22] ing process. All the choices the writer makes. For instance, your choice of subject matter is contingent on your attitude toward life: not everybody would decide to write about broom balancing or birds—my first book was devoted to dwarf parrots—or balding. Your choice of subject and incident, of what a piece is to say or mean, your choice of words—all of these reflect the writer's attitude or tone.

EDITOR: One choice that helped to set the tone in "How to Set a [23] World Record" is that key phrase, "desire fostered by proper attitude." Where did it come from?

ALLEN: Those formulas for success come at us from everywhere. [24] It's probably a distillation of things I heard and read as a child of the Fifties, a period when self-help and free enterprise thrived. The writer in me intends it to be tongue-in-cheek, of course, but my persona believes it with all his heart.

EDITOR: You say point of view influences style as well as tone. [25] What is *style* in writing?

ALLEN: Tone is a characteristic attitude; style is a way of express-   26
ing that attitude in words. Style has to do especially with language—the choice of individual words and the manner in which
they are combined. In the broadest sense, my style might be described as informal rather than formal. I start a lot of sentences
with conjunctions; I use a lot of pronouns and relatively simple
sentences. However, the offhand quality of my style is only an
appearance. My sentences are constructed to seem laid back, but
they are really studied and, I like to think, artful. Like the hair-
cut I had in high school. I plastered my hair with Brylcreem and
spent hours erecting it into a complicated pompadour with a
duck tail. Then I walked around the rest of the day trying to
look cool while avoiding gusts of wind. The style of "How to
Set a World Record" seems casual but it took hours of preparation. Years really. A writer's personal style and tone develop with
trial and error over a period of time. But it's never too early to
start looking for the style and tone that are right for you.

EDITOR: One last question. How much labor did it take, roughly   27
to put together "How to Set a World Record"?

ALLEN: Enough time had gone by between when I wrote the col-   28
umn for my college newspaper and when I wrote the essay as you
have it that the piece came easily. I wrote it in about a week,
and it took three drafts. Having that much distance on the material—and having already written about it once before—saved
me a lot of work. Often I will spend six weeks and as many
drafts on an essay and still have it not work out. If that happens,
I shelve it for a while; then when I go back to it, in say a month
or two, I usually wrap it up fast. I think our subsconscious mind
continues to work at solving problems all the time, whether the
problems have to do with writing or living. As a professional
writer, I have a number of projects going at once and can afford
to shelve some of them. Students don't have the same luxury.

WRITING TOPICS for Chapter Three
Essays That Analyze a Process

Write an essay analyzing one of the following processes or giving directions for one of the following operations:

1. How to play chess
2. How to change a tire
3. How to install an electric circuit in a house
4. How to make wine, beer, or mead
5. How to milk a cow
6. How to keep bees
7. How to thread and operate a sewing machine
8. How to make butter
9. How a piano works
10. How a solar heating system works
11. How to conserve energy in a house
12. How to install and operate a CB radio
13. How to meet a girl or guy
14. How to make a good (or bad) impression on your boyfriend's or girlfriend's parents
15. How to excel in school
16. How to take and develop photographs
17. How iron ore is made into steel
18. How a fuel injection system (or carburetor) works
19. How an internal combustion engine works
20. How to sail a boat
21. How to buy a used car
22. How to buy a horse or other livestock
23. How to buy stocks, bonds, or other securities
24. How to beat inflation in small ways
25. How to get rich

4

Essays That Analyze Cause and Effect

PROCESS ANALYSIS [1] (*Chapter 3*) *is concerned with sequence in time and space. Sequence is one kind of relationship among objects and events; another is causation. When we confuse the two, we are reasoning as Mark Twain's hero does in* Adventures of Huckleberry Finn. *Alone in the woods one night, Huck sees an evil omen:*

Pretty soon a spider went crawling up my shoulder, and I flipped it off and it lit in the candle; and before I could budge it was all shriveled up. I didn't need anybody to tell me that that was an awful bad sign and would fetch me some bad luck, so I was scared and 'most shook the clothes off of me. I got up and turned around in my tracks three times and crossed my breast every time; and then I tied up a little lock of my hair to keep witches away. But I hadn't no confidence.

Huck is right to be scared; all sorts of misadventures are going to befall him and Jim in Mark Twain's masterpiece. But Huck commits the blunder of thinking that because the misadventures follow the burning of the spider, they were necessarily caused by it: he confuses mere sequence with causation. This mistake in logic is commonly known as the post hoc, ergo propter hoc *fallacy—Latin for "after this, therefore because of this."*

Huck Finn does not realize that two conditions have to be met to prove causation:

B can not have happened without A;
Whenever A happens, B must happen.

[1] Terms printed in all capitals are defined in the Glossary.

The chemist who observes again and again that a flammable substance burns (B) only when combined with oxygen (A) and that it always burns when so combined, may infer that oxidation causes combustion. The chemist has discovered in oxygen the "immediate" cause of combustion. The flame necessary to set off the reaction and the chemist himself, who lights the match, are "ultimate" causes.

Often the ultimate causes of an event are more important than the immediate causes, especially when we are dealing with psychological and social rather than purely physical factors. Let us raise the following question about a college freshman: Why does Mary smoke? Depending upon whom we asked, we might get responses like these:

Mary: "I smoke because I need something to do
                       with my hands."
Mary's boyfriend: "Mary smokes because she thinks it looks
                       sophisticated."
Medical doctor: "Because Mary has developed a physical
                       addiction to tobacco."
Psychologist: "Because of peer pressure."
Sociologist: "Because 30 percent of all female Americans
                       under 20 years of age now smoke. Mary is
                       part of a trend."
Advertiser: "Because she's come a long way, baby."

Each of these explanations tells only part of the story. For a full answer to our question about why Mary smokes, we must take all of these answers together. Together they form what is known as the "complex" cause of Mary's behavior.

Most essays in CAUSE AND EFFECT that you will be asked to read or to write will examine the complex cause of an event or phenomenon. There are two reasons for addressing all the contributing causes. The first is to avoid over-simplification. Interesting questions are usually complex, and complex questions probably have complex answers. The second reason is to anticipate objections that might be raised against your argument.

Often a clever writer will run through several causes to show that he or she knows the ground before making a special case for one or two. When a clergyman asked journalist Lincoln Steffens to name the ultimate cause of corruption in city government, Steffens replied with the following analysis:

> Most people, you know, say it was Adam. But Adam, you remember, he said that it was Eve, the woman; she did it. And Eve said no, no, it wasn't she; it was the serpent. And that's where you clergy have stuck ever since. You blame the serpent, Satan. Now I come and I am trying to show you that it was, it is, the apple.

Steffens was giving an original answer to the old question of original sin. Man's fallen state, he said, is due not to innate depravity but to economic conditions.

When explaining causes, be as specific as you can without oversimplifying. When explaining effects, be even more specific. Here is your chance to display the telling fact or colorful detail that can save your essay from the ho-hum response. Consider this explanation of the effects of smoking written by England's King James I (of the King James Bible). His Counter-Blaste to Tobacco (1604) found smoking to be

> A custom lothsome to the eye, hatefull to the Nose, harmefull to the braine, dangerous to the Lungs, and in the blacke stinking fume thereof, neerest resembling the horrible Stigian smoke of the pit that is bottomelesse.

In a more recent essay on the evils of tobacco, Erik Eckholm strikes a grimmer note. "But the most potentially tragic victims of cigarettes," he writes, "are the infants of mothers who smoke. They are more likely than the babies of nonsmoking mothers to be born underweight and thus to encounter death or disease at birth or during the initial months of life."

In singling out the effects of smoking upon unwitting infants, Eckholm has chosen an example that might be just powerful enough to convince some smokers to quit. Your examples need not be so grim, but they must be specific to be powerful. And they must be selected with the interests of your audience in mind. Eckholm is addressing the young women who are smoking more today than ever before. When writing for a middle-aged audience, he points out that smoking causes cancer and heart disease at a rate

70 percent higher among pack-a-day men and women than among nonsmokers.

Your audience must be taken into account because writing a cause and effect analysis is much like constructing a persuasive argument. It is a form of reasoning that carries the reader step by step through a "proof." Your analysis may be instructive, amusing, or startling; but first it must be logical.

Frank Trippett

The Great American Cooling Machine

Frank Trippett is a reporter, photographer, and newspaper editor. He was born in Columbus, Mississippi, in 1926. After World War II, he worked briefly in Meridian, Mississippi, before moving to Virginia and then Florida, where he was a bureau chief for the St. Petersburg Times. In the sixties, Trippett served as an associate editor of Newsweek and senior editor of Look. Since 1971 he has been a free-lance writer, author of The First Horsemen (1974) and Child Ellen (1975). "The Great American Cooling Machine" first appeared in Time; it analyzes some of the chilling effects of air conditioning on American society and character.

"The greatest contribution to civilization in this century may well be air conditioning—and America leads the way." So wrote British Scholar-Politician S.F. Markham 32 years ago when a modern cooling system was still an exotic luxury. In a century that has yielded such treasures as the electric knife, spray-on deodorant and disposable diapers, anybody might question whether air conditioning is the supreme gift. There is not a whiff of doubt, however, that America is far out front in its use. As a matter of lopsided fact, the U.S. today, with a mere 5% of the population, consumes as much man-made coolness as the whole rest of the world put together. [1]

Just as amazing is the speed with which this situation came to be. Air conditioning began to spread in industries as a production aid during World War II. Yet only a generation ago a chilled sanctuary during summer's stewing heat was a happy frill that ordinary people sampled only in movie houses. Today most Americans tend to take air conditioning for [2] granted in homes, offices, factories, stores, theaters, shops, studios, schools, hotels and restaurants. They travel in chilled buses, trains, planes and private cars. Sporting events once associated with open sky and fresh air are increasingly boxed in and air cooled. Skiing still takes place outdoors, but such attractions as tennis, rodeos, football and, alas, even baseball are now often staged in synthetic climates like those of Houston's Astrodome and New Orleans' Superdome. A great many of the country's farming tractors are now, yup, air-conditioned.

It is thus no exaggeration to say that Americans have taken to   3
mechanical cooling avidly and greedily. Many have become all but addicted, refusing to go places that are not air-conditioned. In Atlanta, shoppers in Lenox Square so resented having to endure natural heat while walking outdoors from chilled store to chilled store that the mall management enclosed and air-conditioned the whole sprawling shebang. The widespread whining about Washington's raising of thermostats to a mandatory 78°F suggests that people no longer think of interior coolness as an amenity but consider it a necessity, almost a birthright, like suffrage. The existence of such a view was proved last month when a number of federal judges, sitting too high and mighty to suffer 78°, defied and denounced the Government's energy-saving order to cut back on cooling. Significantly, there was no popular outrage at this judicial insolence; many citizens probably wished that they could be so highhanded.

Everybody by now is aware that the cost of the American way is   4
enormous, that air conditioning is an energy glutton. It uses some 9% of all electricity produced. Such an extravagance merely to provide comfort is peculiarly American and strikingly at odds with all the recent rhetoric about national sacrifice in a period of menacing energy shortages. Other modern industrial nations such as Japan, Germany and France have managed all along to thrive with mere fractions of the man-made coolness used in the U.S., and precious little of that in private dwellings. Here, so profligate has its use become that the air conditioner is almost as glaring a symptom as the automobile of the national tendency to overindulge in every technical possibility, to use every convenience to such excess that the country looks downright coddled.

But not everybody is aware that high cost and easy comfort are   5
merely two of the effects of the vast cooling of America. In fact,

air conditioning has substantially altered the country's character and folkways. With the dog days at hand and the thermostats ostensibly up, it is a good time to begin taking stock of what air conditioning has done besides lower the indoor temperature.

Many of its byproducts are so conspicuous that they are   6 scarcely noticed. To begin with, air conditioning transformed the face of urban America by making possible those glassy, boxy, sealed-in skyscrapers on which the once humane geometries of places like San Francisco, Boston and Manhattan have been impaled. It has been indispensable, no less, to the functioning of sensitive advanced computers, whose high operating temperatures require that they be constantly cooled. Thus, in a very real way, air conditioning has made possible the ascendancy of computerized civilization. Its cooling protection has given rise not only to moon landings, space shuttles and Skylabs but to the depersonalized punch-cardification of society that regularly gets people hot under the collar even in swelter-proof environments. It has also reshaped the national economy and redistributed political power simply by encouraging the burgeoning of the sultry southerly swatch of the country, profoundly influencing major migration trends of people and industry. Sunbelt cities like Phoenix, Atlanta, Dallas and Houston (where shivering indoor frigidity became a mark of status) could never have mushroomed so prosperously without air conditioning; some communities—Las Vegas in the Nevada desert and Lake Havasu City on the Arizona-California border—would shrivel and die overnight if it were turned off.

It has, as well, seduced families into retreating into houses with   7 closed doors and shut windows, reducing the commonalty of neighborhood life and all but obsoleting the front-porch society whose open casual folkways were an appealing hallmark of a sweatier America. Is it really surprising that the public's often noted withdrawal into self-pursuit and privatism has coincided with the epic spread of air conditioning? Though science has little studied how habitual air conditioning affects mind or body, some medical experts suggest that, like other technical avoidance of natural swings in climate, air conditioning may take a toll on the human capacity to adapt to stress. If so, air conditioning is only like many óther greatly useful technical developments that liberate man from nature by increasing his productivity and power in some ways—while subtly weakening him in others.

Neither scholars nor pop sociologists have really got around to charting and diagnosing all the changes brought about by air conditioning. Professional observers have for years been preoccupied with the social implications of the automobile and television. Mere glancing analysis suggests that the car and TV, in their most decisive influences on American habits, have been powerfully aided and abetted by air conditioning. The car may have created all those shopping centers in the boondocks, but only air conditioning has made them attractive to mass clienteles. Similarly, the artificial cooling of the living room undoubtedly helped turn the typical American into a year-round TV addict. Without air conditioning, how many viewers would endure reruns (or even Johnny Carson) on one of those pestilential summer nights that used to send people out to collapse on the lawn or to sleep on the roof? 8

Many of the side effects of air conditioning are far from being fully pinned down. It is a reasonable suspicion, though, that controlled climate, by inducing Congress to stay in Washington longer than it used to during the swelter season, thus presumably passing more laws, has contributed to bloated Government. One can only speculate that the advent of the supercooled bedroom may be linked to the carnal adventurism associated with the mid-century sexual revolution. Surely it is a fact—if restaurant complaints about raised thermostats are to be believed—that air conditioning induces at least expense-account diners to eat and drink more; if so, it must be credited with adding to the national fat problem. 9

Perhaps only a sophist might be tempted to tie the spread of air conditioning to the coincidentally rising divorce rate, but every attentive realist must have noticed that even a little window unit can instigate domestic tension and chronic bickering between couples composed of one who likes it on all the time and another who does not. In fact, perhaps surprisingly, not everybody likes air conditioning. The necessarily sealed rooms or buildings make some feel claustrophobic, cut off from the real world. The rush, whir and clatter of cooling units annoys others. There are even a few eccentrics who object to man-made cool simply because they like hot weather. Still, the overwhelming majority of Americans have taken to air conditioning like hogs to a wet wallow. 10

It might be tempting, and even fair, to chastise that vast majority for being spoiled rotten in their cool ascendancy. It would be more just, however, to observe that their great cooling machine 11 carries with it a perpetual price tag that is going to provide continued and increasing chastisement during the energy crisis. Ultimately, the air conditioner, and the hermetic buildings it requires, may turn out to be a more pertinent technical symbol of the American personality than the car. While the car has been a fine sign of the American impulse to dart hither and yon about the world, the mechanical cooler more neatly suggests the maturing national compulsion to flee the natural world in favor of a technological cocoon.

Already architectural designers are toiling to find ways out of   12
the technical trap represented by sealed buildings with immovable glass, ways that might let in some of the naturally cool air outside. Some have lately come up with a remarkable discovery: the openable window. Presumably, that represents progress.

QUESTIONS

Understanding

1. Why did air conditioning take hold originally in America, according to Trippett?
2. Trippett says that "two of the effects" of America's addiction to air conditioning are "high cost and easy comfort" (par. 5). How has it also had the effect of transforming "the face of urban America" (par. 6)? What is the result of that transformation?
3. What other effects of universal air conditioning does Trippett identify? Which is he less confident about linking directly with air conditioning, rather than some other cause?
4. Why does Trippett think air conditioning may become a symbol of American character even more apt than the automobile? What does it symbolize about us?
5. Does Trippett seem to think the effects of air conditioning the entire country are largely beneficial or largely detrimental?

Strategies and Structure

1. Does Trippett's essay spend more time analyzing causes or analyzing effects? Explain your answer.

2. In paragraph 6, we are told that air conditioning has made it possible to construct enormous "sealed-in" skyscrapers. This effect, in turn, says Trippett, has caused urban America to become less livable because less human in scale. Point out several other examples in his essay of effects that turn into causes.

3. Paragraph 5 here is mainly a TRANSITION paragraph. Which parts look back to the four opening paragraphs? Which look forward to the rest? See if you can find other clearly transitional sentences in Trippett's essay.

4. The opening paragraph of "Cooling Machine" identifies the prime cause of which the author will subsequently trace the effects: the wholesale use of air conditioning in America in recent years. However, when Trippett questions "whether air conditioning is the supreme gift" (par. 1), he sounds more like a writer setting up a PERSUASIVE ARGUMENT than an essay in CAUSE AND EFFECT. What is the point of his implied argument?

5. Explain why Trippett's essay is nevertheless one that uses persuasion to support a cause-and-effect analysis (and not the reverse).

6. How might Trippett's analysis of the effects of universal air conditioning serve to support a full-fledged argument that our air should no longer be "conditioned"?

Words and Figures of Speech

1. What other terms for "effects" does Trippett use in this essay (for instance, "byproducts" in paragraph 6)?

2. Americans, says Trippett, have taken to air conditioning like "hogs to a wet wallow" (par. 11). Point out other places in which Trippett uses SLANG or other informal language. Do such words and phrases belong in an essay on a technical subject such as air conditioning? Why or why not?

3. Does your dictionary list the word *obsoleting* (par. 7)? What part of speech is *obsolete* usually? Should Trippett have written instead "making obsolete"? Why or why not?

4. In ancient Greece, *Sophists* were philosophers known for their exceedingly clever (though sometimes hair-splitting) arguments. How does the word (uncapitalized) apply in this modern context?

Comparing

1. Trippett emphasizes the negative effects of his subject. How does

he compare, in this regard, with Ellen Willis in "Memoirs of a Non-Prom Queen," the next essay in this chapter?

2. Contrast the attitude expressed here toward air conditioning and the architecture it has produced with the attitude of Eugene Raskin toward modern architecture in "Walls and Barriers" (Chapter 6).

3. If Johnson C. Montgomery ("Island of Plenty," Chapter 9) had written an essay on air conditioning and the American way, what differences might you expect between his treatment of the subject and Trippett's?

Discussion and Writing Topics

1. How accurate do you consider the proclamation with which Trippett begins: that air conditioning is America's greatest contribution to civilized living in the twentieth century? What other contenders can you think of?

2. Write an essay in which you analyze the benefits and wholesome effects of air conditioning.

3. Write an essay on the likely effects of some other important technological "advance," such as high-yield fertilizer, containerized freight, wide-body jets, synthetic DNA, or the projected "elevator" that may some day make entry into space easy and inexpensive.

Ellen Willis

Memoirs of
a Non-Prom Queen

*Ellen Willis is a journalist who was born in New York City in 1941
and attended a large "semisuburban" high school in Queens,
before going on to Barnard College and Berkeley. She was a critic
of rock music for the New Yorker from 1968 to 1975, and a staff
writer and columnist for Rolling Stone in the late seventies. She
is the author of Beginning to See the Light (1981), essays
about political and cultural events of the late 1960s and 1970s.
Willis has been an associate or contributing editor of Cheetah
magazine, US magazine, Ms., and the Village Voice and a staff
member of Home Front, a center for antiwar soldiers. Since 1979,
she has been on the staff of the Village Voice, first as a staff
writer and now as senior editor of the Voice Literary Supplement.
"Memoirs of a Non-Prom Queen" is a review essay inspired by
Ralph Keyes's Is There Life after High School? (1976). It analyzes
the lasting psychological effects of Willis's own less-than-ideal high
school years.*

There's a book out called *Is There Life after High School?*   1
It's a fairly silly book, maybe because the subject matter is
the kind that only hurts when you think. Its thesis—that most
people never get over the social triumphs or humiliations of
high school—is not novel. Still, I read it with the respectful
attention a serious hypochondriac accords the lowliest "dear
doctor" column. I don't know about most people, but for me,
forgiving my parents for real and imagined derelictions has
been easy compared to forgiving myself for being a teenage
reject.

Victims of high school trauma—which seems to have af-   2
flicted a disproportionate number of writers, including Ralph
Keyes, the author of this book—tend to embrace the ugly
duckling myth of adolescent social relations: the "innies"

(Keyes's term) are good-looking, athletic mediocrities who will never amount to much, while the "outies" are intelligent, sensitive, creative individuals who will do great things in an effort to make up for their early defeats. Keyes is partial to this myth. He has fun with celebrity anecdotes: Kurt Vonnegut receiving a body-building course as a "gag prize" at a dance; Frank Zappa yelling "fuck you" at a cheerleader; Mike Nichols,[1] as a nightclub comedian, insulting a fan—an erstwhile overbearing classmate turned used-car salesman. In contrast, the ex-prom queens and kings he interviews slink through life, hiding their pasts lest someone call them "dumb jock" or "cheerleader type," perpetually wondering what to do for an encore.

If only it were that simple. There may really be high schools   3 where life approximates an Archie comic, but even in the Fifties, my large (5000 students), semisuburban (Queens, New York), heterogeneous high school was not one of them. The students' social life was fragmented along ethnic and class lines; there was no universally recognized, schoolwide social hierarchy. Being an athlete or a cheerleader or a student officer didn't mean much. Belonging to an illegal sorority or fraternity meant more, at least in some circles, but many socially active students chose not to join. The most popular kids were not necessarily the best looking or the best dressed or the most snobbish or the least studious. In retrospect, it seems to me that they were popular for much more honorable reasons. They were attuned to other people, aware of subtle social nuances. They projected an inviting sexual warmth. Far from being slavish followers of fashion, they were self-confident enough to set fashions. They suggested, initiated, led. Above all—this was their main appeal for me—they knew how to have a good time.

True, it was not particularly sophisticated enjoyment—dancing,   4 pizza eating, hand holding in the lunchroom, the usual. I had friends—precocious intellectuals and bohemians—who were consciously alienated from what they saw as all that teenage crap. Part of me identified with them, yet I badly wanted what they

---

[1] Vonnegut, American novelist, author of *Cat's Cradle* (1963); *God Bless You, Mr. Rosewater* (1964); *Slaughterhouse-Five* (1969); and *Breakfast of Champions* (1973). Zappa was the leader of the rock music group, Mothers of Invention. Nichols is a former night club and television comedian, now a film and stage director.

rejected. Their seriousness engaged my mind, but my romantic and sexual fantasies, and my emotions generally, were obsessively fixed on the parties and dances I wasn't invited to, the boys I never dated. I suppose what says it best is that my "serious" friends hated rock & roll; I loved it.

If I can't rationalize my social ineptitude as intellectual rebellion, neither can I blame it on political consciousness. Feminism has inspired a variation of the ugly duckling myth in which high school wallflower becomes feminist heroine, suffering because she has too much integrity to suck up to boys by playing a phony feminine role. There is a tempting grain of truth in this idea. Certainly the self-absorption, anxiety and physical and social awkwardness that made me a difficult teenager were not unrelated to my ambivalent awareness of women's oppression. I couldn't charm boys because I feared and resented them and their power over my life; I couldn't be sexy because I saw sex as a mine field of conflicting, confusing rules that gave them every advantage. I had no sense of what might make me attractive, a lack I'm sure involved unconscious resistance to the game girls were supposed to play (particularly all the rigmarole surrounding clothes, hair and cosmetics); I was a clumsy dancer because I could never follow the boy's lead.

Yet ultimately this rationale misses the point. As I've learned from comparing notes with lots of women, the popular girls were in fact much more in touch with the reality of the female condition than I was. They knew exactly what they had to do for the rewards they wanted, while I did a lot of what feminist organizers call denying the awful truth. I was a bit schizy. Desperate to win the game but unwilling to learn it or even face my feelings about it, I couldn't really play, except in fantasy; paradoxically, I was consumed by it much more thoroughly than the girls who played and played well. Knowing what they wanted and how to get it, they preserved their sense of self, however compromised, while I lost mine. Which is why they were not simply better game players but genuinely more likable than I.

The ugly duckling myth is sentimental. It may soothe the memory of social rejection, but it falsifies the experience, evades its cruelty and uselessness. High school permanently damaged my self-esteem. I learned what it meant to be impotent; what it meant to be invisible. None of this improved my character, spurred my ambition, or gave me a deeper understanding of life. I know people who were popular in high school who later became serious intellectuals, radicals, artists, even journalists. I regret not being one of those people. To see my failure as morally or politically superior to their success would be to indulge in a version of the Laingian [2] fallacy—that because a destructive society drives people crazy, there is something dishonorable about managing to stay sane.

QUESTIONS

Understanding

1. What was the effect of her high school experience upon the author? In which sentence does she formulate that effect most directly?
2. What specific difficulties during Willis's high school years caused the aftereffects that she describes?
3. Explain the basic idea behind the ugly duckling myth (or the Cinderella story—the two are fundamentally the same). What does the myth have to do with Ralph Keyes's theory (in *Is There Life after High School?*) about the "innies" and the "outies" (par. 2)?
4. Willis agrees that high school can scar its victims for life, but she thinks Keyes's theory about "innies" and "outies" is wrong. Why? What fallacies does she see in Keyes's reasoning?
5. How, according to Willis, has the feminist movement "inspired a variation of the ugly duckling myth" (par. 5)? Who is the swan in this version? How might Willis's essay be interpreted as a more complicated feminist statement?

Strategies and Structure

1. Does Willis devote more attention to causes or to effects in this essay? Assuming that paragraph 1 and 2 constitute her introduction, which specific paragraphs deal with causes? Which deal with effects?

[2] R. D. Laing, the Scottish psychiatrist, argues that personality division is a predictable result of modern life.

2. How efficient do you find the first sentence in paragraph 3 as a TRANSITION sentence? Explain your answer.

3. In paragraph 1 Willis introduces herself as a "serious" hypochondriac, and we smile at the joke. By the end of the essay, how has the non-prom queen's TONE of voice changed?

4. Sentimentality is emotional response out of all proportion to the conditions · that produce it. Willis criticizes the ugly duckling myth for emotional bloat in paragraph 7. Do you think her "memoirs" successfully avoid sentimentality? Why or why not?

5. Why does Willis mention "Archie" comics and the example of her own high school in paragraph 3?

6. In paragraph 3, Willis tells what her high school days look like "in retrospect." What word in the title of her essay alerts us to this backward glance?

Words and Figures of Speech

1. A *rationale* (par. 6) explains the reasons for some course of action. Rationales may turn out to be accurate or inaccurate. *Rationalizations* (par. 5) are always inaccurate. Why? What does the term mean?

2. *Schizy* (par. 6) is short for *schizophrenic*. What psychological condition does the word DENOTE? How does it apply to Willis's state of mind in high school?

3. Willis's vocabulary is sophisticated, even learned; but it includes a smattering of slang and profanity. How might such language be considered appropriate, given the fact that Willis's essay first appeared in *Rolling Stone* magazine?

4. Look up any unfamiliar words in the following list: *thesis* (par. 1), *derelictions* (1), *trauma* (2), *mediocrities* (2), *anecdotes* (2), *erstwhile* (2), *heterogeneous* (3) *hierarchy* (3), *retrospect* (3), *nuances* (3), *slavish* (3), *precocious* (4), *bohemians* (4), *ineptitude* (5), *ambivalent* (5), *impotent* (7).

Comparing

1. Willis says (par. 2) that writers seem especially vulnerable to the traumas of adolescence, and her essay might be seen as a writer's attempt to put a traumatic past into perspective. How does this

therapeutic motive compare with the motive Annie Dillard assigns to the writer in "Transfiguration" (reprinted in "The Writing Process")?

Discussion and Writing Topics

1. Have your high school days left any psychological scars? What traumas caused them?

2. Do you now question any standards or values that you accepted without a second thought in high school? What were they? What caused you to change your mind?

3. Did you know people in high school who were popular for some of the "honorable" reasons Willis mentions in paragraph 3? How did they behave?

4. What is a myth? What kinds of belief do myths reveal within a society or a culture?

James Seilsopour

I Forgot the Words to
the National Anthem

Born in California in 1962, James Seilsopour is an American
citizen whose father is Iranian. After spending most of his early
life in Teheran, he returned to the U.S. with his family during
the Iranian revolution of 1979. Seilsopour entered high school in
Norco, California, the scene of the political discrimination he
describes in "I Forgot the Words to the National Anthem." He
graduated in 1982 and is now an English major at Riverside City
College, where his English teacher, W. F. Hunt, urged him to
submit this essay to a national competition in student writing.
It was selected for publication in Student Writers at Work
(1984). The author discusses the task of composing and revising
his prizewinning essay in "Writers on the Writing Process" at
the end of this chapter.

The bumper sticker read, "Piss on Iran."   1

To me, a fourteen-year-old living in Teheran, the Iranian rev-   2
olution was nothing more than an inconvenience. Although
the riots were just around the corner, although the tanks lined
the streets, although a stray bullet went through my sister's
bedroom window, I was upset because I could not ride at the
Royal Stable as often as I used to. In the summer of 1979 my
family—father, mother, brothers, sister, aunt, and two cousins—were forced into exile. We came to Norco, California.

In Iran, I was an American citizen and considered myself an   3
American, even though my father was Iranian. I loved baseball
and apple pie and knew the words to the "Star-Spangled Banner." That summer before high school, I was like any other kid
my age; I listened to rock 'n' roll, liked fast cars, and thought
Farrah Fawcett was a fox. Excited about going to high school, I
was looking forward to football games and school dances. But

I learned that it was not meant to be. I was not like other kids, and it was a long, painful road I traveled as I found this out.

The American embassy in Iran was seized the fall I started high   4
school. I did not realize my life would be affected until I read that bumper sticker in the high school parking lot which read, "Piss on Iran." At that moment I knew there would be no football games or school dances. For me, Norco High consisted of the goat ropers, the dopers, the jocks, the brains, and one quiet Iranian.

I was sitting in my photography class after the hostages were   5
taken. The photography teacher was fond of showing travel films. On this particular day, he decided to show a film about Iran, knowing full well that my father was Iranian and that I grew up in Iran. During the movie, this teacher encouraged the students to make comments. Around the room, I could hear "Drop the bomb" and "Deport the mothers." Those words hurt. I felt dirty, guilty. However, I managed to laugh and assure the students I realized they were just joking. I went home that afternoon and cried. I have long since forgiven those students, but I have not and can never forgive that teacher. Paranoia set in. From then on, every whisper was about me: "You see that lousy son of a bitch? He's Iranian." When I was not looking, I could feel their pointing fingers in my back like arrows. Because I was absent one day, the next day I brought a note to the attendance office. The secretary read the note, then looked at me. "So you're Jim Seilsopour?" I couldn't answer. As I walked away, I thought I heard her whisper to her co-worker, "You see that lousy son of a bitch? He's Iranian." I missed thirty-five days of school that year.

My problems were small compared to those of my parents. In   6
Teheran, my mother had been a lady of society. We had a palatial house and a maid. Belonging to the women's club, she collected clothes for the poor and arranged Christmas parties for the young American kids. She and my father dined with high government officials. But back in the States, when my father could not find a job, she had to work at a fast-food restaurant. She was the proverbial pillar of strength. My mother worked seventy hours a week for two years. I never heard her complain. I could see the toll the entire situation was taking on her. One day my mother and I went grocery shopping at Stater Brothers Market. After an hour of carefully picking our food, we proceeded to the cashier. The cashier was friendly and began a conversation with my mother. They spoke briefly of the weather as my mother wrote the check. The

cashier looked at the check and casually asked, "What kind of name is that?" My mother said, "Italian." We exchanged glances for just a second. I could see the pain in her eyes. She offered no excuses; I asked for none.

Because of my father's birthplace, he was unable to obtain a job. 7 A naturalized American citizen with a master's degree in aircraft maintenance engineering from the Northrop Institute of Technology, he had never been out of work in his life. My father had worked for Bell Helicopter International, Flying Tigers, and McDonnell Douglas. Suddenly, a man who literally was at the top of his field was unemployable. There is one incident that haunts me even today. My mother had gone to work, and all the kids had gone to school except me. I was in the bathroom washing my face. The door was open, and I could see my father's reflection in the mirror. For no particular reason I watched him. He was glancing at a newspaper. He carefully folded the paper and set it aside. For several long moments he stared blankly into space. With a resigned sigh, he got up, went into the kitchen, and began doing the dishes. On that day, I know I watched a part of my father die.

My father did get a job. However, he was forced to leave the 8 country. He is a quality control inspector for Saudi Arabian Airlines in Jeddah, Saudi Arabia. My mother works only forty hours a week now. My family has survived, financially and emotionally. I am not bitter, but the memories are. I have not recovered totally; I can never do that.

And no, I have never been to a high school football game or 9 dance. The strike really turned me off to baseball. I have been on a diet for the last year, so I don't eat apple pie much anymore. And I have forgotten the words to the national anthem.

QUESTIONS

Understanding

1. How did James Seilsopour expect to be treated when he moved with his family to California during the Iranian revolution of 1979? What incident first made him realize how wrong he had been?

2. Ostracized by his teachers and classmates at Norco High, the

author sums up in a single word in paragraph 5 the immediate effect of their discrimination upon him. What is it?

3. Seilsopour has forgiven the students who taunted him in high school. With whom does he still refuse, however, to let bygones be bygones? Why?

4. Seilsopour's experience at an American high school has not left him bitter, he says; but what lasting effect *has* it had?

5. His own mistreatment is only one reason for the author's regret in "I Forgot the Words to the National Anthem." To what other causes in the past does he also assign his present painful memories?

Strategies and Structure

1. James Seilsopour tells in paragraph 5 how life in America affected *him*. By what two specific incidents does he convey the cumulative effect of their American experience upon each of his parents?

2. The author classifies students at Norco High into "the goat ropers, the dopers, the jocks, the brains, and one quiet Iranian" (par. 4). What purpose does this brief CLASSIFICATION serve in an essay otherwise devoted to cause and effect?

3. Any political statement about the nation's treatment of immigrants remains implicit in Seilsopour's essay. Should he have made it more explicit, as in the persuasive arguments of Chapters 9 and 10? Or do you find his letting the effects of discrimination speak for themselves to be just as persuasive in this case? Explain your answer.

4. Seilsopour can say "I felt dirty, guilty" because he is revealing his own feelings in paragraph 5. How does he elsewhere tell us about his parents' feelings without violating the limited, first-person POINT OF VIEW he has already set up?

5. In paragraph 2 Seilsopour stacks up three clauses beginning with "although." Why? Whose insensitivity to danger signs is he imitating?

6. Most of the time, Seilsopour is writing about the temporary effects of their American experience upon himself and his family. What seems to be his intention in the last two paragraphs of the essay?

Words and Figures of Speech

1. Is the profanity in Seilsopour's essay justified? Why or why not? To whom is he always careful to attribute it?

2. Do you find Seilsopour's use of the CLICHÉ "pillar of strength" (par. 6) to describe his mother's stoicism to be more or less effective than his references to baseball and apple pie? Explain your answer.

3. Why would you suppose Seilsopour chose the national anthem to "forget" rather than some other song?

4. What is surprising about the use of the word *inconvenience* in paragraph 2? Of *exile* in the same paragraph?

Comparing

1. Both James Seilsopour and Deairich Hunter ("Ducks vs. Hard Rocks," Chapter 2) write as beleaguered outsiders in a new school. Contrast the reasons for their discontent.

2. Compare and contrast "I Forgot the Words to the National Anthem" with Mary Mebane's "The Back of the Bus" (Chapter 1) as personal accounts of discrimination.

Topics for Discussion and Writing

1. Judging from the specific acts he mentions, how seriously, in your view, were James Seilsopour and his family discriminated against? Is his essay, therefore, reasonable in its criticism, too forgiving, or unfairly condemning?

2. Have you ever been the victim of political, racial, sexual, or any other form of discrimination? Write a personal account of the experiences that emphasizes the *effects* it had upon you and your family.

3. Have you ever committed or condoned an act of discrimination? Write about the occasion in a personal essay that makes the causes of your behavior understandable without justifying or approving it.

Paul Colinvaux
Why Japan
Bombed Pearl Harbor

Professor of zoology at the Ohio State University, Paul Colinvaux
was born in England and served in the Royal Artillery, where he
acquired a knowledge of soldiering that has served him more
recently as a biological historian for whom warfare is ecology.
Besides England and the United States, Colinvaux has lived or
done field work in Germany, Canada, Portugal, Africa, Bermuda,
the Galapagos, and South America. A contributor to Science,
Nature, Ecology, and other journals, he is the author of Why Big
Fierce Animals Are Rare (1978) and The Fates of Nations (1981),
a Darwinian view of history that links historical change to
variations in national populations and living habits. "Why Japan
Bombed Pearl Harbor" (editor's title), a complete section of this
later book, analyzes the ecological causes leading to an act of
aggression that changed the fate of an ambitious island nation.
The apparently plain style of Colinvaux's essay is eloquent proof
of his contention "that science is so intrinsically interesting that it
only has to be written about beautifully for everybody to
understand all about it."

The Japanese learned of the ways of the European West   I
when their island was feudal, agrarian and crowded. So
crowded were they that, although a country of rural folk and
artisans, Japan actually imported its staple food, rice. Her
feudal masters kept their country and their own power isolated from the expanding West as long as possible, but the
traders came at last. The Americans were first, extracting a
trade treaty with a few thoughtful discharges of their cannon,
and the Europeans were glad enough to follow where the
American cannon went.

It took the Japanese less than ten years to act on the politic   2
maxim, "If you can't beat them join them." In a mild revolution
the feudal chieftains returned their fiefs; their quaint old retainers,
who served as soldiers, were pensioned off, and the people turned
their formidable brains to mastering the techniques of Western
industry. They also bought or manufactured some cannon as they
went along, because they were a trading nation and they had
learned from the civilized West that cannon were a very useful aid
to trade.

The people learned the new ways in a single generation. Their   3
aspirations bounded high, and so did the country's birth rate. Between the revolution of 1868 and the turn of the century the
Japanese bred an extra thirteen million people. They were so
crowded to start with that they had to import rice. Now, as an
industrial state, they had to import raw materials too. The people
felt that they needed to be sure of their supply of resources; they
needed to own land with raw materials in it, to control outlets for
some of their trade and, perhaps, to have some land where they
could deposit surplus people too. They prepared to take what they
wanted by force. They studied Western war, made what Western
weapons they could, and bought the rest. Britain had the best
navy, so the Japanese bought British warships. Germany had
Krupp,[1] so they bought German artillery, and so on. Then they
beat up some primitive Chinese forces to let them have their way
over some minor matters on the mainland, which gave them a
chance to try their hands at the new form of soldiering. Practice
was necessary because they knew that they must tackle Western
power eventually.

What the Japanese wanted first was Korea, a long-coveted piece   4
of land which could supply many of their immediate wants. Curious as it may sound, they had to fight Russia for the privilege of
conquering Korea, because the Russians felt their vital interest was
involved. So they fought the Russians and beat them handsomely
in a campaign of 1904, known as the Siege of Port Arthur. They
had read the very latest military writers more carefully than had
the Russians, and were that much more modern. The Russians let
them have Korea. It was a very successful aggression.

[1] Industrial giant known for manufacturing armaments, founded and for 150
years run by the Krupp family.

But, as the population went on growing so did the needs of the   5
people. The Japanese got some more land out of the First World
War when, by a very sensible arrangement for mutual benefit, they
were allied to the British. Their purchase of cannon and warships
was paying off very nicely. No other Asiatic power stood a chance
against Western methods of war, whether these were used by Japanese or by the Europeans who had invented them; and the Japanese had carefully avoided a clash with a major Western power.
Even in their battle with the Russians they had prudently kept
themselves to very limited objectives, avoiding such provocation
that the Russians might think a major war effort was necessary.

But aggressive war was now a Japanese habit, as it is to all   6
nations who pursue it successfully. And the Japanese numbers and
aspirations still continued to grow. Some of the thinking then
common in Japan was written down for us by a young Japanese
naval officer in a book published in 1935 and called *Japan Must
Fight Britain*. The theme is that Japan must expand; therefore,
someone must move over. If not, "Japan must fight Britain," and
if Japan loses that first fight "It is as clear as day that, with her
population and her insufficient resources, it would not be long
before she had to draw her sword and stand up to fight for her
life."

The Japanese were convinced that they must take by force what   7
was needed to give an ever-growing population the standard of life
it thought it deserved. And they did fight. In choosing Britain for
an enemy they were, of course, tackling a weakened power, one
with incompetent generals who had lately preferred horses to tanks
and who had not thought it necessary for Singapore to have guns
on the land side as well as on the sea side. Even so, it was a
dangerous thing to do. But tackling the United States of America
at the same time was so hazardous an undertaking as to be
scarcely believable. The reasons for this desperate venture must
have been very strong indeed.

A wealthy island state, as Japan then was, is predicted by the   8
ecological hypothesis[2] to be extremely prone to start an aggressive
war. The opportunities for a broad niche on the island base must

---

[2] The theory that changes in human history are caused in part by changes in a
people's numbers and living habits, as with any other animal.

be limited, putting a strong pressure on those desiring wealth to find opportunity elsewhere. Trade must, and always does, become part of the niche-space of the affluent on all islands that achieve moderate wealth. But part of the success in winning niche-space through trade must be spent, through the breeding strategy, in the production of more potential traders. The numbers of the affluent grow, but there is also a worse population consequence as well because imports always include cheap food, which allows the poorer classes to maintain their own, larger breeding effort. The country then becomes dependent on free access to markets to maintain its traditional affluence and must be ready to fight for those markets. A few generations later rising numbers of the wealthier classes find it difficult to provide affluence for their own descendants, which is the essential condition for an aggressive war. Island folk can educate, trade, and breed their way into this condition very easily.

It was clear to the Japanese of 1941 that they had real need of   9
access to other people's land if their new and better way of life was to be maintained. They were quite right. They still need that access forty years later, and are getting it. The large continents of Europe and America are yielding to the Japanese much of their continental living space, welcoming Japanese traders, keeping the sea lanes safe for Japanese commerce with their own navies, accepting Japanese manufactures even at the cost of destroying their own currencies and industries. It is, perhaps, a moot point how long they will feel content to go on doing so. But in 1941 the Japanese were not being so warmly welcomed in the world.

The Japanese had long been fighting to take provinces from   10
China, expanding the continental land they already held in Korea. It was, of course, blatant aggression, sired of ecological necessity and mothered in imitation of the Anglo-Saxon example. Success in this war, long and drawn-out as it came to be, was vital to those who controlled the Japanese government. The people too were deeply conscious of their need, schooled to accept the new Western ways, building a high standard of living by fighting for it. And they were proud.

Then the United States did two things for Japan. They placed an   11
embargo on the sale of the oil needed to sustain Japanese armies, and they put all American warships into one handy disposable package in a harbor in Hawaii. A better combination of stick and

carrot to drive the Japanese into war would be hard to imagine. The war chiefs saw their opportunity and struck, and Japan was committed to the forlorn, hopeless adventure. They would take their oil from the British in Burma, by force. They did that. Then they would use valor and skill to make the United States agree to their keeping the loot. But this could not be.

QUESTIONS

Understanding

1. What immediate cause, according to Colinvaux, produced Japan's sudden turn in the 1860s from ancient feudalism to Western ways?
2. One cause of Japan's expansionism early in this century, says Colinvaux, was the unavailability of new land within its own borders. What other causes does he cite?
3. If Colinvaux is right, why are island nations like Japan and England "extremely prone to start an aggressive war" (par. 8)?
4. With any nation, according to Colinvaux, the practice of successful aggression typically has what effect?
5. Of all the causes of aggression that Colinvaux analyzes with the aid of ecological theory, which is "the essential condition" (par. 8) necessary to send an ambitious country to war?
6. In the broadest terms, what other causes of aggression does Colinvaux analyze here by using the example of Japan?
7. In the particular case of Japan's attack on Pearl Harbor, what two immediate causes produced this catastrophic effect?

Strategies and Structure

1. Historians are supposed to be objective toward their subject. Point out additional sentences like the following in which Colinvaux gives the impression of even-handed judgment and sympathy: "It was clear to the Japanese of 1941 that they had real need of access to other people's land. . . . They were quite right" (par. 9).
2. Colinvaux is both a historian and a zoologist. In his essay, how does the scientist accustomed to studying the habits of animals affect the historian who is studying the behavior of a people?

3. The habits of people living in groups are affected by their joint use of tools. Since Colinvaux is studying the Japanese habits of war, he pays special attention to the tools of war. Point out several examples you find especially pertinent.

4. Would you describe the scope of Colinvaux's historical analysis as broad or narrow? Approximately how many years does he cover? For the number of conclusions he draws, does he cite many documentary sources or relatively few, in your opinion?

5. Judging from the number of documentary references in Colinvaux's essay, would you say he is writing primarily for historians, zoologists, or a general audience? Explain your answer.

6. Paragraph 6 cites a book written by a young Japanese naval officer shortly before the bombing of Pearl Harbor. Why do you suppose Colinvaux chose to cite this source rather than other examples of "the thinking then common in Japan" (par. 6), written, say, by army officers or government officials?

7. How effective do you find the reference to rice in paragraph 1? How skillful in general do you find this author at choosing his examples? Explain your answer.

8. America originally opened trade with Japan, writes Colinvaux, by administering some "thoughtful" cannon blasts (par. 1). Try to find other examples of a similar IRONY in this essay. Why might Colinvaux adopt such a TONE when writing for an American readership?

Words and Figures of Speech

1. Both *ecology* and *biology* are words having to do with living things. What are the principal differences in meaning between the two terms?

2. "Agrarianism" (par. 1) refers to a way of making a living. From what? What is *feudalism*? How do these two related words differ in DENOTATION? In CONNOTATION?

3. In the first sentence of paragraph 11, why does Colinvaux use the preposition "for" instead of "to"?

4. What is the difference, exactly, between "politic" (par. 2) and "political"?

5. What are the connotations of the word *bred* in paragraph 3? How can Colinvaux use it here without being insulting?

6. A "maxim" is usually a sober, high-sounding rule for guiding conduct. How would you describe Colinvaux's tone when he says the

Japanese acted on the maxim, "If you can't beat them join them" (par. 2)?

7. Consult your dictionary for any of the following words that are not in your working vocabulary: *artisans* (par. 1), *fiefs* (par. 2), *retainers* (par. 2), *pensioned off* (par. 2), *formidable* (par. 2), *coveted* (par. 3), *provocation* (par. 5), *niche* (par. 8), *moot* (par. 9), *blatant* (par. 10), *embargo* (par. 11).

Comparing

1. How is Colinvaux's analysis of the causes of human aggression confirmed by Loren Eiseley's account of animal behavior in "The Angry Winter" (Chapter 1)?

2. Colinvaux's essay studies a prime example of *offensive* behavior. Desmond Morris's "Barrier Signals" (Chapter 5), on the other hand, looks at *defensive* behavior. What common cause lies behind these contrasting responses of action and reaction as explained in these two essays?

Discussion and Writing Topics

1. Besides changes in breeding and living habits, what other forces do you think can shape and even alter history? (One example might be the emergence of a great leader, such as Abraham Lincoln.)

2. Are you convinced by Colinvaux's analysis of why Japan bombed Pearl Harbor? Why or why not? If not, give your own causal analysis.

3. Who was to blame for Pearl Harbor, according to Colinvaux's account?

4. Is Colinvaux right or wrong to leave out questions of morality when discussing history? Explain your answer.

Writers on the Writing Process:
James Seilsopour

James Seilsopour's "I Forgot the Words to the National An- 1
them" is an example of dealing with pain by writing about it.
When the author returned with his family to the United States
during the Iranian revolution of 1979, he expected to be what
he had been in Teheran: an American citizen who "loved baseball and apple pie and knew the words to the 'Star-Spangled
Banner.' " He was "excited" about entering high school and
"looking forward to football games and school dances." Unprepared for the anti-Iranian sentiment in this country, Seilsopour
was stunned by the treatment he received at Norco High, California.

After Seilsopour entered Riverside City College in 1982, he 2
felt the need "to talk about that part of my life." He planned
to deal with it by writing poetry but turned to the essay form
to meet a course assignment. ("I had fallen behind in my English class," he explains, "and needed a paper to turn in.")
Seilsopour's teacher encouraged him to write as if for publication and guided him through several revisions. Revising the
essay was almost as "painful" as the experience it describes—
"like cutting yourself with a hot blade."

The author survived and his essay improved with such ex- 3
cisions as the one he made at the end of paragraph 7. In his
first draft, Seilsopour ended the paragraph with the line, "To
this day we have never spoken of that incident." The sentence
specifies no particular feeling, but it makes the mistake Annie
Dillard identifies in the introduction to this book. It stops
evoking and starts to *describe* emotion.

Another revision in Seilsopour's essay is harder to justify. 4
Seilsopour's teacher recommended the finished essay for a
prize in a national competition of student writers. It was se-

lected and eventually published, along with the other prize essays. As he submitted it, Seilsopour's final, typed version located what is now the first paragraph in a different place. In the typescript, the line about the bumper sticker is centered a few lines above the rest, as a sort of epigraph. The author apparently intended for the body of his essay to begin with what is now paragraph 2.

Epigraphs are fine for books but out of place in most short pieces; so when Seilsopour's typed version was prepared for the printer, the raised line was dropped down to become the opening paragraph. This "solution," however, raises a problem of its own, for Seilsopour encountered the bumper sticker after he moved to America, yet his essay proper begins with his experience in Iran. Since the obscene bumper sticker is mentioned again in paragraph 4, would it not have been better to omit the first reference altogether? The blemish hardly disfigures a fine essay, but you might consider how to fix it. 5

Writing to cope with painful experience can be good therapy. As the considered revisions in Seilsopour's essay attest, however, good writing holds the writer's experience at sufficient distance to consider the reader's needs, too. The real problem he had to work out during the writing process, says Seilsopour, "was toning the paper down from an angry commentary to a straightforward personal essay." When it was chosen to be published, Seilsopour was happy that the story of his personal trial "will finally get told." His main task as a writer, however, was not to rail about the pain his experience caused him but to make the reader feel its effects: "When people read my essay, I want them to imagine themselves in my place for just a moment—then never think about it again." 6

WRITING TOPICS for Chapter Four
Essays That Analyze Cause and Effect

Write an essay analyzing the probable causes or effects (or both) of one of the following:

1. The energy crisis

2. Pollution

3. Urban blight

4. Drug or alcohol abuse

5. Heart disease, sickle cell anemia, or some other disease

6. Divorce within the first year or two of marriage

7. Loss of religious faith

8. Loss of self-esteem

9. Racial discrimination or ethnic jokes and slurs

10. Success in college

11. Student cheating

12. Sibling rivalry

13. The Civil War or other historical event

14. Invention of the assembly line system

15. Dropping out of high school or college

16. A sudden shift in status: from high school senior to college freshman, for example

5
Essays That Define

To make a basic DEFINITION,[1] put whatever you are defining into a class and then list the characteristics that distinguish it from all other members of that class. The Greek philosopher Plato, for example, defined man by putting him in the class "biped." Then Plato thought of a quality that sets man off from other two-legged creatures. "Man," he said, "is a featherless biped."

When the rival philosopher Diogenes heard this definition, he brought a plucked chicken into the lecture room and observed, "Here is Plato's man." Plato responded by adding that man is a featherless biped "having broad nails." The general principle that Plato was obeying holds for the basic definitions you will write. If at first you choose qualities that do not sufficiently distinguish your subject from others in the same class, refine those attributes until they do.

You can tell when a basic definition is essentially complete by testing whether it is true if reversed. "Man is a biped" proves to be an incomplete definition when we turn it around, for it is not true that "all bipeds are men." Likewise, we know that the final version of Plato's definition is sound because it is truly reversible. All featherless bipeds having broad nails (instead of claws) are indeed humans.

When it can be reversed, a basic definition is complete enough to be accurate; but it still may be scanty or undeveloped. One way of developing a basic definition is by listing qualities or attributes of a thing beyond those needed merely to identify it. Food expert Raymond Sokolov defines

[1] Terms printed in all capitals are defined in the Glossary.

the Florida tomato, for example, as a vegetable that is "mass-produced, artificially ripened, mechanically picked, long-hauled" (all qualities or attributes). "It has no taste and it won't go splat" (more qualities, though negative ones). Sokolov advises that we grow our own tomatoes if we want them to be "antique-style, squishable, blotchy, tart, and sometimes green-dappled."

Another common strategy of basic definition is to define the whole by naming its parts. "Ketchup is long-haul tomatoes combined with sugar, vinegar, salt, onion powder, and 'natural' flavoring." Or you might define a word by tracing its origins: "The English ketchup (or catsup) comes from the Malay word kechap, derived in turn from the Chinese word meaning 'fish brine.'" This word history may seem to take us far from the tomatoes at the base of America's favorite sauce, but it suggests where ketchup originally got its salty taste. Such word histories (or ETYMOLOGIES) can be found in parentheses or brackets before many of the definitions in your dictionary.

Yet another way of developing a basic definition is to give synonyms for the word or concept being defined. A botanist might well tell us that the tomato is a plant used as a vegetable. But if pushed, he would add that the tomato is actually a "berry," or "fleshy fruit," akin to the "hesperidium" and the "pepo." His botanical definition would then proceed to explain what these closely related terms have in common, as well as the shades of difference among them. You can find synonyms for the word you are defining in any good desk dictionary or dictionary of synonyms. (The etymologies usually come at the beginning of a dictionary entry; the "synonymies," or lists of synonyms, at the end.)

The definitions we have discussed so far are short and limited to defining a basic word or phrase. When the strategy of an entire essay is to define something, the author produces what is called an extended definition. Extended definitions seek first and last to explain the nature or meaning of a thing, but they often use many of the other strategies of exposition. An extended definition of the detective story, for example, might divide it into types according to the kind of detective involved: the hard-boiled cop, the bumbling private eye, the clever priest. This would be an example of supporting a definition by CLASSIFICATION.

If we distinguished the detective story from the mystery story or the thriller, we might go on to define it by COMPARISON AND CONTRAST with similar forms. If we noted that Edgar Allan Poe invented the detective story and we gave the history of great detectives from Poe's Dupin to Sherlock Holmes to Columbo, we might draw upon NARRATIVE. Or if we speculated that the detective story came into being because Poe wanted to discover a walk of life in which the scientific mind blended with the poetic mind, we would be analyzing CAUSE AND EFFECT.

There is no set formula for writing an extended definition, but here are some questions to keep in mind when working one up: What is the essential nature or purpose of the thing you are defining? What are its qualities? How does it work? How is it different from others like it? Why do we need to know about it? In answering these questions, be as specific as you can. Vivid details make definitions interesting, and interest (after accuracy) is the best test of a good definition. Plato's definition of man surprises us into attention by reducing a lofty concept to the homely term "featherless." The poet Emily Dickinson does the same when she defines Hope as "the thing with feathers." It is the vivid specific detail that startles us here, as Woody Allen well knows when he reduces Dickinson's definition to absurdly specific terms: "The thing with feathers has turned out to be my nephew. I must take him to a specialist in Zurich."

Jeremy Rifkin
The Christian World View

Jeremy Rifkin grew up in Chicago. He studied finance at Penn State and earned a Master's in International Affairs at Tufts. In 1967 Rifkin helped organize the first national rally against the war in Vietnam. Since then, he has been an economic advisor to Congress, labor and business leaders, and the President's Commission on the Agenda for the 1980s. Author of The Emerging Order *(1979) and* Algeny *(1983), Rifkin has written about genetic engineering, labor relations, modern evangelism, and the first two laws of thermodynamics as applied to broad cultural trends. The following complete chapter from* Entropy *(1980) tells how a medieval Christian serf would have defined the universe.*

I magine, if you will, a time warp that could put you face to face with a medieval Christian serf. Now, the thirteenth century is not so very long ago. Only forty generations separate us from the feudal world. In fact, there's much about that world that you would immediately recognize. In England, students were already graduating from Cambridge, *Beowulf* had been written, and a form of English was being spoken—although we would find it difficult to understand. Still, even without a language barrier you and the serf would have very little of interest to say to each other after the usual chitchat about the weather. That's because you would probably be interested in finding out what his goals in life were. What contribution did he hope to make to the world? How was he bettering his lot in life? What kind of largesse did he expect to leave to his children? What were his ideas about happiness and the good life?

You might even want to probe a little deeper into his psyche, asking him about his personality traits and identity problems.

Of course, you shouldn't expect much in the way of a response. 2 In fact, if all you see in his eyes is a blank expression, it's not because you're talking over his head, or because his mind isn't developed enough for the exchange of ideas. It's just that his ideas about life, history, and reality are so utterly different from our own.

The Christian view of history, which dominated western Europe 3 throughout the Middle Ages, perceived life in this world as a mere stopover in preparation for the next. The Christian world view abandoned the Greek concept of cycles but retained the notion of history as a decaying process. In Christian theology, history has a distinct beginning, middle, and end in the form of the Creation, the Redemption, and the Last Judgment. While human history is linear, not cyclical, it is not believed to be progressing toward some perfected state. On the contrary, history is seen as an ongoing struggle in which the forces of evil continue to sow chaos and disintegration in the earthly world.

Equally important, the doctrine of original sin precluded the 4 possibility of humanity ever improving its lot in life. In fact, the idea of people making or changing history would have been unthinkable. After all, to the medieval mind, the world was a tightly ordered structure in which God controlled every single event. The Christian God was a personal God who intervened in every aspect of life. If things happened or didn't happen it was because God willed it. God made history, not people.

There were no personal goals, no desire to get ahead or to leave 5 something behind. There were only God's decrees to be faithfully carried out. As historian John Randall points out, for the medieval Christian "everything must possess significance not in and for itself, but for man's pilgrimage." The purpose of every action, of every unfolding event, was tied to the "purpose it served in the divine scheme."

The Christian world view provided a unified and all-encompass- 6 ing picture of history. There was no room for the individual in this grand theological synthesis. It was duties and obligations, not freedoms and rights, that cemented and unified the historical frame of medieval life. Like the Greeks', the medieval concept of history was not one of growth and material gain. The human purpose was not to "achieve things" but to seek salvation. Toward this end, society was viewed as an organic whole, a kind of divinely directed moral organism in which each person had a part to play.

QUESTIONS

Understanding

1. You are walking in the woods one day, and you come upon a medieval Christian serf in a clearing. Why, according to Jeremy Rifkin, would the two of you have little of importance to say to each other?

2. Until recently, *progress* has been a controlling idea in the American view of history. We were thought to be moving ever forward toward material perfection. How does this aspect of the modern world view differ from the ancient Christian view (also linear) as described by Rifkin?

3. According to the ancient Greeks, human history cycled from a Golden Age through periods of greater and greater decay until the gods intervened to start the earthly spiral over again. In what particular does this view of the world contradict the Christian view? About the relative power of mortals as compared with immortal deities, nevertheless, the two theories agree. How so?

4. What do all the questions that Rifkin assumes we would first ask a medieval Christian have in common? If Rifkin is right, what do they reveal about the way we moderns define the world?

5. How is the role of the individual defined in the traditional Christian scheme of things as interpreted by Rifkin?

Strategies and Structure

1. Formal disquisitions upon vast theories of human endeavor can overwhelm the reader in lofty abstraction. How effective do you find Jeremy Rifkin's hypothetical Christian serf as a device for avoiding this pitfall?

2. Who else does the author of "The Christian World View" introduce as a means of bringing his sweeping generalizations down to earth? Why is this an especially clever strategy?

3. Rifkin begins his definition with a little NARRATIVE about entering

a time warp. Where does the narrative end and his formal definition begin? With which phrase does the author tell us what he is
defining?

4. After beginning with narration, Rifkin develops his definition by
the use of comparison and contrast. What is he comparing to what
in paragraphs 1 and 2? In most of paragraph 3?

5. What order in time does Rifkin follow in paragraphs 1–3? When
does he implicitly return to the modern period?

6. Definitions work by identifying the distinguishing features that set
apart whole classes of objects, persons, or ideas from other classes.
Rifkin's serf is representative of his breed. By what main distinguishing characteristics of thought does Rifkin define him and it?
By what contrasting characteristics does he identify us moderns in
paragraphs 4–6?

7. Rifkin cites historian John Randall in paragraph 5. Why do you
think he limits this reference to a few phrases only? Why not
quote a whole paragraph or more here?

Words and Figures of Speech

1. Look up the root meaning of *medieval* in your dictionary. Why
is the term appropriate to the period of history known as "the
Middle Ages"? When, approximately, did that period begin and
end in Europe?

2. What is a "serf"? Why do you think Rifkin chose a representative
of this class of medieval society as his model Christian?

3. Cyclical theories of history (such as the Greeks') are sometimes
described as "periodic." What does the term mean and how does
it apply to human events?

4. In Greek mythology "Chaos" was a proper name. Of whom? How
did the word acquire its present meaning of disorder, utter confusion?

5. A "pilgrimage" (par. 5) is a journey to a sacred destination. Why
is a journey an appropriate METAPHOR for the Christian way of
life as defined by Rifkin? (If you are familiar with John Bunyan's
The Pilgrim's Progress, where does Christian's journey lead him?)

6. What is the difference between an "organism" (par. 6) and a
"mechanism"? Which model of organization do you think Rifkin
would be more likely to assign to the modern world view? Why so?

Comparing

1. How do you think Rifkin's medieval Christian serf would react to Desmond Morris's definitions of barrier signals as emblems of social distance and cohesion in the next essay in this chapter?

2. In what way does Rifkin's use of the serf resemble Mary Mebane's use of the man in the porkpie hat in "The Back of the Bus" (Chapter 1)? Which world view does the figure in her essay clearly adhere to? What do you suppose the serf would think of the conflict she describes?

Discussion and Writing Topics

1. To the Puritans of early America, no event in a person's experience was too trivial to set down, as attested by the many surviving journals and diaries of their daily lives. Why did the Puritans and other pious colonists record such minutiae of the self? Were they being more like medieval Christians in their views of the self's place in the world or like modern Americans? Explain your answer.

2. How accurate do you consider Rifkin's definition of the Christian viewpoint? What details would you add? Which would you delete if any?

3. Should Rifkin's definition take into account such matters of Christian doctrine as grace, faith-versus-works, and transubstantiation? Why or why not?

4. "The Modern World View" is an enormous topic—Rifkin himself has written an entire book exploring it, in fact—but what main points would you cover if you were assigned an essay on the subject? What hints for dealing with expansive ideas in a small compass might you take from Rifkin's example?

Desmond Morris
Barrier Signals

*Born in Wiltshire, England, in 1928, Desmond Morris is a
zoologist who applies his knowledge of animal behavior to human
beings. Since 1968 he has been a full-time writer, but he maintains an office in the Department of Psychology, Oxford University.
An associate of the Tinbergen zoological research group at Oxford,
he is also an artist, and once organized a gallery sale in London of
abstract paintings by chimpanzees. Morris is best known in this
country as the author of* The Naked Ape *(1967), a study of the
human animal that was filmed by Universal studios in 1973. His
other books include* The Human Zoo *(1969);* Intimate Behavior
(1971); Manwatching: A Field Guide to Human Behavior
(1977); and the forthcoming Animal Days. *"Barrier Signals," a
complete section from* Manwatching, *is about the gestures we
unconsciously use to say no. It is an extended definition, developed
largely by the use of examples.*

People feel safer behind some kind of physical barrier. If a   1
social situation is in any way threatening, then there is an immediate urge to set up such a barricade. For a tiny child faced
with a stranger, the problem is usually solved by hiding behind its mother's body and peeping out at the intruder to see
what he or she will do next. If the mother's body is not
available, then a chair or some other piece of solid furniture
will do. If the stranger insists on coming closer, then the peeping face must be hidden too. If the insensitive intruder continues to approach despite these obvious signals of fear, then
there is nothing for it but to scream or flee.

This pattern is gradually reduced as the child matures. In   2
teenage girls it may still be detected in the giggling cover-up
of the face, with hands or papers, when acutely or jokingly em-

barrassed. But by the time we are adult, the childhood hiding which dwindled to adolescent shyness, is expected to disappear altogether, as we bravely stride out to meet our guests, hosts, companions, relatives, colleagues, customers, clients, or friends. Each social occasion involves us, once again, in encounters similar to the ones which made us hide as scared infants and, as then, each encounter is slightly threatening. In other words, the fears are still there, but their expression is blocked. Our adult roles demand control and suppression of any primitive urge to withdraw and hide ourselves away. The more formal the occasion and the more dominant or unfamiliar our social companions, the more worrying the moment of encounter becomes. Watching people under these conditions, it is possible to observe the many small ways in which they continue to 'hide behind their mother's skirts'. The actions are still there, but they are transformed into less obvious movements and postures. It is these that are the Barrier Signals of adult life.

The most popular from of Barrier Signal is the Body-cross. In   3
this, the hands or arms are brought into contact with one another in front of the body, forming a temporary 'bar' across the trunk, rather like a bumper or fender on the front of a motor-car. This is not done as a physical act of fending off the other person, as when raising a forearm horizontally across the front of the body to push through a struggling crowd. It is done, usually at quite a distance, as a nervous guest approaches a dominant host. The action is performed unconsciously and, if tackled on the subject immediately afterwards, the guest will not be able to remember having made the gesture. It is always camouflaged in some way, because if it were performed as a primitive fending-off or covering-up action, it would obviously be too transparent. The disguise it wears varies from person to person. Here are some examples:

The special guest on a gala occasion is alighting from his official   4
limousine. Before he can meet and shake hands with the reception committee, he has to walk alone across the open space in front of the main entrance to the building where the function is being held. A large crowd has come to watch his arrival and the press cameras are flashing. Even for the most experienced of celebrities this is a slightly nervous moment, and the mild fear that is felt expresses itself just as he is halfway across the 'greeting-space'. As he walks forward, his right hand reaches across his body and makes

a last-minute adjustment to his left cuff-link. It pauses there momentarily as he takes a few more steps, and then, at last, he is close enough to reach out his hand for the first of the many hand-shakes.

On a similar occasion, the special guest is a female. At just the point where her male counterpart would have fiddled with his cuff, she reaches across her body with her right hand and slightly shifts the position of her handbag, which is hanging from her left forearm.

There are other variations on this theme. A male may finger a button or the strap of a wristwatch instead of his cuff. A female may smooth out an imaginary crease in a sleeve, or re-position a scarf or coat held over her left arm. But in all cases there is one essential feature: at the peak moment of nervousness there is a Body-cross, in which one arm makes contact with the other across the front of the body, constructing a fleeting barrier between the guest and the reception committee.

Sometimes the barrier is incomplete. One arm swings across but does not actually make contact with the other. Instead it deals with some trivial clothing-adjustment task on the opposite side of the body. With even heavier camouflage, the hand comes up and across, but goes no further than the far side of the head or face, with a mild stroking or touching action.

Less disguised forms of the Body-cross are seen with less experienced individuals. The man entering the restaurant, as he walks across an open space, rubs his hands together, as if washing them. Or he advances with them clasped firmly in front of him.

Such are the Barrier Signals of the greeting situation, where one person is advancing on another. Interestingly, field observations reveal that it is most unlikely that both the greeter *and* the greeted will perform such actions. Regardless of status, it is nearly always the new arrival who makes the body-cross movement, because it is he who is invading the home territory of the greeters. They are on their own ground or, even if they are not, they were there first and have at least temporary territorial 'rights' over the place. This gives them an indisputable dominance at the moment of the greeting. Only if they are extremely subordinate to the new arrival, and perhaps in serious trouble with him, will there be a likelihood of them taking the 'body-cross role'. And if they do, this will mean that the new arrival on the scene will omit it as he enters.

These observations tell us something about the secret language [10] of Barrier Signals, and indicate that, although the sending and receiving of the signals are both unconsciously done, the message gets across, none the less. The message says: 'I am nervous but I will not retreat'; and this makes it into an act of subordination which automatically makes the other person feel slightly more dominant and more comfortable.

The situation is different after greetings are over and people are [11] standing about talking to one another. Now, if one man edges too close to another, perhaps to hear better in all the noise of chattering voices, the boxed-in companion may feel the same sort of threatening sensation that the arriving celebrity felt as he walked towards the reception committee. What is needed now, however, is something more long-lasting than a mere cuff-fumble. It is simply not possible to go fiddling with a button for as long as this companion is going to thrust himself forward. So a more composed posture is needed. The favorite Body-cross employed in this situation is the arm-fold, in which the left and right arms intertwine themselves across the front of the chest. This posture, a perfect, frontal Barrier Signal, can be held for a very long time without appearing strange. Unconsciously it transmits a 'come-no-farther' message and is used a great deal at crowded gatherings. It has also been used by poster artists as a deliberate 'They-shall-not-pass!' gesture, and is rather formally employed by bodyguards when standing outside a protected doorway.

The same device of arm-folding can be used in a sitting rela- [12] tionship where the companion is approaching too close, and it can be amplified by a crossing of the legs *away* from the companion. Another variant is to press the tightly clasped hands down on to the crotch and squeeze them there between the legs, as if protecting the genitals. The message of this particular form of barrier is clear enough, even though neither side becomes consciously aware of it. But perhaps the major Barrier Signal for the seated person is that ubiquitous device, the desk. Many a businessman would feel naked without one and hides behind it gratefully every day, wearing it like a vast, wooden chastity-belt. Sitting beyond it he feels fully protected from the visitor exposed on the far side. It is the supreme barrier, both physical and psychological, giving him an immediate and lasting comfort while he remains in its solid embrace.

QUESTIONS

Understanding

1. What is a "barrier signal" as defined by Morris?
2. Why must barrier signals be disguised? What do they mask?
3. Barrier signals as defined by Morris are part of a "secret language" (par. 10) of gestures or signs. How does a sign differ from an action like screaming or running away?
4. In a greeting situation, according to Morris, why is it usually the new arrival who sets up barriers, even when his status is higher than the greeter's?
5. Why are barrier signals of interest to sociologists and anthropologists? What kind of information can they provide?

Strategies and Structure

1. Which sentence in paragraph 2 signals that the author has been constructing a definition?
2. Is the definition in paragraphs 1 and 2 developed primarily by CLASSIFICATION, PROCESS ANALYSIS, CAUSE AND EFFECT analysis, or some combination of these methods? Explain your answer.
3. This essay refers to several different kinds of barrier signals, but it is not really an essay in classification. Why not?
4. The examples in paragraphs 3–8 illustrate "the Body-cross." What else do they also illustrate?
5. In paragraph 12, Morris says that the desk is "the major Barrier Signal for the seated person." Is a desk really a good example of a "signal"? Why or why not?

Words and Figures of Speech

1. Morris is an "ethologist." Look up the definition of this specialty in an unabridged dictionary. How does "Barrier Signals" help to demonstrate what an ethologist does?
2. When he writes such a phrase as "clothing-adjustment task" (par. 7), Morris might be accused of "excess noun-overusage." Point out other examples and suggest less awkward ways for rewriting these phrases-used-as-nouns.

3. How does Morris's METAPHOR of hiding behind mother's skirts (par. 2) apply to barrier signals as he defines them?

4. If you are not sure of any of these words, see how your dictionary defines them: *colleagues* (par. 2), *suppression* (2), *camouflaged* (3), *gala* (4), *status* (9), *subordination* (10), *ubiquitous* (12).

Comparing

1. When you read Barry Lopez's "My Horse" in Chapter 7, look for barrier signals and other symbolic gestures among the Plains Indians that he describes.

2. Compare and contrast Morris's essay with Susan Allen Toth's "Cinematypes" (Chapter 2) as essays about social signals.

Discussion and Writing Topics

1. Elsewhere, Morris defines a "tie" signal as a gesture that indicates a close relationship between two or more people (holding hands, for example). Write an extended definition of "tie signals" in which you cite examples that you have actually observed "in the field."

2. Define *language*. In what sense are most written languages sign languages?

Charles Panati

Nature's Building Blocks: Stalking the Quark

Born in Baltimore, Maryland, in 1943 and educated at Villanova and Columbia, Charles Panati was a research physicist at Columbia Medical Center and RCA before he became Newsweek's science editor from 1971 to 1977. He has written on scientific subjects for NBC and such magazines as Redbook, Reader's Digest, and New York. His books include Supersenses (1974), The Geller Papers (1976), and Links (1978), a novel based on experiments in mutual hypnosis. "Nature's Building Blocks" (with editor's subtitle) is a chapter from Breakthroughs (1980). It defines one of the fundamental puzzles of physics: after Truth and Beauty comes . . .

Is there a fundamental particle in nature out of which all matter is composed? Or is matter an endless series of seeds within seeds within smaller seeds? To physicists, this 2,000-year-old question is the most basic to their science. Many times over the centuries they thought they had solved this conundrum, only to discover later that they had complicated the issue. Well, the answer may be forthcoming within the next two decades. Not only would this constitute the century's biggest breakthrough in physics, but it could drastically alter the way in which we regard all matter.

At the beginning of this century, physicists considered atoms the ultimate and indivisible building blocks of nature. Before the middle of the century, they had changed their minds, for they had delineated the basic building blocks of atoms—electrons, protons, and neutrons. When scientists began colliding these new "elementary" particles head on in accelerators, they unwittingly unleashed at least 200 even "more elementary" particles within a few years' time. This was as exciting a discovery as it was frustrating. Nature seemed to delight in being devious, and the very term "elementary matter" appeared to be a joke.

Currently, many physicists believe that the structure of matter   3
can be ultimately explained by the existence of six kinds of building blocks called quarks. Whimsically named for the properties (quantum numbers) of particles they represent, the six quarks are Up, Down, Strange, Charm, Truth, and Beauty. Quarks are colored, figuratively speaking, red, blue, and yellow, so that certain assortments yield tan gossamerlike neutrinos, and other combinations yield neutral-colored stable particles. This is supposed to be fact, not fiction. Two physicists at the University of Chicago have even suggested that certain combinations of quarks could be manipulated to form stable and very strange gases. What they are labeling "Beauty-Up" gas and "Anti-Beauty [Ugly?]-Up" gas could, supposedly, be safely stored in containers, and minuscule quantities could form a veritable power plant, since mixing just two molecules would result in their annihilation into ten billion volts of pure energy. In their technical report the physicists write: "Stable quarks would, therefore, offer the possibility of storing very high useable energies within small volumes. The technological possibilities are self-evident."

Quarks are so abstruse that physicist Murray Gell-Mann lifted   4
their name from an equally abstruse phrase in James Joyce's *Finnegans Wake*: "Three quarks for Muster Mark." Having recently uncovered convincing, though indirect, evidence for the existence of five quarks, physicists are pushing their accelerators to the limit to find evidence for the still elusive Beauty. California physicists at the two-mile-long Stanford Linear Accelerator are building a sensitive new detector, Mark III, to search for her (the only creature in physics with a sex) in the early 1980s.

Finding Beauty, though, may not end the game. A new genera-   5
tion of more powerful accelerators will be appearing in the late 1980s; some of them will make it possible for the first time to collide matter with beams of antimatter. The offspring of these strange unions, some physicists contend, may reveal quarks to be merely another intermediate limb of nature's family tree. Will this

regression ever end? Physicists are divided over this dilemma. According to Geoffrey Chew of the University of California, matter has no bottom level; the most definite answer physicists can ever hope to possess is the immutable law that governs the behavior of matter. Theoretician T. D. Lee at Columbia University has solved the riddle by changing the rules of the game. He has proposed a mathematical model that expresses matter not as discrete particles, but as continuous waves called solitons, which by their very nature cannot be subdivided. A still more simple hypothesis is the theory of "nuclear democracy," which holds that all particles are fundamental.

Despite this uncertain state of affairs, most physicists remain   6
optimistic that, one way or another, they will solve the dilemma soon. If matter has a definable essence—and deep in his or her heart every physicist hopes this is true—finding that essence will permit physicists to erect a new theory of matter anchored to sturdy and permanent foundations. At the moment no one is certain quite what form the theory will take, what new facets of nature it will reveal, or what revolutions in physics it may usher in.

On the other hand, if matter turns out to be infinitely reducible;   7
that is, if every mysterious new particle is just a known particle wearing a different disguise selected from an infinitely diverse and fanciful wardrobe, that news will be greeted more warmly by philosophers than by physicists. Two thousand years ago the Greek philosopher Democritus argued that nature was composed of individual particles called atoms; his opponent, Anaxagoras, claimed that matter consisted of seeds nested in seeds, ad infinitum. We will be supremely fortunate if the ancient riddle is solved in our lifetime.

QUESTIONS

Understanding

1. Charles Panati's essay assumes that one distinguishing feature above all will define the essential building block of nature if it exists. What is that characteristic?

2. What is a quark? Approximately how many kinds are there, according to recent theories of subatomic physics?

3. Why are physicists hotly pursuing the quark? What ancient debate about the nature of matter do they hope to settle?

4. Which of the two fundamental views of matter cited by Panati do scientists favor today?

5. Even if they discover no single building block, scientists generally agree that a great breakthrough in subatomic physics is likely to be made in the next decade or so. What will it be?

Strategies and Structure

1. "Nature's Building Blocks" is an extended definition of an as yet undefined and perhaps indefinable substance. How does the author handle the problem of identifying the unknown?

2. A physicist himself, Charles Panati takes no side in the great debate about the ultimate definition of matter. Should he have, do you think? Why or why not?

3. Definitions usually assign distinguishing features to the class of objects or ideas being defined. In which paragraph especially does Panati touch on the peculiar characteristics of quarks? Why, in your opinion, doesn't he spend more time identifying their specific traits?

4. Why do you think Panati introduced into paragraph 3 the sentence, "This is supposed to be fact, not fiction"? Is this statement more or less neutral than the rest of his essay?

5. How does Panati's final paragraph recall his first one? Do you find this way of concluding to be effective or overly predictable? Explain your answer.

Words and Figures of Speech

1. Abstruse (par. 4) denotes a thing or idea that is not clearly understood. How does it differ in exact meaning from such related words as esoteric, ambiguous, and mystical?

2. The names of quarks, says Panati (par. 3), were assigned "whimsically." What is whimsy, and how appropriate is this attitude to such lofty pursuits as defining the essence of matter?

3. How helpful do you find Panati's ANALOGY between subatomic particles and clothes in paragraph 7? Explain your reaction.

4. What is the effect of Panati's inserting "Ugly?" in brackets in paragraph 3?

5. How technical do you find Panati's vocabulary in the title of his essay and elsewhere? Judging from his language, would you say he is writing for an audience of specialists or for the general reader?

6. What is a "nuclear democracy" (par. 5)? Where do you suspect this theory of subatomic physics got its name?

7. Look up any of the following words that are unfamiliar to you: *conundrum* (par. 1), *delineated* (par. 2), *unwittingly* (par. 2), *devious* (par. 2), *quantum* (par. 3), *gossamerlike* (par. 3), *minuscule* (par. 3), *veritable* (par. 3), *annihilation* (par. 3), *regression* (par. 5), *dilemma* (par. 5), *immutable* (par. 5), *discrete* (par. 5), *hypothesis* (par. 5), *ad infinitum* (par. 7).

Comparing

1. Would you say that the intended audience for "Nature's Building Blocks" is essentially the same, more specialized, or less specialized than the audience of Isaac Asimov's "What Do You Call a Platypus?" in Chapter 2? Explain your answer.

2. Is Asimov more or less willing than Panati to take sides in the scientific debate he is reporting? Cite your evidence.

3. How do Panati's assumptions about nature and natural processes differ from Alexander Petrunkevitch's in "The Spider and the Wasp" (Chapter 3)?

Discussion and Writing Topics

1. In your opinion should scientific definitions be limited to known quantities or can they legitimately be used to inquire into the unknown?

2. Write an extended definition of one of the following elusive components of nature: black holes, antimatter, quasars, antigravity, supergravity, neutrinos, the fourth dimension.

3. Whose definition of matter do you consider the more accurate one, Democritus' or Anaxagoras'? Why?

Ellen Goodman

The Just-Right Wife

*A columnist for the Boston Globe, Ellen Goodman (b. 1941)
writes about national but also "private" affairs of home, marriage
and the family, school, and work. Her syndicated column, carried
in over two hundred newspapers throughout the country, was
awarded the 1980 Pulitzer Prize for Commentary. A graduate of
Radcliffe College and a former Nieman Fellow at Harvard,
Goodman is a sometime radio and television commentator and the
author of* Turning Points *(1979) and* At Large *(1981). "The Just-
Right Wife" is Goodman's definition of what some marriageable
American (and Arab) men are looking for in a mate. This essay
in definition is reprinted from a collection of her essays on familiar,
personal topics,* Close to Home *(1979). In "Writers on the Writing Process," Goodman explains how she wrote it and other
columns.*

The upper-middle-class men of Arabia are looking for just   1
the right kind of wife. Arabia's merchant class, reports the
Associated Press, finds the women of Libya too backward, and
the women of Lebanon too forward, and have therefore gone
shopping for brides in Egypt.

Egyptian women are being married off at the rate of thirty   2
a day—an astonishing increase, according to the Egyptian
marriage bureau. It doesn't know whether to be pleased or
alarmed at the popularity of its women. According to one recent Saudi Arabian groom, the Egyptian women are "just
right."

"The Egyptian woman is the happy medium," says Aly   3
Abdul el-Korrary of his bride, Wafaa Ibrahiv (the happy medium herself was not questioned). "She is not too inhibited
as they are in conservative Moslem societies, and not too liberal
like many Lebanese."

Is this beginning to sound familiar? Well, the upper-middle-   **4**
class, middle-aged, merchant-professional-class man of America
also wants a "happy medium" wife. He is confused. He, too, has a
problem and he would like us to be more understanding.

If it is no longer chic for a sheik to marry a veiled woman, it is   **5**
somehow no longer "modern" for a successful member of the
liberal establishment to be married to what he used to call a
"housewife" and what he now hears called a "household drudge."

As his father once wanted a wife who had at least started col-   **6**
lege, now he would like a wife who has a mind, and even a job,
of her own. The younger men in his office these days wear their
wives' occupations on their sleeves. He thinks he, too, would like a
wife—especially for social occasions—whose status would be his
status symbol. A lady lawyer would be nice.

These men, you understand, now say (at least in private to   **7**
younger working women in their office) that they are bored with
women who "don't do anything." No matter how much some of
them conspired in keeping them at home Back Then, many are
now saying, in the best Moslem style, "I divorce thee." They are
replacing them with more up-to-date models. A Ph.D. candidate
would be nice.

The upper-middle-class, middle-aged man of today wants a wife   **8**
who won't make him feel guilty. He doesn't want to worry if she's
happy. He doesn't want to hear her complain about her dusty
American history degree. He doesn't want to know if she's crying
at the psychiatrist's office. He most definitely doesn't want to be
blamed. He wants her to fulfill herself already! He doesn't mean
that maliciously.

On the other hand, Lord knows, he doesn't want a wife who is   **9**
too forward. The Saudi Arabian merchant believes that the Egyptian woman adapts more easily to his moods and needs. The
American merchant also wants a woman who adapts herself to his
moods and needs—his need for an independent woman and a
traditional wife.

He doesn't want to live with a "household drudge," but it would   **10**
be nice to have an orderly home and well-scrubbed children. Certainly he wouldn't want a wife who got high on folding socks—he
is not a Neanderthal—but it would be nice if she arranged for
these things to get done. Without talking about marriage contracts.

He wants a wife who agreed that "marriage is a matter of give   **11** and take, not a business deal and 50–50 chores." It would help if she had just enough conflict herself (for not being her mother) to feel more than half the guilt for a full ashtray.

Of course, he sincerely would like her to be involved in her own   12
work and life. But on the other hand, he doesn't want it to siphon away her energy for him. He needs to be taken care of, nurtured. He would like her to enjoy her job, but be ready to move for his, if necessary (after, of course, a long discussion in which he feels awful about asking and she ends up comforting him and packing).

He wants a wife who is a sexually responsive and satisfied   13
woman, and he would even be pleased if she initiated sex with him. Sometimes. Not too often, however, because then he would get anxious.

He is confused, but he does, in all sincerity (status symbols   14
aside), want a happy marriage to a happy wife. A happy medium. He is not sure exactly what he means, but he, too, would like a wife who is "just right."

The difference is that when the upper-middle-class, middle-aged   15
man of Arabia wants his wife he goes out and buys one. His American "brother" can only offer himself as the prize.

QUESTIONS

Understanding

1. What qualities, as reported by Goodman, make Egyptian women "just-right" in the eyes of today's middle-class Arab men?
2. How have the requirements of American men who go shopping for wives changed since their fathers' day, according to Goodman? By what new standards do they define the just-right wife?
3. What traditional qualities do American men still look for in their wives?
4. Whose needs and opinions are slighted, in Goodman's view, when the ideal American wife gets defined by today's changing standards? What are some of those needs?
5. Goodman treats marriage as a transaction here. Considered as such, what is the main difference she sees between the way Amer-

ican men do business and the practice of their Arab "brothers"? Who offers the better deal for the wife in her view?

Strategies and Structure

1. Who is Goodman addressing primarily when she asks in paragraph 4, "Is this beginning to sound familiar?"
2. In paragraph 3, Goodman writes that "the happy medium herself was not questioned." What pronoun would this construction normally require? Why do you think Goodman used *herself* instead?
3. How do the last sentences in paragraphs 6, 7, and 8 resemble each other in structure? In TONE? Do you find this sort of repetition an effective device? Why or why not?
4. It was Goldilocks who sampled everything in the Three Bears' house until she found the porridge and bed that seemed "just-right" to her taste. What effect does Goodman achieve here by putting Goldilocks's standard of definition in the mouths of men?
5. Goodman's main strategy here is to compare the taste of American men with that of Moslem men, who traditionally prefer wives so subservient that they go about veiled from all other male eyes. Does the comparison work because the parallel is so close and obvious or because it is so unexpected? Explain your answer.
6. Despite the comparison between Moslem men and American men, why is this nevertheless an essay in definition rather than COM-PARISON AND CONTRAST (the strategy defined in Chapter 6)?

Words and Figures of Speech

1. American men, says this essay, want a "medium" wife—not too traditional but not too "forward" either. From the wife's point of view, what is the IRONY in repeatedly calling this kind of standard (and standardizing) "happy"?
2. Do you find "chic for a sheik" (par. 5) just-right or a little too-much?
3. Who was Neanderthal man (par. 10)? What qualities have been (erroneously) associated with him?
4. To what is Goodman comparing women in the METAPHOR "more up-to-date models" (par. 7)? What does the comparison imply about men's treatment of women?

Comparing

1. What might Calvin Trillin do with the phrase "happy medium" if it turned up among the "aphorisms" in "Literally" (Chapter 7)?
2. In what ways does Goodman's point of view resemble that of Susan Allen Toth as she looks at the preferences of men in "Cinematypes" (Chapter 2)?

Discussion and Writing Topics

1. To what extent do you think Goodman is right about what American men want from a wife these days? On what grounds, if any, do you disagree with her definition of the just-right wife?
2. Write your own definition of the perfect spouse.
3. Write a definition of the "just-right" husband that exposes women's selfish demands when looking for a mate.

Writers on the Writing Process:
Ellen Goodman

Asked if she revises much during the writing process, Ellen Goodman responds: "I rewrite, rewrite, rewrite." Her comments on her methods, however, are mainly about choosing a subject.

Most syndicated columnists, Goodman feels, write about "important" topics like politics. But for Goodman, politics is "basically a game men play like any other sport." "The Just-Right Wife" deals with the kinds of issues that Goodman considers actually "much more important" than the political "trivia" of the editorial page. These are "the family and what I call life-and-death issues." Instead of politics and economics, Goodman's subjects are "the underlying values by which the country exists."

The idea of the "just-right" wife (not too traditional, not too liberated) was suggested, says Goodman, by Associated Press news reports of marriage brokering in Saudi Arabia. But news agency sources only sparked the author's imagination, like the recollection of Goldilocks and the "just-right" porridge. Besides her own marriage, which ended in divorce after eight years, the ultimate source of her subject in this essay is Goodman's lingering concern with "the vast social changes in the way men and women lead their lives and deal with each other." (She has devoted an entire book to this subject: *Turning Points* [1979].)

Goodman professes to a "lousy memory" for the history of her news stories and essays, including "The Just-Right Wife." "Alas, I have to write the next column rather than analyzing the old one," she confides. Goodman recalls one story she wrote before becoming a columnist, however, that may have nudged her toward editorial writing. It was on abortion, and it was written for *The Boston Globe*. The article, says Goodman, took a "radical" form for a news story. It was written more like an opinion piece than straight reportage. After interviewing a woman who had had an abortion, Goodman wrote her story "very much like a narrative and I didn't use one quote from her, which is very unusual. In a lot of papers, I wouldn't have been able to get that through."

When did she become a columnist? "I started writing a column   5
about 1970 when the *Globe* first opened up its op-ed page [the one across from the editorial page] to inside columns [that is, columns written by the newspaper's own staff]. I wrote about six the first year and after that I was asked if I could do it once a week and I said yes."

Distinct from a feature writer, a columnist is responsible for dis-   6
covering her or his own subjects. "With features stories," explains Goodman, "very often you wait until someone gives you the idea, and you're not putting yourself on the line all the time, either." It's different for the columnist and essayist. "You're totally self-starting, totally dependent on your own ideas, when you write a column."

Goodman used to write three columns per week; now she writes   7
two. Still she is "constantly having to think and figure out what you think." Which is both the burden and the reward of her kind of work. "Why do I write? I like to," she asserts; "it helps me form my own thoughts. It's the only work I've done as an adult and it is, as Pete Hamill once said, the hardest work in the world that doesn't include heavy lifting."

WRITING TOPICS for Chapter Five
Essays That Define

Write extended definitions of one or more of the following:

1. Photosynthesis or mitosis
2. Obscenity
3. A liberal education
4. Success
5. A happy marriage
6. A liberated woman
7. A true friend
8. Self-reliance
9. Inertia (physical or spiritual)
10. Non-Euclidian geometry
11. Calculus
12. The big-bang theory of creation
13. Your idea of the ideal society
14. Blues music
15. Tragedy, comedy, romance, novel, satire, or some other literary form

6
Essays That Compare and Contrast

Before you begin an essay in COMPARISON AND CONTRAST,[1]
it is a good idea to make a list of the qualities of the two
objects or ideas to be compared. Suppose, for example, that
our "objects" were all-time basketball greats Wilt ("The
Stilt") Chamberlain and Bill Russell. Our lists might look
like this:

Chamberlain	Russell
7-feet-3-inches tall	6-feet-9-inches tall
good team	better team
fast	faster
style	discipline
loser (almost)	winner (almost)
Goliath	David

Each of these lists is an abbreviated DESCRIPTION of the
player whose attributes it compiles. At this early stage, our
comparison and contrast essay seems indistinguishable from
descriptive writing. As soon as we bring our two lists
together, however, the descriptive impulse yields to the
impulse to explain. Consider the following excerpt from
an actual comparison of Chamberlain with Russell by sports-
writer Jeremy Larner:

Wilt's defenders could claim with justice that Russell played
with a better team, but it was all too apparent that Boston was
better partly because Russell played better with them. Russell
has been above all a team player—a man of discipline, self-
denial and killer instinct; in short, a *winner*, in the best American
Calvinist tradition. Whereas Russell has been able somehow to

---

[1] Terms printed in all capitals are defined in the Glossary.

squeeze out his last ounce of ability, Chamberlain's performances have been marked by a seeming nonchalance—as if, recognizing his Giantistic fate, he were more concerned with personal style than with winning. "I never want to set records. The only thing I strive for is perfection" Chamberlain has said. When Wilt goes into his routine, his body proclaims from tip to toe, it's not my fault, folks, honestly—and though I've got to lose, if you look close, you'll see I'm beautiful through and through!

Even though it describes the two men in some detail, this passage is EXPOSITION rather than description. Like most comparative writing, its comparisons are cast as statements or propositions: Russell is more efficient than Chamberlain; Chamberlain is concerned with style, while Russell plays to win. The controlling proposition of Larner's entire essay is that Chamberlain was a Goliath "typecast" by fans to lose to Russell the giant-killer; but Chamberlain broke the stereotype to become the greatest basketball player ever.

We can take a number of hints from Jeremy Larner about writing comparison and contrast essays. First, stick to two and only two subjects at a time. Second, choose subjects that invite comparison because they belong to the same general class: two athletes, two religions, two sororities, two mammals. You might point out many differences between a mattress and a steamboat, but no one is likely to be impressed by this exercise in the obvious. The third lesson is that you do not have to give equal weight to similarities and differences. Larner assumes the similarities between Chamberlain and Russell (both are towering champions), but he works carefully through the differences. An essay that compares a turtle to a tank, on the other hand, might concentrate upon the similarities of the two if it proposes that both belong to the class of moving things with armor.

Our example suggests, finally, that comparison and contrast essays proceed by alternation. From paragraph to paragraph, Larner dispenses his subject in "slices." His assertion that Russell is a team player is followed immediately by the counterassertion that Chamberlain plays to a private standard. Chamberlain's free throws are always uncertain; Russell's are accurate in the clutch. And so on, point by point. Another way of comparing and contrasting is in "chunks." Larner might have said all he had to say about Russell in several paragraphs and then followed up with all of his remarks on Chamberlain. Either method (or a combination of the two) is correct if it works. The aim is to set forth clear alternatives.

Bruce Catton

Grant and Lee: A Study in Contrasts

A native of Michigan who attended Oberlin College, Bruce
Catton was a former newspaper reporter, a one-time editor of
American Heritage, and a noted historian of the Civil War. A
Stillness at Appomattox (1953) won both the Pulitzer Prize and
the National Book Award for history in 1954. It was not, said
Catton, "the strategy or political meanings" that fascinated him
but the "almost incomprehensible emotional experience which
this war brought to our country." Among Catton's many other
books are This Hallowed Ground (1956); The Coming Fury
(1961); The Army of the Potomac (1962); Terrible Swift Sword
(1963); Never Call Retreat (1965); Grant Takes Command
(1969); and Michigan: A Bicentennial History (1976). "Grant
and Lee: A Study in Contrasts" is reprinted from a collection of
essays by distinguished historians. Catton died in 1979.

When Ulysses S. Grant and Robert E. Lee met in the   1
parlor of a modest house at Appomattox Court House, Virginia, on April 9, 1865, to work out the terms for the surrender of Lee's Army of Northern Virginia, a great chapter
in American life came to a close, and a great new chapter
began.

These men were bringing the Civil War to its virtual finish.   2
To be sure, other armies had yet to surrender, and for a few
days the fugitive Confederate government would struggle desperately and vainly, trying to find some way to go on living
now that its chief support was gone. But in effect it was all

over when Grant and Lee signed the papers. And the little room where they wrote out the terms was the scene of one of the poignant, dramatic contrasts in American history.

They were two strong men, these oddly different generals, and 3 they represented the strengths of two conflicting currents that, through them, had come into final collision.

Back of Robert E. Lee was the notion that the old aristocratic 4 concept might somehow survive and be dominant in American life.

Lee was tidewater Virginia, and in his background were family, 5 culture, and tradition . . . the age of chivalry transplanted to a New World which was making its own legends and its own myths. He embodied a way of life that had come down through the age of knighthood and the English country squire. America was a land that was beginning all over again, dedicated to nothing much more complicated than the rather hazy belief that all men had equal rights and should have an equal chance in the world. In such a land Lee stood for the feeling that it was somehow of advantage to human society to have a pronounced inequality in the social structure. There should be a leisure class, backed by ownership of land; in turn, society itself should be keyed to the land as the chief source of wealth and influence. It would bring forth (according to this ideal) a class of men with a strong sense of obligation to the community; men who lived not to gain advantage for themselves, but to meet the solemn obligations which had been laid on them by the very fact that they were privileged. From them the country would get its leadership; to them it could look for the higher values—of thought, of conduct, of personal deportment—to give it strength and virtue.

Lee embodied the noblest elements of this aristocratic ideal. 6 Through him, the landed nobility justified itself. For four years, the Southern states had fought a desperate war to uphold the ideals for which Lee stood. In the end, it almost seemed as if the Confederacy fought for Lee; as if he himself was the Confederacy . . . the best thing that the way of life for which the Confederacy stood could ever have to offer. He had passed into legend before Appomattox. Thousands of tired, underfed, poorly clothed Confederate soldiers, long since past the simple enthusiasm of the early days of the struggle, somehow considered Lee the symbol of everything for which they had been willing to die. But they could not quite put this feeling into words. If the Lost Cause, sanctified by so much heroism and so many deaths, had a living justification, its justification was General Lee.

Grant, the son of a tanner on the Western frontier, was every-   7 thing Lee was not. He had come up the hard way and embodied nothing in particular except the eternal toughness and sinewy fiber of the men who grew up beyond the mountains. He was one of a body of men who owed reverence and obeisance to no one, who were self-reliant to a fault, who cared hardly anything for the past but who had a sharp eye for the future.

These frontier men were the precise opposites of the tidewater   8 aristocrats. Back of them, in the great surge that had taken people over the Alleghenies and into the opening Western country, there was a deep, implicit dissatisfaction with a past that had settled into grooves. They stood for democracy, not from any reasoned conclusion about the proper ordering of human society, but simply because they had grown up in the middle of democracy and knew how it worked. Their society might have privileges, but they would be privileges each man had won for himself. Forms and patterns meant nothing. No man was born to anything, except perhaps to a chance to show how far he could rise. Life was competition.

Yet along with this feeling had come a deep sense of belonging   9 to a national community. The Westerner who developed a farm, opened a shop, or set up in business as a trader, could hope to prosper only as his own community prospered—and his community ran from the Atlantic to the Pacific and from Canada down to Mexico. If the land was settled, with towns and highways and accessible markets, he could better himself. He saw his fate in terms of the nation's own destiny. As its horizons expanded, so did his. He had, in other words, an acute dollars-and-cents stake in the continued growth and development of his country.

And that, perhaps, is where the contrast between Grant and Lee   10 becomes most striking. The Virginia aristocrat, inevitably, saw himself in relation to his own region. He lived in a static society which could endure almost anything except change. Instinctively, his first loyalty would go to the locality in which that society existed. He would fight to the limit of endurance to defend it, because in defending it he was defending everything that gave his own life its deepest meaning.

The Westerner, on the other hand, would fight with an equal   11 tenacity for the broader concept of society. He fought so because everything he lived by was tied to growth, expansion, and a constantly widening horizon. What he lived by would survive or fall with the nation itself. He could not possibly stand by unmoved in the face of an attempt to destroy the Union. He would combat it with everything he had, because he could only see it as an effort to cut the ground out from under his feet.

So Grant and Lee were in complete contrast, representing two   12 diametrically opposed elements in American life. Grant was the modern man emerging; beyond him, ready to come on the stage, was the great age of steel and machinery, of crowded cities and a restless burgeoning vitality. Lee might have ridden down from the old age of chivalry, lance in hand, silken banner fluttering over his head. Each man was the perfect champion of his cause, drawing both his strengths and his weaknesses from the people he led.

Yet it was not all contrast, after all. Different as they were—in   13 background, in personality, in underlying aspiration—these two great soldiers had much in common. Under everything else, they were marvelous fighters. Furthermore, their fighting qualities were really very much alike.

Each man had, to begin with, the great virtue of utter tenacity   14 and fidelity. Grant fought his way down the Mississippi Valley in spite of acute personal discouragement and profound military handicaps. Lee hung on in the trenches at Petersburg after hope itself had died. In each man there was an indomitable quality . . . the born fighter's refusal to give up as long as he can still remain on his feet and lift his two fists.

Daring and resourcefulness they had, too; the ability to think   15 faster and move faster than the enemy. These were the qualities which gave Lee the dazzling campaigns of Second Manassas and Chancellorsville and won Vicksburg for Grant.

Lastly, and perhaps greatest of all, there was the ability, at the   16 end, to turn quickly from war to peace once the fighting was over. Out of the way these two men behaved at Appomattox came the possibility of a peace of reconciliation. It was a possibility not wholly realized, in the years to come, but which did, in the end, help the two sections to become one nation again . . . after a war whose bitterness might have seemed to make such a reunion wholly impossible. No part of either man's life became him more than the part he played in this brief meeting in the McLean house

at Appomattox. Their behavior there put all succeeding generations of Americans in their debt. Two great Americans, Grant and
Lee—very different, yet under everything very much alike. Their
encounter at Appomattox was one of the great moments of
American history.

QUESTIONS

Understanding

1. Catton writes that generals Lee and Grant represented two opposing currents (par. 3) of American culture. What were they?
   Describe the contrasting qualities and ideals that Catton associates
   with each man.
2. What qualities, according to Catton, did Grant and Lee have in
   common?
3. With Lee's surrender, says Catton, "a great new chapter" (par.
   1) of American history began. He is referring, presumably, to the
   period of expansion between the Civil War and World War I,
   when industrialization really took hold in America. What characteristics of the new era does his description of Grant anticipate?
4. Catton does not describe, in any detail, how Grant and Lee behaved as they worked out the terms of peace at Appomattox; but
   what does he *imply* about the conduct of the two generals? Why
   was their conduct important to "all succeeding generations" (par.
   16) of Americans?
5. Catton gives no specific reasons for the Confederacy's defeat. He
   says nothing, for example, about the Union's greater numbers or
   its superior communications system. What general explanation
   does he imply, however, when he associates Lee with a "static"
   society (par. 10) and Grant with a society of "restless burgeoning
   vitality" (par. 12)?

Strategies and Structure

1. Beginning with paragraph 3, Catton gets down to the particulars
   of his contrast between the two generals. Where does the contrast end? In which paragraph does he begin to list similarities
   between the two men?

2. Except for mentioning their strength, Catton says little about the unique physical appearance of either Grant or Lee. Is this a weakness in his essay or is there some justification for avoiding such details? Explain your answer.

3. Which sentence in paragraph 16 brings together the contrasts and the similarities of the preceding paragraphs? How does this final paragraph recall the opening paragraphs of the essay? Why might Catton end with an echo of his beginning?

4. Would you say that the historian's voice in this essay is primarily DESCRIPTIVE, NARRATIVE, or EXPOSITORY? Explain your answer.

Words and Figures of Speech

1. Catton describes the parlor where Grant and Lee met as the *scene* of a *dramatic* contrast (par. 2), and he says in paragraph 12 that the post–Civil War era was "ready to come on stage." Where do such METAPHORS come from, and what view of history do they suggest?

2. What is the Lost Cause of paragraph 6, and what does the phrase (in capital letters) CONNOTE?

3. Catton does not use the phrase *noblesse oblige*, but it could be applied to General Lee's beliefs as Catton defines them. What does the phrase mean?

4. What is the precise meaning of *obeisance* (par. 7), and why might Catton have chosen it instead of the more common *obedience* when describing General Grant?

5. Look up any of these words with which you are not on easy terms: *fugitive* (par. 2), *poignant* (2), *chivalry* (5), *sinewy* (7), *implicit* (8), *tenacity* (11), *diametrically* (12), *acute* (14), *profound* (14), and *indomitable* (14).

Comparing

1. Both Catton and Howard Means in "The Terror and the Honor at UVa" (Chapter 10) are writing about the past from vantage points in the present. How do they differ in their approaches to the past and in their roles as historians?

2. Catton speaks often of the "conduct" and "deportment" of Grant and Lee. How does his idea of human behavior compare with

that of sociologist Desmond Morris in "Barrier Signals" (Chapter 5)?

Discussion and Writing Topics

1. Write an essay contrasting Thomas Jefferson and Alexander Hamilton (or John F. Kennedy and Richard Nixon) as men who represented the conflicting forces of their time.
2. "America," Catton writes, "was a land that was beginning all over again . . ." (par. 5). Discuss this idea as one way of formulating the "American dream."
3. Grant, we are told, saw the nation's "destiny" (par. 9) as coinciding with his own. What was the notion of "Manifest Destiny," and how did it help to shape American history?
4. Do you agree with Catton's assessment of General Lee as a man of the past and, therefore, a fitting emblem of the South? Why or why not?
5. Is history the story of forces acting through great personalities (as Catton assumes) or of great personalities who control forces? Or neither? Explain your answer.

Russell Baker

A Nice Place to Visit

For many years now, Russell Baker has lived and worked in New York City. To an insider's familiarity with the manners and folkways of that city, however, he brings the perspective of a relative late-comer who was born in Virginia in 1925 and lived in Baltimore and Washington, D.C., before coming to the Big Apple. Since 1962, Baker has contributed to the New York Times his nationally syndicated "Observer" column, known both for its keen eye upon American politics and its attentive ear to the English language. Baker is also the author of numerous books and collections of essays, including Baker's Dozen (1964), and The Rescue of Miss Yashell and Other Pipe Dreams (1983). He is the recipient of two Pulitzer Prizes. "A Nice Place to Visit" was collected in So This Is Depravity (1980). Baker here contrasts his mannerly Canadian neighbor, Toronto, with the American metropolis he loves to hate. The author explains how he wrote the column in the final section of this chapter.

Having heard that Toronto was becoming one of the continent's noblest cities, we flew from New York to investigate. New Yorkers jealous of their city's reputation and concerned about challenges to its stature have little to worry about.

After three days in residence, our delegation noted an absence of hysteria that was almost intolerable and took to consuming large portions of black coffee to maintain our normal state of irritability. The local people to whom we complained in hopes of provoking comfortably nasty confrontations declined to become bellicose. They would like to enjoy a gratifying big-city hysteria, they said, but believed it would seem ill-mannered in front of strangers.

Extensive field studies—our stay lasted four weeks—persuaded   3
us that this failure reflects the survival in Toronto of an ancient
pattern of social conduct called "courtesy."

"Courtesy" manifests itself in many quaint forms appalling to   4
the New Yorker. Thus, for example, Yankee fans may be astonished to learn that at the Toronto baseball park it is considered
bad form to heave rolls of toilet paper and beer cans at players on
the field.

Official literature inside Toronto taxicabs includes a notification   5
of the proper address to which riders may mail the authorities not
only complaints but also compliments about the cabbie's behavior.

For a city that aspires to urban greatness, Toronto's entire taxi   6
system has far to go. At present, it seems hopelessly bogged down
in civilization. One day a member of our delegation listening to a
radio conversation between a short-tempered cabbie and the dispatcher distinctly heard the dispatcher say, "As Shakespeare said,
if music be the food of love, play on, give me excess of it."

This delegate became so unnerved by hearing Shakespeare   7
quoted by a cab dispatcher that he fled immediately back to New
York to have his nerves abraded and his spine rearranged in a real
big-city taxi.

What was particularly distressing as the stay continued was the   8
absence of shrieking police and fire sirens at 3 A.M.—or any other
hour, for that matter. We spoke to the city authorities about this.
What kind of city was it, we asked, that expected its citizens to
sleep all night and rise refreshed in the morning? Where was the
incentive to awaken gummy-eyed and exhausted, ready to scream
at the first person one saw in the morning? How could Toronto
possibly hope to maintain a robust urban divorce rate?

Our criticism went unheeded, such is the torpor with which   9
Toronto pursues true urbanity. The fact appears to be that
Toronto has very little grasp of what is required of a great city.

Consider the garbage picture. It seems never to have occurred to   10
anybody in Toronto that garbage exists to be heaved into the
streets. One can drive for miles without seeing so much as a ba-
nana peel in the gutter or a discarded newspaper whirling in the
wind.

Nor has Toronto learned about dogs. A check with the authori-   11
ties confirmed that, yes, there are indeed dogs resident in Toronto,

but one would never realize it by walking the sidewalks. Our delegation was shocked by the presumption of a town's calling itself a city, much less a great city, when it obviously knows nothing of either garbage or dogs.

The subway, on which Toronto prides itself, was a laughable   12
imitation of the real thing. The subway cars were not only spotlessly clean, but also fully illuminated. So were the stations. To New Yorkers, it was embarrassing, and we hadn't the heart to tell the subway authorities that they were light-years away from greatness.

We did, however, tell them about spray paints and how effec-   13
tively a few hundred children equipped with spray-paint cans could at least give their subway the big-city look.

It seems doubtful they are ready to take such hints. There is a   14
disturbing distaste for vandalism in Toronto which will make it hard for the city to enter wholeheartedly into the vigor of the late twentieth century.

A board fence surrounding a huge excavation for a new high-   15
rise building in the downtown district offers depressing evidence of Toronto's lack of big-city impulse. Embedded in the fence at intervals of about fifty feet are loudspeakers that play recorded music for passing pedestrians.

Not a single one of these loudspeakers has been mutilated.   16
What's worse, not a single one has been stolen.

It was good to get back to the Big Apple. My coat pocket was   17
bulging with candy wrappers from Toronto and—such is the lingering power of Toronto—it took me two or three hours back in New York before it seemed natural again to toss them into the street.

QUESTIONS

Understanding

1. When Toronto authorities pay no attention to Baker's advice about the need for sirens at 3:00 A.M., he remarks how slowly the city "pursues true urbanity" (par. 9). What definition of "urbanity" is Baker humorously assuming here and throughout his comparison of New York and Toronto?

2. What are some of the main conditions in Toronto that seem particularly backward to a New Yorker? How might New Yorkers define the idea of "civilization" in which the Canadian city is "hopelessly bogged down" (par. 6).

3. What specific living conditions does Baker attribute to New York by contrast with the appallingly genteel ways of life in Toronto?

4. When Baker returns home from Canada, it takes "two or three hours" (par. 17) before he can start throwing litter in the streets again. How "lingering," actually, is the influence of the Canadian city upon the true New Yorker?

Strategies and Structure

1. In comparing the two cities, Baker does not so much tell us what New York is like as what Toronto is *not* like. How, then, does he nevertheless get across a clear picture of life in the American city?

2. Baker's IRONY is especially thick in sentences such as this, "What kind of a city was it, we asked, that expected its citizens to sleep all night and rise refreshed in the morning" (par. 8)? Point out other examples in which his mock exasperation is particularly transparent. Do you find such irony an effective device? Why or why not?

3. Why does the author of this essay adopt the plural pronoun "we" instead of saying "I"? Is his reason solely that he went to Canada with several other people?

4. Why does Baker refer to his ramblings in Toronto as "extensive field studies" (par. 3)? What is the difference between an expedition and a trip, or visit?

5. Baker uses a number of highly formal constructions: "our delegation noted an absence" (par. 2), "local people . . . declined to become bellicose" (par. 2), " 'courtesy' manifests itself in many quaint forms" (par. 4). Why might Baker adopt such ponderous SYNTAX, given the role he assumes in this essay.

6. Point out grammatical constructions that show Baker knows how to write in a plainer style.

7. What is a parody? What sort of language and general point of view is Baker having fun with here?

Words and Figures of Speech

1. Baker's title is the first half of an observation that returning travel-

ers often make about strange, impressive places. What is the other half? How does it apply to the case of a dyed-in-the-wool New Yorker?

2. Why does Baker put the word *courtesy* (pars. 5 and 6) in quotation marks?

3. How would you describe Baker's vocabulary most of the time in this essay? Which is more typical of his diction throughout: words like *gummy-eyed* (par. 8) or like *bellicose* (par. 2)? Why the preponderance of such words?

4. What are the CONNOTATIONS of *robust* (par. 8)? Has Baker failed to consider the implications of the word? What reason might he have for choosing it in the context of divorce rates?

5. "What's worse" (par. 16) is a good example of verbal irony, that is, words that say one thing and mean another. In Baker's opening paragraph, what phrase is to be taken equally ironically? What is Baker really saying in both cases?

Comparing

1. Baker's assumed attitude toward the subject of his field studies closely resembles that of Horace Miner in "Body Ritual among the Nacirema" (Chapter 8). What do the assumed roles of both writers have in common? What similar effects do they achieve by adopting them?

Discussion and Writing Topics

1. What is your opinion of the true American urbanite's understanding of urbanity, as reported by Baker? Is Baker being fair to New York and New Yorkers?

2. Confirmed urban dwellers, especially those born and bred in New York City have been called the country's greatest provincials. Do you agree? Why or why not?

3. Compare and contrast two cities or towns of your acquaintance by assuming the prejudices of one and revealing the "faults" of the other in the glaring light of those prejudices.

Colman McCarthy

Phasing Out Campus Idealism

Colman McCarthy was born in Glen Head, New York, in 1938.
A journalist and an attorney, McCarthy worked in the Office of
Economic Opportunity in Washington before turning to writing.
He began reporting for the Washington Post in 1969 and, ten
years later, became a syndicated columnist with the Washington
Post Writer's Group. McCarthy is the author of Disturbers of
the Peace (1973), Inner Companions (1975), and The Pleasures of
the Game (1977). In "Phasing Out Campus Idealism," a seasoned
campus watcher compares the atmosphere at American colleges
today, as he sees it, with the mood of the 1960s.

At first, it seemed like old times at Sproul Plaza. It was at   1
this storm center on the University of California campus where
student radicalism peaked in the free-speech movement of the
mid-1960s and the antiwar protests shortly after. On the announcement board at Sproul Plaza was a poster that looked to
be a definite call to action.

"In Defense of Marxism," read the top line in bold letters.   2
Underneath was a quote from the master himself, "Marx on
the party." "A party? You call this a party? The beer is warm,
the women are cold and I'm hot under the collar."

The Marx being quoted at Sproul 1982 was Groucho, not   3
Karl. The last line, also in bold letters, called out: "Smirkers
of the World Unite."

One goof-off poster hardly represents a Sociological Shift of   4
Large Import. Nor are my eyes much given to student watching. But in the 15 years since my last visit to Berkeley, the difference between students then and now is like the night and
day between the Marxes, Groucho and Karl.

In 1967, the tumult on the Berkeley campus was against the gov-   5
ernment's war policies in Vietnam. Now the antigovernment protest is against the Berkeley town council for passing a municipal
noise ordinance. The campus Interfraternity Council, it seems, believes that the new anti-noise policy means the end of frat house
parties on Friday and Saturday nights.

Elsewhere on this campus that generated so much of the na-   6
tion's anti-war feeling just when that was needed, the military's
ROTC program is flourishing. Business courses are popular, and a
professor in the journalism department says he is regularly challenged by students who see nothing disturbing—as does the professor—in the increasing control of the daily press by newspaper
chains. Reading The Wall Street Journal has replaced reading the
Berkeley Barb, now defunct.

The sharp contrasts here help focus what I've seen in more   7
muted regressions on the dozen or so other campuses I've visited in
the past two years: the phasing out of idealism. It is still present
in many students, but they keep it inside. Nursing students, for
example, don't dare say that they are studying medicine to help
people by easing their suffering. Instead, they express individual career hopes of being supervisors by the time they are 35. Why can't
they say they want to be nurses because they love people?

Students don't talk of service to others, but of benefits to them   8
selves. Personal growth is out, intellectual self-grooming for corporate recruiters is in. Courses are taken to get a marketable skill, not
to acquire skills for reasoning or for human understanding.

The tension between idealism and careerism isn't new, or un-   9
necessary. But seldom has it seemed this one-sided. The students
aren't to blame. They are trapped. As the colleges and universities
have less and less resources to devote to the humanities and liberal
arts, where a sensitivity toward social advancement has traditionally
been nurtured, they are forced to look to private industry for
money. Edward E. David, Jr., president of Exxon Research and
Engineering Company, reports in Change magazine that corpora-
tions are becoming the big men on campus. In the 1980s, he projects a tripling of industry support for academic research, from
$200 million a year to about $600 million a year. He emphasizes
that this is not mere industrial philanthropy; the money goes to research "consistent with a commercial 'mission.' "

The main industry objective is to ensure a supply of "excellent   10 people" among the graduates. David cited a study that "showed that the disciplines most aligned with conservative political ideas and favorable to the private sector are engineering, medicine, physics and mathematics."

Among the most horrified at how students have fewer alterna-   11
tives as the campuses become corporate annexes are the faculty members in their 40s who themselves were idealists in the 1960s. At every college I've visited, I've met professors who speak of their frustration. They want to pass on their ideals about public service to their students. But they can't. The imbalance now favors private industries that have the economic might to tell the students, "Serve us."

QUESTIONS

Understanding

1. Colman McCarthy is comparing the attitudes of college students today with those of students at what earlier time?
2. Back then, according to McCarthy, "idealism" determined behavior and expectations on college campuses; what is the motivating force now in his view?
3. Why has this shift in attitude taken place? List several of the reasons McCarthy cites.
4. In your opinion, how does the author of "Phasing Out Campus Idealism" feel about the changes he is chronicling? Does he seem to be saying that more ground has been gained or lost?

Strategies and Structure

1. Why do you think Colman McCarthy begins his comparison with the University of California, Berkeley? Why not some other college?
2. Is his comparison restricted to the Berkeley campus at different times, or does McCarthy's essay have a wider basis of comparison? Which paragraph lets you know for sure?
3. In which paragraph does McCarthy begin explicitly to develop his essay by comparison and contrast? Which sentence in that paragraph draws the comparison most directly?

4. Does "Phasing Out Campus Idealism" pay more attention to the similarities or to the differences between students in the sixties and students in the eighties? As an exercise, go through the essay and put an "S" in the margin each time you encounter a point of similarity, a "D" each time you encounter a difference.

5. McCarthy analyzes the root causes of the changes he has observed on college campuses. Why is this, nevertheless, an essay in comparison and contrast rather than an essay in cause and effect (discussed in Chapter 4)?

6. By what phrase in paragraph 1 does the author efficiently alert you to suspect that his essay is not going to come out where it seems to be heading? Is some such notice-to-readers a courtesy or a necessity in your opinion?

7. How effective do you find McCarthy's reference to the Marx poster (pars. 1–4) as a way of setting up his comparison and contrast? How and how well does McCarthy here and elsewhere anticipate that some readers will say he is jumping to conclusions from insufficient evidence?

8. Would you describe the speaker in this essay as a political "liberal" or a conservative"? Define these terms as you give your reasons.

Words and Figures of Speech

1. In paragraph 4 of "Phasing Out Campus Idealism," why does the author capitalize "Sociological Shift of Large Import"? Who is he gently mocking?

2. What are the CONNOTATIONS of the phrase "Phasing Out" in McCarthy's title?

3. Of the two controlling terms in McCarthy's essay, "idealism" and "careerism," which is more likely to have negative connotations for most people? How does this verbal contrast serve his purpose here?

4 Would you describe the dominant TONE of "Phasing Out Campus Idealism" as biting, factual, or wistful? Explain your choice.

5. What does McCarthy mean by "muted regressions" in paragraph 7? How well does this phrase fit with the METAPHOR of focusing in the same paragraph?

Comparing

1. In "The Terror and the Honor at UVa "(Chapter 10), Howard

Means looks at changes in the student honor code since his own college days. Do his observations seem to confirm or deny the contrast that McCarthy is pointing up?

2. How closely does the campus atmosphere described by James Seilsopour in "I Forgot the Words to the National Anthem" (Chapter 4) resemble the atmosphere described by Colman McCarthy? What resemblance, if any, do you discern between the causes both writers assign to the current feelings on campus?

Discussion and Writing Topics

1. McCarthy does not charge that idealism on college campuses is dead, only slumbering. Do you agree or disagree with his assessment?

2. If you agree with McCarthy's views, what additional reasons can you give to explain the disappearance of idealism from college campuses?

3. Do you agree that students themselves are as free of responsibility for their new attitudes as McCarthy says, or would you say they are partly to blame? Why?

4. If you disagree with McCarthy's views, write a comparison and contrast essay in which you stress the fundamental similarities between students today and ten or twenty years ago.

5. How important is it, would you say, that "careerism" be informed by "idealism"? To what extent do you think the study of history, literature, and other "humanities" contributes to this tempering effect?

Eugene Raskin

Walls and Barriers

Eugene Raskin is an architect, playwright, and composer. Born in New York in 1909, he was educated at Columbia University and the University of Paris. He joined the Columbia faculty as a professor of architecture in 1942, became a Langley fellow of the American Institute of Architects in 1952, and in 1963 won first prize at the American Film Festival for the documentary, How to Look at a City. *Author of* Architecturally Speaking *(1954),* The Post-Urban Society *(1969), and* Architecture and People *(1974), Raskin also writes novels and plays. Among his published songs was the international hit "Those Were the Days." "Walls and Barriers" contrasts the modern notion of wall-as-window with the ancient conception of wall-as-barrier. Professor Raskin explains how he wrote it in the section following the questions on his essay.*

$\mathbf{M}$y father's reaction to the bank building at 43rd Street and Fifth Avenue in New York City was immediate and definite: "You won't catch me putting my money in *there!*" he declared. "Not in that glass box!"

Of course, my father is a gentleman of the old school, a member of the generation to whom a good deal of modern architecture is unnerving; but I suspect—I more than suspect, I am convinced—that his negative response was not so much to the architecture as to a violation of his concept of the nature of money.

In his generation money was thought of as a tangible commodity—bullion, bank notes, coins—that could be hefted, carried, or stolen. Consequently, to attract the custom of a sensible man, a bank had to have heavy walls, barred windows, and bronze doors, to affirm the fact, however untrue, that money would be safe inside. If a building's design made it appear impregnable, the institution was necessarily sound, and the meaning of the heavy wall as an architectural symbol dwelt in the prevailing attitude toward money, rather than in any aesthetic theory.

But that attitude toward money has of course changed. Excepting pocket money, cash of any kind is now rarely used; money as a tangible commodity has largely been replaced by credit; a book-keeping-banking matter. A deficit economy, accompanied by huge expansion, has led us to think of money as a product of the creative imagination. The banker no longer offers us a *safe*, he offers us a *service*—a service in which the most valuable elements are dash and a creative flair for the invention of large numbers. It is in no way surprising, in view of this change in attitude, that we are witnessing the disappearance of the heavy-walled bank. The Manufacturers Trust, which my father distrusted so heartily, is a great cubical cage of glass whose brilliantly lighted interior challenges even the brightness of a sunny day, while the door to the vault, far from being secluded and guarded, is set out as a window display. 4

Just as the older bank asserted its invulnerability, this bank *by its architecture* boasts of its imaginative powers. From this point of view it is hard to say where architecture ends and human assertion begins. In fact, there is no such division; the two are one and the same. 5

It is in the understanding of architecture as a medium for the expression of human attitudes, prejudices, taboos, and ideals that the new architectural criticism departs from classical aesthetics. The latter relied upon pure proportion, composition, etc., as bases for artistic judgment. In the age of sociology and psychology, walls are not simply walls but physical symbols of the barriers in men's minds. 6

In a primitive society, for example, men pictured the world as large, fearsome, hostile, and beyond human control. Therefore they built heavy walls of huge boulders, behind which they could feel themselves to be in a delimited space that was controllable and safe; these heavy walls expressed man's fear of the outer world and his need to find protection, however illusory. It might be argued that the undeveloped technology of the period precluded the construction of more delicate walls. This is of course true. 7

Still, it was not technology, but a fearful attitude toward the world, which made people want to build walls in the first place. The greater the fear, the heavier the wall, until in the tombs of ancient kings we find structures that are practically all wall, the fear of dissolution being the ultimate fear.

And then there is the question of privacy—for it *has* become 8 questionable. In some Mediterranean cultures it was not so much the world of nature that was feared, but the world of men. Men were dirty, prying, vile, and dangerous. One went about, if one could afford it, in guarded litters; women went about heavily veiled, if they went about at all. One's house was surrounded by a wall, and the rooms faced not out, but in, toward a patio, expressing the prevalent conviction that the beauties and values of life were to be found by looking inward, and by engaging in the intimate activities of a personal as against a public life. The rich intricacies of the decorative arts of the period, as well as its contemplative philosophies, are as illustrative of this attitude as the walls themselves.

We feel different today. For one thing, we place greater reliance 9 upon the control of human hostility, not so much by physical barriers, as by the conventions of law and social practice—as well as the availability of motorized police. We do not cherish privacy as much as did our ancestors. We are proud to have our women seen and admired, and the same goes for our homes. We do not seek solitude; in fact, if we find ourselves alone for once, we flick a switch and invite the whole world in through the television screen. Small wonder, then, that the heavy surrounding wall is obsolete, and we build, instead, membranes of thin sheet metal or glass.

The principal function of today's wall is to separate possibly 10 undesirable outside air from the controlled conditions of temperature and humidity which we have created inside. Glass may accomplish this function, though there are apparently a good many people who still have qualms about eating, sleeping, and dressing under conditions of high visibility; they demand walls that will at least give them a sense of adequate screening. But these shy ones are a vanishing breed. The Philip Johnson [1] house in Connecticut,

---

[1] American architect, born 1906; in 1949 he designed and constructed the Glass House for his residence in New Canaan, Connecticut.

which is much admired and widely imitated, has glass walls all the way around, and the only real privacy is to be found in the bathroom, the toilette taboo being still unbroken, at least in Connecticut.

To repeat, it is not our advanced technology, but our changing conceptions of ourselves in relation to the world that determine how we shall build our walls. The glass wall expresses man's conviction that he can and does master nature and society. The "open plan" and the unobstructed view are consistent with his faith in the eventual solution of all problems through the expanding efforts of science. This is perhaps why it is the most "advanced" and "forward-looking" among us who live and work in glass houses. Even the fear of the cast stone has been analyzed out of us.   11

QUESTIONS

Understanding

1. Raskin is contrasting ancient walls and modern walls. According to him, what was the function of walls in primitive society? What attitude toward nature is expressed by the glass walls of modern society?
2. Why has the function of walls changed, according to Raskin?
3. Raskin is also contrasting "classical" and "new" (par. 6) theories of architecture. Which stresses form? Which stresses function?
4. How, according to Raskin, has our culture's view of money changed since his father's day?

Strategies and Structure

1. Why do you think Raskin begins by quoting his father? Do you think this is an effective opening? Why or why not?
2. Is Raskin's father in any way a confusing example? He has an old-fashioned view of money; what is his view of architecture?
3. The "cast stone" (par. 11) of Raskin's last sentence echoes the proverb, "People who live in glass houses should not throw stones." How does this reference to traditional wisdom at the end resemble Raskin's reference to his father at the beginning?

4. Which phrase in his last paragraph (par. 11) signals that the author is summing up what he has to say?

5. Does the paragraph on Mediterranean houses (par. 8) continue or diverge from the preceding paragraph (par. 7) on walls in primitive culture?

Words and Figures of Speech

1. What is the meaning of the proverb about glass houses? Under what conditions might it be applied?

2. Which of the two key words in the title applies to primitive walls as Raskin describes them?

3. Paragraph 6 mentions "architectural criticism." What does *criticism* mean here and in phrases like "art criticism" or "literary criticism"?

4. In paragraph 4, Raskin says that the bright interior of the new bank "challenges" the daylight. How does that word apply to modern man's attitude toward nature as Raskin defines it?

5. Look up any of the following words that you do not already know: *tangible* (par. 3), *impregnable* (3), *aesthetic* (3), *deficit* (4), *taboos* (6), *composition* (6), *illusory* (7), *dissolution* (7), and *membrane* (9).

Comparing

1. How does Desmond Morris's explanation of the origin of barrier signals in Chapter 5 confirm what Raskin says about the original purpose of walls?

Discussion and Writing Topics

1. Raskin says we do not cherish privacy as much as our fathers did. Agree or disagree with this view by comparing and contrasting life in an old-fashioned single-family dwelling with life in a high-rise apartment or condominium.

2. What is the "international style" in modern architecture? Contrast it with what Raskin calls the "classical" style.

3. American architect Louis Sullivan (1856–1924) said that "form

follows function" in architecture. By "follows" he meant "depends upon." Is his theory modern or classical by Raskin's standards?

4. Recall an old building in your hometown (a high school, library, or courthouse, for example) that has been replaced by a new building. Compare and contrast the two.

5. What is a proverb? How does it differ from a parable?

Writers on the Writing Process:
Russell Baker and Eugene Raskin

I could tell stories of agonizing complication about a hundred others you might have chosen," Russell Baker replies to inquiries about the composition of "A Nice Place to Visit": "but this particular one was simply a piece of cake." [1]

Baker's ironic comparison of two major North American cities appeared after a layoff from writing his regular columns for the *New York Times*. He was working, Baker explains, as a writer on a musical bound for Broadway if it could get off the ground in Canada. "It was my first stay in Toronto. I was impressed." [2]

The play failed, and Baker returned to New York with a deadline to meet the next day. Having grown "rusty" during his time-off from writing columns, he hoped to ease into the old routine. "I knew a piece comparing Toronto and New York would be a snap. The slobbishness of New York is an old familiar subject. I had written about it in earlier columns and have written about it since. New Yorkers seem to take perverse pleasure in reading about it and even to be slightly proud of their ability to thrive in it. After four weeks in Toronto, which many consider the finest city in North America, it seemed very easy to have another stab at New York's swinishness by invoking the charms of Toronto." [3]

The original typescript of "A Nice Place to Visit"—the essay was composed from scratch at the typewriter apparently—shows why the author remembers it as "a very easy piece to write." The original ran to five pages, triple-spaced to allow room for editing. On three of those pages, Baker made only minor corrections in ballpoint pen: a practiced writer proofreading deftly, altering a verb tense here, inserting an adjective there, deleting stray marks from the typewriter. Only two [4] pages bear revisions that gave the author pause.

When he defined "courtesy" in paragraph 4, Baker originally 5
referred to its "curious forms appalling to the New Yorker in their
small town quaintness." Perhaps to clear up any possible ambiguity
in "their"—Toronto's or New York's?—Baker changed "curious"
to "quaint" and crossed out the last five words. In the next sentence (about Toronto baseball parks), he then had to insert
"Yankee fans may be astonished to learn that. . . ."

The next paragraph (about Toronto taxicabs) went smoothly 6
until Baker reached the part that now reads "mail the authorities
not only complaints but also compliments upon the cabbie's behavior." First he tried "mail compliments to the hack licensing
authorities." Then he went back and added "for the driver" after
"compliments." Still dissatisfied, Baker crossed out the whole
phrase and tried again before making the final emendations: "mail
the hack licensing authorities not only complaints but also compliments upon the service."

After this brief editorial stall, all went smoothly until the end- 7
ing (even more troublesome sometimes than the beginning of an
essay). Baker launched it with: "It makes you proud to get back
to the Big Apple." Then: "It's good to be back in the Big Apple
where the worms are. . . ." And again: "It was good to get back to
the Big Apple, and we listened ["worms" scratched out] happily to
the cabbie's radio blaring 'I Love New York' and threw candy
wrappers out the window" [amended to "pulled out the candy
wrappers"]. On the fourth try, Baker sailed into the version that
concludes the essay as we have it, and his false starts lie neatly
inked out behind him. The title, he reports, was added after the
entire piece was written and corrected.

Often his essays take much longer. Was he gratified by the 8
speedy delivery of this one? "Too easy," says Baker. "Afterwards, I
thought the irony was a bit ham-handed and the quality of the
piece not much above what a slick college newspaper columnist
could have done."

Spoken like the true author of *Growing Up*. 9

The author of "Walls and Barriers" does not recall where he first 10
got the idea for the essay. "What I Know," writes Eugene Raskin,
"is that it has been my lifelong habit to look at the world around
me, especially the works of man, and wonder how and why things

get to be as they are. Thus, for example, I wonder why we so often feel we need a spire to help worship God, or how an arch became a symbol of victory. (I also wonder why I wonder about such things, but I get nowhere with that query and have given it up.)"

How much revising did he do on the essay? "Very little, since [11] I don't begin to write until I know pretty well what I'm going to say. But I rarely do less than three drafts of anything.

Where did he get the title? "I don't remember, but I think it [12] was suggested by my editor, Eric Wensberg. Obviously, since the title came last, it did not serve me in the composing process."

The beginning? "I find in general it is better to begin with some- [13] thing personal than with some abstraction, so I began with my father, but as you see, I got to the abstraction fairly soon."

The ending? "Again I followed a common practice: Tell them [14] what you just told them."

What kind of audience did he have in mind? "Actually, at the [15] time I was (and still am) passionately interested in explaining that architecture is more than a matter of structure and style, but is deeply dependent on social customs and attitudes. This approach, which is fairly well accepted now, was considered quite radical when I wrote the piece, and earned me many detractors, of which I am proud, remembering who they were!"

Why, in general, does he write? "Ah, there's a question! I write [16] because I am alive. Because my eyes see. My brain thinks. My mouth speaks. And if my words are on paper, they will be heard by many beyond the reach of my voice. It's also a living."

WRITING TOPICS for Chapter Six
Essays That Compare and Contrast

Write a comparison and contrast essay on one of the following topics:

1. Two different cities (for example, New York and Washington, D.C.)
2. The same city at different times of day or in different seasons
3. Two World War II generals (for example, Patton and Eisenhower)
4. Two teachers you have admired
5. Two neighborhoods you have lived in
6. The haves and the have-nots in your hometown
7. Two of your classmates from different geographical regions
8. Two roommates you have had
9. A job versus a profession
10. Modern versus old-fashioned families (or marriages)
11. Two churches or synagogues in your hometown
12. Life in a democracy versus life under some other form of government
13. Two styles of playing football, baseball, tennis, or golf
14. The styles of two political (or social) leaders on your campus
15. The styles of two national politicians
16. The work of two painters, singers, musicians, or writers
17. Two newspaper columns or magazines that you read
18. Two comic strips

7

Essays That Use
Metaphor and Analogy

METAPHORS [1] and ANALOGIES are FIGURES OF SPEECH or "turns" of language that use words symbolically rather than literally. The poet Carl Sandburg created a metaphor when he wrote, "The woman named Tomorrow/sits with a hairpin in her teeth/and takes her time. . . ." His friend and fellow poet, Robert Frost, was developing an analogy when he told Sandburg that writing poetry without regular meter and rhyme is like playing tennis with the net down. Metaphors and analogies (or "extended metaphors"), then, are comparisons that reveal an object, event, or quality by identifying it with another object, event, or quality (usually one more familiar than the first, as tennis is more familiar to most of us than the rules of poetry).

The kinds of comparisons that metaphors and analogies make, however, should not be confused with those discussed in the last chapter ("Essays That Compare and Contrast"). When Bruce Catton compared Grant and Lee, he was as much interested in one general as the other. COMPARISON AND CONTRAST essays may not attend equally to the similarities and differences between their subjects, but they usually give equal weight to the subjects themselves. Essays that use metaphor and analogy, on the other hand, have a primary subject, which the object of comparison is introduced to explain. When Ernest Hemingway declared, for example, that a fine English sentence has the clean grace of a matador's sweeping cape, he was talking about writing, not bullfighting.

[1] Terms printed in all capitals are defined in the Glossary.

One common use of such comparisons is to advance an ARGU-
MENT. If you were trying to convince a friend that the government
should spend more money on the space program, you might argue
that Americans have a pioneering spirit and that outer space is like
the western frontier of a century ago; to advance across this new
frontier is simply to fulfill our national destiny. Such a line of
reasoning is an "argument by analogy." It assumes that, because
two entities or ideas are alike in some ways, they are alike in other
significant ways. An argument by analogy is the most vulnerable
form of argument; it is only as strong as the analogy is close and
complete. Your argument would collapse if your friend observed
that spaceships are much more expensive than covered wagons and
that the original frontier was conquered by exploiting the first
Americans.

Another common function of analogies is to explain; the EXPOSI-
TORY essays in the following pages are used for this purpose. "On
Societies as Organisms" by Lewis Thomas, for example, teaches us
something about humans in groups by comparing their social
activity to the bustle of an insect colony. In finished essays, such
analogies are primarily organizing devices; but when you are preparing an essay, they may actually aid you in finding something
to say.

Suppose you were getting ready to write an essay on the expansion of the universe, and you were puzzled by the problem of
locating the center of expansion. From our galaxy, all the other
galaxies seem to be rushing out and away; yet astrophysicists tell
us that we would experience the same sense of being left behind
if we visited any other galaxy in the universe. To write your essay,
you must resolve this apparent contradiction.

Now, suppose you hit upon the analogy of the balloon. (Your
subject is the universe, remember, not balloons; an analogy illumi-
nates a primary subject, it does not replace it with another.) You
might begin to think of the many galaxies of our expanding universe as spots of dark paint dotting the surface of the inflating
balloon. As the rubber surface expands, every dot draws apart from
every other dot. Whichever dot you single out will appear to be
the "center" of a surface that has no fixed middle point. Having
used this analogy to grasp your subject, you may then turn around
and use it to explain your complicated ideas to the reader.

Keep the following pointers in mind when developing an essay by analogy. Although an analogy will not "hold" if it compares objects that are too disparate, avoid obvious, trivial, or tired comparisons: life to a brief parade, a face without a smile to a day without sunshine. Analogies often liken the unfamiliar and the complicated to the common and the simple, but an analogy may also compare its primary subject with something exotic in order to discover the unexpected in the familiar. (This is Barry Lopez's strategy in "My Horse," an essay that is really about his Dodge van.) And, finally, try to compare your primary subject with something that is interesting and original in its own right. You are not likely to impress your reader if you explain the idea of blind choice by analogy with a stab in the dark or a number drawn from a hat.

Lewis Thomas

On Societies as Organisms

Lewis Thomas, M.D., a neurologist by training, is president and chief executive officer of the Memorial Sloan-Kettering Cancer Center in New York City. He was born in Flushing, New York, and attended Princeton University and Harvard Medical School (M.D., 1937). In 1971, Thomas began writing "Notes of a Biology Watcher" for less specialized readers of the New England Journal of Medicine. Lives of a Cell (1974), a collection of those "notes" from which the following essay is taken, won the National Book Award for arts and letters in 1975. The Medusa and the Snail (1979) and Late Night Thoughts on Listening to Mahler's Ninth Symphony (1983) bring together still more of Thomas's essays. In 1983 Thomas also published his autobiography, The Youngest Science. "On Societies as Organisms" begins by comparing ants to humans—not the other way around—and goes on to draw an extended analogy between all social groups and the activity of living beings.

Viewed from a suitable height, the aggregating clusters of   1
medical scientists in the bright sunlight of the boardwalk at
Atlantic City, swarmed there from everywhere for the annual
meetings, have the look of assemblages of social insects. There
is the same vibrating, ionic movement, interrupted by the
darting back and forth of jerky individuals to touch antennae
and exchange small bits of information; periodically, the mass
casts out, like a trout-line, a long single file unerringly toward
Childs's.[1] If the boards were not fastened down, it would not
be a surprise to see them put together a nest of sorts.

It is permissible to say this sort of thing about humans.   2
They do resemble, in their most compulsively social behavior,

[1] A local restaurant.

ants at a distance. It is, however, quite bad form in biological circles to put it the other way round, to imply that the operation of insect societies has any relation at all to human affairs. The writers of books on insect behavior generally take pains, in their prefaces, to caution that insects are like creatures from another planet, that their behavior is absolutely foreign, totally unhuman, unearthly, almost unbiological. They are more like perfectly tooled but crazy little machines, and we violate science when we try to read human meanings in their arrangements.

It is hard for a bystander not to do so. Ants are so much like   3
human beings as to be an embarrassment. They farm fungi, raise aphids as livestock, launch armies into wars, use chemical sprays to alarm and confuse enemies, capture slaves. The families of weaver ants engage in child labor, holding their larvae like shuttles to spin out the thread that sews the leaves together for their fungus gardens. They exchange information ceaselessly. They do everything but watch television.

What makes us most uncomfortable is that they, and the bees   4
and termites and social wasps, seem to live two kinds of lives: they are individuals, going about the day's business without much evidence of thought for tomorrow, and they are at the same time component parts, cellular elements, in the huge, writhing, ruminating organism of the Hill, the nest, the hive. It is because of this aspect, I think, that we most wish for them to be something foreign. We do not like the notion that there can be collective societies with the capacity to behave like organisms. If such things exist, they can have nothing to do with us.

Still, there it is. A solitary ant, afield, cannot be considered to   5
have much of anything on his mind; indeed, with only a few neurons strung together by fibers, he can't be imagined to have a mind at all, much less a thought. He is more like a ganglion on legs. Four ants together, or ten, encircling a dead moth on a path, begin to look more like an idea. They fumble and shove, gradually moving the food toward the Hill, but as though by blind chance. It is only when you watch the dense mass of thousands of ants, crowded together around the Hill, blackening the ground, that you begin to see the whole beast, and now you observe it thinking, planning, calculating. It is an intelligence, a kind of live computer, with crawling bits for its wits.

At a stage in the construction, twigs of a certain size are needed,   6 and all the members forage obsessively for twigs of just this size. Later, when outer walls are to be finished, thatched, the size must change, and as though given new orders by telephone, all the workers shift the search to the new twigs. If you disturb the arrangement of a part of the Hill, hundreds of ants will set it vibrating, shifting, until it is put right again. Distant sources of food are somehow sensed, and long lines, like tentacles, reach out over the ground, up over walls, behind boulders, to fetch it in.

Termites are even more extraordinary in the way they seem to accumulate intelligence as they gather together. Two or three termites in a chamber will begin to pick up pellets and move them from place to place, but nothing comes of it; nothing is built. As more join in, they seem to reach a critical mass, a quorum, and the thinking begins. They place pellets atop pellets, then throw up columns and beautiful, curving, symmetrical arches, and the crystalline architecture of vaulted chambers is created. It is not known how they communicate with each other, how the chains of termites building one column know when to turn toward the crew on the adjacent column, or how, when the time comes, they manage the flawless joining of the arches. The stimuli that set them off at the outset, building collectively instead of shifting things about, may be pheromones[2] released when they reach committee size. They react as if alarmed. They become agitated, excited, and then they begin working, like artists.

Bees live lives of organisms, tissues, cells, organelles, all at the same time. The single bee, out of the hive retrieving sugar (instructed by the dancer: "south-southeast for seven hundred meters, clover—mind you make corrections for the sundrift") is still as much a part of the hive as if attached by a filament. Building the hive, the workers have the look of embryonic cells organizing a developing tissue; from a distance they are like the viruses inside a cell, running off row after row of symmetrical polygons as though laying down crystals. When the time for swarming comes, and the old queen prepares to leave with her part of the population, it is as though the hive were involved in mitosis. There is an agitated moving of bees back and forth, like granules in cell sap. They distribute themselves in almost precisely equal parts, half to the departing queen, half to the new one. Thus, like an egg, the great,

7

8

---

[2] Hormones secreted by insects when communicating with other insects.

hairy, black and golden creature splits in two, each with an equal
share of the family genome.

The phenomenon of separate animals joining up to form an   9
organism is not unique in insects. Slime-mold cells do it all the
time, of course, in each life cycle. At first they are single amebocytes swimming around, eating bacteria, aloof from each other,
untouching, voting straight Republican. Then, a bell sounds, and
acrasin [3] is released by special cells toward which the others
converge in stellate ranks, touch, fuse together, and construct the
slug, solid as a trout. A splendid stalk is raised, with a fruiting
body on top, and out of this comes the next generation of amebocytes, ready to swim across the same moist ground, solitary and
ambitious.

Herring and other fish in schools are at times so closely inte-   10
grated, their actions so coordinated, that they seem to be func-
tionally a great multi-fish organism. Flocking birds, especially the
seabirds nesting on the slopes of offshore islands in Newfoundland,
are similarly attached, connected, synchronized.

Although we are by all odds the most social of all social animals   11
—more interdependent, more attached to each other, more in-
separable in our behavior than bees—we do not often feel our
conjoined intelligence. Perhaps, however, we are linked in circuits
for the storage, processing, and retrieval of information, since this
appears to be the most basic and universal of all human enter-
prises. It may be our biological function to build a certain kind
of Hill. We have access to all the information of the biosphere,
arriving as elementary units in the stream of solar photons. When
we have learned how these are rearranged against randomness, to
make, say, springtails, quantum mechanics, and the late quartets,
we may have a clearer notion how to proceed. The circuitry seems
to be there, even if the current is not always on.

The system of communications used in science should provide   12
a neat, workable model for studying mechanisms of information-
building in human society. Ziman, in a recent *Nature* essay, points
out, "the invention of a mechanism for the systematic publication
of *fragments* of scientific work may well have been the key event
in the history of modern science." He continues:

---

[3] Chemical attractant named after the class (Acrasiae) to which these special
slime molds belong.

A regular journal carries from one research worker to another the various . . . observations which are of common interest. . . . A typical scientific paper has never pretended to be more than another little piece in a larger jigsaw—not significant in itself but as an element in a grander scheme. *This technique, of soliciting many modest contributions to the store of human knowledge, has been the secret of Western science since the seventeenth century, for it achieves a corporate, collective power that is far greater than any one individual can exert* [italics mine].

With some alternation of terms, some toning down, the passage could describe the building of a termite nest. 13

It is fascinating that the word "explore" does not apply to the searching aspect of the activity, but has its origins in the sounds we make while engaged in it. We like to think of exploring in science as a lonely, meditative business, and so it is in the first stages, but always, sooner or later, before the enterprise reaches completion, as we explore, we call to each other, communicate, publish, send letters to the editor, present papers, cry out on finding. 14

QUESTIONS

Understanding

1. In paragraph 1, what is Thomas comparing to what? In paragraph 3? Which of the two paragraphs formulates the ANALOGY that Thomas will develop throughout his essay?

2. The title of Thomas's essay expresses his main analogy in its most general terms. Which term applies to individual human beings? Which applies to *groups* of insects, fish, birds, or humans?

3. What is an organism? How does it differ from a mechanism, one of the "crazy little machines" that Thomas refers to in paragraph 2?

4. Why, according to Thomas, are we reluctant to attribute human characteristics to insect colonies? How might people in Russia or Communist China be expected to react to such comparisons?

5. Thomas says that, like the ant's, mankind's biological function is "to build a certain kind of Hill" (par. 11). What, specifically, is

the basic enterprise of human society in Thomas's view? What kind of hill is the human community erecting?

Strategies and Structure

1. In the opening paragraph, Thomas looks down upon his fellow medical scientists from a "suitable height." Why do you suppose he establishes this perspective? Why does Thomas call himself a "bystander" in paragraph 3?

2. How might paragraph 5 be interpreted as a mini-version of Thomas's entire essay?

3. Thomas develops a single elaborate analogy by building upon a number of smaller analogies. To what specialized human beings does he compare the builder termites in paragraph 7? Why does an egg provide a fitting analogy for describing the swarming bee colony in paragraph 8? What analogy is suggested by "voting straight Republican" in paragraph 9?

4. Throughout most of this essay, the author is applying what he knows about human society to learn more about insect behavior. When does he begin to reverse this procedure? In what sense is Thomas's essay not about insects at all?

5. Thomas is writing here for a more general audience than a convention of medical specialists at Atlantic City, but he nevertheless speaks with the authority of a trained scientist. How is that authority conveyed to us?

6. Explain the analogy in paragraphs 12, 13, and 14. Does it make for a satisfying ending to Thomas's essay? Why or why not?

Words and Figures of Speech

1. Look up the root meaning of *explore* (par. 14). Applied to scientific investigation, how does the word in its original meaning support Thomas's analogy in paragraphs 12–14?

2. Look up *biology* in your dictionary. In which sense is Thomas using the word when he refers to insects as "unbiological" (par. 2) and to the "biological function" of humanity (par. 11)?

3. Why do you think Thomas applies such terms as *quorum* and *committee* (par. 7) to groups of insects that begin to act intelligently?

4. In paragraph 11, when Thomas says that "the current is not always on," to what circuit is he referring? Why is the METAPHOR amusing?

5. Consult your dictionary for definitions of the following words: *ionic* (par. 1), *ruminating* (1), *ganglion* (5), *critical mass* (7), *organelles* (8), *embryonic* (8), *mitosis* (8), *genome* (8), *amebocytes* (9), *stellate* (9), *biosphere* (11), *photons* (11), *springtails* (11), and *quantum mechanics* (11).

Comparing

1. If you compare Thomas's essay with Alexander Petrunkevitch's "The Spider and the Wasp" (Chapter 3), which reads more like a technical scientific report? Explain your answer.

2. In its use of analogy does Thomas's essay more closely resemble Petrunkevitch's or Virginia Woolf's "The Death of the Moth" (Chapter 8)? Explain your answer.

Discussion and Writing Topics

1. Describe some human social enterprise—a party, field trip, class session, convention, or bargain sale—by analogy with a collective gathering of insects.

2. Thomas suggests that human beings work collectively to gather information. Speculate on other motives for human social activity —companionship, for example.

3. If societies are organisms with a group mind or will, what becomes of the individual's responsibility for his or her behavior when he or she acts as part of a group? Is a lynch mob, say, an amoral thing like a cold virus?

Barry Lopez

My Horse

Barry Lopez is a full-time writer. He was born in Port Chester, New York, in 1945, but now lives with his wife in Finn Rock, Oregon. He was educated at Notre Dame and the University of Oregon. A contributor to Harper's, the North American Review, and Audubon, he is the author of a collection of American Indian trickster tales and of Desert Notes: Reflections in the Eye of a Raven (1976), Of Wolves and Men (1978), and River Notes: The Dance of Herons (1979). He is now at work on a book about the Arctic and a book of fiction set on the northern plains of two centuries ago. "My Horse" originally appeared in the North American Review. It draws an analogy between the author's Dodge Sportsman 300 van and Coke High, a quarter horse that he rode as a wrangler in Wyoming. Lopez recalls the process of writing "My Horse" at the end of this chapter.

It is curious that Indian warriors on the northern plains in the nineteenth century, who were almost entirely dependent on the horse for mobility and status, never gave their horses names. If you borrowed a man's horse and went off raiding for other horses, however, or if you lost your mount in battle and then jumped on mine and counted coup [1] on an enemy—well, those horses would have to be shared with the man whose horse you borrowed, and that coup would be mine, not yours. Because even if I gave him no name, he was my horse.

If you were a Crow warrior and I a young Teton Sioux out after a warrior's identity and we came over a small hill some-

[1] The custom among the Plains Indians of striking or touching an enemy as a sign of courage.

235

where in the Montana prairie and surprised each other, I could tell a lot about you by looking at your horse.

Your horse might have feathers tied in his mane, or in his tail, [3] or a medicine bag tied around his neck. If I knew enough about the Crow, and had looked at you closely, I might make some sense of the decoration, even guess who you were if you were well-known. If you had painted your horse I could tell even more, because we both decorated our horses with signs that meant the same things. Your white handprints high on his flanks would tell me you had killed an enemy in a hand-to-hand fight. Small horizontal lines stacked on your horse's foreleg, or across his nose, would tell me how many times you had counted coup. Horse hoof marks on your horse's rump, or three-sided boxes, would tell me how many times you had stolen horses. If there was a bright red square on your horse's neck I would know you were leading a war party and that there were probably others out there in the coulees behind you.

You might be painted all over as blue as the sky and covered [4] with white dots, with your horse painted the same way. Maybe hailstorms were your power—or if I chased you a hailstorm might come down and hide you. There might be lightning bolts on the horse's legs and flanks, and I would wonder if you had lightning power, or a slow horse. There might be white circles around your horse's eyes to help him see better.

Or you might be like Crazy Horse,[2] with no decoration, no [5] marks on your horse to tell me anything, only a small lightning bolt on your cheek, a piece of turquoise tied behind your ear.

You might have scalps dangling from your rein. [6]

I could tell something about you by your horse. All this would [7] come to me in a few seconds. I might decide this was my moment and shout my war cry—*Hoka hey!* Or I might decide you were like the grizzly bear: I would raise my weapon to you in salute and go my way, to see you again when I was older.

I do not own a horse. I am attached to a truck, however, and I [8] have come to think of it in a similar way. It has no name; it never occurred to me to give it a name. It has little decoration; neither

[2] (1849?–1877), a Sioux chief, born in Nebraska; he fought General Custer at the Little Big Horn.

of us is partial to decoration. I have a piece of turquoise in the truck because I had heard once that some of the southwestern tribes tied a small piece of turquoise in a horse's hock to keep him from stumbling. I like the idea. I also hang sage in the truck when I go on a long trip. But inside, the truck doesn't look much different from others that look just like it on the outside. I like it that way. Because I like my privacy.

For two years in Wyoming I worked on a ranch wrangling horses. The horse I rode when I had to have a good horse was a quarter horse and his name was Coke High. This name came with him. At first I thought he'd been named for the soft drink. I'd known stranger names given to horses by whites. Years later I wondered if some deviant Wyoming cowboy wise to cocaine had not named him. Now I think he was probably named after a rancher, an historical figure of the region. I never asked the people who owned him for fear of spoiling the spirit of my inquiry.

We were running over a hundred horses on this ranch. They all had names. After a few weeks I knew all the horses and the names too. You had to. No one knew how to talk about the animals or put them in order or tell the wranglers what to do unless they were using the names—Princess, Big Red, Shoshone, Clay.

My truck is named Dodge. The name came with it. I don't know if it was named after the town or the verb or the man who invented it. I like it for a name. Perfectly anonymous, like Rex for a dog, or Old Paint. You can't tell anything with a name like that.

The truck is a van. I call it a truck because it's not a car and because "van" is a suburban sort of consumer word, like "oxford loafer," and I don't like the sound of it. On the outside it looks like any other Dodge Sportsman 300. It's a dirty tan color. There are a few body dents, but it's never been in a wreck. I tore the antenna off against a tree on a pinched mountain road. A boy in Midland, Texas, rocked one of my rear view mirrors off. A logging truck in Oregon squeeze-fired a piece of debris off the road and shattered my windshield. The oil pan and gas tank are pug-faced from high-centering on bad roads. (I remember a horse I rode for a while named Targhee whose hocks were scarred from tangles in barbed wire when he was a colt and who spooked a lot in high grass, but these were not like "dents." They were more like bad tires.)

I like to travel. I go mostly in the winter and mostly on two-   13
lane roads. I've driven the truck from Key West to Vancouver,
British Columbia, and from Yuma to Long Island over the past
four years. I used to ride Coke High only about five miles every
morning when we were rounding up horses. Hard miles of twisting
and turning. About six hundred miles a year. Then I'd turn him
out and ride another horse for the rest of the day. That's what was
nice about having a remuda.[3] You could do all you had to do and
not take it all out on your best horse. Three car family.

My truck came with a lot of seats in it and I've never really   14
known what to do with them. Sometimes I put the seats in and go
somewhere with a lot of people, but most of the time I leave them
out. I like riding around with that empty cavern of space behind
my head. I know it's something with a history to it, that there's
truth in it, because I always rode a horse the same way—with
empty saddle bags. In case I found something. The possibility
of finding something is half the reason for being on the road.

The value of anything comes to me in its use. If I am not using   15
something it is of no value to me and I give it away. I wasn't
always that way. I used to keep everything I owned—just in case.
I feel good about the truck because it gets used. A lot. To haul
hay and firewood and lumber and rocks and garbage and animals.
Other people have used it to haul furniture and freezers and dirt
and recycled newspapers. And to move from one house to another.
When I lend it for things like that I don't look to get anything
back but some gas (if we're going to be friends). But if you go way
out in the country to a dump and pick up the things you can still
find out there (once a load of cedar shingles we sold for $175 to
an architect) I expect you to leave some of those things around
my place when you come back—if I need them.

When I think back, maybe the nicest thing I ever put in that   16
truck was timber wolves. It was a long night's drive from Oregon
up into British Columbia. We were all very quiet about it; it was
like moving clouds across the desert.

Sometimes something won't fit in the truck and I think about   17

---

[3] In the Southwest, a herd of horses from which ranch hands choose their
mounts.

improving it—building a different door system, for example. I am forever going to add better gauges on the dash and a pair of driving lamps and a sunroof, but I never get around to doing any of it. I remember I wanted to improve Coke High once too, especially the way he bolted like a greyhound through patches of cottonwood on a river flat. But all I could do with him was to try to rein him out of it. Or hug his back.

Sometimes, road-stoned in a blur of country like southwestern [18] Wyoming or North Dakota, I talk to the truck. It's like wandering on the high plains under a summer sun, on plains where, George Catlin [4] wrote, you were "out of sight of land." I say what I am thinking out loud, or point at things along the road. It's a crazy, sun-stroked sort of activity, a sure sign it's time to pull over, to go for a walk, to make a fire and have some tea, to lie in the shade of the truck.

I've always wanted to pat the truck. It's basic to the relation- [19] ship. But it never works.

I remember when I was on the ranch, just at sunrise, after I'd [20] saddled Coke High, I'd be huddled down in my jacket smoking a cigarette and looking down into the valley, along the river where the other horses had spent the night. I'd turn to Coke and run my hand down his neck and slap-pat him on the shoulder to say I was coming up. It made a bond, an agreement we started the day with.

I've thought about that a lot with the truck, because we've gone [21] out together at sunrise on so many mornings. I've even fumbled around trying to do it. But metal won't give.

The truck's personality is mostly an expression of two ideas: [22] "with-you" and "alone." When Coke High was "with-you" he and I were the same animal. We could have cut a rooster out of a flock of chickens, we were so in tune. It's the same with the truck: rolling through Kentucky on a hilly two-lane road, three in the morning under a full moon and no traffic. Picture it. You roll like water.

There are other times when you are with each other but there's [23] no connection at all. Coke got that way when he was bored and we'd fight each other about which way to go around a tree. When

[4] (1796–1872), American artist and writer who lived among the Indians.

the truck gets like that—"alone"—it's because it feels its Detroit fat-ass design dragging at its heart and making a fool out of it.

I can think back over more than a hundred nights I've slept in   24 the truck, sat in it with a lamp burning, bundled up in a parka, reading a book. It was always comfortable. A good place to wait out a storm. Like sleeping inside a buffalo.

The truck will go past 100,000 miles soon. I'll rebuild the engine   25 and put a different transmission in it. I can tell from magazine advertisements that I'll never get another one like it. Because every year they take more of the heart out of them. One thing that makes a farmer or a rancher go sour is a truck that isn't worth a shit. The reason you see so many old pickups in ranch country is because these are the only ones with any heart. You can count on them. The weekend rancher runs around in a new pickup with too much engine and not enough transmission and with the wrong sort of tires because he can afford anything, even the worst. A lot of them have names for their pickups too.

My truck has broken down, in out of the way places at the worst   26 of times. I've walked away and screamed the foulness out of my system and gotten the tools out. I had to fix a water pump in a blizzard in the Panamint Mountains in California once. It took all day with the Coleman stove burning under the engine block to keep my hands from freezing. We drifted into Beatty, Nevada, that night with it jury-rigged together with—I swear—baling wire, and we were melting snow as we went and pouring it in to compensate for the leaks.

There is a dent next to the door on the driver's side I put there   27 one sweltering night in Miami. I had gone to the airport to meet my wife, whom I hadn't seen in a month. My hands were so swollen with poison ivy blisters I had to drive with my wrists. I had shut the door and was locking it when the window fell off its runners and slid down inside the door. I couldn't leave the truck unlocked because I had too much inside I didn't want to lose. So I just kicked the truck a blow in the side and went to work on the window. I hate to admit kicking the truck. It's like kicking a dog, which I've never done.

Coke High and I had an accident once. We hit a badger hole   28 at a full gallop. I landed on my back and blacked out. When I came to, Coke High was about a hundred yards away. He stayed a hundred yards away for six miles, all the way back to the ranch.

I want to tell you about carrying those wolves, because it was a 29 fine thing. There were ten of them. We had four in the truck with us in crates and six in a trailer. It was a five hundred mile trip. We went at night for the cool air and because there wouldn't be as much traffic. I could feel from the way the truck rolled along that its heart was in the trip. It liked the wolves inside it, the sweet odor that came from the crates. I could feel that same tireless wolf-lope developing in its wheels; it was like you might never have to stop for gas, ever again.

The truck gets very self-focused when it works like this; its 30 heart is strong and it's good to be around it. It's good to be *with* it. You get the same feeling when you pull someone out of a ditch. Coke High and I pulled a Volkswagen out of the mud once, but Coke didn't like doing it very much. Speed, not strength, was his center. When the guy who owned the car thanked us and tried to pat Coke, the horse snorted and swung away, trying to preserve his distance, which is something a horse spends a lot of time on.

So does the truck. 31

Being distant lets the truck get its heart up. The truck has been 32 cold and alone in Montana at 38 below zero. It's climbed horrible, eroded roads in Idaho. It's been burdened beyond overloading, and made it anyway. I've asked it to do these things because they build heart, and without heart all you have is a machine. You have nothing. I don't think people in Detroit know anything at all about heart. That's why everything they build dies so young.

One time in Arizona the truck and I came through one of the 33 worst storms I've ever been in, an outrageous, angry blizzard. But we went down the road, right through it. You couldn't explain our getting through by the sort of tires I had on the truck, or the fact that I had chains on, or was a good driver, or had a lot of weight over my drive wheels or a good engine, because it was more than this. It was a contest between the truck and the blizzard— and the truck wouldn't quit. I could have gone to sleep and the truck would have just torn a road down Interstate 40 on its own. It scared the hell out of me; but it gave me heart, too.

We came off the Mogollon Rim that night and out of the storm 34 and headed south for Phoenix. I pulled off the road to sleep for a few hours, but before I did I got out of the truck. It was raining. Warm rain. I tied a short piece of red avalanche cord into the grill. I left it there for a long time, like an eagle feather on a horse's tail. It flapped and spun in the wind. I could hear it ticking against the grill when I drove.

When I have to leave that truck I will just raise up my left   35
arm—*Hoka hey!*—and walk away.

QUESTIONS

Understanding

1. Which is the *primary* subject of Lopez's ANALOGY, his truck or his horse? Explain your answer.

2. What does Lopez mean by "heart" (par. 32)? How does his account of the drive through the blizzard (par. 33) help to define this virtue?

3. Why does Lopez admire Crazy Horse (par. 5)? How is his truck like Crazy Horse's mount?

4. How does Lopez resemble the young Teton Sioux at the beginning of his essay? How has he changed (almost) by the end? What accounts for the change?

5. Lopez says of riding in his empty truck that "it's something with a history to it, that there's truth in it" (par. 14). What does he mean by this statement? How has it been anticipated earlier?

6. What does Detroit come to signify in this essay?

7. When friends borrow Lopez's truck, they are expected to share what they find with it, even though he otherwise shuns possessions. Why? What tradition does this custom recall?

Strategies and Structure

1. Lopez's analogy between truck and horse is largely unstated; he does not often refer explicitly to the fact of resemblance. Instead, he proceeds by alternating between his two subjects until they blend and merge. Cite several examples of this technique.

2. Sometimes Lopez's analogy shifts unexpectedly from one subject

back to the other. Which examples do you find particularly surprising? How does Lopez use this technique to end his essay?

3. In what sense does the last line of paragraph 13 reverse Lopez's
basic analogy? Where else in his essay does this sort of reversal
occur?

4. Lopez's basic analogy is between his truck and a horse, but this
is not the only analogy in his essay. To what else, particularly
animals, does he compare his truck?

5. Lopez admits that his basic analogy breaks down in one respect.
How is his truck *not* like a horse? How does he turn this exception to advantage?

6. Lopez is drawing analogies here, but his essay also uses many of
the techniques of NARRATION. What are some of these techniques?
Point to specific examples.

Words and Figures of Speech

1. Names usually signify identity, but Lopez is glad that his truck
is named "Dodge" because it is thus *anonymous* (par. 11), like an
Indian pony. Look up the root meaning of this word. Why is it
appropriate here?

2. In a way, this is an essay about sign language. To whose language
does the word *van* (par. 12) belong, according to Lopez? What
does it signify or "sign"?

3. Some cultures assume that "signs" and the ideas they represent
are separate and distinct. Other cultures blur this distinction and
tend to *identify* a sign with what it refers to. Which is the case
with Lopez and his Indians? Explain your answer.

4. Is Coke High a METAPHOR for Lopez's truck or a SIMILE? Explain
your opinion.

5. If Lopez's horse stands for his truck, what does his truck stand
for?

Comparing

1. Describe how Barry Lopez's use of language resembles that of
Chief Seattle in his "Reply to the U.S. Government" (Chapter
10).

2. How does the sign language of Lopez's Indians resemble the

"secret language" that Desmond Morris defines in "Barrier Signals" (Chapter 5)?

3. Compare Lopez's attitude toward new-fangled gadgets and soft living with that of Frank Trippett in "The Great American Cooling Machine" (Chapter 4).

Discussion and Writing Topics

1. If you know someone who identifies with his or her car, motorcycle, or bike, develop an analogy between them.

2. Develop an analogy between someone you know and his or her pet.

3. Some tasks and responsibilities (raising a colt, harvesting a crop, maintaining a boat) have been considered as aids to growing up. Describe some such task as a metaphor for coming-of-age.

Calvin Trillin
Literally

Calvin Trillin was born in Kansas City, Missouri, in 1935 and educated at Yale. Since 1963, when he left Time magazine, he has been a staff member of the New Yorker, where he writes a column entitled "U.S. Journal." Trillin is also a regular contributor to the Nation, Atlantic, Harper's, and Esquire. Uncivil Liberties (1982), from which "Literally" is taken, is a collection of his essays for the Nation. Trillin likes to eat and has written three books on American cuisine: American Fried (1974), Alice, Let's Eat, and Third Helpings (1983). He maintains that the best restaurant in the country is Arthur Bryant's barbecue house in Kansas City. "Literally" shows the confusion that can result from assuming that a phrase like "soup to nuts" has something to do with food.

M y problem with country living began innocently enough   1
when our well ran dry and a neighbor said some pump
priming would be necessary.

"I didn't come up here to discuss economics," I said. Actu-   2
ally, I don't understand economics. There's no use revealing
that, though, to every Tom, Dick and Harry who interrupts
his dinner to try to get your water running, so I said, "I come
up here to get away from that sort of thing." My neighbor gave
me a puzzled look.

"He's talking about the water pump," Alice told me. "It   3
needs priming."

I thought that experience might have been just a fluke—   4
until, on a fishing trip with the same neighbor, I proudly pulled
in a fish with what I thought was a major display of deep-sea
angling skill, only to hear a voice behind me say, "It's just a
fluke."

"This is dangerous," I said to Alice, while helping her weed the   5
vegetable garden the next day. I had thought our problem was limited to the pump-priming ichthyologist down the road, but that
morning at the post office I had overheard a farmer say that since
we seemed to be in for a few days of good weather he intended to
make his hay while the sun was shining. "These people are robbing
me of aphorisms," I said, taking advantage of the discussion to rest
for a while on my hoe. "How can I encourage the children to take
advantage of opportunities by telling them to make hay while the
sun shines if they think that means making hay while the sun
shines?"

"Could you please keep weeding those peas while you talk," she   6
said. "You've got a long row to hoe."

I began to look at Alice with new eyes. By that, of course, I   7
don't mean that I actually went to a discount eye outlet, acquired
two new eyes (20/20 this time), replaced my old eyes with the new
ones and looked at Alice. Having to make that explanation is just
the sort of thing I found troubling. What I mean is that I was
worried about the possibility of Alice's falling into the habit of
rural literalism herself. My concern was deepened a few days later
by a conversation that took place while I was in one of our apple
trees, looking for an apple that was not used as a *dacha*[1] by the
local worms. "I just talked to the Murrays, and they say that the
secret is picking up windfalls," Alice said.

"Windfalls?" I said. "Could it be that Jim Murray has taken over   8
Exxon since last time I saw him? Or do the Murrays have a natural-
gas operation in the back forty I didn't know about?"

"Not those kinds of windfalls," Alice said. "The apples that fall   9
from the tree because of the wind. They're a breeding place for
worms."

"There's nothing wrong with our apples," I said reaching for a   10
particularly plump one.

"Be careful," she said. "You may be getting yourself too far out   11
on a limb."

"You may be getting yourself out on a limb yourself," I said to   12
Alice at breakfast the next morning.

She looked around the room. "I'm sitting at the kitchen table,"   13
she said.

---

[1] A Russian country house.

"I meant it symbolically," I said. "The way it was meant to be [14]
meant. This has got to stop. I won't have you coming in from the
garden with small potatoes in your basket and saying that what
you found was just small potatoes. 'Small potatoes' doesn't mean
small potatoes."

"Small potatoes doesn't mean small potatoes?" [15]

"I refuse to discuss it," I said. "The tide's in, so I'm going fish- [16]
ing, and I don't want to hear any encouraging talk about that fluke
not being the only fish in the ocean."

"I was just going to ask why you have to leave before you finish [17]
your breakfast," she said.

"Because time and tide wait for no man," I said. "And I mean [18]
it."

Had she trapped me into saying that? Or was it possible that I [19]
was falling into the habit myself? Was I, as I waited for a bite,
thinking that there were plenty of other fish in the sea? Then I
had a bite—then another. I forgot about the problem until after I
had returned to the dock and done my most skillful job of filleting.

"Look!" I said, holding up the carcass of one fish proudly, as [20]
Alice approached the dock. "It's nothing but skin and bones."

The shock of realizing what I had said caused me to stumble [21]
against my fish-cleaning table and knock the fillets off the dock.
"Now we won't have anything for dinner," I said.

"Don't worry about it," Alice said. "I have other fish to fry." [22]

"That's not right!" I shouted. "That's not what that means. It [23]
means you have something better to do."

"It can also mean that I have other fish to fry," she said. "And [24]
I do. I'll just get that other fish you caught out of the freezer. Even
though it was just a fluke."

I tried to calm myself. I apologized to Alice for shouting and [25]
offered to help her pick vegetables from the garden for dinner.

"I'll try to watch my language," she said, as we stood among the [26]
peas.

"It's all right, really," I said. [27]

"I was just going to say that tonight it seems rather slim pick- [28]
ings," she said. "Just about everything has gone to seed."

"Perfectly all right," I said, wandering over toward the garden [29]
shed, where some mud seemed to be caked in the eaves. I pushed
at the mud with a rake, and a swarm of wasps burst out at me. I
ran for the house, swatting at wasps with my hat. Inside, I suddenly

had the feeling that some of them had managed to crawl up the legs of my jeans, and I tore the jeans off. Alice found me there in the kitchen, standing quietly in what the English call their smalls.

"That does it," I said. "We're going back to the city."   30

"Just because of a few stings?"   31

"Can't you see what happened?" I said. "They scared the pants   32
off me."

QUESTIONS

Understanding

1. What is an "aphorism" (par. 5)? By what means are his wife, Alice, and their neighbors robbing Trillin of aphorisms?

2. If, as Trillin says, " 'small potatoes' doesn't mean small potatoes" (par. 15), what does it mean? How about "priming the pump" (pars. 1–3), "just a fluke" (par. 4), and "windfalls" (par. 8)?

3. If literal language rules in the country, how, according to Trillin, do people back in the city use language? Why is Trillin's confirmed city-dweller anxious to leave?

4. What is happening to Trillin's wife, Alice, in the country? How does he feel about this transformation?

Strategies and Structure

1. Is Calvin Trillin as exasperated (literally) as he seems? How would you describe the TONE of his essay?

2. In which paragraph and with what phrase does Trillin first find himself, to his "horror," falling into the literalism he is pretending to abhor?

3. We laugh in paragraph 32 when Trillin is stripped of more than just his normal resources of language; but the humor in this essay is primarily verbal, deriving from what Trillin sees as the consistent misuse of METAPHOR. Metaphors are verbal comparisons in which an object or idea (the "vehicle") stands in for the one that is actually being discussed (the "tenor"). Which element (TENOR or VEHICLE, as defined in the Glossary) do Trillin's rural friends tend to ignore? Explain your answer by analyzing several of the sample phrases that "horrify" the author.

4. Why must *both* tenor and vehicle be recognized if a metaphor or other verbal comparison is to work figuratively?

5. Are the "literalists" incorrect in their use of the English language, or do aphorisms usually have a literal as well as a metaphoric meaning? Put your nose to the grindstone, and recall several aphorisms you have heard or read. Analyze how they work verbally.

6. What is the role of Alice in "Literally"?

Words and Figures of Speech

1. What is the figurative meaning of the phrase "to watch my language" (par. 26)? Why does Trillin note that Alice is standing among the peas when asked to mind her words?

2. After consulting a good dictionary, explain the difference between an *aphorism* and a *proverb*.

3. Look up FIGURES OF SPEECH in the Glossary at the back of this book. Besides metaphor, what other types of figurative language is Trillin using for comic effect here?

4. Judging from its context in paragraph 5, what is an *ichthyologist*? What is the meaning of rural *literalism* (par. 7)?

Comparing

1. Compare the language of Garrison Keillor's comic essay, "Attitude" (Chapter 3), with that of Trillin's "Literally." Which seems more like the language of speech than of formal writing? How might the author's subject in each case influence the form of diction he chooses?

2. In what sense are Trillin and Colman McCarthy ("Phasing Out Campus Idealism," Chapter 6) representing the same political point of view despite their difference in tone?

Discussion and Writing Topics

1. Write an essay in which you encounter the same kind of literalism that frustrated Trillin. You do not have to set it in the country, but exercise your verbal license in some definite place. A few dead metaphors you may want to revive: "Don't beat around the bush"; "Draw the bottom line"; "Eat your heart out"; "To pull a long face"; "To fiddle while Rome burns"; "To live in a fool's paradise"; "What's good for the goose is good for the gander."

2. Reverse Trillin's strategy and write an essay in which other people insist upon interpreting everything you say figuratively when you mean it to be taken literally.

Writers on the Writing Process:
Barry Lopez

When Barry Lopez examines artifacts of civilization (such as a truck), he finds traces of the natural world. When he studies the wilderness or the plains, he discovers metaphors for human behavior. Thus one of his books, a closer look at the unusual cargo of "My Horse," bears the title *Of Wolves and Men*. Thus, too, the subject of Lopez's essay is a machine that comes alive. The truck of "My Horse" is sometimes a truck and sometimes a horse because it is a vehicle for the author's double vision.

Asked to comment on the process of writing the essay, Lopez did not explain how he acquired this distinctive way of seeing; but in the following factual account, it takes over at the end.

"It is unusual [writes Lopez] for me to draft a story away from home. The comparison in 'My Horse,' however, insisted on being set down in a cafe in Fort Morgan, Colorado, December 3, 1974. (The day and the place I know because notes about drafts are part of a daily journal.) I wrote the piece out in longhand, on a white Formica table in a booth, over three or four cups of hot chocolate.

"I was traveling that winter to Oklahoma City to attend the National Finals Rodeo, where I would complete the research for a piece about bull riders. I was alone, traveling in the truck I was writing about, and I had come by way of Fort Morgan to see the country along the South Fork of the Platte River.

"The essay reflects an interest in areas that were, and continue to be, part of my work—the lives of animals, cultures of various North American tribes, and features of the Western American landscape. Also here, obviously, is evidence of the great pleasure I take in traveling by road.

" 'My Horse' went through four drafts before I sent it to Robley 6
Wilson at the *North American Review* in the spring of 1975. He
accepted it without changes, though, as it turned out, a small
change I did want to make never got to the printer. You learn to
live with these things.

"The truck is still in use, but mostly to haul firewood. On damp 7
winter mornings it's hard to get it started. The red cord, bleached
and washed by weather to a faded mauve, is still tied to the grill.
An old horse now."

WRITING TOPICS for Chapter Seven
Essays That Use Metaphor and Analogy

1. Explain your inner self by analogy with a car, truck, motorcycle, boat, or other vehicle that you consider to be a means of self-expression.

2. Write an essay using the shrinking size of American automobiles as indexes to the country's economic condition.

3. Describe a house you have seen as an emblem of the people that you know or imagine to inhabit it.

4. Define several different kinds of human intelligence by associating each type with a game that exemplifies it.

5. Explain how to develop self-confidence by comparing the process of acquiring it to weaving a design, cultivating a garden, or building a fire.

6. Explain the kind of education your college or university offers by comparing it to a meal in a restaurant or cafeteria.

7. Describe a typical day in your life as if you were threading your way through a maze.

8. Compare the maneuvers and challenges of the dating game to the activities of a disco lounge or other night spot.

9. Recall formative events of your past life by associating them with objects in an attic or pictures in a photo album.

10. Explain the typical life cycle of a human being by likening it to that of an insect or animal.

Description

8

Essays That Appeal to the Senses

DESCRIPTION [1] is the MODE of writing that appeals most directly to the senses either by telling us the qualities of a person, place, or thing or by showing them. For example, here are two descriptions of cemeteries. The first, from Natural History magazine, is written in the language of detached observation:

An old and popular New England tradition for resident and visitor alike, is a relaxing walk through one of our historical cemeteries. . . .

Haphazard rows of slate tablets give way in time to simple marble tablets bearing urn and willow motifs. The latter in turn lose popularity to marble gravestones of a variety of sizes and shapes and often arranged in groups or family plots. The heyday of ornate marble memorials lasted into the 1920s, when measured rows of uniformly sized granite blocks replaced them.

Compare this passage with novelist John Updike's far-from-detached description of the cemetery in the town where he lives:

The stones are marble, modernly glossy and simple, though I suppose that time will eventually reveal them as another fashion, dated and quaint. Now, the sod is still raw, the sutures of turf are unhealed, the earth still humped, the wreaths scarcely withered. . . . I remember my grandfather's funeral, the hurried cross of sand the minister drew on the coffin lid, the whine of the lowering straps, the lengthening, cleanly cut sides of clay, the thought of air, the lack of air forever in the close dark space lined with pink satin. . . .

---

[1] Terms printed in all capitals are defined in the Glossary.

Our first example relies heavily upon adjectives: "historical," "haphazard," "simple," "ornate," "measured," "uniformly sized." Except when they identify minerals—slate tablets, marble memorials—these adjectives tend to be ABSTRACT. Indeed, the movement of the entire passage is away from the particular. No single grave is described in detail. Even the "urn and willow motifs" adorn a number of tombs. The authors seem interested in the whole sweep of the cemetery from the haphazard rows of the oldest section to the ordered ranks of modern headstones in the newest. It is the arrangement, or shift in arrangement, that most concerns them.

Arrangement is an abstract concept, and we should remember that description is not limited to people or things that can be perceived directly by the physical senses. Description may also convey ideas: the proportions of a building, the style of a baseball player, the infinitude of space. Our first description of cemeteries, in fact, moves from the concrete to the abstract because it was written to support ideas. It is part of a sociological study of cemeteries as they reveal changing American attitudes toward death, family, and society. The authors take their "relaxing walk" not because they want to examine individual tombstones but because they want to generalize from a multitude of physical evidence. As reporters, they stand between us and the actual objects they tell about.

By contrast, the movement of the Updike passage is from the general to the particular. Starting where the other leaves off—with a field of glossy modern slabs—it focuses quickly upon the new-dug graves and then narrows even more sharply to a single grave kept fresh in the author's memory. This time the adjectives are CONCRETE: "raw," "unhealed," "humped," "withered," "hurried," "close," "dark." The nouns are concrete too: "sod" and "earth" give way to the "space" lined with satin. Death is no abstraction for Updike; it is the suffocating loss of personal life. Updike makes us experience the finality of death by recreating his own sensations of claustrophobia at his grandfather's funeral.

Different as they are, these two passages illustrate a single peculiarity of description as a mode: it seldom stands alone. As in our first example, "scientific" description shades easily into exposition. As in our second, "evocative" description shades just as easily into narration. The authors of example number one describe the changes in a cemetery in order to explain (EXPOSITION) what those changes mean for American culture. After evoking his feelings about a past event, the author of example number two goes on in later lines to show what happened (NARRATION) when his reverie was interrupted by his son, who was learning to ride a bicycle in the peaceful cemetery. Which kind of description is better—telling or showing, scientific or evocative? Neither is inherently better or worse than the other. The kind of description that a writer chooses depends upon what he wants to do with it.

Updike's reference to the "sutures" of "unhealed" turf suggests how easily description also falls into METAPHOR, SIMILE, and ANALOGY. This is hardly surprising, for we often describe a thing in everyday speech by telling what it is like. A thump in your closet at night sounds like an owl hitting a haystack. A crowd stirs like a jellyfish. The seams of turf on new graves are like the stitches binding a human wound.

The ease with which description shifts into other MODES does not mean that a good description has no unity or order of its own, however. When writing description, keep in mind that every detail should contribute to a dominant impression, mood, or purpose. The dominant impression he wanted to convey when describing his grandfather's funeral, says Updike, was "the foreverness, the towering foreverness." Updike creates this impression by moving from the outside to the inside of the grave. Depending upon the object or place you are describing, you may want to move from the inside out, from left to right, top to bottom, or front to back. Whatever arrangement you choose, present the details of your description systematically; but do not call so much attention to your system of organization that it dominates the thing you are describing.

What impression, mood, or purpose is your description intended to serve? What specific objects can contribute to it? What do they look, feel, smell, taste, or sound like? Does your object or place suggest any natural order of presentation? These are the questions to ask when you begin a descriptive essay.

William Least Heat Moon
Driving Through Nevada

In March 20, 1978, William Trogdon stepped into his Econoline van with a sleeping bag, a camp stove, $450 in cash, and two books—Walt Whitman's Leaves of Grass and John Neihardt's Black Elk Speaks. Leaving behind a marriage and a job as an English professor at Stephens College in Missouri, Trogdon had begun his epic 14,000-mile trip along the back roads of America. His record of that journey was published in 1982 as Blue Highways, after the color of secondary roads on old maps. Part Osage, Trogdon had sometime before taken the Indian name that appears on the title page. "My father calls himself Heat Moon, my elder brother Little Heat Moon," Trogdon explains. "I, coming last, am therefore Least. It has been a long lesson of a name to learn." "Driving Through Nevada" (editor's title) is a complete chapter from Blue Highways. It describes the highway at night, the town of Ely, the Hotel Nevada, and one phase of the author's long journey into the self.

A third of the land mass of earth is desert of one kind or another. After my bout with the mountain, I found that a comforting statistic as I started across the Escalante Desert west of Cedar City. Utah 56 went at the sagebrush flats seriously, taking up big stretches before turning away from anything.

A car whipped past, the driver eating and a passenger clicking a camera. Moving without going anywhere, taking a trip instead of making one. I laughed at the absurdity of the photographs and then realized I, too, was rolling effortlessly along, turning the windshield into a movie screen in which I, the viewer, did the moving while the subject held still. That was the temptation of the American highway, of the American vacation (from the Latin *vacare*, "to be empty"). A woman in Texas had told me that she often threatened to write a book about her family vacations. Her title: *Zoom!* The drama of their trips, she said, occurred on the inside of the windshield with one family crisis after another. Her husband drove a thousand miles, much of it with his right arm over the backseat to hold down one of the children. She said, "Our vacations take us."

She longed for the true journey of an Odysseus or Ishmael or   3
Gulliver or even a Dorothy of Kansas,[1] wherein passage through space and time becomes only a metaphor of a movement through the interior of being. A true journey, no matter how long the travel takes, has no end. What's more, as John Le Carré, in speaking of the journey of death, said, "Nothing ever bridged the gulf between the man who went and the man who stayed behind."

Within a mile of the Nevada stateline, the rabbit brush and sage   4
stopped and a juniper forest began as the road ascended into cooler air. I was struck, as I had been many times, by the way land changes its character within a mile or two of a stateline. I turned north on U.S. 93, an empty highway running from Canada nearly to Mexico. I'm just guessing, but, for its great length, it must have fewer towns per mile than any other federal highway in the country. It goes, for example, the length of Nevada, more than five hundred miles, passing through only seventeen towns—and that's counting Jackpot and Contact.

Pioche, one of the seventeen, was pure Nevada. Its elevation of   5
six thousand feet was ten times its population; but during the peak of the mining boom a century ago, the people and the feet above sea level came to the same number. The story of Pioche repeats itself over Nevada: Indian shows prospector a mountain full of metal; prospector strikes bonanza; town booms for a couple of decades with the four "G's": grubstakes, gamblers, girls, gunmen (seventy-five people died in Pioche before anyone died a natural death); town withers. By 1900, Pioche was on its way to becoming a ghost town like Midas, Wonder, Bullion, Cornucopia. But, even

[1] These great travelers of literature appear, respectively, in Homer's *Odyssey*, Herman Melville's *Moby-Dick*, Jonathan Swift's *Gulliver's Travels*, and Frank Baum's *The Wizard of Oz*. John Le Carré writes spy thrillers that are also journeys of consciousness.

with the silver and gold gone, technological changes in the forties made deposits of lead and zinc valuable, and cheap power from Boulder Dam (as it was then) kept Pioche alive.

A citizen boasted to me about their "Million Dollar Courthouse"—a plain yet pleasing century-old fieldstone building sitting high on the mountainside—albeit a little cynically, since construction cost a fraction of that; but through compound interest and refinancing, the price finally hit a million. The courthouse was condemned three years before the mortgage was paid off.

6

The highway went down into a narrow and immensely long, thunder-of-hooves valley, then, like a chalkline, headed north, running between two low mountain ranges, the higher eastern one still in snow. A sign: NEXT GAS 80 MILES. In the dusk, the valley showed no evidence of man other than wire fences, highway, and occasional deer-crossing signs that looked like medieval heraldic devices: on a field of ochre, a stag rampant, sable. The signs had been turned into colanders by gunners, almost none of whom hit the upreared bucks.

7

Squat clumps of white sage, wet from a shower out of the western range, sweetened the air, and gulches had not yet emptied. Calm lay over the uncluttered openness, and a damp wind blew everything clean. I saw no one. I let my speed build to sixty, cut the ignition, shifted to neutral. Although Ghost Dancing[2] had the aerodynamics of an orange crate, it coasted for more than a mile across the flats. When it came to a standstill, I put it back in gear and left it at roadside. There was no one. Listening, I walked into the scrub. The desert does its best talking at night, but on that spring evening it kept God's whopping silence; and that too is a desert voice.

8

I've read that a naked eye can see six thousand stars in the hundred billion galaxies, but I couldn't believe it, what with the sky white with starlight. I saw a million stars with one eye and two million with both. Galileo proved that the rotation and revolution of the earth give stars their apparent movements. But on that night his evidence wouldn't hold. Any sensible man, lying on his back among new leaves of sage, in the warm sand that had already dried, even he could see Arcturus and Vega and Betelgeuse just above, not

9

2 The name of the van in which the author made his journey through America.

far at all, wheeling about the earth. Their paths cut arcs, and there was no doubt about it.

The immensity of sky and desert, their vast absences, reduced   10
me. It was as if I were evaporating, and it was calming and cleansing to be absorbed by that vacancy. Whitman says:

> O *to realize space!*
> *The plenteousness of all, that there are no bounds,*
> *To emerge and be of the sky, of the sun and moon and*
>   *flying clouds,*
> *as one with them.*

On the highway a car came and went, sounding a pitiful brief   11
whoosh as it ran the dark valley. When I drove back onto the road, I saw in the headlights a small desert rodent spin across the pavement as if on wheels; from the mountains, my little machine must have looked much the same. Ahead hung the Big Dipper with a million galaxies, they say, inside its cup, and on my port side, atop the western range, the evening star held a fixed position for miles until it swung slowly around in front of me and then back to port. I had followed a curve so long I couldn't see the bend. Only Vesper showed the truth. The highway joined U.S. 6—from Cape Cod to Long Beach, the longest federal route under one number in the days before interstates—then crossed the western mountains. Below lay the mining town of Ely.

Not everything that happens in Ely happens at the Hotel Ne-   12
vada, but it could. The old place is ready for it. But that night the blackjack tables were empty, the slots nearly so, and the marbelized mirrors reflected the bartender's slump and a waitress swallowing a yawn. Yet I did see these things:

Item: a woman, face as blank as a nickel slug, pulling dutifully   13
on the slot handles. She had stood before the gears so many times she herself had become a mechanism for reaching, dropping, pulling. Her eyes were dark and unmoving as if unplugged. The periodic jangle of change in the winner's cup moved her only to reach into the little coffer without looking and deposit the coins again.

Item: a man moseyed in wearing leather from head to toe;   14
attempting cowpuncher macho, he looked more like a two-legged first baseman's mitt. With him a bored blonde. "I'm a very com-

petitive person. I'm in it to win," he said, and the blonde yawned again.

Item: in a glass case hung a cross-section of bristlecone pine. At _15_ its center a card said 3000 B.C. BUILDING OF THE PYRAMIDS. A seedling today could be alive in the year 7000. That put a perspective on things.

Over another beer I watched faces that would be lucky to see _16_ A.D. 2000. When I left, a man in a white goatee whispered, "No games of chance, cowboy?"

"Haven't finished losing the first one," I said.   _17_

QUESTIONS

Understanding

1. What is the nature of the all-too-typical American vacation, according to William Least Heat Moon? How does he define a "true journey" (par. 3)?

2. In what way, as described by Moon, does Pioche resemble Ely (and a host of other towns in Nevada)? How is the courthouse like the town?

3. What abstract idea is Moon conveying when he pulls off the road to observe the heavens and when he quotes (par. 10) from Walt Whitman, the chief American poet of the self and the road?

4. Moon is on a journey of self-discovery in his solitary trek across the nation. What does he learn about the self on this starry night in Nevada?

5. What game of chance would you guess Moon is referring to in paragraph 17 when he declines to gamble with the man in the goatee?

Strategies and Structure

1. Around what physical object does Moon organize and unify most of this description of a night journey? In which paragraph does the author shift to another principle of organization? What word does he use to indicate the new system?

2. In which paragraph does Moon's traveler leave the highway? In which does he start on his journey again? How has his perception of the universe changed in the meantime?

3. A description must be presented from a definable vantage point or points. Find several passages in which Moon alters the physical relation (especially distance) between the perceiver and the universe in his descriptive essay. Upon what or whom is the author seeking new perspectives?

4. What is the function of the desert rodent in paragraph 11?

5. In paragraph 8 of his description, Moon draws upon most of the five senses. Go through the paragraph sentence by sentence and indicate where each is used.

6. What single sense dominates paragraph 9? The essay as a whole?

7. How does the author give his journey a sense of open-endednes? Where is he going as he leaves the hotel?

8. What is the dominant impression of Moon's description of the woman at the slot machine (par. 13)? How is that impression confirmed by our glimpse of the people in the next paragraph?

9. Moon's description of the Nevada nightscape is devoted more to space than time. By the use of what specific details does he nevertheless convey a sense of the vastness of time by human measure?

Words and Figures of Speech

1. The brief etymology in paragraph 2 is a stinging commentary on the American "vacation" as construed by Moon. Explain the aptness of the word from his perspective. Why is *Zoom!* (par. 2) such a good title in his view?

2. Moon's journey is a conceit, or extended metaphor, as defined among the FIGURES OF SPEECH in the Glossary at the end of this book. What is he comparing to what here? Why is it important that the journey have no end?

3. How appropriate do you find the ALLUSION to Whitman in paragraph 10? From what you know of Whitman's work, why might he of all American poets appeal to the author of this essay?

4. Consult your dictionary for the root meaning of *mortgage* (par. 6). Why is it IRONIC that the boom town died before the mortgage was paid off?

5. Why do you suppose Moon named his van "Ghost Dancing"?

Comparing

1. William Least Heat Moon and Barry Lopez ("My Horse," Chapter 7), ride similar steeds. Comment on their likenesses and on the common purposes they serve.

2. Contrast Moon's night journey with Mary Meban's wild daytime excursion in "The Back of the Bus" (Chapter 1). In what ways does Meban's public bus resemble the Hotel Nevada in Moon's essay?

Discussion and Writing Topics

1. Why do you suppose so many accounts of the self in America—from Huck Finn's *Adventures* to Steinbeck's *Travels with Charley*—have taken the form of a journey?

2. Spend an hour or so in a field, desert, or other natural region in which "nothing" is happening; make an itemized list of everything you see, hear, touch, taste, and smell there. Write an essay describing this "empty" place.

3. Write an essay about a journey of self-discovery you have made; link your insights closely to the physical setting of your journey.

Horace Miner

Body Ritual
among the Nacirema

*Horace Miner is professor of social anthropology at the University
of Michigan; he is an authority on African cultures. A native of
St. Paul, Minnesota, he studied at the University of Kentucky and
the University of Chicago (Ph.D., 1937). He joined the faculty
at Michigan in 1946 after teaching at Wayne State University
and serving in the wartime army. Miner is the author of* The
Primitive City of Timbuctoo *(1953);* Oasis and Casbah *(1960);
and* The City in Modern Africa *(1967). "Body Ritual among the
Nacirema" first appeared in* The American Anthropologist; *it
uses the methods and language of social anthropology to describe
a curious North American tribe. Professor Miner describes the
composition of the essay in "Writers on the Writing Process."*

The anthropologist has become so familiar with the diversity   1
of ways in which different peoples behave in similar situations
that he is not apt to be surprised by even the most exotic customs. In fact, if all of the logically possible combinations of
behavior have not been found somewhere in the world, he is
apt to suspect that they must be present in some yet unde-
scribed tribe. This point has, in fact, been expressed with
respect to clan organization by Murdock.[1] In this light, the
magical beliefs and practices of the Nacirema present such
unusual aspects that it seems desirable to describe them as an
example of the extremes to which human behavior can go.

   Professor Linton first brought the ritual of the Nacirema   2
to the attention of anthropologists twenty years ago, but the

[1] American anthropologist George Peter Murdock (b. 1897), authority ♠
on primitive cultures.

culture of this people is still very poorly understood. They are a North American group living in the territory between the Canadian Cree, the Yaqui and Tarahumare of Mexico, and the Carib and Arawak of the Antilles.[2] Little is known of their origin, although tradition states that they came from the east. . . .

Nacirema culture is characterized by a highly developed market   3
economy which has evolved in a rich natural habitat. While much of the people's time is devoted to economic pursuits, a large part of the fruits of these labors and a considerable portion of the day are spent in ritual activity. The focus of this activity is the human body, the appearance and health of which loom as a dominant concern in the ethos of the people. While such a concern is certainly not unusual, its ceremonial aspects and associated philosophy are unique.

The fundamental belief underlying the whole system appears to   4
be that the human body is ugly and that its natural tendency is to debility and disease. Incarcerated in such a body, man's only hope is to avert these characteristics through the use of the powerful influences of ritual and ceremony. Every household has one or more shrines devoted to this purpose. The more powerful individuals in the society have several shrines in their houses and, in fact, the opulence of a house is often referred to in terms of the number of such ritual centers it possesses. Most houses are of wattle and daub construction, but the shrine rooms of the more wealthy are walled with stone. Poorer families imitate the rich by applying pottery plaques to their shrine walls.

While each family has at least one such shrine, the rituals as-   5
sociated with it are not family ceremonies but are private and secret. The rites are normally only discussed with children, and then only during the period when they are being initiated into these mysteries. I was able, however, to establish sufficient rapport with the natives to examine these shrines and to have the rituals described to me.

The focal point of the shrine is a box or chest which is built   6
into the wall. In this chest are kept the many charms and magical potions without which no native believes he could live. These preparations are secured from a variety of specialized practitioners.

---

[2] Native American tribes formerly inhabiting the Saskatchewan region of Canada, the Sonora region of Mexico, and the West Indies.

The most powerful of these are the medicine men, whose assistance must be rewarded with substantial gifts. However, the medicine men do not provide the curative potions for their clients, but
decide what the ingredients should be and then write them down
in an ancient and secret language. This writing is understood only
by the medicine men and by the herbalists who, for another gift,
provide the required charm.

The charm is not disposed of after it has served its purpose, but   7
is placed in the charm-box of the household shrine. As these
magical materials are specific for certain ills, and the real or imagined maladies of the people are many, the charm-box is usually
full to overflowing. The magical packets are so numerous that
people forget what their purposes were and fear to use them again.
While the natives are very vague on this point, we can only
assume that the idea in retaining all the old magical materials is
that their presence in the charm-box, before which the body rituals
are conducted, will in some way protect the worshipper.

Beneath the charm-box is a small font. Each day every member   8
of the family, in succession, enters the shrine room, bows his head
before the charm-box, mingles different sorts of holy water in the
font, and proceeds with a brief rite of ablution. The holy waters
are secured from the Water Temple of the community, where the
priests conduct elaborate ceremonies to make the liquid ritually
pure.

In the hierarchy of magical practitioners, and below the medi-   9
cine men in prestige, are specialists whose designation is best translated "holy-mouth-men." The Nacirema have an almost pathological horror of and fascination with the mouth, the condition
of which is believed to have a supernatural influence on all social
relationships. Were it not for the rituals of the mouth, they
believe that their teeth would fall out, their gums bleed, their
jaws shrink, their friends desert them, and their lovers reject them.
They also believe that a strong relationship exists between oral
and moral characteristics. For example, there is a ritual ablution
of the mouth for children which is supposed to improve their
moral fiber.

The daily body ritual performed by everyone includes a mouth-   10
rite. Despite the fact that these people are so punctilious about
care of the mouth, this rite involves a practice which strikes the
uninitiated stranger as revolting. It was reported to me that the

ritual consists of inserting a small bundle of hog hairs into the mouth, along with certain magical powders, and then moving the bundle in a highly formalized series of gestures.

In addition to the private mouth-rite, the people seek out a [11] holy-mouth-man once or twice a year. These practitioners have an impressive set of paraphernalia, consisting of a variety of augers, awls, probes, and prods. The use of these objects in the exorcism of the evils of the mouth involves almost unbelievable ritual torture of the client. The holy-mouth-man opens the client's mouth and, using the above mentioned tools, enlarges any holes which decay may have created in the teeth. Magical materials are put into these holes. If there are not naturally occurring holes in the teeth, large sections of one or more teeth are gouged out so that the supernatural substance can be applied. In the client's view, the purpose of these ministrations is to arrest decay and to draw friends. The extremely sacred and traditional character of the rite is evident in the fact that the natives return to the holy-mouth-men year after year, despite the fact that their teeth continue to decay.

It is to be hoped that, when a thorough study of the Nacirema [12] is made, there will be careful inquiry into the personality structure of these people. One has but to watch the gleam in the eye of a holy-mouth-man, as he jabs an awl into an exposed nerve, to suspect that a certain amount of sadism is involved. If this can be established, a very interesting pattern emerges, for most of the population shows definite masochistic tendencies. It was to these that Professor Linton referred in discussing a distinctive part of the daily body ritual which is performed only by men. This part of the rite involves scraping and lacerating the surface of the face with a sharp instrument. Special women's rites are performed only four times during each lunar month, but what they lack in frequency is made up in barbarity. As part of this ceremony, women bake their heads in small ovens for about an hour. The theoretically interesting point is that what seems to be a preponderantly masochistic people have developed sadistic specialists.

The medicine men have an imposing temple, or *latipso*, in [13] every community of any size. The more elaborate ceremonies required to treat very sick patients can only be performed at this temple. These ceremonies involve not only the thaumaturge but a permanent group of vestal maidens who move sedately about the temple chambers in distinctive costume and headdress.

The *latipso* ceremonies are so harsh that it is phenomenal that [14] a fair proportion of the really sick natives who enter the temple ever recover. Small children whose indoctrination is still incomplete have been known to resist attempts to take them to the temple because "that is where you go to die." Despite this fact, sick adults are not only willing but eager to undergo the protracted ritual purification, if they can afford to do so. No matter how ill the supplicant or how grave the emergency, the guardians of many temples will not admit a client if he cannot give a rich gift to the custodian. Even after one has gained admission and survived the ceremonies, the guardians will not permit the neophyte to leave until he makes still another gift.

The supplicant entering the temple is first stripped of all his or [15] her clothes. In everyday life the Nacirema avoids exposure of his body and its natural functions. Bathing and excretory acts are performed only in the secrecy of the household shrine, where they are ritualized as part of the body-rites. Psychological shock results from the fact that body secrecy is suddenly lost upon entry into the *latipso*. A man, whose own wife has never seen him in an excretory act, suddenly finds himself naked and assisted by a vestal maiden while he performs his natural functions into a sacred vessel. This sort of ceremonial treatment is necessitated by the fact that the excreta are used by a diviner to ascertain the course and nature of the client's sickness. Female clients, on the other hand, find their naked bodies are subjected to the scrutiny, manipulation and prodding of the medicine men.

Few supplicants in the temple are well enough to do anything [16] but lie on their hard beds. The daily ceremonies, like the rites of the holy-mouth-men, involve discomfort and torture. With ritual precision, the vestals awaken their miserable charges each dawn and roll them about on their beds of pain while performing ablutions, in the formal movements of which the maidens are highly trained. At other times they insert magic wands in the supplicant's mouth or force him to eat substances which are supposed to be healing. From time to time the medicine men come to their clients and jab magically treated needles into their flesh. The fact that these temple ceremonies may not cure, and may even kill the neophyte, in no way decreases the people's faith in the medicine men.

There remains one other kind of practitioner, known as a   [17] "listener." This witchdoctor has the power to exorcise the devils that lodge in the heads of people who have been bewitched. The Nacirema believe that parents bewitch their own children. Mothers are particularly suspected of putting a curse on children while teaching them the secret body rituals. The counter-magic of the witchdoctor is unusual in its lack of ritual. The patient simply tells the "listener" all his troubles and fears, beginning with the earliest difficulties he can remember. The memory displayed by the Nacirema in these exorcism sessions is truly remarkable. It is not uncommon for the patient to bemoan the rejection he felt upon being weaned as a babe, and a few individuals even see their troubles going back to the traumatic effects of their own birth.

In conclusion, mention must be made of certain practices which   [18] have their base in native esthetics but which depend upon the pervasive aversion to the natural body and its functions. There are ritual fasts to make fat people thin and ceremonial feasts to make thin people fat. Still other rites are used to make women's breasts larger if they are small, and smaller if they are large. General dissatisfaction with breast shape is symbolized in the fact that the ideal form is virtually outside the range of human variation. A few women afflicted with almost inhuman hyper-mammary development are so idolized that they make a handsome living by simply going from village to village and permitting the natives to stare at them for a fee.

Reference has already been made to the fact that excretory   [19] functions are ritualized, routinized, and relegated to secrecy. Natural reproductive functions are similarly distorted. Intercourse is taboo as a topic and scheduled as an act. Efforts are made to avoid pregnancy by the use of magical materials or by limiting intercourse to certain phases of the moon. Conception is actually very infrequent. When pregnant, women dress so as to hide their condition. Parturition takes place in secret, without friends or relatives to assist, and the majority of women do not nurse their infants.

Our review of the ritual life of the Nacirema has certainly   [20] shown them to be a magic-ridden people. It is hard to understand how they have managed to exist so long under the burdens which they have imposed upon themselves. But even such exotic customs as these take on real meaning when they are viewed with the insight provided by Malinowski [3] when he wrote:

"Looking from far and above, from our high places of safety in   21
the developed civilization, it is easy to see all the crudity and irrelevance of magic. But without its power and guidance early man could not have mastered his practical difficulties as he has done, nor could man have advanced to the higher stages of civilization."

QUESTIONS

Understanding

1. Who are these strange people, the Nacirema? How did they get their name?

2. What are "shrine rooms" (par. 4) and "charm-boxes"(par. 7) used in the morning rituals of the Nacirema?

3. Why do the Nacirema put "hog hairs" (par. 10) in their mouths? What is the "ritual ablution of the mouth" (par. 9) believed to improve the moral fiber of children?

4. Who is the "listener" (par. 17), and why do the Nacirema think that "parents bewitch their own children" (par. 17)?

5. Having closely observed their private behavior, Miner concludes that the Nacirema base their body rituals on the belief that "the human body is ugly" (par. 4) in its natural state. Do you agree? Why or why not?

6. What is the "real meaning" (par. 20) of the Nacirema's exotic customs when viewed in the light of Malinowski's statement in paragraph 21?

Strategies and Structure

1. When did you first suspect that Miner is writing tongue-in-cheek? What specific details in his DESCRIPTION tipped you off?

2. From what perspective is Miner describing the Nacirema? How

[3] Bronislaw Kasper Malinowski (1884–1942), Polish-born anthropologist, who came to America in 1938.

do paragraphs 1, 3, and 21 help to establish his "cultural" and professional vantage point?

3. Descriptions often strive to make the strange seem familiar, but Miner's makes the familiar seem strange. Give several examples, and analyze how they reverse the usual procedure.

4. What is the serious purpose behind Miner's "joke"? Do you think a mock-scientific paper is an effective means of accomplishing that purpose? Why or why not?

5. A social anthropologist, Miner originally wrote his "study" for *The American Anthropologist*, a journal whose audience expected writing in their field to follow conventional forms. How does Miner give his essay the flavor of a scientific (as opposed to a "literary") article or report? Pay special attention to paragraphs 1–3 and 18–21.

6. How can Miner's essay be seen in any way to SATIRIZE the methods and language of social anthropology?

Words and Figures of Speech

1. Where did the Nacirema get the word *latipso* (par. 13) for their temples of the sick?

2. Miner's last paragraph could be considered a non-sequitur, or conclusion that does not logically follow from the evidence it is built upon. What is wrong, logically, with the quoted statement? Why might Miner choose to end his essay with this device?

3. What is a *thaumaturge* (par. 13)? Given his true subject, what is the effect of Miner's using that term and such related terms as *herbalist* (par. 6), *medicine men* (par. 6), *holy-mouth-men* (par. 9), and *diviner* (par. 15)?

4. For which one of these practitioners does Miner have to invent a name? What does the lack of a standard term for it in the language of anthropology suggest about this role in modern society?

5. Why do you think Miner uses such clinical terms as *excreta* (par. 15), *hyper-mammary* (par. 18), and *parturition* (par. 19)?

6. Consult your dictionary for any of the following words you do not already know: *ethos* (par. 3), *incarcerated* (4), *opulence* (4), *ablution* (8), *pathological* (9), *punctilious* (10), *paraphernalia* (11), *sadism* (12), *masochistic* (12), *supplicant* (14), *neophyte* (14), *scrutiny* (15), *aversion* (18), *taboo* (19), *parturition* (19).

Comparing

1. Both Miner and Russell Baker ("A Nice Place to Visit," Chapter 6) describe "alien" cultures. What does the language of both "interpreters" have in common?

2. How does Miner's perspective here resemble Jeremy Rifkin's in "The Christian World View" in Chapter 5?

3. Miner's irony is similar to Jonathan Swift's in "A Modest Proposal" ("Essays For Further Reading"); when you read Swift, ask yourself how the speakers in the two essays resemble each other.

Discussion and Writing Topics

1. Describe other rituals of the Nacirema—for example, those associated with wearing clothes and with transportation—that bear out Miner's findings about the tribe's distaste for the human body.

2. Although Miner says that the Nacirema have a "highly developed market economy" (par. 3), he says little about it. Describe their "economic pursuits" (par. 3) in such a way as to "prove" that these people who find the body ugly nevertheless find treasure beautiful.

3. Describe a barber or beauty shop or an exercise salon as if you were seeing one for the first time and so did not know the names or purposes of anything. Make up descriptive names for people and objects and assign causes according to the surface appearance of events.

Richard Selzer

The Discus Thrower

Richard Selzer is a surgeon. From his native Troy, New York, he attended Union College and Albany Medical College (M.D., 1953). After postdoctoral study at Yale, he entered private practice in 1960. A fellow of Ezra Stiles College of Yale University, he also teaches surgery at Yale Medical School. Selzer has contributed stories and essays to Harper's, Esquire, Redbook, Mademoiselle, and other popular magazines. His Rituals of Surgery, a collection of short stories, appeared in 1974. Selzer is best known for his essays of the doctor's life, some of which are collected in Mortal Lessons (1977) and Confessions of a Knife (1979). He is now at work on more essays and stories and on a mythological treatment of the Civil War. "The Discus Thrower" was published in Harper's with the subtitle "Do Not Go Gentle"; it describes a terminally ill patient in a bare hospital room. Dr. Selzer's own description of writing the essay is to be found at the end of the chapter.

I spy on my patients. Ought not a doctor to observe his patients by any means and from any stance, that he might the more fully assemble evidence? So I stand in the doorways of hospital rooms and gaze. Oh, it is not all that furtive an act. Those in bed need only look up to discover me. But they never do.

From the doorway of Room 542 the man in the bed seems deeply tanned. Blue eyes and close-cropped white hair give him the appearance of vigor and good health. But I know that his skin is not brown from the sun. It is rusted, rather, in the last stage of containing the vile repose within. And the blue eyes are frosted, looking inward like the windows of a snowbound cottage. This man is blind. This man is also leg-

274

less—the right leg missing from midthigh down, the left from just below the knee. It gives him the look of a bonsai, roots and branches pruned into the dwarfed facsimile of a great tree.

Propped on pillows, he cups his right thigh in both hands. Now 3 and then he shakes his head as though acknowledging the intensity of his suffering. In all of this he makes no sound. Is he mute as well as blind?

The room in which he dwells is empty of all possessions—no 4 get-well cards, small, private caches of food, day-old flowers, slippers, all the usual kickshaws of the sickroom. There is only the bed, a chair, a nightstand, and a tray on wheels that can be swung across his lap for meals.

"What time is it?" he asks. 5
"Three o'clock." 6
"Morning or afternoon?" 7
"Afternoon." 8
He is silent. There is nothing else he wants to know. 9
"How are you?" I say. 10
"Who is it?" he asks. 11
"It's the doctor. How do you feel?" 12
He does not answer right away. 13
"Feel?" he says. 14
"I hope you feel better," I say. 15
I press the button at the side of the bed. 16
"Down you go," I say. 17
"Yes, down," he says. 18
He falls back upon the bed awkwardly. His stumps, unweighted 19 by legs and feet, rise in the air, presenting themselves. I unwrap the bandages from the stumps, and begin to cut away the black scabs and the dead, glazed fat with scissors and forceps. A shard of white bone comes loose. I pick it away. I wash the wounds with disinfectant and redress the stumps. All this while, he does not speak. What is he thinking behind those lids that do not blink? Is he remembering a time when he was whole? Does he dream of feet? Of when his body was not a rotting log?

He lies solid and inert. In spite of everything, he remains im- 20 pressive, as though he were a sailor standing athwart a slanting deck.

"Anything more I can do for you?" I ask. 21

For a long moment he is silent.   22

"Yes," he says at last and without the least irony. "You can   23
bring me a pair of shoes."

In the corridor, the head nurse is waiting for me.   24

"We have to do something about him," she says. "Every morn-   25
ing he orders scrambled eggs for breakfast, and, instead of eating
them, he picks up the plate and throws it against the wall."

"Throws his plate?"   26

"Nasty. That's what he is. No wonder his family doesn't come   27
to visit. They probably can't stand him any more than we can."

She is waiting for me to do something.   28

"Well?"   29

"We'll see," I say.   30

The next morning I am waiting in the corridor when the   31
kitchen delivers his breakfast. I watch the aide place the tray on
the stand and swing it across his lap. She presses the button to
raise the head of the bed. Then she leaves.

In time the man reaches to find the rim of the tray, then on to   32
find the dome of the covered dish. He lifts off the cover and places
it on the stand. He fingers across the plate until he probes the
eggs. He lifts the plate in both hands, sets it on the palm of his
right hand, centers it, balances it. He hefts it up and down
slightly, getting the feel of it. Abruptly, he draws back his right
arm as far as he can.

There is the crack of the plate breaking against the wall at the   33
foot of his bed and the small wet sound of the scrambled eggs
dropping to the floor.

And then he laughs. It is a sound you have never heard. It is   34
something new under the sun. It could cure cancer.

Out in the corridor, the eyes of the head nurse narrow.   35

"Laughed, did he?"   36

She writes something down on her clipboard.   37

A second aide arrives, brings a second breakfast tray, puts it on   38
the nightstand, out of his reach. She looks over at me shaking her
head and making her mouth go. I see that we are to be accomplices.

"I've got to feed you," she says to the man.   39

"Oh, no you don't," the man says.   40

"Oh, yes I do," the aide says, "after the way you just did. Nurse   41
says so."

"Get me my shoes," the man says. 42

"Here's oatmeal," the aide says. "Open." And she touches the 43
spoon to his lower lip.

"I ordered scrambled eggs," says the man. 44

"That's right," the aide says. 45

I step forward. 46

"Is there anything I can do?" I say. 47

"Who are you?" the man asks. 48

In the evening I go once more to that ward to make my rounds. 49
The head nurse reports to me that Room 542 is deceased. She
has discovered this quite by accident, she says. No, there had been
no sound. Nothing. It's a blessing, she says.

I go into his room, a spy looking for secrets. He is still there in 50
his bed. His face is relaxed, grave, dignified. After a while, I turn
to leave. My gaze sweeps the wall at the foot of the bed, and I see
the place where it has been repeatedly washed, where the wall
looks very clean and very white.

QUESTIONS

Understanding

1. Why does Selzer's dying patient throw his breakfast against the
   wall?

2. What is the significance of the patient's repeatedly calling for
   shoes? Of his reminding the aide in paragraph 44 that he had
   ordered scrambled eggs?

3. Selzer says that the discus thrower is "impressive" (par. 19) despite his mutilation. Why is he impressive to the doctor?

4. What is the significance of the patient's question about time in
   paragraph 7?

5. What attitude is revealed by the doctor's questions to his patient?
   What is revealed by the dying patient's responses, "Who is it?"
   (par. 11) and "Who are you?" (par. 48)?

6. How might the doctor's response to the nurse (par. 30) be interpreted to carry the "mortal lesson" of Selzer's entire essay?

Strategies and Structure

1. The doctor's role throughout this essay is to DESCRIBE without interpreting. How is this role anticipated in paragraph 1? Why do you think Selzer adopts it?

2. How does the doctor's physical stance during much of the essay contribute to the POINT OF VIEW from which it is told?

3. Selzer's essay alternates between dialogue and description, with little commentary on the meaning of what he describes. Point out the few passages of actual commentary or interpretation. Would Selzer's essay have been more or less successful with more such commentary? Explain your answer.

4. Analyze the TONE of Selzer's description of dressing his patient's stumps in paragraph 19. How well does the tone comport with the doctor's role throughout the essay?

5. How does Selzer avoid sentimentality in his description of the dying man?

6. Describe the function of the head nurse in this essay.

7. What is the effect of Selzer's using the second PERSON "you" in paragraph 34?

8. Why does Selzer end his essay with a reference to the wall?

Words and Figures of Speech

1. An *epithet* is a descriptive title or name for a person, such as "giant-killer" for Jack in the fairy tale. What are the implications of Selzer's main epithet for this patient?

2. Why is the "rotting log" METAPHOR appropriate (par. 19)?

3. The second nurse's aide and the doctor are said to be "accomplices" (par. 38). What does this term CONNOTE? Why does Selzer use it? What similar term does he use in paragraph 1?

4. A *kickshaw* (par. 4) is a trinket or other little gift, often of food. What does Selzer's reference to kickshaws show about his patient? About the doctor?

5. HYPERBOLE is exaggeration. How effective is Selzer's use of this figure of speech in paragraph 34? Explain your answer.

6. Selzer's alternate title, or subtitle, for "The Discus Thrower" is "Do Not Go Gentle," an ALLUSION to the Dylan Thomas poem,

"Do Not Go Gentle into That Good Night." Find a copy of the poem in your school library and explain why Selzer refers to it.

Comparing

1. Both Selzer's essay and the next one (by Virginia Woolf), deal with death; but Woolf's essay, you will find, includes much more commentary on what it describes. What accounts for this difference, and how does it influence our response in each case?
2. What attitudes (both physical and intellectual) does the speaker in Selzer's essay share with the speaker in Lewis Thomas's "On Societies as Organisms" (Chapter 7)?

Discussion and Writing Topics

1. Write a description of a person in a place or situation that is characteristic of him or her. Use dialogue to support your description.
2. Describe the "kickshaws" of any sickroom or rooms with which you have been acquainted. Try to suggest the emotions that those objects represent or fail to represent.
3. Define and describe the role of the physician, as you see it, after his or her patient is beyond the help of medicine.

Virginia Woolf

The Death of the Moth

Virginia Woolf (1882–1941), the distinguished novelist, was the
daughter of Leslie Stephen, a Victorian literary critic. She became the center of the "Bloomsbury Group" of writers and artists
that flourished in London from about 1907 to 1930. Terrified by
the return of her recurring mental depression, she drowned herself
in the river Ouse near her home at Rodmell, England. The
Voyage Out (1915), Mrs. Dalloway (1925), To the Lighthouse
(1927), Orlando (1928), and The Waves (1931) are among the
works with which she helped to alter the course of the English
novel. Today she is recognized as a psychological novelist especially gifted at exploring the minds of her female characters.
"The Death of the Moth" is the title essay of a collection published soon after her suicide; it describes "a tiny bead of pure
life."

Moths that fly by day are not properly to be called moths;   1
they do not excite that pleasant sense of dark autumn nights
and ivy-blossom which the commonest yellow underwing
asleep in the shadow of the curtain never fails to rouse in us.
They are hybrid creatures, neither gay like butterflies nor
sombre like their own species. Nevertheless the present specimen, with his narrow hay-coloured wings, fringed with a tassel
of the same colour, seemed to be content with life. It was a
pleasant morning, mid-September, mild, benignant, yet with
a keener breath than that of the summer months. The plough
was already scoring the field opposite the window, and where
the share had been, the earth was pressed flat and gleamed
with moisture. Such vigour came rolling in from the fields

and the down beyond that it was difficult to keep the eyes strictly turned upon the book. The rooks too were keeping one of their annual festivities; soaring round the tree-tops until it looked as if a vast net with thousands of black knots in it has been cast up into the air; which, after a few moments sank slowly down upon the trees until every twig seemed to have a knot at the end of it. Then, suddenly, the net would be thrown into the air again in a wider circle this time, with the utmost clamour and vociferation, as though to be thrown into the air and settle slowly down upon the tree-tops were a tremendously exciting experience.

The same energy which inspired the rooks, the ploughmen, the horses, and even, it seemed, the lean bare-backed downs, sent the moth fluttering from side to side of his square of the window-pane. One could not help watching him. One was, indeed, conscious of a queer feeling of pity for him. The possibilities of pleasure seemed that morning so enormous and so various that to have only a moth's part in life, and a day moth's at that, appeared a hard fate, and his zest in enjoying his meagre opportunities to the full, pathetic. He flew vigorously to one corner of his compartment, and, after waiting there a second, flew across to the other. What remained for him but to fly to a third corner and then to a fourth? That was all he could do, in spite of the size of the downs, the width of the sky, the far-off smoke of houses, and the romantic voice, now and then, of a steamer out at sea. What he could do he did. Watching him, it seemed as if a fiber, very thin but pure, of the enormous energy of the world had been thrust into his frail and diminutive body. As often as he crossed the pane, I could fancy that a thread of vital light became visible. He was little or nothing but life.

Yet, because he was so small, and so simple a form of the energy that was rolling in at the open window and driving its way through so many narrow and intricate corridors in my own brain and in those of other human beings, there was something marvelous as well as pathetic about him. It was as if someone had taken a tiny bead of pure life and decking it as lightly as possible with down and feathers, had set it dancing and zigzagging to show us the true nature of life. Thus displayed one could not get over the strangeness of it. One is apt to forget all about life, seeing it humped and bossed and garnished and cumbered so that it has to move with the greatest circumspection and dignity. Again, the thought

of all that life might have been had he been born in any other
shape caused one to view his simple activities with a kind of pity.

After a time, tired by his dancing apparently, he settled on the   4
window ledge in the sun, and the queer spectacle being at an end,
I forgot about him. Then, looking up, my eye was caught by him.
He was trying to resume his dancing, but seemed either so stiff
or so awkward that he could only flutter to the bottom of the
window-pane; and when he tried to fly across it he failed. Being
intent on other matters I watched these futile attempts for a time
without thinking, unconsciously waiting for him to resume his
flight, as one waits for a machine, that has stopped momentarily,
to start again without considering the reason for its failure. After
perhaps a seventh attempt he slipped from the wooden ledge and·
fell, fluttering his wings, on to his back on the window-sill. The
helplessness of his attitude roused me. It flashed upon me that he
was in difficulties; he could no longer raise himself; his legs
struggled vainly. But, as I stretched out a pencil, meaning to help
him to right himself, it came over me that the failure and awkwardness were the approach of death. I laid the pencil down again.

The legs agitated themselves once more. I looked as if for the   5
enemy against which he struggled. I looked out of doors. What
had happened there? Presumably it was midday, and work in the
fields had stopped. Stillness and quiet had replaced the previous
animation. The birds had taken themselves off to feed in the
brooks. The horses stood still. Yet the power was there all the
same, massed outside indifferent, impersonal, not attending to
anything in particular. Somehow it was opposed to the little hay-
coloured moth. It was useless to try to do anything. One could
only watch the extraordinary efforts made by those tiny legs
against an oncoming doom which could, had it chosen, have sub-
merged an entire city, not merely a city, but masses of human
beings; nothing, I knew, had any chance against death. Nevertheless after a pause of exhaustion the legs fluttered again. It was
superb this last protest, and so frantic that he succeeded at last in
righting himself. One's sympathies, of course, were all on the side
of life. Also, when there was nobody to care or to know, this
gigantic effort on the part of an insignificant little moth, against
a power of such magnitude, to retain what no one else valued or
desired to keep, moved one strangely. Again, somehow, one saw
life, a pure bead. I lifted the pencil again, useless though I knew it

to be. But even as I did so, the unmistakable tokens of death showed themselves. The body relaxed, and instantly grew stiff. The struggle was over. The insignificant little creature now knew death. As I looked at the dead moth, this minute wayside triumph of so great a force over so mean an antagonist filled me with wonder. Just as life had been strange a few minutes before, so death was now as strange. The moth having righted himself now lay most decently and uncomplainingly composed. O yes, he seemed to say, death is stronger than I am.

QUESTIONS

Understanding

1. The author of this essay is describing much more than just an insect. What is the true object of her studied observation? What name does she give it in paragraph 3?

2. What does Woolf's tiny moth have in common with the rooks, ploughmen, horses, and fields? Why does the moth's dance seem "strange" (par. 3) to Woolf?

3. If "the true nature of life" (par. 3) is animation, or mere movement, what is the essence of death as Woolf describes it?

4. What role is the speaker in Woolf's essay vainly assuming when she starts to interpose a pencil between the moth and death? Why does she tell us so little about who or what set the moth dancing in the first place?

Strategies and Structure

1. Woolf's essay opens with a DESCRIPTION of moths in general. In which sentence does she begin to describe a particular moth? Through what specific details?

2. How does Woolf use the window to help organize her description?

3. Paragraphs 1 and 3 picture the same scene outside Woolf's window. How has the picture altered in the second version? How does she convey the change?

4. What is the observer in this essay doing when she is not watching the moth or looking out the window?

5. Approximately how much time elapses during the course of this essay? How does Woolf indicate the passage of time?

6. What time of year is Woolf describing here? How does she give us a sense of the season?

7. At first, the speaker in this essay feels pity for the limitations of the moth's life. When the moth struggles against death at the end, how has her attitude changed?

8. Woolf does not use the first PERSON until she says (almost half-way through her essay), "I could fancy that a thread of vital light became visible" (par. 2). What effect does she achieve with such phrases as "in us," "the eyes," "one was," and "one could" (pars. 1 and 2)?

Words and Figures of Speech

1. Paragraph 3 describes the moth's "down and feathers." Why does Woolf choose to "deck" her specimen in the lightest of garments? What property or quality is expressed by "humped," "bossed," "garnished," and "cumbered" (also in par. 3)?

2. Which of the following possible definitions of *vigor* (par. 1) best fits the content of Woolf's essay: 1) physical or mental strength; 2) healthy growth; 3) intensity or force; 4) validity? Explain your choice.

3. Why does Woolf use the METAPHOR of the dance to describe the moth's frantic movements? How does the moth's dance resemble the flight of the rooks?

Comparing

1. Which essay—Woolf's or Annie Dillard's in "The Writing Process"—do you find more effective as a description of a physical phenomenon? Explain your preference.

2. Woolf equates the moth's life with movement; to what does Dillard compare the "moth-essence" in "Transfiguration"? Which of the two essays seems more "religious"? Why?

Discussion and Writing Topics

1. Describe a pond, a dance, a journey, or a mountain as an emblem of life or one of life's phases.
2. Have you ever been tempted to interfere with a natural process or to save some animal from a natural enemy? Describe what you did and how you felt.

Writers on the Writing Process:
Richard Selzer and Horace Miner

"The Discus Thrower," says Richard Selzer, is "based on an actual patient. The events really did take place." When he is not writing, Dr. Selzer's time is devoted to "the multitude of the sick and those who tend them." "The Discus Thrower" was intended as a tribute to one of these. "I wanted," he writes, "to portray the character as a kind of defiant hero who refuses to accept his fate politely and who summons up his manhood in an act of rebellion." Between such events and the printed page, Dr. Selzer considers himself "but their conduit."

The flow is hardly automatic. In this case the author remembers "endless" rewriting. The overall form of the essay, in particular, gave him trouble. It was only after a struggle that he "lit upon the device of four appointments." Why this form of organization? Because it seemed "congenial" and "because doctors do have appointments with their patients."

The "major difficulty" that Richard Selzer encountered in the composition of his essay was not a matter of structure, however. It was "the portrayal of the nurse. I do not see nurses as insensitive. Not at all. But it seemed necessary for literary purposes to cast her in the role of villainess."

When did he hit upon the title? The title came "afterwards," he says. "It is an ironic title, isn't it? What conjoins the blind amputee and the discus thrower is the act of hurling. One is in the very prime of youth and vigor; the other a mere remnant, but no less a contestant."

What about the *language* of the piece? "The language is 'high,'" according to the author, "because the subject is high. Metaphor abounds in the few descriptive passages. The rest is terse, clipped, almost monosyllabic dialogue, used to heighten the dramatic effect. Each phrase, word even, was selected and arranged for powerful effect."

Was such attention to language paid with the reader in mind? The reader is primary in Selzer's view. "I try to write so that the reader will taste my voice at the back of his throat." 6

Other motives for writing? "I write about misery in order to endear it. I write to exorcise my demons by making something beautiful and strong." 7

And what about that blank spot on the wall at the end of this case history? "Here, the patient is victorious over his diminution and death. The spot on the wall is clean and white next to the rest, which is merely gray." 8

Dr. Selzer is a surgeon writing for a general audience of nonspecialists. A professional anthropologist, the author of "The Nacirema," on the other hand, originally intended his essay for a limited readership. "I write," Professor Miner confides, "to communicate with professional colleagues, and the piece was written for publication in *The American Anthropologist*, the principal journal of my profession." 9

One message of "The Nacirema" (pronounced, he explains, Nah-se-ray-mah) is that the cultural biases of an outside observer tend to color not only how the observer looks at an alien culture but also what he or she sees. This is a message of special interest to anthropologists; but by making America the primitive culture of his "study," Miner found that "what I had to say to my colleagues happened to have a much wider audience." As it turned out, he notes, "Americans, generally, found it amusing." 10

Over the years, says Miner, "my manner of writing has not changed." What is that manner? "As for how I write," says Miner, "I only do so when I think I have something new to say and have a rough idea in mind of the general structure of what I want to say. Of course, new relevant material occurs to me as I write." 11

What about rewriting? Does he revise as he goes or later, in a separate stage? "I normally do it as I progress. It seems to me that I should not move on to new ideas (paragraphs) until I have said what I want to say as clearly and effectively as possible." 12

What then? "Finally, I ask my wife to read and comment on my draft. She has a Ph.D. in Germanics, but has been a partner in all my field work." 13

WRITING TOPICS for Chapter Eight
Essays That Appeal to the Senses

Describe one of the following:

1. The oldest person you know

2. Your dream house

3. The place you associate most closely with family vacations

4. A ghost town or dying neighborhood you have visited

5. A shipyard, dock, or harbor you have seen

6. The worst storm you can remember and its aftermath

7. A room in a hospital or rest home

8. An old-fashioned general store, hardware store, or drugstore

9. A carnival or fair

10. A building, street, or town that has given you a glimpse of foreign culture

11. A statue that seems out of place to you

12. A tropical garden

13. The waiting room of a bus or train station

14. The main reading room of a public library

15. An expensive sporting goods store

16. A factory or plant you have worked in or visited

17. A well-run farm

18. A junkyard

Persuasion and Argumentation

9

Essays That
Appeal to Reason

PERSUASION [1] is the strategic use of language to move an audience to action or belief. In persuasive writing, readers can
be moved in three ways: (1) by appealing to their reason;
(2) by appealing to their emotions; and (3) by appealing to
their sense of ethics (their standards of what constitutes
proper behavior). The first of these, often called ARGUMEN-
TATION, is discussed in this chapter; the other two will be
taken up in Chapter 10.

Argumentation, as the term is used here, refers both to
logical thinking and to the expression of that thought in
such a way as to convince others to accept it. Argumentation, in other words, analyzes a subject or problem in order
to induce belief. It may or may not go on to urge a course of
action. Whether they induce action or belief or both, however,
persuasive arguments appeal through logic to our capacity to
reason. There are two basic kinds of logical reasoning: IN-
DUCTION and DEDUCTION. When we deduce something, we
reason from general premises to particular conclusions.
When we reason by induction, we proceed the other way—
from particulars to generalities.

In Edgar Allan Poe's "The Murders in the Rue Morgue," master detective Auguste Dupin is investigating two brutal killings.
One victim has been jammed up a chimney further than the
strength of a normal man could have shoved her; the other lies in
the courtyard below. Dupin notices a lightning-rod extending from
the courtyard past the victims' window, but it is too far for an escaping man to negotiate. Putting these and other particulars together, Dupin reasons inductively that the murderer is not a man

[1] Terms printed in all capitals are defined in the Glossary.

but a giant ape. Yet how did the animal escape?—the two windows of the apartment are nailed shut and the doors are locked from the inside. Reasoning deductively now, Dupin begins with the premise that a "material" killer—not the supernatural agent the authorities half-suspect—must have "escaped materially." Thus the closed windows must have the power of closing themselves: Dupin examines one window and finds a hidden spring; but the nail fastening the window is still intact. Therefore, Dupin reasons, the ape "must have escaped through the other window" and "there must be found a difference between the nails." Dupin examines the nail in the second window and, sure enough, it is broken; outside, moreover, hangs a shutter on which the animal could have swung to the lightning-rod. Dupin advertises for the owner of a missing orangutang, and that very night, a sailor appears at his door.

Inductive reasoning, then, depends upon examples—like the minute clues that lead Poe's Dupin to suspect an orangutang—and in many cases the validity of an inductive argument increases as the sheer number of examples increases. We are more likely to believe that UFOs exist if they have been sighted by ten thousand witnesses than by one thousand. In a short essay we seldom have room for more than a few examples, however. (You will be surprised how often they are reduced to the "magic" number three.) So we must select the most telling and representative ones.

Deductive reasoning depends upon the "syllogism." Here is Aristotle's famous example of this basic pattern of logical thinking:

Major premise: All men are mortal.
Minor premise: Socrates is a man.
Conclusion: Therefore, Socrates is mortal.

If we grant Aristotle's major assumption that all men must die and his minor (or narrower) assumption that Socrates is a man, the conclusion follows inevitably that Socrates must die. (Since Socrates had died about fifteen years before Aristotle was born, Aristotle was reasonably confident that his example would not be seriously challenged.)

When a conclusion follows from the premises or (in inductive reasoning) from the examples, we say that the argument is "valid." An invalid argument is one that jumps to conclusions: the conclusion does not follow logically from the premises or examples. Inductive arguments (from particulars to generalizations) are often invalid because they use too few examples, because the examples are not representative, or because the examples depend upon faulty authorities or faulty comparisons of the sort the Duchess makes in Lewis Carroll's Alice in Wonderland. In your own reasoning, strive to think like Alice:

> "Very true," said the Duchess: "flamingoes and mustard both bite. And the moral of that is—'Birds of a feather flock together.' "
> "Only mustard isn't a bird," Alice remarked.
> "Right, as usual," said the Duchess: "what a clear way you have of putting things!"

A deductive argument may be valid without being true, of course. Consider this valid argument by satirist Ambrose Bierce:

> Major Premise: Sixty men can do a piece of work sixty times as quickly as one man.
> Minor Premise: One man can dig a posthole in sixty seconds; therefore—
> Conclusion: Sixty men can dig a posthole in one second.

As Bierce was aware, this argument is valid but untrue. It would get too crowded around that posthole for efficiency. The trouble here, and with all deductive arguments that are valid but untrue, is a faulty premise. Sixty men cannot do work sixty times as fast as one if they have no place to stand. We can see why Bierce's Devil's Dictionary defines the syllogism as a "logical formula consisting of a major and a minor assumption and an inconsequent." The syllogism provides a manner for thinking logically; but as Bierce's irony would warn us, it does not provide the matter of logical thought. We have to supply that ourselves.

In real-life persuasive arguments, we seldom use the formal syllogism. We are much more likely to assert, "If one man can dig a posthole in sixty seconds, sixty men can do it in one." Or: "You know he is an atheist because he doesn't go to church." We can meet such faulty arguments more effectively if we realize that they are abbreviated syllogisms with one premise left unsaid. Stated as a formal syllogism, our second example would look like this:

> Major premise: All people who do not go to church are atheists.
> Minor premise: He does not go to church.
> Conclusion: Therefore, he is an atheist.

The implied premise here is the major premise: "All people who do not go to church are atheists." Usually the implied premise is the weak spot in your opponent's argument. If you can challenge it, your own position has won an excellent foothold.

Most extended debates in real life arise because the parties disagree over the truth or untruth of one or more primary assumptions. "The U.S. should stay out of South American affairs." "Inflation will drop sharply next year." "All women should work." Propositions like these cannot be assumed; they must be debated. But in your own persuasive writing, be sure of your logic first. If it can be shown that your conclusions do not follow from your premises, the debate will be over before the crucial issue of truth can be raised.

In a short essay, you should not depend rigidly upon logical forms, and you cannot hope to prove anything worth proving to an absolute certainty. But an argumentative essay does not have to prove, remember. It has only to convince. Be as convincing as you reasonably can by appealing to your audience's reason.

Thomas Jefferson

The Declaration of Independence

The third American president, Thomas Jefferson (1743–1826) was born in Virginia, attended William and Mary College, and practiced law for several years. He entered local politics in 1769, was elected to the Continental Congress, and drafted the Declaration of Independence in 1776. After serving as Virginia's governor during the revolution, he became American minister to France and later Washington's secretary of state. His conflict with Alexander Hamilton contributed to the formation of separate political parties in America. Jefferson became vice-president of the United States in 1796 and president in 1801. During the first (and more successful) of his two terms, he engineered the Louisiana Purchase. Retiring to his estate, Monticello, in 1809, he died there on the fiftieth anniversary of American independence, July 4, 1826. Jefferson preferred the role of the philosopher to that of the politician, and the Declaration of Independence, which announced the thirteen colonies' break with England, was as much an essay on human rights as a political document. It is based upon the natural-rights theory of government, derived from eighteenth-century rationalism. The Declaration, written by Jefferson, was revised by Benjamin Franklin, John Adams, and the Continental Congress at large. The fifty-six colonial representatives signed it on August 2, 1776.

When in the course of human events, it becomes necessary 1
for one people to dissolve the political bands which have connected them with another, and to assume among the Powers of the earth, the separate and equal station to which the Laws of Nature and of Nature's God entitle them, a decent respect

to the opinions of mankind requires that they should declare the causes which impel them to the separation.

We hold these truths to be self-evident, that all men are created   2
equal, that they are endowed by their Creator with certain un-alienable Rights, that among these are Life, Liberty and the pursuit of Happiness. That to secure these rights, Governments are instituted among Men, deriving their just powers from the consent of the governed. That whenever any Form of Government becomes destructive of these ends, it is the Right of the People to alter or to abolish it, and to institute new Government, laying its foundation on such principles and organizing its powers in such form, as to them shall seem most likely to effect their Safety and Happiness. Prudence, indeed, will dictate that Governments long established should not be changed for light and transient causes; and accordingly all experience hath shown, that mankind are more disposed to suffer, while evils are sufferable, than to right themselves by abolishing the forms to which they are accustomed. But when a long train of abuses and usurpations pursuing invariably the same Object evinces a design to reduce them under absolute Despotism, it is their right, it is their duty, to throw off such government, and to provide new Guards for their future security. Such has been the patient sufferance of these Colonies; and such is now the necessity which constrains them to alter their former Systems of Government. The history of the present King of Great Britain [1] is a history of repeated injuries and usurpations, all having in direct object the establishment of absolute Tyranny over these States. To prove this, let Facts be submitted to a candid world.

He has refused his Assent to Laws, the most wholesome and   3
necessary for the public good.

He has forbidden his Governors to pass Laws of immediate and   4
pressing importance, unless suspended in their operation till his Assent should be obtained; and when so suspended, he has utterly neglected to attend to them.

He has refused to pass other Laws for the accommodation of   5
large districts of people, unless those people would relinquish the right of Representation in the Legislature, a right inestimable to them and formidable to tyrants only.

[1] George III (ruled 1761–1820).

He has called together legislative bodies at places unusual, un- 6
comfortable, and distant from the depository of their Public Records, for the sole purpose of fatiguing them into compliance with
his measures.

He has dissolved Representative Houses repeatedly, for opposing 7
with manly firmness his invasions on the rights of the people.

He has refused for a long time, after such dissolutions, to cause 8
others to be elected; whereby the Legislative Powers, incapable of
Annihilation, have returned to the People at large for their exercise; the State remaining in the mean time exposed to all the
dangers of invasion from without, and convulsions within.

He has endeavoured to prevent the population of these States; 9
for that purpose obstructing the Laws of Naturalization of For-
eigners; refusing to pass others to encourage their migration hither,
and raising the conditions of new Appropriations of Lands.

He has obstructed the Administration of Justice, by refusing 10
his Assent to Laws for establishing Judiciary Powers.

He has made Judges dependent on his Will alone, for the tenure 11
of their offices, and the amount and payment of their salaries.

He has erected a multitude of New Offices, and sent hither 12
swarms of Officers to harass our People, and eat out their substance.

He has kept among us, in time of peace, Standing Armies with- 13
out the Consent of our Legislature.

He has affected to render the Military independent of and 14
superior to the Civil Power.

He has combined with others to subject us to jurisdictions 15
foreign to our constitution, and unacknowledged by our laws;
giving us Assent to their acts of pretended Legislation:

For quartering large bodies of armed troops among us: 16

For protecting them, by a mock Trial, from Punishment for any 17
Murders which they should commit on the Inhabitants of these
States:

For cutting off our Trade with all parts of the world: 18

For imposing Taxes on us without our Consent: 19

For depriving us in many cases, of the benefits of Trial by Jury: 20

For transporting us beyond Seas to be tried for pretended of- 21
fenses:

For abolishing the free System of English Laws in a Neighbour- 22
ing Province, establishing therein an Arbitrary government, and
enlarging its boundaries so as to render it at once an example and

fit instrument for introducing the same absolute rule into these Colonies:

For taking away our Charters, abolishing our most valuable   23
Laws, and altering fundamentally the Forms of our Governments:

For suspending our own Legislatures, and declaring themselves   24
invested with Power to legislate for us in all cases whatsoever.

He has abdicated Government here, by declaring us out of his   25
Protection and waging War against us.

He has plundered our seas, ravaged our Coasts, burnt our towns   26
and destroyed the Lives of our people.

He is at this time transporting large Armies of foreign Mer-   27
cenaries to complete the works of death, desolation and tyranny,
already begun with circumstances of Cruelty & perfidy scarcely
paralleled in the most barbarous ages, and totally unworthy the
Head of a civilized nation.

He has constrained our fellow Citizens taken Captive on the   28
high Seas to bear Arms against their Colony, to become the exe-
cutioners of their friends and Brethren, or to fall themselves by
their Hands.

He has excited domestic insurrections amongst us, and has en-   29
deavoured to bring on the inhabitants of our frontiers, the merci-
less Indian Savages, whose known rule of warfare, is an undistin-
guished destruction of all ages, sexes and conditions.

In every stage of these Oppressions We have Petitioned for   30
Redress in the most humble terms: Our repeated petitions have
been answered only by repeated injury. A Prince, whose character
is thus marked by every act which may define a Tyrant, is unfit to
be the ruler of a free People.

Nor have We been wanting in attention to our British brethren.   31
We have warned them from time to time of attempts by their
legislature to extend an unwarrantable jurisdiction over us. We
have reminded them of the circumstances of our emigration and
settlement here. We have appealed to their native justice and
magnanimity and we have conjured them by the ties of our common kindred to disavow these usurpations, which would inevitably
interrupt our connections and correspondence. They too have been
deaf to the voice of justice and of consanguinity. We must, therefore acquiesce in the necessity, which denounces our Separation,
and hold them, as we hold the rest of mankind, Enemies in War,
in Peace Friends.

We, therefore, the Representatives of the United States of ³² America, in General Congress, Assembled, appealing to the Supreme Judge of the world for the rectitude of our intentions, do, in the Name, and by Authority of the good People of these Colonies, solemnly publish and declare, That these United Colonies are, and of Right ought to be Free and Independent States; that they are Absolved from all Allegiance to the British Crown, and that all political connection between them and the State of Great Britain, is and ought to be totally dissolved; and that as Free and Independent States, they have full power to levy War, conclude Peace, contract Alliances, establish Commerce, and to do all other Acts and Things which Independent States may of right do. And for the support of this Declaration, with a firm reliance on the protection of Divine Providence, we mutually pledge to each other our lives, our Fortunes and our sacred Honor.

QUESTIONS

Understanding

1. What is the purpose of government, according to Thomas Jefferson?
2. Where, in Jefferson's view, does a ruler get his authority?
3. "We hold these truths to be self-evident . . ." (par. 2). Another name for a self-evident "truth" granted at the beginning of an ARGUMENT is a *premise*. Briefly summarize the initial premises on which Jefferson's entire argument is built.
4. Which of Jefferson's premises is most crucial to his logic?
5. What is the ultimate conclusion of Jefferson's argument? Where is it stated?
6. Which of the many "injuries and usurpations" (par. 2) attributed by Jefferson to the British king seem most intolerable to you? Why?

Strategies and Structure

1. Jefferson gives the impression that the colonies are breaking away with extreme reluctance and only because of forces beyond any

colonist's personal power to overlook them. How does he create this impression?

2. What is the function of paragraph 31, which seems to be a digression from Jefferson's main line of argument?

3. A *hypothesis* is a theory or supposition to be tested by further proof. What is the hypothesis, introduced in paragraph 2, that Jefferson's long list of "Facts" is adduced to test?

4. Where is Jefferson's hypothesis restated (indirectly) as an established conclusion? Is the process of arriving at this conclusion basically INDUCTION (from examples to generalizations) or DEDUCTION (from premises to particular conclusions)?

5. Jefferson's conclusion to this line of argument might be restated simply as, "King George is a tyrant." We can take this conclusion as the *minor premise* of the underlying argument of the entire Declaration. If the *major premise* is "Tyrannical governments may be abolished by the People," what is the *conclusion* of that underlying argument?

6. Which sentence in paragraph 2 states Jefferson's major premise in so many words?

7. Is this underlying argument of the Declaration basically inductive or deductive? Explain your answer.

8. The signers of the Declaration of Independence wanted to appear as men of right reason, and they approved the logical form that Jefferson gave that document. Many of the specific issues their reason addressed, however, were highly emotional. What traces of strong feelings can you detect in Jefferson's wording of individual charges against the king?

9. The eighteenth-century is said to have admired and imitated "classical" balance and symmetry (as in the facade of Jefferson's Monticello). Does the form of the Declaration confirm or deny this observation? Explain your answer.

Words and Figures of Speech

1. Look up *unalienable* (or *inalienable*) in your dictionary. Considering that the Declaration was addressed, in part, to a "foreign" tyrant, why might Jefferson have chosen this adjective (par. 2) instead of, say, *natural*, *God-given*, or *fundamental*?

2. A *proposition* is a premise that is waiting to be approved. What single word signals us each time that Jefferson introduces a new proposition in his argument?

3. What is *consanguinity* (par. 31)? How may it be said to have a "voice"?

4. Look up *metonymy* under FIGURES OF SPEECH in the Glossary. What example of this figure can you find in paragraph 32?

5. For any of the following words you are not quite sure of, consult your dictionary: *transient* (par. 2), *usurpations* (2), *evinces* (2), *despotism* (2), *constrains* (2), *candid* (2), *abdicated* (25), *perfidy* (27), *redress* (30), *magnanimity* (31), *conjured* (31), *acquiesce* (31), *rectitude* (32).

Comparing

1. Like the Declaration of Independence, Chief Seattle's "Reply" (Chapter 10) is addressed to a "superior" head of state. Unlike Jefferson's, however, Chief Seattle's nation was toppling instead of rising. How does this difference in circumstances change the way the two speakers address their adversaries?

Discussion and Writing Topics

1. Compose a reply to Jefferson's charges by King George in defense of his actions and policies toward the colonies.

2. Jefferson lists "the pursuit of Happiness" (par. 2) as one of our basic rights. Construct an argument urging that this promise was unwise, that happiness cannot be guaranteed, and, therefore, that Americans have been set up for inevitable disappointment by the founding fathers. Your argument will have to anticipate the objection that the Declaration protects the *pursuit* of happiness, not happiness itself.

3. Some "loyalists" remained true to England at the time of the American Revolution. How might they have justified their "patriotism"?

Afton Blake

Sperm Banks: The Duty of Germinal Choice

In 1983, when she was past forty years of age, Afton Blake became the second woman in the world to bear a child ("Doron," meaning "gift") through artificial insemination conducted by the Repository for Germinal Choice. Known as the "Nobel sperm bank" because of the high I.Q.s of its donors (some of them Nobel laureates), the Repository was Blake's choice because it was willing to tell her more than just the race and religion of her future child's father. "Sperm Banks: The Duty of Germinal Choice" (editor's title) appeared in Omni soon after Blake's child was born. It sets forth her ideas on nurturance and argues that parenting is no longer the simple right it was once assumed to be. The author is a clinical psychologist practicing in California.

I am a woman who has always known that she would have a [1] child. My thirties rushed by me in a whirl of professional involvements. I was finishing graduate school, building a practice, acquiring economic stability, as well as experiencing emotional and spiritual growth.

In 1981 I realized I was approaching forty without a rela- [2] tionship or a child. Yet the time appeared right in all respects to have a baby. A relationship seemed superfluous. How would I create my family? I contemplated several options: inviting a friend whom I loved and respected to be a father and coparent; a voyage around the world to befriend a mysterious stranger I would never see again, an option that presumed that such a man would be capable of insemination on demand; placing a personal ad in *The New York Review of Books*; or a sperm bank. After careful deliberation, I chose the sperm bank as appropriate for my own needs. I would remain uncommitted—free to continue the search for that ideal relationship and free to instill my own parenting values in my child without conflict from a spouse.

But which sperm bank? I began to investigate the alternatives. 3 It was paramount that I know a great deal about the father's background, and that he be a man I could admire and respect: His emotional, intellectual, spiritual, and physical well-being were important to me.

Unfortunately, the first few sperm banks assured me only that I 4 could choose the father's race and religion, neither of which seemed relevant to me, and that the donor would most likely be a medical student. I was uncomfortable with so nebulous a profile. My quest then led me to the Repository for Germinal Choice, or the "Nobel sperm bank," as it is affectionately called after the Nobel laureates who were the first donors in the Seventies. Located in Escondido, California, and founded by Herman Muller, the repository believes that a woman has the right to select genetic qualities for her offspring and is firmly committed to making such choices available.

I was able to find a "father" for my child who was unquestion- 5 ably a man I would value as a vital human being, a man who was intelligent, creative, healthy, attractive, cultured, and psychologically well-balanced, as evidenced by his family history. The donor also shared many of my interests and values. I felt comfortable that this person could contribute the genetic material that I believed was needed to invite a soul into the world.

The rest was up to me. Nurturance, I believe, probably accounts 6 for about 50 percent of what a person becomes. My son, Doron, is about 75 percent my responsibility—25 percent my genes and 50 percent the environment I've created for him, if you accept my childrearing equation.

Once I was certain of my choice, the artificial-insemination pro- 7 cess was a joyous ritual, made so largely through the encouragement of my friends and family and the staff of the Nobel sperm bank. For ten successive months I inseminated myself with the donor's frozen sperm before my son was conceived.

I did not get the sense of being a pioneer until the media de- 8 scended on me in my eighth month of pregnancy. I had not comprehended that I was different. Now I understand the uniqueness of my venture and the symbol I have become to other single professional women—and men, too—who find themselves alone in their late thirties or forties without the child they desire. No longer does the deliberate creation of a single parent family remain a fantasy.

Doron (the name is from the Greek and Hebrew words for *gift*) 9 will celebrate his first birthday this month. He is more than I thought I could ever have. Through his coming, I know a deeper love. I am more awed by life. I have a greater investment in the future of our planet than I could have known was possible. For the first time in my life, I do not feel I am missing something. And there are positive aspects of such a relationship exclusive to the single parent. The dyadic intimacy between mother and child would be difficult to duplicate in the marriage triad. The symbiosis of the first 18 months of life, so essential for psychological health, can immerse one completely.

My choice of bringing Doron into the world in this deliberate 10 manner is an implicit statement, one that raises moral and ethical considerations. I feel that having a child in this age is no longer a right but a privilege that demands grave considerations. An unborn child should be guaranteed the best genetic material. Potential "quality of life" must be assessed before a soul is invited in.

Ideally, an individual, after experiencing a well-nourished child- 11 hood, should be able to emerge as an adult who can give more than he takes from humanity. The likes of Churchill and Gandhi must be more abundant if the imbroglio that our planet has fallen into is to be corrected. Individuals *invited* into the world at this time— and each birth should be meditated on as if it were a careful invitation—must have a capacity for broad vision. Deliberate genetic selection is one way of accomplishing this. The family, as we have known it throughout history, will remain as one alternative. Single parenthood, when all the economic and emotional considerations have been understood, is now another option.

Would I do it the same way again? In another couple of years, I 12 will contemplate whether or not I should invite another person into this world.

QUESTIONS

Understanding

1. What "implicit statement" (par. 10) is Afton Blake making about germinal choice for the single woman? Does she see it as a right or an obligation?

2. What options for becoming a single parent does she consider? Which one does she finally choose, and where does she go for assistance?

3. In Blake's opinion, what is wrong with the way many sperm banks are administered? Which qualities does she consider most important in a sperm donor?

4. Summarize Blake's "equation" (par. 6) for determining the degree of a single parent's influence upon the rearing of a child.

5. Why does Blake feel that deliberate genetic selection is needed now more than ever before? What quality in particular doe she believe the times will demand of a new generation?

6. In Blake's view, what will happen to the traditional   nt family in the future?

Strategies and Structure

1. Much of Blake's essay explains her personal reasons for choosing to become a parent through artificial insemination. In which paragraphs, however, does she embark upon a more general argument about the present need for germinal selection?

2. Besides the major point that conditions of modern life demand careful genetic planning, Blake is arguing a minor (in the sense of "narrower") point about the management of sperm banks. Where is this part of her argument developed?

3. To which part of Blake's argument do you find her account of her own deliberations more pertinent? Why?

4. Artificial insemination and single parenthood are emotionally charged issues to some people, yet Blake seemingly treats them with the coolest detachment. "I contemplated several options," she says (par. 2). And again: "I began to investigate the alternatives" (par. 3). Point to similar passages that lend a sense of dispassionate rationality to her writing.

5. Describe the effect of Blake's statement (par. 9), "For the first time in my life, I do not feel I am missing something." Where else do you find evidence of suppressed feelings in her essay?

6. Which, would you say, is a more representative of the language and TONE of Blake's essay as a whole, her statement about not missing anything or the following from the same paragraph: "The dyadic intimacy between mother and child would be difficult to duplicate in the marriage triad."

7. What is the dominant pronoun in Blake's essay? Is it justified or overworked in your estimation? Explain your judgment.

Words and Figures of Speech

1. How appropriate do you consider Blake's choice of the name "Doron" (par. 9) for her child?

2. Look up the meaning of the word *imbroglio* (par. 11). In what literal sense is Blake using it here? How well do you think the CONNOTATIONS of the word fit what she is saying?

3. What are the connotations of *superfluous* and *conflict* in paragraph 2?

4. A *symbiosis* is a natural relationship so close that to disturb either partner will threaten the life or well-being of the other. How appropriate do you find this term from biology (often applied loosely to denote any close relationship) as a term for the tie between mother and child in the first eighteen months after birth?

5. Afton Blake is a professional psychologist. How technically scientific do you find her vocabulary here? Explain by citing specific words and phrases.

6. Were you surprised by the author's use of *soul* (pars. 5, 10)? Why or why not?

7. Turn to your dictionary for assistance with any of the following terms you don't know for sure: *superfluous* (par. 2); *paramount* (par. 3), *nebulous* (par. 4), *repository* (par. 4), *genetic* (pars. 4, 5, 10, 11), *nurturance* (par. 6), *dyadic* (par. 9), *symbiosis* (par. 9).

Comparing

1. In the next chapter, Roger Verhulst appeals to emotion on an issue where he might be expected instead to appeal to reason. Does

Afton Blake's essay follow the same strategy or its obverse? Explain your answer?

2. Compare and contrast Blake's attitude toward childrearing with Joyce Maynard's in "Four Generations" (Chapter 1).

Discussion and Writing Topics

1. Do you accept Afton Blake's childrearing "equation" (par. 6)? How would you modify it, if at all?

2. What additional "moral and ethical considerations" (par. 10), if any, would you associate with artificial insemination? With single parenthood in general, however achieved?

3. Write an essay in defense of the two-parent family.

4. Write an essay in defense of single parenthood, but make your appeal to emotion (as defined in the next chapter) instead of right reason.

5. How effective do you find it, as a strategy of debate, for an author to adopt the form and TONE of logical argument when he or she feels a strong emotional commitment to the subject? How *ethical* is it? Why do you think so?

Johnson C. Montgomery

The Island of Plenty

*Johnson C. Montgomery was a California attorney and an early
member of the Zero Population Growth organization. Born in
1934, Montgomery attended Harvard University and the Stanford
University Law School; he was admitted to the California bar in
1960. "The Island of Plenty," in his own words, is an "elitist"
argument in favor of American social isolationism. Until we have
enough food to feed ourselves, he says, we owe it to future
generations not to share our material resources with other countries of the world.*

The United States should remain an island of plenty in a sea   1
of hunger. The future of mankind is at stake. We are not
responsible for the rest of humanity. We should not accept responsibility for all humanity. We owe more to the hundreds
of billions of *Homo futurans* than we do to the hungry millions—soon to be billions—of our own generation.

Ample food and resources exist to nourish man and all   2
other creatures indefinitely into the future. This planet is indeed an Eden—to date our only Eden. Admittedly our Eden
is plagued by pollution. Some of us have polluted the planet
by reproducing too many of us. Too many people have made
excessive demands on the long-range carrying capacity of our
garden; and during the last 200 years there has been dramatic,
ever-increasing destruction of the web of life on earth. If we
try to save the starving millions today, we will simply destroy
what's left of Eden.

The problem is not that there is too little food. The problem   3
is there are too many people—many too many. It is not that the
children should never have been born. It is simply that we have
mindlessly tried to cram too many of us into too short a time
span. Four billion humans are fine—but they should have been
spread over several hundred years.

But the billions are already here. What should we do about   4
them? Should we send food, knowing that each child saved in
Southeast Asia, India or Africa will probably live to reproduce and
thereby bring more people into the world to live even more miserably? Should we eat the last tuna fish, the last ear of corn and
utterly destroy the garden? That is what we have been doing for a
long time and all the misguided efforts have merely increased the
number who go to bed hungry each night. There have never been
more miserable, deprived people in the world than there are right
now.

It was obvious even in the late 1950s that the famine the world   5
now faces was coming unless people immediately began exercising
responsibility for reducing population levels. It was also obvious
that too many people contributed to the risk of nuclear war, global
pestilence, illiteracy and even to many problems that are usually
classified as purely economic. For example, unemployment is having too many people for the available jobs. Inflation is in part the
result of too much demand from too many people. But in the
1950s, population control was taboo and those who warned of
impending disasters received a cool reception.

By the time Zero Population Growth, Inc., was formed, those of   6
us who wanted to do something useful decided to concentrate our
initial efforts on our own families and friends and then on the
white American middle and upper classes. Our belief was that by
setting an example, we could later insist that others pay attention
to our proposals.

I think I was the first in the original ZPG group to have had a   7
vasectomy. Nancy and I had two children—each doing superbly
well and each getting all the advantages of the best nutrition,
education, attention, love and other resources available. I think
Paul Ehrlich [1] (one child) was the next. Now don't ask me to

---

[1] Biology professor at Stanford, founder and past-president of Zero Population
Growth.

cut my children back to the same number of calories that children from large families eat. In fact, don't ask me to cut my children back on anything. I won't do it without a fight; and in today's world, power is in knowledge, not numbers. Nancy and I made a conscious decision to limit the number of our children so each child could have a larger share of whatever we could make available. We intend to keep the best for them.

The future of mankind is indeed with the children. But it is   8
with the nourished, educated and loved children. It is not with the starving, uneducated and ignored. This is of course a highly elitist point of view. But that doesn't make the view incorrect. As a matter of fact, the lowest reproductive rate in the nation is that of one of the most elite groups in the world—black, female Ph.D.'s. They had to be smart and effective to make it. Having made it, they are smart enough not to wreck it with too many kids.

We in the United States have made great progress in lowering   9
our birth rates. But now, because we have been responsible, it seems to some that we have a great surplus. There is, indeed, waste that should be eliminated, but there is not as much fat in our system as most people think. Yet we are being asked to share our resources with the hungry peoples of the world. But why should we share? The nations having the greatest needs are those that have been the least responsible in cutting down on births. Famine is one of nature's ways of telling profligate peoples that they have been irresponsible in their breeding habits.

Naturally, we would like to help; and if we could, perhaps we   10
should. But we can't be of any use in the long run—particularly if we weaken ourselves.

Until we have at least a couple of years' supply of food and   11
other resources on hand to take care of our own people and until those asking for handouts are doing at least as well as we are at reducing existing excessive population-growth rates, we should not give away our resources—not so much as one bushel of wheat. Certainly we should not participate in any programs that will increase the burden that mankind is already placing on the earth. We should not deplete our own soils to save those who will only die equally miserably a decade or so down the line—and in many cases only after reproducing more children who are inevitably doomed to live and die in misery.

We know the world is finite. There is only so much pie. We 12
may be able to expand the pie, but at any point in time, the pie
is finite. How big a piece each person gets depends in part on how
many people there are. At least for the foreseeable future, the
fewer of us there are, the more there will be for each. That is
true on a family, community, state, national and global basis.

At the moment, the future of mankind seems to depend on our 13
maintaining the island of plenty in a sea of deprivation. If everyone shared equally, we would all be suffering from protein-defi-
ciency brain damage—and that would probably be true even if we
ate every last animal on earth.

As compassionate human beings, we grieve for the condition of 14
mankind. But our grief must not interfere with our perception of
reality and our planning for a better future for those who will
come after us. Someone must protect the material and intellectual
seed grain for the future. It seems to me that that someone is the
U.S. We owe it to our children—and to their children's children's
children's children.

These conclusions will be attacked, as they have been within 15
Zero Population Growth, as simplistic and inhumane. But truth
is often very simple and reality often inhumane.

QUESTIONS

Understanding

1. What is Montgomery's main proposition in this essay? In which
   two paragraphs is it stated most directly?
2. What other general propositions does he put forth in support of
   his main proposition?
3. In paragraph 4, what is the last sentence (about the number of
   miserable people in the world) intended to prove?
4. Montgomery warns us not to "ask me to cut my children back on
   anything" (par. 7). How is this position consistent with what he
   says about the planet's not having enough to go around?

Strategies and Structure

1. The logic of Montgomery's basic ARGUMENT can be represented by a syllogism. *Major premise:* To provide undamaged human stock for the future, some people must remain healthy. *Minor premise:* All will suffer if all share equally in the world's limited bounty. *Conclusion:* Some must not share what they have. How sound is this logic? Will you grant Montgomery's premises? Why or why not?

2. Montgomery's hard-headed realism would show us the "truth" (par. 15) of the human condition; but it would also move us to action. What would Montgomery have us do?

3. Logic is only part of Montgomery's persuasive arsenal. Which paragraphs in his essay appeal more to emotion and ethics than to logic?

4. Montgomery seems to be speaking from authority. Where does he get his authority, and how much weight should it carry?

5. Montgomery admits that his position is "elitist" (par. 8). How does he head off the charge that it is racist?

6. Is Montgomery's last paragraph necessary? Why or why not?

7. Are you persuaded by Montgomery's essay? Why or why not?

Words and Figures of Speech

1. How does the METAPHOR of the island contribute to Montgomery's argument? Is there any IRONY in his title?

2. For the sake of the future, says Montgomery, we must save some "material and intellectual seed grain" (par. 14). Explain this metaphor: What is being compared to what? Why is the metaphor appropriate?

3. How is Montgomery altering the traditional definition of Eden? Is he rejecting the traditional idea altogether? Explain your answer.

4. *Homo futurans* (par. 1), meaning "man of the future," is modeled after such scientific terms as *Homo erectus* ("upright man") and *Homo sapiens* ("thinking man"). Why might Montgomery choose to use the language of science at the beginning of his argument?

5. How does Montgomery's use of the word *mindlessly* (par. 3) fit in with his entire argument?

6. What is the meaning of *profligate* (par. 9)?

Comparing

1. By comparison with Afton Blake's "Sperm Banks," does "The Island of Plenty" seem more concerned with analyzing a condition or with persuading the reader to act? Explain.
2. Opponents of Montgomery's argument might charge that he has written "a modest proposal." What would they mean by this? Would they be justified? (See Jonathan Swift's "A Modest Proposal" in "Essays For Further Reading.")

Discussion and Writing Topics

1. Attack Montgomery's position on the grounds that he is confusing compassion with weakness.
2. Defend Montgomery's assertion that "there is not as much fat in our system as most people think" (par. 9).
3. Write your own "modest proposal" (for feeding the world, curing inflation, regulating human breeding habits, or some other "simple" task).

Richard M. Restak
The Other Difference between Boys and Girls

Born in Wilmington, Delaware, in 1942 and trained at hospitals
in New York City and Washington, D.C., Dr. Richard Restak
is a Washington neurologist. He is the author of Premeditated
Man (1945), The Brain (1979), The Self Seekers (1982), and a
new book about the brain that will accompany a forthcoming
television series on PBS. The most controversial of Restak's con-
clusions from his studies in neurology is that the brains of men
and women function differently—the "other difference" between
the sexes proclaimed in the following essay from the Washington
Post. Restak argues for social and educational changes based
upon an open recognition that men and women do not think alike.
For a rebuttal attacking his argument on logical grounds, see the
next essay in this chapter, "The Sexes Are Not Born with Differ-
ent Brains," by Martha Mednick and Nancy Felipe Russo. Dr.
Restak's remarks on the process of writing his own essay appear
at the end of the chapter.

Boys think differently from girls. Recent research on brain   1
behavior makes that conclusion inescapable, and it is unrealistic to keep denying it.

I know how offensive that will sound to feminists and others   2
committed to overcoming sexual stereotypes. As the father of
three daughters, I am well aware of the discrimination girls
suffer. But social equality for men and women really depends
on recognizing these differences in brain behavior.

At present, schooling and testing discriminate against both   3
boys and girls in different ways, ignoring differences that have
been observed by parents and educators for years. Boys suffer
in elementary school classrooms, which are ideally suited to

314

the way girls think. Girls suffer later on, in crucial ways, taking scholarship tests that are geared for male performance.

Anyone who has spent time with children in a playground or   4
school setting is aware of differences in the way boys and girls respond to similar situations. Think of the last time you supervised a birthday party attended by five-year-olds. It's not usually the girls who pull hair, throw punches or smear each other with food.

Usually such differences are explained on a cultural basis. Boys   5
are expected to be more aggressive and play rough games, while girls are presumably encouraged to be gentle, nonassertive and passive. After several years of exposure to such expectations, the theory goes, men and women wind up with widely varying behavioral and intellectual repertoires. As a corollary to this, many people believe that if child-rearing practices could be equalized and sexual stereotypes eliminated, most of these differences would eventually disappear. As often happens, however, the true state of affairs is not that simple.

Undoubtedly, many of the differences traditionally believed to   6
exist between the sexes are based on stereotypes. But despite this, evidence from recent brain research indicates that many behavioral differences between men and women are based on differences in brain functioning that are biologically inherent and unlikely to be modified by cultural factors alone.

The first clue to brain differences between the sexes came from   7
observations of male and female infants. From birth, female infants are more sensitive to sounds, particularly to their mother's voice. In a laboratory, if the sound of the mother's voice is displaced to another part of the room, female babies will react while male babies usually seem oblivious to the displacement. Female babies are also more easily startled by loud noises. In fact, their enhanced hearing performance persists throughout life, with females experiencing a fall-off in hearing much later than males.

Tests involving girls old enough to cooperate show increased   8
skin sensitivity, particularly in the fingertips, which have a lower threshold for touch identification. Females are also more proficient at fine motor performance. Rapid tapping movements are carried out quickly and more efficiently by girls than by boys.

In addition, there are differences in what attracts a girl's atten-   9
tion. Generally, females are more attentive to social contexts—

faces, speech patterns and subtle vocal cues. By four months of age, a female infant is socially aware enough to distinguish photographs of familiar people, a task rarely performed well by boys of that age. Also at four months, girls will babble to a mother's face, seemingly recognizing her as a person, while boys fail to distinguish between a face and a dangling toy, babbling equally to both.

Female infants also speak sooner, have larger vocabularies and 10
rarely demonstrate speech defects. Stuttering, for instance, occurs almost exclusively among boys.

Girls can also sing in tune at an earlier age. In fact, if we think 11
of the muscles of the throat as muscles of fine control—those in which girls excel—then it should come as no surprise that girls exceed boys in language abilities. This early linguistic bias often prevails throughout life. Girls read sooner, learn foreign languages more easily and, as a result, are more likely to enter occupations involving language mastery.

Boys, in contrast, show an early visual superiority. They are 12
also clumsier, performing poorly at something like arranging a row of beads, but excel at other activities calling on total body coordination. Their attentional mechanisms are also different. A boy will react to an inanimate object as quickly as he will to a person. A male baby will often ignore the mother and babble to a blinking light, fixate on a geometric figure and, at a later point, manipulate it and attempt to take it apart.

A study of nursery preschool children carried out by psycholo- 13
gist Diane McGuinness of Stanford University found boys more curious, especially in regard to exploring their environment. McGuinness' studies also confirmed that males are better at manipulating three-dimensional space. When boys and girls are asked to mentally rotate or fold an object, boys overwhelmingly outperform girls. "I folded it in my mind" is a typical male response. Girls, when explaining how they perform the same task, are likely to produce elaborate verbal descriptions which, because they are less appropriate to the task, result in frequent errors.

In an attempt to understand the sex differences in spatial ability, 14
electroencephalogram (EEG) measurements have recently been made of the accompanying electrical events going on within the brain.

Ordinarily, the two brain hemispheres produce a similar electri- 15 cal background that can be measured by an EEG. When a person is involved in a mental task—say, subtracting 73 from 102—the hemisphere that is activated will demonstrate a change in its electrical background. When boys are involved in tasks employing spatial concepts, such as figuring out mentally which of three folded shapes can be made from a flat, irregular piece of paper, the right hemisphere is activated consistently. Girls, in contrast, are more likely to activate both hemispheres, indicating that spatial ability is more widely dispersed in the female brain.

When it comes to psychological measurements of brain functioning between the sexes, unmistakable differences emerge. In 11 subtests of the most widely used test of general intelligence, only two subtests reveal similar mean scores for males and females. These sex differences have been substantiated across cultures and are so consistent that the standard battery of this intelligence test now contains a masculinity-femininity index. [16]

Further support for sex differences in brain functioning comes from experience with subtests that eventually had to be omitted from the original test battery. A cube-analysis test, for example, was excluded because, after testing thousands of subjects, a large sex bias appeared to favor males. In all, over 30 tests eventually had to be eliminated because they discriminated in favor of one or the other sex. One test, involving mentally working oneself through a maze, favored boys so overwhelmingly that, for a while, some psychologists speculated that girls were totally lacking in a "spatial factor." [17]

Most thought-provoking of all is a series of findings by Eleanor Maccoby and Carol Nagly Jacklin of Stanford on personality traits and intellectual achievement. They found that girls whose intellectual achievement is greatest tend to be unusually active, independent, competitive and free of fear or anxiety, while intellectually outstanding boys are often timid, anxious, not overtly aggressive and less active. [18]

In essence, Maccoby and Jacklin's findings suggest that intellectual performance is incompatible with our stereotype of femininity in girls or masculinity in boys. [19]

Research evidence within the last six months indicates that many of these brain sex differences persist over a person's lifetime. In a study at the University Hospital in Ontario that compared [20] verbal and spatial abilities of men and women after a stroke, the women did better than men in key categories tested. After the stroke, women tended to be less disabled and recovered more quickly.

Research at the National Institute of Mental Health is even un-   21
covering biochemical differences in the brains of men and women. Women's brains, it seems, are more sensitive to experimentally administered lights and sounds. The investigator in charge of this research, Dr. Monte Buchsbaum, speculates that the enhanced response of the female brain depends on the effect of sex hormones on the formation of a key brain chemical. This increased sensibility to stimuli by the female brain may explain why women more often than men respond to loss and stress by developing depression.

It's important to remember that we're not talking about one sex   22
being generally superior or inferior to another. Rather, psychobiological research is turning up important functional differences between male and female brains. The discoveries might possibly contribute to further resentments and divisions in our society. But must they? Why are sex differences in brain functioning disturbing to so many people? And why do women react so vehemently to findings that, if anything, indicate enhanced capabilities in the female brain?

It seems to me that we can make two responses to these findings   23
on brain-sex differences. First, we can use them to help bring about true social equity. One way of doing this might be to change such practices as nationwide competitive examinations. If boys, for instance, truly do excel in right-hemisphere tasks, then tests such as the National Merit Scholarship Examination should be radically redesigned to assure that both sexes have an equal chance. As things now stand, the tests are heavily weighted with items that virtually guarantee superior male performance.

Attitude changes are also needed in our approach to "hyperac-   24
tive" or "learning disabled" children. The evidence for sex differences here is staggering: More than 95 percent of hyperactives are males. And why should this be surprising in light of the sex differences in brain function that we've just discussed?

The male brain learns by manipulating its environment, yet the   25
typical student is forced to sit still for long hours in the classroom. The male brain is primarily visual, while classroom instruction

demands attentive listening. Boys are clumsy in fine hand coordination, yet are forced at an early age to express themselves in writing. Finally, there is little opportunity in most schools, other than during recess, for gross motor movements or rapid muscular responses. In essence, the classrooms in most of our nation's primary grades are geared to skills that come naturally to girls but develop very slowly in boys. The results shouldn't be surprising: a "learning disabled" child who is also frequently "hyperactive."

"He can't sit still, can't write legibly, is always trying to take things apart, won't follow instructions, is loud, and, oh yes, terribly clumsy," is a typical teacher description of male hyperactivity. We now have the opportunity, based on emerging evidence of sex differences in brain functioning, to restructure elementary grades so that boys find their initial educational contacts less stressful.   26

At more advanced levels of instruction, efforts must be made to develop teaching methods that incorporate verbal and linguistic approaches to physics, engineering and architecture (to mention only three fields where women are conspicuously underrepresented and, on competitive aptitude tests, score well below males).   27

The second alternative is, of course, to do nothing about brain differences and perhaps even deny them altogether. Certainly there is something to be said for this approach too. In the recent past, enhanced social benefit has usually resulted from stressing the similarities between people rather than their differences. We ignore brain-sex differences, however, at the risk of confusing biology with sociology, and wishful thinking with scientific facts.   28

The question is not, "Are there brain-sex differences?" but rather, "What is going to be our response to these differences?" Psychobiological research is slowly but surely inching toward scientific proof of a premise first articulated by the psychologist David Wechsler more than 20 years ago: 29

"The findings suggest that women seemingly call upon different resources or different degrees of like abilities in exercising whatever it is we call intelligence. For the moment, one need not be concerned as to which approach is better or 'superior.' But our findings do confirm what poets and novelists have often asserted, and the average layman long believed, namely, that men not only behave, but 'think' differently from women."   30

QUESTIONS

Understanding

1. The major premise of Restak's essay is that "Boys think differently from girls" (par. 1). What does he mean when he says, "Usually such differences are explained on a cultural basis" (par. 5)?

2. How would Restak, as a neurologist, explain the "difference in brain functioning" (par. 6) between boys and girls?

3. Why might some women be disturbed by Restak's explanation for intellectual differences between males and females? (He says he makes no judgments about "inferior" and "superior" brains and that his findings might even be interpreted to favor women.)

4. What answer does Restak give in advance to "feminists" and others who may be expected to take exception to his views?

5. Neurologists believe that the right hemisphere of the brain dominates our handling of visual and spatial data and that the left hemisphere has more to do with language acquisition and use. By comparison with girls, do boys tend to be more "right-brained' or "left-brained," according to Restak's analysis of the research? How about girls? Which are they?

6. Restak has examined research dealing with both physiological and psychological data. Which kind is provided by electroencephalograms (pars. 14 and 15)? By intelligence tests and subtests (pars. 16 and 17)? By recent research with lights and sounds at the National Institute of Mental Health (par. 21)?

7. According to Restak, what were the conclusions of the thought-provoking Maccoby-Jacklin experiments at Stanford (par. 18)? How does Restak himself interpret their findings? What conclusion does he draw from their conclusion?

8. One public response to the new understanding of brain differences, says Restak, is to do nothing or "perhaps even deny them altogether" (par. 28). What advantage might conceivably be gained from this negative response? Why is doing nothing, however, the wrong way to react in Restak's opinion?

9. What does Restak consider the proper, positive reaction to the new findings? How, specifically, would he change traditional teaching and testing methods in the schools?

Strategies and Structure

1. A good strategy in logical argument is always to anticipate objections that might be raised against your reasoning. Restak begins

almost immediately to defend his position against "feminists and others committed to overcoming sexual stereotypes" (par. 2). What concession does he make to the opposition? Where does he take up the line of defense again toward the end of his essay? Is he still making concessions, or is he arguing more aggressively? Explain your answer.

2. Why does Restak mention that he is the father of three daughters (par. 2)?

3. Restak's essay combines INDUCTIVE reasoning (from particular observations to general principles) with DEDUCTIVE reasoning (from general principles to conclusions). If the "inescapable" conclusion of his inductive argument is that "boys think differently from girls" (anticipated in par. 1), which paragraph begins to recite the specific bits of evidence upon which this conclusion rests?

4. Where does Restak end the survey of the evidence (and thus the deductive part of his argument)?

5. The conclusion of Restak's inductive argument—that the sexes have different brains—becomes the major premise of a deductive argument in the last third of his essay. If the implied minor premise is that differences among the sexes are socially undesirable, what is the conclusion of Restak's deductive argument? Where is it stated?

6. When Restak launches into his inductive argument in paragraph 7, he suspends the deductive part for some time. We know to expect it eventually, however, because of clear signals in the opening six paragraphs. Where exactly does Restak anticipate his deductive argument in favor of reform in educating and testing the sexes?

7. There is a considerable difference between arguing that males and females develop different brains and arguing that they are *born* with those differences. In which early paragraph does Restak switch ground toward the second, more radical view?

8. Restak notes that boys activate the right hemisphere of the brain when working with shapes, while girls activate both hemispheres. From such data he concludes (par. 15) that "spatial ability is more widely dispersed" in girls (and therefore, presumably, more watered down). Is this a logical conclusion? Why or why not? What different conclusion is possible from these same data?

9. Should Restak have cited more or less research to buttress his findings, or has he selected about the right amount? What do you think and why?

Words and Figures of Speech

1. Which single word in paragraph 1 anticipates Restak's later con-

tention that people who ignore brain differences between the sexes confuse "biology with sociology, and wishful thinking with scientific facts" (par. 28)?

2. What are the implications of the phrase "biologically inherent" (par. 6)? Why is it a crucial part of Restak's argument? Does he call attention to the importance of this phrase or leave it to be discovered by the reader? Why?

3. Do you find Restak's title effective and accurate? Why or why not?

4. The word *stereotypes* (pars. 2, 5, 6, 19) comes from printing; it refers to metal plates of type, or other design, cast from a mold. What does the word mean when applied to people? Why is it appropriate here for describing behavior that is imposed rather than inherited?

5. Sociologists and psychologists speak not only of "behavior" but also of "behaviors" (plural). The way male babies respond to lights is one behavior; to sounds, another. What is meant by the technical use of this term?

6. Look up in a good desk dictionary any of these words that you do not recognize immediately: *cultural* (par. 5), *repertoires* (par. 5), *corollary* (par. 5), *modified* (par. 6), *oblivious* (par. 7), *enhanced* (pars. 7, 21, 22), *threshold* (par. 8), *inanimate* (par. 12), *fixate* (par. 12), *stimuli* (par. 21), *depression* (par. 21), *equity* (par. 23), *hyperactivity* (par. 26), *linguistic* (par. 27).

7. Judging from this list, how would you characterize Dr. Restak's vocabulary?

Comparing

1. How does Restak's premise that intelligence is inherent rather than learned compare with Ellen Willis's explanation of how personalities are formed in "Memoirs of a Non-Prom Queen" (Chapter 4)?

2. Examine the following counter argument ("The Sexes Are Not Born with Different Brains") in which Martha Mednick and Nancy Felipe Russo directly respond to Dr. Restak's argument. On what grounds do they disagree? Where do they concur, if at all?

3. Like Thomas Jefferson in the "Declaration of Independence" (earlier in this chapter), Restak combines inductive and deductive reasoning. How close is the parallel as far as logic is concerned?

Discussion and Writing Topics

1. From Restak's argument, are you convinced that the sexes have different brains? That they are *born* with them? That the differences should be acknowledged and taken into account? Explain your answer to each of these separate questions.

2. Are most scientific arguments based on the evidence of research more like to be inductive or deductive? Why?

3. Using Restak's own report of the research, attack or defend his conclusions.

Martha Mednick
and Nancy Felipe Russo

The Sexes Are Not Born with Different Brains

Born in New York City, Martha Mednick (Ph.D., Northwestern) is professor of psychology at Howard University and co-author of Women and Achievement (1975). A native Californian, her collaborator, Nancy Felipe Russo (Ph.D., Cornell), has administered the women's programs of the American Psychological Association since 1977. She is the author of The Motherhood Mandate (1979). As research psychologists, teachers, and writers, Mednick and Russo share a common interest in the psychology of women and in social influences upon women's careers and sex-roles. "The Sexes Are Not Born with Different Brains" first appeared in the Washington Post as a direct response to neurologist Richard Restak's "The Other Difference between Boys and Girls." The titles of the two essays neatly demarcate the grounds on which their authors disagree about the psychology of sex. The subtitle of the essay by Mednick and Russo is "How Misleading Thinking Can Lead to Illogical Results." For Professor Mednick's remarks on its composition, see "Writers on the Writing Process" at the end of this chapter.

For many years some people have been searching for differ- [1]
ences in the brains of men and women in an attempt to explain
differences in behavior between the sexes.

For a while in the 19th century it was thc smaller absolute [2]
brain size of females that was said to account for a supposed
lesser ability among women. In the mid-1800s some researchers
concentrated on the fact that men have more developed frontal lobes than women. Then attention switched to the parietal
lobes, which were regarded as the seat of the intellect at that
time.

Now we have neurologist Richard Restak reviewing a large   3
number of research findings and researching the "inescapable"
conclusion that in many respects boys and girls think differently.
As there are male and female reproductive systems, Restak tells us
in the June 24 "Outlook," so there are in effect male and female
brains.

Restak contends that "many behavioral differences between   4
men and women are based on differences in brain functioning that
are biologically inherent and unlikely to be modified by cultural
factors alone." "We ignore brain-sex differences," he says, "at
the risk of confusing biology with sociology, and wishful thinking
with scientific fact."

But if ever there was an example of wishful thinking disguised   5
as scientific objectivity, it is in the distorted evidence and shaky
logic exhibited by Restak.

Granted, Restak asserts that "we're not talking about one sex   6
being superior or inferior to the other," and he says that his proposal to restructure the educational, social and work worlds of
men and women is intended to help every person fully realize his
or her own potential. But he is naïve if he believes that his work
will not be used by some to help justify the low numbers of women
in many professions, and his proposal could not conceivably accomplish what he says he intends.

Let us begin, then, with his misleading review of the research.   7
If we look at children just after birth, before the sexes have been
extensively exposed to differential treatment, we do not find the
sex differences in sensation, perception and motor behavior that
Restak suggests are inherent.

Yvonne Brackbill, a noted authority on infant development, re-   8
cently completed a major review of all recent research published in
the United States and England dealing with the behavior of babies
from 1 to 30 days of age. She could find no sex difference in *any* of
these important aspects of behavior. Even sleep patterns, indi-
cators of brain activity, were not found to differ for the sexes.

Similarly, Restak's assertion that females are more sensitive to   9
sound while males show an "early visual superiority" is based on
an incomplete evaluation of the literature. In a comprehensive
review of research in these areas, for one example, Eleanor
Maccoby and Carol Nagly Jacklin of Stanford University con-

cluded that "it has not been demonstrated that either sex is more 'visual' or more 'auditory' than the other."

It would be surprising, of course, if different treatment of boys   10
and girls did not in time have some effect. As Restak notes, in American society girls on the average eventually achieve verbal superiority over boys, while boys eventually excel on the average in spatial ability. But he is sorely mistaken in suggesting that these differences are universal or immodifiable.

The female verbal superiority in this country which Restak at- ·   11
tributes to "the female brain" is not found in Germany, as Michele Wittig and Anne Petersen report in their recent book, "Sex-Related Cognitive Differences." Amiah Lieblich of Hebrew University similarly has found that boys in Israel perform equal to or better than girls at all ages on measures of verbal ability.

Nor is male superiority in spatial ability found in all cultures.   12
J. W. Berry and R. McArthur, for example, conducted separate and independent studies among Canadian Eskimos and found no sex differences in measures of spatial ability. Moreover, there is no doubt that where lower female performance in spatial ability is found among adolescents, in this country or elsewhere, it can be changed by training.

A more serious error by Restak, though, is the way he leaps to   13
cause-and-effect conclusions in linking behavior differences between the sexes to "biologically inherent" differences in brain functioning. It is believed, for example, that the left hemisphere of the brain plays a dominant role in language functions and that the right hemisphere is dominant for processing spatial information. Restak reports that on tests of spatial ability, boys used the right sides of their brains while girls were more likely to activate both sides. Fine.

But then he jumps to the unfounded conclusion that this differ-   14
ence is caused by something inherent about male and female brains, and that it is related to a detriment in performance for females. He does not even consider the fact that after boys are "trained" for years in our society to emphasize tasks involving spatial abilities, it would be surprising if their brains did not react differently to spatial tasks. Which is really the cause and which the effect?

Any weight watcher or body builder will tell you that one's   15
biological status at any moment is a complex expression of the

effect of both one's heredity and one's environment. The brain is not exempt from this principle. It is exceedingly difficult to sort out the contributions of genetics, biology and environment to the development of sex differences in hemispheric activity.

In the same way, it cannot automatically be *assumed* that a sex [16] difference in one area such as the brain's hemispheric activity is linked to another area such as spatial tasks. For example, a study that recently appeared in *Science*, the journal of the American Association for the Advancement of Science, raises questions about the behavioral effects of sex differences in hemispheric activity that Restak cites so definitively.

In that study, psychologists Joseph Cioffi and Gilray Kandel of [17] the Rensselaer Polytechnic Institute found that in contrast to earlier work, both boys and girls identify shapes better by touch with their left hand than with their right. Both sexes also identified words better by touch with their right hand than with their left. Girls performed no differently on these tasks than boys.

The researchers did find a difference in the hand best used to [18] identify bigrams (two letters that do not form a word, such as XH), but both sexes nonetheless were equally accurate in identifying the bigrams. Further, some girls did better with their left hand, and some boys did better with their right. The authors concluded that any assertions about the differential organization of the brains of boys and girls must be carefully qualified.

Perhaps the most profound and consequential mistake Restak [19] makes, however, is in his confusion between groups and individuals, particularly as it affects his prescriptions for general changes in education and elsewhere.

When group differences are found, it is always an average com- [20] paring large numbers of people. While a small average difference can be significant to a statistician, it tells very little about individuals. As Leona E. Tyler, past president of the American Psychological Association and a noted authority on individual differences, has observed, average differences in tests "are trifling as compared with the individual differences in each sex."

Any approach that ignores individual variation is naive and [21] harmful. It also leads to tortured semantics. In dealing with hemispheric activities, for example, Restak says that girls, on the average, are more *likely* to demonstrate such differences, yet he talks about "biologically inherent" characteristics of male and female brains. Does he mean to imply that the many girls within the average who perform the tasks "the way the boys do it" (on the average) have inherited "male brains"? Do the many boys who do better than many other girls on verbal measures have "female brains"?

When society bases educational, occupational and social poli- 22
cies on studies of group differences, there obviously are devastating consequences for individuals.

Whether one is talking about brain size in the 19th century or 23
hemispheric activity in the 20th, then, there is no body of scientific fact proving that sex differences in behavior are caused by inherent differences in brain characteristics. The failure of science to establish this link is not surprising, given the powerful forces that have been demonstrated to shape boys and girls into fulfilling the expectations of our sex-role stereotypes.

That is not to say that both genetic and biological considera- 24
tions for individuals are not important. But the strength of the contribution of genetic factors depends directly on how differently people are treated on the basis of their sex. If society treated the sexes in a totally equivalent fashion, differences between male and females would reflect inherent characteristics. We do not live in such a society.

What it comes down to is that some boys think differently from 25
some girls. They also think differently from each other. The same holds for girls. We are beginning to understand the many factors that create this rich diversity. There is a new sophistication in much of the research that focuses on the interaction of genetic, biological and environmental factors, and the results of this work may, indeed, eventually lead to the full realization of the potential within each person.

QUESTIONS

Understanding

1. Mednick and Russo agree with neurologist Richard M. Restak ("The Other Difference between Boys and Girls," preceding essay) that the brains of males and females may respond differently to the

same task (for example, learning a language or solving problems in spatial relations). They vehemently disagree, however, with Restak's "unfounded conclusion" (par. 14) about the cause of such differences. To what ultimate cause does Restak attribute brain differences between the sexes? To what do Mednick and Russo attribute them?

2. Mednick and Russo are reluctant even to grant Restak's basic premise, that "boys think differently from girls." How would they qualify this assertion about *uniform* brain differences between the sexes?

3. Mednick and Russo accuse Restak of misevaluating research on sensation and perception among infants. What conclusions do they reach from their own evaluation of the research in paragraphs 7–12? What conclusions do they attribute to Dr. Restak?

4. What social effects do Mednick and Russo fear from the "biologically inherent" theory of intellectual differences between males and females?

5. Restak argues that those who reject the notion of male and female brains are "unrealistic." What quality of mind do Mednick and Russo, in turn, charge against Restak for believing that his interpretation of the evidence will not be misused?

6. What is Restak's most serious error as Mednick and Russo see it? How does this "mistake" (par. 19), in their view, nullify Restak's argument that all girls need to be educated differently from all boys?

Strategies and Structure

1. Why do you think Mednick and Russo begin with a historical perspective?

2. Which part of Restak's thesis do they contest more vigorously— the proposition that the sexes have different brains or that they are born with those differences? Where is the issue first raised in their rebuttal?

3. Mednick and Russo accuse Restak of distorting evidence (par. 5). The first evidence they themselves cite is the research compiled by Yvonne Brackbill (par. 8). What makes this study especially helpful to their case against Dr. Restak?

4. What is the evidence cited in paragraphs 11 and 12 intended to prove? Where else in the essay do Mednick and Russo address the issue of brain modification?

5. Mednick and Russo also chide Restak for "shaky logic" (par. 5). The logical blunder they cite is that of "leaping" to a false conclusion about causation (par. 13), a fallacy that usually occurs with INDUCTIVE rather than DEDUCTIVE arguments. The portion of Restak's argument that Mednick and Russo seem to have in mind is that set forth in paragraphs 13–17 of the preceding essay. Look closely at those paragraphs. Is the charge of shaky logic justified? Why or why not?

6. In paragraph 4, Mednick and Russo quote from Dr. Restak's argument and then (par. 5) turn his words back on him. How effective do you consider this as a technique of rebuttal?

7. In paragraph 23, Mednick and Russo argue a negative: "there is no body of scientific fact proving that sex differences in behavior are caused by inherent differences in brain characteristics." What would be the positive version of this proposition? Would their argument have been stronger if they had cast it this way? Why didn't they?

8. What counter arguments, if any, might be raised against the argument set forth here by Mednick and Russo?

Words and Figures of Speech

1. When applied to language, "semantics" refers to the study of the *meanings* of words. Mednick and Russo say that ignoring brain differences among individuals of the same sex leads to "tortured semantics" (par. 21). What new, clumsy meanings of *male* and *female* do they make fun of?

2. How effective do you find the ANALOGY between brain performance and body building or weight watching (par. 15)?

3. In logic, what is a *non sequitur*? (Your dictionary will tell you.) What *non sequitur*, in particular, do Mednick and Russo attribute to Dr. Restak's argument?

4. Which single word in paragraph 6 lets you know that the authors are agreeing with their opponent only to disagree with him soon after?

5. A single word, *fine*, does duty for a whole sentence at the end of paragraph 13 of this essay. Why are the authors so terse? Is the device "correct" or "incorrect"? Why?

6. Consult your dictionary for the following words if you do not know them already: *parietal* (par. 2), *spatial* (par. 12), *detriment* (par. 14), *genetics* (par. 15), *consequential* (par. 19), *prescriptions*

(par. 19), *statistician* (par. 20), *verbal* (par. 21), *sophistication* (par. 25).

7. What is the difference between *verbal* (par. 21) and *oral*?

Comparing

1. "The Sexes Are Not Born with Different Brains" is a direct rebuttal to the preceding essay by Richard Restak, "The Other Difference between Boys and Girls." Which do you find more convincing as a logical argument (even if you do not agree with the truth of the conclusions or premises). Why?

2. Both Restak (pars. 18 and 19 of the preceding essay) and the coauthors of this essay cite the work of Maccoby and Jacklin at Stanford University. How do their interpretations of this research compare? Who is right? Is there enough evidence to tell?

Discussion and Writing Topics

1. How would you go about resolving differences in the interpretation of the same evidence, reported in brief, by different experts? Is it possible for well-informed, well-intentioned people to interpret the same body of evidence diversely? Explain your opinion?

2. What advantages might an unanswered rebuttal (like Mednick's and Russo's) have in debate over the original argument it attacks? Can you think of any disadvantages or limitations imposed upon the author of a rebuttal?

3. Take a side in this debate about inherent differences in male and female brains and argue your case using different evidence or the same evidence interpreted differently.

4. Inductive arguments can lead to faulty generalizations when they are based on insufficient evidence, bad authorities, or good authorities quoted inaccurately or out of context. Do any of these fallacies apply to the logic of this essay or the preceding one by Richard Restak? If so, how might they be corrected?

Writers on the Writing Process:
Martha Mednick and Richard M. Restak

Martha Mednick and Nancy Felipe Russo composed "The 1
Sexes Are Not Born with Different Brains" in direct response
and rebuttal to Dr. Richard M. Restak's "The Other Difference between Boys and Girls." "We wrote the piece," says
Martha Mednick, "after Restak's had appeared in the [*Washington*] *Post*'s Sunday 'Outlook' section. Several friends who
were, as was I, very upset by the misrepresentation, called that
day to urge that we launch a protest."

Mednick's first step was to approach her friend and colleague 2
Nancy Russo, who in turn contacted an editor at the *Washington Post*. "He told us to write something," Mednick recalls,
"and 'he would see.' " As Mednick remembers the process, she
wrote a draft of the response to Dr. Restak's article, and her
collaborator "added and revised." Then the amended essay was
returned to Mednick. "I polished it a bit after that and she
[Nancy Russo] sent it over. The editor came back to us with
several questions and suggestions; we revised it again and sent it
back. I believe the process took three weeks."

The title of the finished essay—"headline is more accurate," 3
according to Mednick—was not the choice of the authors but
was furnished later by the newspaper. Mednick does "not remember one section as being more difficult than any other"
to produce during the writing process. "The most difficult
aspect of the process," she says, was a matter of adjusting the
whole presentation of a technical subject to the demands of "a
general audience." "I must confess," Mednick reports, "that
the editor helped with this part of the problem."

Does she stand by her argument? "I would write almost the 4
same article today, perhaps including some of the newer research." Mednick believes that the "issues have not changed,

nor have the data. I wrote this out of conviction and dedication to a point of view."

Why, in general, does she write? "I want to persuade and educate a wider audience than I can reach in my classroom or in professional journals." 5

"The essay 'The Other Difference between Boys and Girls,' " says its author, "was excerpted from my book *The Brain: The Last Frontier*." Dr. Restak writes that the subject interested him "because at that time brian research findings were squaring with my own observations that men and women think differently." Since the publication of the essay, he reports, his observations have only been confirmed: "evidence has continued to mount that brain organization accounts for certain behavioral differences between the sexes." These include "hyper-activity and learning disability in males." According to Restak, "these sex differences are not cultural, don't depend on sexual stereotypes, and aren't based on politics or social considerations." 6

How does he respond to "The Sexes Are Not Born with Different Brains"? "The essay by Mednick and Russo is based on a mixture of misinformation and ignorance," in Restak's view. "My piece was on neurobiology," he writes. "Neither of the authors" of the rebuttal, he continues, "has any training in the evaluation of neurologic data nor does the essay reflect any familiarity with the literature." Restak feels that the counterstatement assumes, "quite incorrectly, that my position was based on sexism." The Mednick and Russo rebuttal, in Restak's opinion, is thus founded upon "resentment" rather than fact. 7

Since the publication of the essay on brain sex differences, Restak continues to write about the human brian and related subjects. Where does he find the time? He writes "only in the morning between 7:00 and 8:00 a.m." He usually does "only one draft of my essays," and he follows "a single rule: Don't write anything unless you have something to say . . . after that, things progress along according to their own inscrutable ways." 8

WRITING TOPICS for Chapter Nine
Essays That Appeal to Reason

Write a logical argument defending one of the following propositions:

1. Buying a house, condominium, or trailer makes (does not make) better sense in the long run than renting one

2. Grading standards are (are not) slipping in American colleges and universities

3. College students are (are not) as bright now as they used to be

4. College graduates get (do not get) better jobs than those who do not go to college

5. Graduate or professional school is (is not) worth the expense these days

6. Smoking is (is not) hazardous to your health

7. America has (has not) developed into a "welfare state"

8. Farm-life is (is not) a dying institution in America

9. Cities are (are not) dying in America

10. Women's liberation has (has not) produced desirable results

11. The "revolution" in sexual morality is (is not) a myth

12. Religion is (is not) reviving in America

13. Pollution is (is not) avoidable

14. Our society has (has not) curtailed racism

10

Essays That Appeal
to Emotion and Ethics

PERSUASION,[1] *we have said, is the strategic use of language
to move an audience to action or belief. It works by appealing to our reason through logical* ARGUMENT *(the* MODE OF
PERSUASION *discussed in Chapter 9). It also works by appealing to our emotions and to our sense of ethics.*

The APPEAL TO EMOTION *is nicely exemplified in "Being
Prepared in Suburbia," the first essay in this chapter. Writing about gun-control legislation, Roger Verhulst deliberately sets aside reason and logic. He could produce statistics
to show how many deaths will soon be caused by privately
owned firearms, says Verhulst; but he finds "no point in
citing those statistics again; they may prove something, but
they're not likely to prompt any concrete action. There is
nothing moving about statistics."*

Here is the essence of the emotional appeal. It assumes,
in Verhulst's words, that "what is needed to produce results
is passion"; it aims at "the gut." Even if his own passion has
cooled in the process of *writing it down—and what passion
can flare through several rewritings?—the author* of an emotional appeal must kindle his original feelings in the reader.
He cannot do this, however, simply by being emotional.

It is a fallacy to think that you can appeal to an emotion
in your reader by imitating it: hysteria by being hysterical,
anger by raging. Often the best measure is to appear calm,
detached, thoroughly in control of your feelings—now. However intensely felt, your testimony must be orderly, or at
least coherent. You may want to recreate the circumstances
or perception that first excited in you the emotions that you

---

[1] Terms printed in all capitals are defined in the Glossary.

want to excite in your readers (as Fred Reed does so viscerally in "A Veteran Writes"); but here again your narrative must be controlled and directed toward its desired effect. Even your choice of individual words cannot be haphazard; you must pay close attention to their CONNOTATIONS. If you are addressing a labor union, for example, it will make a great difference whether you refer to the members as drones, workers, comrades, or just people.

The APPEAL TO ETHICS is an appeal to the reader's sense of how people ought to behave. This mode of persuasion convinces the reader that it is written by a person of good character whose judgment should be heeded. We are moved by the force of the speaker's personality.

Because the author's personality is so important in an appeal to ethics, great care must be taken to measure his or her tone of voice. TONE is an author's revealed attitude toward the material; it conveys his or her temper. A writer can be a decent human being and may have the reader's best interests at heart; but the reader may not trust the writer if the tone clashes with the message. Sincerity is the soul of the ethical appeal, and a writer must take pains to appear trustworthy as well as to be so.

To appear trustworthy, the writer must seem to be not only a person of good character and even temper but also a person who is well-informed. When noted attorney F. Lee Bailey tells us to "watch out for trial lawyers" because too many are competent only in the research library, we tend to believe him. Bailey's own expertise in the courtroom makes him an expert witness. The appeal of the expert witness, in fact, is one of the most common modern forms of the appeal to ethics. We are won over not by the moral uprightness of the expert but by his or her knowledge and intellectual integrity.

For study purposes, the appeals to emotion and to ethics have been separated here from the appeal to reason and from each other. (The first two essays in this chapter appeal to emotions; the last two appeal to ethics; and George Will's "Why Not Use Food as Food?" begins as an appeal to reason but ends with an emotional appeal to ethical behavior.) In practice you may want to combine all three modes of persuasion in the same essay (as George Will does). The goal of persuasive writing is to bring others around to your way of thinking in a good cause. Any honest means to this end is sound RHETORIC.

Roger Verhulst
Being Prepared in Suburbia

*Roger Verhulst lives with his wife and children in Grand Rapids,
Michigan. Most of his professional writing is in advertising,
though he also contributes essays to newspapers and magazines,
including Newsweek (from which the following is reprinted).
Verhulst has long believed in gun-control legislation, but "Being
Prepared in Suburbia" testifies to a conversion of sorts. After
acquiring a Crossman 760 because his Cub Scout den wanted
target practice, Verhulst found owners of guns to have an irrational attachment to their weapons that, he says, is stronger than
the rational arguments against owning deadly firearms. Analyzing
the emotion it arouses, his essay argues that gun control is as dead
as the victims of uncontrolled guns. How he came to this conclusion and how he wrote about it are examined in detail by
Verhulst himself in "Writers on the Writing Process" at the
end of this chapter.*

Gun legislation is dead for another year. As a result, if sta- 1
tistics are any guide, there's every likelihood that a lot of people now living will also be dead before the year is over.

There's no point in citing those statistics again; they may 2
prove something, but they're not likely to prompt any concrete action. There is nothing very moving about statistics.

What is needed to produce results is passion—and that's 3
where the antigun-control lobby has it all over the rest of
us. Those who favor stronger gun legislation—a solid majority
of Americans—can't hold a candle to the lovers of guns when
it comes to zeal.

I had a taste of that passion recently, and I begin to under- 4
stand something of what it is that fosters in gun libbers such
dedicated resolve. Thanks to a bunch of Cub Scouts and an
absurd little creature that went bump in the night, I've begun
to realize why cold, unemotional tabulations of gun deaths will

never lead to effective gun control. It's because of what can happen to people—even sane, rational, firearm-hating people like me—when they get their hands on a genuine, authentic, real-life gun.

Until last fall, I had never owned any weapon more lethal than   5
a water pistol. I opposed guns as esthetically repugnant, noisy, essentially churlish devices whose only practical purpose was to blast holes of various sizes in entities that would thereby be rendered less functional than they would otherwise have been. I didn't object merely to guns that killed people; I also objected to guns that killed animals, or shattered windows, or plinked away at discarded beer bottles. Whenever a gun was put to effective use, I insisted, something broke; and it seemed absurd to go through life breaking things.

With arguments such as these, bolstered by assorted threats, I   6
tried to instill holey terror also in my sons. Initially, I imposed an absolute ban on even toy guns. When that didn't work—their determination to possess such toys exceeding by scores of decibels my determination to ban them—I tried substituting lectures on the merits of nonviolence and universal love. Nice try.

Then, last fall, I became co-leader of a Cub Scout den here in   7
Grand Rapids, Mich., consisting of half a dozen 9-, 10- and 11-year-old boys. Sharing the leadership responsibilities with me was a kind and gentle man named Mickey Shea, who happens to be extremely fond of outdoor activities—including, of course, hunting.

It was in Mickey's basement, in full view of an imposing gun   8
rack, that I yielded to the pressure of pleading Cubbers and agreed to add target shooting to our scheduled activities. (Though I should make it clear that it wasn't Mickey who forced, or even strongly urged, that agreement; it was rather a wish to be accepted by the boys—to be regarded as appropriately adult and masculine —that prompted my decision. I've no one to blame but myself.)

So, for the sake of my kids and under the auspices of the Boy   9
Scouts of America, I bought a gun—a Crossman Power Master 760 BB Repeater pump gun, with bolt action, adjustable sight and a satisfying heft. It was capable of putting holes in all sorts of things.

A few nights later we got the Cubs together and spent an hour   10
or two aiming and firing at targets taped to paper-filled cardboard cartons. After which I unloaded the gun and locked it in my study, intending to leave it there until future target shoots came along

to justify bringing it out again. But a roving opossum that took up residence in our garage for a few cold nights in January undermined my good intentions.

We were entertained, at first. We called the kids down to see   11
our visitor perched on the edge of the trash barrel; we recorded the event on film. We regarded the presence of authentic wild animals in our corner of suburbia as delightfully diverting.

Almost at once, however, the rat-faced prowler began to make   12
himself obnoxious. There was the midnight clatter of falling objects, and the morning-after disarray of strewn garbage. The possum, we decided, would have to go.

But he proved to be not only an unwelcome but also a recal-   13
citrant guest. It was cold outside, and rather than waddling willingly back through the open garage door he took refuge behind a pile of scrap lumber; my vigorous thrusts with a broomstick were parried by obstinacy, and an occasional grunt.

I was cold, too, by now; and tired; and becoming frustrated.   14
Drastic action was indicated; I poured a handful of BB's into the Crossman 760, pumped it up, pointed the barrel blindly into the woodpile and pulled the trigger.

Nothing happened. The opossum did not move. Shivering, I   15
went back inside the house, still holding my weapon. I sat down with a drink and a cigarette to warm up.

With little else to do, I put the gun to my shoulder and aimed   16
it idly at the clock above the fireplace; I aimed it at a light fixture across the room, pressing gently against the trigger; I aimed it at a row of glasses behind the bar, imagining the snap and shatter of breaking glass; I aimed it at my own reflection in the TV set, thinking how absurdly easy it would be to eliminate television from my life.

The more imaginary targets I selected, the stronger became the   17
urge to shoot—something, anything. The gun extended my potential range of influence to everyone within sight; I could alter the world around me without even moving from the couch, simply by pulling the trigger. Gun in hand, I was bravely prepared to defend myself against any intruder, man or beast. I felt omnipotent as Zeus,[1] with lightning bolts at my fingertips.

No wonder, I thought, that people become hooked on guns.   18

---

[1] Ruler of the Greek gods; lightning was his special weapon.

This is the feeling that explains their passion, their religious fervor, their refusal to yield. It's rooted in the gut, not in the head. And in the recurrent struggle over gun legislation it is no wonder that their stamina exceeds mine.

I can understand that passion because I've felt it in my own 19 gut. I've felt the gun in my hand punch psychic holes in my intellectual convictions. And having felt all that, I do not have much hope that private ownership of deadly weapons will be at all regulated or controlled in the foreseeable future.

QUESTIONS

Understanding

1. According to Verhulst, what is the appeal of guns to those who own them? In which paragraph does he explain that appeal most explicitly?

2. Verhulst thinks that gun-control legislation is doomed. Why? What is his main reason?

3. Verhulst says that he yielded to the scouts' demand for target practice because he wished "to be accepted by the boys—to be regarded as appropriately adult and masculine" (par. 8). How far does this motive go toward explaining why some men like guns? How "sane" is it?

4. Why do you think Verhulst takes pains to point out that he came into contact with guns through the Cub Scouts?

5. In paragraph 19, Verhulst says that his gun opened "psychic holes" in his resolve. Which earlier paragraphs of his essay does this statement hark back to? How? With what unexpected twist has Verhulst's original theory about guns been confirmed?

6. Why is Verhulst's subject especially suited to an appeal to emotion?

Strategies and Structure

1. Verhulst writes as a "convert," an opponent of free guns who has come reluctantly to understand the appeal of firearms. Would his prediction about the failure of gun control be more or less con-

vincing if he were speaking as a long-time gun enthusiast? Explain your answer.

2. By telling the story of the author's conversion, this essay uses NARRATION to help achieve its persuasive purpose. Where does the narration begin? Where does it end? How compelling do you find Verhulst's narrative? Why?

3. As a general rule, do you think narration is more likely to be found in an APPEAL TO REASON or an APPEAL TO EMOTION? Why?

4. What is the strategy of Verhulst's first and second paragraphs? How successful is it?

5. Verhulst says that his sons' demand for toy guns exceeded "by scores of decibels" (par. 6) his resistance. What is the TONE of this remark? Of "Nice try" in the same paragraph? Describe Verhulst's TONE throughout the essay.

6. Why does Verhulst make himself look foolish, even mean, in the encounter with the "possum"?

7. How do the length and rhythm of the single sentence in paragraph 16 capture the author's state of mind at that point in his essay?

8. Far from assuming that a writer stirs emotion simply by being emotional, Verhulst comes across as remarkably cool-headed. How does he create this impression?

9. Whom do you take to be Verhulst's audience? In which paragraph does he, in effect, define it? Why is his cool-headed approach a good one for this audience?

10. When do you think a writer is better advised to be emotional (not just to describe emotions and appeal to them in the reader)— when he is addressing an audience that essentially agrees with him or one that disagrees? Why?

Words and Figures of Speech

1. Why does Verhulst use the word *hooked* in paragraph 18? What are the CONNOTATIONS of the term?

2. "Holey terror" (par. 6) and "delightfully diverting" (par. 11) represent two different LEVELS OF DICTION. Define the two levels and point out other examples of each. Why do you think Verhulst mixes the two?

3. *Psychic* (par. 19) has two basic meanings. What are they? Which one is intended here?

4. Look up the following words in your dictionary: *churlish* (par. 5), *decibels* (6), *auspices* (9), *obnoxious* (12), *recalcitrant* (13), *obstinacy* (13), *frustrated* (14), *omnipotent* (17), *fervor* (18).

Comparing

1. Compare and contrast "Being Prepared in Suburbia" with Afton Blake's "Sperm Banks: The Duty of Germinal Choice" (Chapter 9) as representative examples of two different MODES OF PERSUASION: the appeal to reason and the appeal to emotion, respectively.

2. Consider both Verhulst's essay and Deairich Hunter's "Ducks vs. Hard Rocks" (Chapter 2) as commentaries on why people resort to violence. Do they square with each other?

Discussion and Writing Topics

1. Write a persuasive essay in favor of gun-control legislation that appeals to emotion and that argues that guns are "esthetically repugnant, noisy, essentially churlish devices" (par. 5).

2. Construct a persuasive rational argument *against* gun-control legislation, the sort of argument, though on the opposite side, that Verhulst declines to make at the start of his essay.

3. If Verhulst's experience is at all typical, under what circumstances do our irrational impulses come forth? Are they any less real for being irrational? Why or why not?

Fred Reed

A Veteran Writes

Fred Reed is a former U. S. Marine, a veteran of the Vietnam War. As a stringer for the Army Times he witnessed the fall of Saigon and Phnom Penh. Reed lingered in Southeast Asia because, like many veterans, he liked it there. When he came home, he felt bored and angry that veterans were not really welcome to those who knew nothing of war at first-hand; he drifted for a while until he learned "that aberrant behavior, when written about, is litera-ture." His memories of Vietnam are as lush, vivid, and frightening as a napalm flash. "A Veteran Writes," from Harper's, might have been placed in the "Description" section of this book—its pictures are so powerful—but even more powerful is the message of silence it carries for non-veterans who criticize G.I.'s for not adjusting gracefully to "real" life back home.

I begin to weary of the stories about veterans that are now in vogue with the newspapers, the stories that dissect the veteran's psyche as if prying apart a laboratory frog—patroniz-ing stories written by style-section reporters who know all there is to know about chocolate mousse, ladies' fashions, and the wonderful desserts that can be made with simple jello. I weary of seeing veterans analyzed and diagnosed and explained by people who share nothing with veterans, by people who, one feels intuitively, would regard it as a harrowing experience to be alone in a backyard.

Week after week the mousse authorities tell us what is wrong with the veteran. The veteran is badly in need of adjust-ment, they say—lacks balance, needs fine tuning to whatever it is in society that one should be attuned to. What we have here, all agree, with omniscience and veiled condescension, is a victim: The press loves a victim. The veteran has bad dreams, say the jello writers, is alienated, may be hostile, doesn't socialize well—isn't, to be frank, quite right in the head.

But perhaps it is the veteran's head to be right or wrong in, and   3
maybe it makes a difference what memories are in the head. For the jello writers the war was a moral fable on Channel Four, a struggle hinging on Nixon and Joan Baez and the inequities of this or that. I can't be sure. The veterans seem to have missed the war by having been away in Vietnam at the time and do not understand the combat as it raged in the internecine cocktail parties of Georgetown.[1]

Still, to me Vietnam was not what it was to the jello writers, not   4
a ventilation of pious simplisms, not the latest literary interpretation of the domino theory. It left me memories the fashion writers can't imagine. It was the slums of Truong Minh Ky, where dogs' heads floated in pools of green water and three-inch roaches droned in sweltering back-alley rooms and I was happy. Washington knows nothing of hot, whorerich, beery Truong Minh Ky. I remember riding the bomb boats up the Mekong to Phnom Penh, with the devilish brown river closing in like a vise and rockets shrieking from the dim jungle to burst against the sandbagged wheelhouse, and crouching below the waterline between the diesel tanks. The mousse authorities do not remember this. I remember the villa on Monivong in Phnom Penh, with Sedlacek, the balding Australian hippie, and Naoki, the crazy freelance combat photographer, and Zoco, the Frenchman, when the night jumped and flickered with the boom of artillery and we listened to Mancini on shortwave and watched Nara dance. Washington's elite did not know Nara. They know much of politicians and of furniture.

If I try to explain what Vietnam meant to me—I haven't for   5
years, and never will again—they grow uneasy at my intensity. *My God*, their eyes say, *he sounds as though he liked it over there. Something in the experience clearly snapped an anchoring ligament in his mind and left him with odd cravings, a perverse view of life—nothing dangerous, of course, but. . . . The war did that to them*, they say. *War is hell.*

Well, yes, they may have something there. When you have seen   6

---

[1] A well-to-do section of Washington, D.C., where many high government officials reside.

a peasant mother screaming over three pounds of bright red mush that, thanks to God and a Chicom 107, is no longer precisely her child, you see that Sherman may have been on to something.[2] When you have eaten fish with Khmer troops in charred Cambodian battlefields, where the heat beats down like a soft rubber truncheon and a wretched stink comes from shallow graves, no particular leap of imagination is necessary to notice that war is no paradise. I cannot say that the jello writers are wrong in their understanding of war. But somehow I don't like hearing pieties about the war from these sleek, wise people who never saw it. It offends propriety.

There were, of course, veterans and veterans. Some hated the war, some didn't. Some went around the bend down in IV Corps, where leeches dropped softly down collars like green sausages and death erupted unexpected from the ungodly foliage. To the men in the elite groups—the Seals, Special Forces, Recondos, and Lurps who spent years in the Khmer bush, low to the ground where the ants bit hard—the war was a game with stakes high enough to engage their attention. They liked to play.

To many of us there, the war was the best time of our lives, almost the only time. We loved it because in those days we were alive, life was intense, the pungent hours passed fast over the central event of the age and the howling jets appeased the terrible boredom of existence. Psychologists, high priests of the mean, say that boredom is a symptom of maladjustment; maybe, but boredom has been around longer than psychologists have.

The jello writers would say we are mad to remember fondly anything about Nixon's war that Kennedy started. They do not remember the shuddering flight of a helicopter high over glowing green jungle that spread beneath us like a frozen sea. They never made the low runs a foot above treetops along paths that led like rivers through branches that clawed at the skids, never peered down into murky clearings and bubbling swamps of sucking snake-ridden muck. They do not remember monsoon mornings in the

7

8

9

[2] General William Tecumseh Sherman (1820–1891): "I am tired and sick of war. Its glory is all moonshine. It is only those who have neither fired a shot nor heard the shrieks and groans of the wounded who cry aloud for blood, more vengeance, more desolation. War is hell." Chicom 107: Chinese communist rocket.

highlands where dragons of mist twisted in the valleys, coiling lazily on themselves, puffing up and swallowing whole villages in their dank breath. The mousse men do not remember driving before dawn to Red Beach, when the headlights in the blackness caught ghostly shapes, maybe VC,[3] thin yellow men mushroom-headed in the night, bicycling along the alien roads. As nearly as I can tell, jello writers do not remember anything.

Then it was over. The veterans came home. Suddenly the world   10
seemed to stop dead in the water. Suddenly the slant-eyed hookers were gone, as were the gunships and the wild drunken nights in places that the jello writers can't picture. Suddenly the veterans were among soft, proper people who knew nothing of what they had done and what they had seen, and who, truth to be told, didn't much like them.

Nor did some of us much like the people at home—though it   11
was not at first a conscious distaste. Men came home with wounds and terrible memories and dead friends to be greeted by that squalling she-ass of Tom Hayden's,[4] to find a country that viewed them as criminals. Slowly, to more men than will admit to it, the thought came: *These are the people I fought for?* And so we lost a country.

We looked around us with new eyes and saw that, in a sense the   12
mousse people could never understand, we had lost even our dignity. I remember a marine corporal at Bethesda Naval Hospital who, while his wounds healed, had to run errands for the nurses, last year's co-eds. "A hell of a bust," he said with the military's sardonic economy of language. "Machine gunner to messenger boy."

It wasn't exactly that we didn't fit. Rather, we saw what there   13
was to fit with—and recoiled. We sought jobs, but found offices where countless bureaucrats shuffled papers at long rows of desks, like battery hens awaiting the laying urge, their bellies billowing over their belts. Some of us joined them but some, in different ways, fled. A gunship pilot of my acquaintance took to the law, and to drink, and spent five years discovering that he really wanted to be in Rhodesia. Others went back into the death-in-the-bushes outfits, where the hard old rules still held. I drifted across Asia,

[3] Viet Cong, communist guerillas.
[4] Hayden is married to actress and antiwar activist Jane Fonda.

Mexico, Wyoming, hitchhiking and sleeping in ditches a lot until I learned that aberrant behavior, when written about, is literature.

The jello writers were quickly upon us. We were morose, they said, sullen. We acted strangely at parties, sat silently in corners and watched with noncommittal stares. Mentally, said the fashion experts, we hadn't made the trip home. 14

It didn't occur to them that we just had nothing to say about jello. Desserts mean little to men who have lain in dark rifle pits over Happy Valley in rainy season, watching mortar flares tremble in low-lying clouds that flickered like the face of God, while in the nervous evening safeties clicked off along the wire and amtracs rumbled into alert idles, coughing and waiting. 15

Once, after the GIs had left Saigon, I came out of a bar on Cach Mang and saw a veteran with a sign on his jacket: VIET NAM: IF YOU HAVEN'T BEEN THERE, SHUT THE FUCK UP. Maybe, just maybe, he had something. 16

QUESTIONS

Understanding

1. Why, according to Reed, did he (and some other veterans) love a war that he recognized as hellish?

2. If this essay is right, why have Reed and many other veterans had trouble getting over their experiences in Vietnam? What do they carry home with them?

3. What aspect of "normal" life back home did Reed himself find hardest to adjust to?

4. What are some examples of the kind of behavior, according to Reed, that non-veterans consider disturbing and anti-social?

5. The newspaper commentators are right, Reed agrees, when they say that war is hell. Why, then, does he get angry with them for mouthing "pieties" (par. 6) anyway? What disqualifies them from commenting, even accurately, on the war in Reed's opinion?

6. How does Reed's opinion of psychologists resemble his opinion of the commentators?

7. Reed's essay is a vivid piece of descriptive writing, but it is also an essay in persuasion. What is Reed trying to persuade readers unacquainted directly with Vietnam to do or accept?

8. Does Reed claim that all veterans reacted as he did to the business of returning to civilian life? How did some others react?

9. How much faith does Reed appear to place in the importance of political forces and policies upon the war in Vietnam?

Strategies and Structure

1. The thrust of Reed's appeal to emotion is that those who have not fought in Vietnam should not presume to explain the experience to those who have. On what authority does he base this appeal? Is he convincing? Why or why not?

2. Why does Reed end his essay by referring to the veteran with the sign on his jacket? Is the profanity justified or not? Why or why not?

3. Reed does not organize his essay according to the steps of a logical proof—logicality is one of the attitudes Reed is attacking here— but as a series of memories. What emotions do these memories appeal to? Which passages do you find most effective, given the author's purpose.

4. In what sense is Reed's persuasive appeal also a definition? What is he defining and for whom?

5. Where do you see traces of a chronological ordering in Reed's essay?

6. Reed's essay at times resembles a harangue, a form of speech in which the speaker faces his audience and repeatedly confronts them with his complaint. Point out other repetitive elements like the following that give Reed's essay the feeling of being spoken, almost chanted: "They do not remember the shuddering flight . . ."; "They do not remember monsoon mornings . . ."; "The mousse men do not remember driving before dawn . . ." (par. 9).

7. What do the italicized portions signify in Reed's essay? What is his TONE in them?

8. "It offends propriety," says Reed (par. 7) of non-veterans who pronounce truisms about war. Why do you suppose Reed chooses this particular defense? How might he respond to the charge that his essay offends propriety with its undisguised anger and unwholesome images?

9. What indications of emotional sensitivity do you discern in this veteran's tough stand against uncomprehending non-veterans?

10. What reason for being sore does Reed suggest when he says of

veterans like himself that some non-veteran critics of the war "viewed them as criminals" (par. 11)?

Words and Figures of Speech

1. What is the effect of Reed's repetition of epithets such as "mousse men" and "jello writers" (par. 9)?
2. Why might epithets (name-calling) fit neatly into a harangue?
3. What is the effect of Reed's choosing the word *precisely* in paragraph 6? Of his choice of *ventilation* in paragraph 4?
4. "And so we lost a country" (par. 11) is a good example of UNDER-STATEMENT. Point out other examples of Reed's use of this device.
5. "They know much of politicians and of furniture," says Reed of non-veterans he meets or overhears at cocktail parties. What is the effect of juxtaposing the last two nouns in this biting sentence?
6. Which sense of *mean* is Reed using in paragraph 8?
7. Explain the METAPHOR, "the world seemed to stop dead in the water" (par. 10). To what is Reed comparing the world? Also explain his "fine tuning" metaphor in paragraph 2.
8. Look up any of the following words that you may have paused over: *psyche* (par. 1), *patronizing* (par. 1), *omniscience* (par. 2), *condescension* (par. 2), *alienated* (par. 2), *internecine* (par. 3), *perverse* (par. 5), *pieties* (par. 6), *appeased* (par. 8), *sardonic* (par. 12), *aberrant* (par. 13), *morose* (par. 14).

Comparing

1. Contrast Reed's presence and voice in this essay with those of another veteran soldier delivering a harangue, Chief Seattle in his "Reply to the U. S. Government" at the end of this chapter.
2. How does "A Veteran Writes" confirm George Orwell's charge in "Politics and the English Language" ("Essays for Further Reading") that political lies erode the power of language to aid clear thinking?

Discussion and Writing Topics

1. Do you find Reed's descriptions of his experience in Vietnam to be beautiful or appalling or both? Explain your reaction?

2. Do you agree with Reed's assumption that one must be an eye-witness of events in order to understand them? Why or why not?

3. If you are a veteran, use your experience to refute or support the position of non-veterans who say that those who fought in Vietnam or elsewhere are criminals.

4. If you are not a veteran, try to get a friend or relative who is to confide his or her experiences to you. Then take a position on this same issue using what you have learned about how one veteran feels.

George Will

Why Not Use Food as Food?

Born in 1941 in Champaign, Illinois, George Will was educated
at Trinity College (B.A., 1962), Oxford University, and Princeton
(Ph.D., 1967). He taught politics at Michigan State and the
University of Toronto, came to Washington first as a congressional
aide, then stayed on as Washington editor of the National Review. Paid to be, as he says, "professionally opinionated," Will
has been a syndicated columnist since 1974 and a contributing
editor of Newsweek since 1975. In 1977, Will was awarded a
Pulitzer Prize for distinguished commentary. His latest book is
Statecraft and Soulcraft: What Government Does (1983). Often
called a "conservative," Will does "not believe that journalists
should be in an adversary relationship with the government," but
the following essay shows that he distinguishes between being an
adversary and being a critic. In "Why Not Use Food as Food?"
Will defends the position attacked by Johnson C. Montgomery
in "The Island of Plenty" (Chapter 9).

The federal government is nibbling at the cheese glut. The   1
Agriculture Department has proposed requiring that frozen
pizzas contain a certain minimum amount of cheese and that
the use of cheese substitutes be clearly confessed on packages.

The frozen pizza industry regards this proposal as the kind   2
of Leninism that Ronald Reagan was elected to stop. But the
cheese glut (which is just a portion of the dairy products surplus, which is just a bit of the agriculture surplus) demands
boldness.

Jeffrey Birnbaum, a Wall Street Journal reporter, recently   3
toured a dormant limestone mine in Missouri. There, the government "stores so much surplus cheese, butter and powdered

milk that a visitor would be hard pressed to walk past it all in one day." A tour by golf cart reveals canyons of cheddar cheese in 500-pound barrels, towers of frozen butter in 68-pound boxes, endless aisles of 100-pound sacks of dried milk—61 million pounds of dairy products, enough to cover 13 football fields 17 feet deep, or fill a train stretching from Manhattan to Toledo.

This is just two percent of the 2.9 billion pounds of dairy products that taxpayers have bought. In recent years they have paid $3 billion, or $13,000 for every dairy farmer. Taxpayers are currently paying $275,000 an hour to buy more surpluses, and are paying $5 million a month to store the stuff.   4

Well, now. Perhaps a dozen-trillion pizzas would cut the current cheese glut, but that many pizzas would lead to a terrible pepperoni shortage. We need another idea.   5

Perhaps we should sell frozen pizzas to the Soviet Union. Moscow might send some of our pizzas, as it sends grain, to Nicaragua, but that is commerce in fungible goods. If Moscow cannot afford pizzas, we can do what we do regarding grain: give them credits and generally fiddle things so that pizzas (like the grain) cost Moscow less than it costs Americans to produce them.   6

Here is another whimsical idea: we could stop paying farmers to inundate markets and limestone mines with dairy products. Today the government is taxing consumers (everyone) to pay farmers to produce food that is, because of price supports, unnecessarily expensive when taxpayers buy it at supermarkets and is expensive when taxpayers pay to store it.   7

One study says that a $1-per-hundredweight reduction in the support price would knock nine cents off a gallon of milk and a pound of cheese, and 11 cents off a pound of butter, and $1.2 billion off consumers' food bills in a year. Furthermore, dairy products, being cheaper, would be more exportable, so there would be less to store.   8

But here is a better idea: use the food as food. America does not have enough productivity. Government should not pay people, as it today is paying farmers, to produce less—less of something that parts of the world need desperately. Surely it is not beyond the capacity of public policy to make America's agricultural bounty an asset to American policy. Indeed, it is a scandal not to.   9

Today in 18 black African countries (Morocco and Algeria, too, have desperate needs), 20 million persons face starvation unless   10

600,000 tons of extra food reach them. Since 1960, Africa's food production has increased less than 2 percent a year—less than population growth. In nine countries, food production is more than 10 percent below 1960 levels.

The World Bank estimates that nearly 200 million persons—60　11 percent of all Africans—eat fewer calories daily than the United Nations considers a survival diet.

Drought is only part of the problem. Governments have made　12 Africa unnecessarily vulnerable to such natural phenomena. Urban mobs demand food at artificially low prices, thus discouraging production. Government planners have tried to spur industrialization by holding down food prices in the hope that this would hold down urban wages. If someone could leash Africa's governments and unleash American farmers on Africa, the continent could produce 100 times more food than it does today.

Logistical problems (including problems posed by African bu-　13 reaucracies) involved in even distributing food are staggering, and there is the danger that American food could produce dependency and further depress African agriculture. But an American attempt to solve these problems is as close as one can come in this world to an absolute moral imperative.

I am staring at a photograph of what looks, at first glance, to be　14 a bold, wizened old man. Actually it is a child. The child is sucking the withered breast of a woman who could be 19 years old. It is a sight to concentrate the mind on limestone mines full of food.

QUESTIONS

Understanding

1. George Will offers three "whimsical" ideas for getting rid of the country's surplus dairy products. What are they?

2. What serious solution does he propose?

3. In paragraph 9 Will writes, "America does not have enough productivity." This statement seems at first to contradict the author's basic premise: that we already have a surplus of food. How can this apparent contradiction be resolved?

4. According to Will, drought is only part of the reason that Africa cannot produce enough food to feed herself. What is the rest of the reason in his view?

5. Why, according to Will, does America have "an absolute moral imperative" to help feed starving countries?

Strategies and Structure

1. Why do you think Will begins his essay with several "whimsical" solutions to the food problem instead of starting with the "better idea" of paragraph 9?

2. "Why Not Use Food as Food? quotes statistics by the pound, beginning with paragraph 3. Point out several other paragraphs in which the author buttresses his argument heavily with numbers. Why do you think Will knowingly cointributes to the statistics glut here?

4. Where else in his essay, besides the array of facts and figures, does Will appeal to reason and logic? Where does he appeal most directly to emotion and ethnics?

5. How and where in his argument does Will tip the balance away from reason and toward emotion?

6. To which kind of appeal is a reason like "absolute moral imperative" (par. 13) more likely to apply? Why?

7. Should Will have devoted as much space to the photograph of the starving child (par. 14) as he does to the size and cost of the dairy surplus? Why or why not?

Words and Figures of Speech

1. Is the title of George Will's essay an actual query or a RHETORICAL QUESTION? Explain your answer.

2. How would you describe the TONE of "Well, now" (par. 5)? How about the SYNTAX? Do they complement or conflict with one another?

3. What are the connotations of *unleash* (par. 12)? How do they change when Will uses the positive form of the word (*leash*) in the same paragraph?

4. Why is it a joke to call pizzas "fungible" goods (par. 6)?

5. Would Will's opening sentence be better if he had said "attempting to alleviate" instead of "nibbling at"? Why or why not? How about his description of the starving child; would it be blunted or improved by using the word *wrinkled* in place of *wizened* (par. 14)?

6. What is "Leninism" (par. 2)? How appropriate do you find the term here?

Comparing

1. "Why Not Use Food as Food?" turns an appeal to reason into an appeal to emotion. To what extent might "The Island of Plenty" (Chapter 9) be said to do the reverse?
2. As strategies of debate, what does Afton Blake's reference to her son Doron in the previous chapter ("Sperm Banks: The Duty of Germinal Choice") have in common with George Will's reference to the African child?

Discussion and Writing Topics

1. Whose arguments about America's role as a provider to the world do you find more persuasive (and why)—George Will's or Johnson C. Montgomery's ("The Island of Plenty," Chapter 9)?
2. Write a rebuttal to Will's argument in which you assert that he begs the question of America's ability to provide enough food for the third world.
3. Write a rebuttal to Montgomery's argument in which you assert that *he* begs this crucial question.

Chief Seattle

Reply to the
U.S. Government

Chief Seattle (c. 1786–1866) was the leader of the Dwamish, Suquamish, and allied Native American tribes living in the region of the city that now bears his name. He welcomed white settlers from the time of their first arrival and loyally resisted uprisings against them. He later converted to Roman Catholicism and began holding morning and evening services among the tribe. He was not pleased when the village of Seattle, Washington, took his name because he believed that his spirit would be disturbed in the afterlife each time his name was spoken by mortals. Toward the end of his life, Seattle exacted compensation for his broken sleep by seeking gifts among citizens of the region. The "Reply" printed here was Chief Seattle's response to the U.S. government's offer to buy two million acres of Indian land. The offer was made in 1854 through Governor Isaac Stevens of the Washington Territory. For his formal answer, spoken in the Dwamish language, Seattle gathered the tribe around him and placed his hand on Governor Stevens's head. He stood a foot taller than the governor, and his voice could be heard for half a mile. Henry A. Smith translated the speech. Seattle considered the government's proposal (as he promises to do here), decided to accept it, and signed the treaty of Point Elliott on January 22, 1855.

Yonder sky that has wept tears of compassion upon my people for centuries untold, and which to us appears changeless and eternal, may change. Today is fair. Tomorrow may be overcast with clouds. My words are like the stars that never change. Whatever Seattle says the great chief at Washington

can rely upon with as much certainty as he can upon the return
of the sun or the seasons. The White Chief says that Big Chief
at Washington sends us greetings of friendship and goodwill.
That is kind of him for we know he has little need of our
friendship in return. His people are many. They are like the
grass that covers vast prairies. My people are few. They resemble
the scattering trees of a storm-swept plain. The great, and—I presume—good, White Chief sends us word that he wishes to buy
our lands but is willing to allow us enough to live comfortably.
This indeed appears just, even generous, for the Red Man no
longer has rights that he need respect, and the offer may be wise
also, as we are no longer in need of an extensive country. . . . I
will not dwell on, nor mourn over, our untimely decay, nor re-
proach our paleface brothers with hastening it, as we too may have
been somewhat to blame.

Youth is impulsive. When our young men grow angry at some   2
real or imaginary wrong, and disfigure their faces with black paint,
it denotes that their hearts are black, and then they are often cruel
and relentless, and our old men and old women are unable to
restrain them. Thus it has ever been. Thus it was when the white
men first began to push our forefathers further westward. But let
us hope that the hostilities between us may never return. We
would have everything to lose and nothing to gain. Revenge by
young men is considered gain, even at the cost of their own lives,
but old men who stay at home in times of war, and mothers who
have sons to lose, know better.

Our good father at Washington—for I presume he is now our   3
father as well as yours, since King George [1] has moved his boundaries further north—our great good father, I say, sends us word
that if we do as he desires he will protect us. His brave warriors
will be to us a bristling wall of strength, and his wonderful ships
of war will fill our harbors so that our ancient enemies far to the
northward—the Hydas and Tsimpsians—will cease to frighten our
women, children, and old men. Then in reality will he be our
father and we his children. But can that ever be? Your God is not
our God! Your God loves your people and hates mine. He folds
his strong and protecting arms lovingly about the paleface and
leads him by the hand as a father leads his infant son—but He

---

[1] George IV, king of England from 1820 to 1830.

has forsaken His red children—if they really are his. Our God, the Great Spirit, seems also to have forsaken us. Your God makes your people wax strong every day. Soon they will fill the land. Our people are ebbing away like a rapidly receding tide that will never return. The white man's God cannot love our people or He would protect them. They seem to be orphans who can look nowhere for help. How then can we be brothers? How can your God become our God and renew our prosperity and awaken in us dreams of returning greatness? If we have a common heavenly father He must be partial—for He came to his paleface children. We never saw Him. He gave you laws but He had no word for His red children whose teeming multitudes once filled this vast continent as stars fill the firmament. No; we are two distinct races with separate origins and separate destinies. There is little in common between us.

To us the ashes of our ancestors are sacred and their resting place is hallowed ground. You wander far from the graves of your ancestors and seemingly without regret. Your religion was written upon tables of stone by the iron finger of your God so that you could not forget. The Red Man could never comprehend nor remember it. Our religion is the traditions of our ancestors—the dreams of our old men, given them in solemn hours of night by the Great Spirit; and the visions of our sachems; and it is written in the hearts of our people.

Your dead cease to love you and the land of their nativity as soon as they pass the portals of the tomb and wander way beyond the stars. They are soon forgotten and never return. Our dead never forget the beautiful world that gave them being.

Day and night cannot dwell together. The Red man has ever fled the approach of the White Man, as the morning mist flees before the morning sun. However, your proposition seems fair and I think that my people will accept it and will retire to the reservation you offer them. Then we will dwell apart in peace, for the words of the Great White Chief seem to be the words of nature speaking to my people out of dense darkness.

It matters little where we pass the remnant of our days. They will not be many. A few more moons; a few more winters—and not one of the descendants of the mighty hosts that once moved over this broad land or lived in happy homes, protected by the Great Spirit, will remain to mourn over the graves of a people once more powerful and hopeful than yours. But why should I mourn at the untimely fate of my people? Tribe follows tribe, and nation follows nation, like the waves of the sea. It is the order of nature, and regret is useless. Your time of decay may be distant, but it will surely come, for even the White Man whose God walked and talked with him as friend with friend, cannot be exempt from the common destiny. We may be brothers after all. We will see.

We will ponder your proposition, and when we decide we will **8** let you know. But should we accept it, I here and now make this condition that we will not be denied the privilege without molestation of visiting at any time the tombs of our ancestors, friends and children. Every part of this soil is sacred in the estimation of my people. Every hillside, every valley, every plain and grove, has been hallowed by some sad or happy event in days long vanished. . . . The very dust upon which you now stand responds more lovingly to their footsteps than to yours, because it is rich with the blood of our ancestors and our bare feet are conscious of the sympathetic touch. . . . Even the little children who lived here and rejoiced here for a brief season will love these somber solitudes and at eventide they greet shadowy returning spirits. And when the last Red Man shall have perished, and the memory of my tribe shall have become a myth among the White Men, these shores will swarm with the invisible dead of my tribe, and when your children's children think themselves alone in the held, the store, the shop, upon the highway, or in the silence of the pathless woods, they will not be alone. . . . At night when the streets of your cities and villages are silent and you think them deserted, they will throng with the returning hosts that once filled and still love this beautiful land. The White Man will never be alone.

Let him be just and deal kindly with my people, for the dead **9** are not powerless. Dead, did I say? There is no death, only a change of worlds.

QUESTIONS

Understanding

1. For what is Chief Seattle appealing to the White Man? What slightly veiled threat does he make in the last two paragraphs of his speech?

2. Describe the single condition that Chief Seattle puts upon his probable acceptance of the government's offer to buy the tribe's land. Why does he make this condition? What does it show about the basis of his religion?

3. How does this belief help to explain why many Native Americans moved onto the reservation only with the greatest reluctance?

4. The last paragraph of Chief Seattle's speech sounds at first like a Christian denial of death and affirmation of heavenly life, but what does he mean by "a change of worlds" (par. 9)? What other differences does Chief Seattle mention between his religion and Christianity?

5. Why does the Dwamish chief doubt that the White Man and the Red Man will ever be brothers? In what grim sense may they prove "brothers after all" (par. 7)?

6. Why, according to Chief Seattle, did the young men of his tribe paint their faces and go to war? What was their motive, and what was the meaning of their war-paint?

7. Chief Seattle refuses to mourn the "untimely fate" (par. 7) of his people or to grant the eternal supremacy of his conquerors. Why? Explain the pervasive theme of his speech.

Strategies and Structure

1. Does Chief Seattle appear trustworthy to you? Why or why not?

2. How does he attempt to establish his authority and trustworthiness in paragraph 1? What equivalent devices might you find in a modern speech?

3. What personal qualities do you attribute to Chief Seattle after reading his entire speech? Point out specific statements and phrases that help to characterize him.

4. How does paragraph 2 show Chief Seattle's wisdom?

5. What distinction is Chief Seattle making when he refers to the "great, and—I presume—good, White Chief" (par. 1)? How does his being anxious to draw this distinction help to qualify the chief as a person worthy to make an APPEAL TO ETHICS?

6. The Dwamish chief shows his respect for the Big Chief at Washington by thanking him for "his greetings of friendship and goodwill" (par. 1) and by addressing him as "our good father" (par. 3). How does he also show that he is not afraid of the Big Chief?

7. Seattle's voice is said to have rumbled like the iron engine of a train when he delivered his speech. How is this rumbling quality conveyed in the sentence patterns of paragraphs 1 and 7? Why is an "iron" pace appropriate to Seattle's message?

8. Seattle begins his appeal by acknowledging the justice (even the generosity) and the power of the government; but he declines to make up his mind at once, and ends by asserting that the Red Man retains a degree of power. Is the order significant here? How would Seattle's speech have been changed if the order had been reversed?

9. When arguing at a disadvantage (against a popular opinion, for example), should you admit that disadvantage early on, mention it in closing, or not acknowledge it at all? Explain your answer.

10. Chief Seattle's ethical appeal also makes use of the APPEAL TO EMOTION. Discuss where and how the two work together. What emotion or emotions does his oration speak to?

Words and Figures of Speech

1. The White Man, we are told, is like "the grass that covers vast prairies" (par. 1) and the Indian is like "scattering trees" (par. 1) or the "receding tide" (par. 3), though once he was like the "stars" (par. 3). How do these natural METAPHORS fit in with Chief Seattle's general references to decay and to the cycle of the seasons?

2. What are the implications of the metaphor, "Day and night cannot dwell together" (par. 6)?

3. In what sense is the translator using the word *sympathetic* when he reports Seattle as saying that "our bare feet are conscious of the sympathetic touch" (par. 8)?

4. What analogy does Chief Seattle draw when he describes the role of the ideal leader or chief in paragraph 3?

Comparing

1. A representative of the old, dying order, Seattle resembles General Lee as Bruce Catton portrays him in "Grant and Lee: A Study in Contrasts" (Chapter 6). Pursue the parallel between the two men and the cultures they represent.

2. Analyze and explain what Barry Lopez in "My Horse" (Chapter 7) has "learned" from Chief Seattle's braves.

3. Compare and contrast Seattle's view of nature with Annie Dillard's in "Transfiguration." (Chapter 7)

4. Apply Horace Miner's explanation of how superstition and magic work in a primitive society ("Body Ritual Among the Nacirema," Chapter 8) to the society of the Dwamish tribe as revealed by Chief Seattle.

Discussion and Writing Topics

1. Speaking on behalf of the government, compose an appropriate reply to Chief Seattle's speech.

2. Write a persuasive ethical appeal in which you contend that it is not possible to restore all their lands to the Native Americans but that some reparation for past injustices is due them.

3. Judging from Chief Seattle's speech, why do you think Indian literature is full of natural metaphors?

Howard Means
The Terror and the Honor at UVa

Howard Means is a senior editor of the Washingtonian. He
attended the University of Virginia, Charlottesville, in the early
1960s, before Vietnam and campus radicalism altered the temper
of the decade. The temper of those times, as Means recalls them
here, was practically "medieval." Campus life in the bastion of
Jeffersonism was governed by an honor code as strict as any
knight's. Those days are gone, even at UVa, Means concedes,
but he laments the passing of the old code in this essay in moral
nostalgia from the Washington Post.

I went to college at the University of Virginia in the early   1
1960s, in what was effectively a reign of terror. On the first day
of orientation, new undergraduates were grouped together in
the presence of the student body president to be told that certain unyielding principles were at work in this miniature world
of ours. Chief among them—chief because deviation from it
was punished the most severely—was the matter of honor: a
university man did not lie, cheat, or steal, nor would the community tolerate a liar, cheat or thief in its midst.

For suspected honor violations, official action was swift and   2
surgical. The accused was informed of the charges lodged
against him, lodged always by another student, and given the
choice of leaving school or appearing before the student-run
honor committee. Should the accused be found guilty by the
honor committee, there was but one penalty: expulsion.

We received the news that first day with a studied casual-   3
ness, much as the members of a high school football team are

likely to shrug off the announcement of some impossible blocking-sled drill while terror secretly grabs their vitals. Something important was to be put to the test here, some vision of what we would like our own best selves to be; and it was to be put to the test time and again for as long as we endured the place.

A kind of giant situation ethics game played itself out on our private boards, a world of what-ifs overlaid by the Draconian system we had fallen into—overlaid finally with the specter of expulsion, disgrace, with the fear of finding ourselves wanting at the core. And yet we managed to go about the business of being undergraduates with much of that same studied casualness. We crammed late, often futilely, did our term papers, took our examinations, even carried them with us when we went out for a coffee and doughnut halfway through; and at the end we pledged on our honor as gentlemen that we had neither given nor received aid, and sealed that pledge with our signatures.

Honor, gentlemen, pledges and sacred troths—it all sounds so quaint now, so nearly medieval. But what seems most antiquated of all is the absolutism that colored the system. Just as there were no gradations of punishment with the university's honor system, so there were no gradations of guilt. One wasn't a little dishonest where the system was concerned, larceny wasn't understood in its social context, a lie was a lie was a lie. Mitigating circumstances entered hardly a whit into the honor council's deliberations; Robin Hood was as guilty as Willie Sutton.[1] And the violations, if they were found to have occurred, brought them all—liar, cheat, and thief, petty ones and grand ones—to the same end.

What occasions these thoughts is the news that a study committee—acting in part on the basis of a Gallup poll of university alumni and students—has now recommended a number of changes in the honor system. Many of them are procedural, but one is fundamental: henceforth, should the committee's changes be enacted, an honor violation shall be punishable either by a one-year suspension or by expulsion, at the trial panel's discretion. A second violation shall be met with expulsion.

One shouldn't be too surprised. We live in a world where too

[1] Robin Hood, the legendary British outlaw of the twelfth century, robbed the rich to give to the poor. Willie ("the actor") Sutton wore disguises when he robbed banks in the 1930s; police found it impossible to keep him jailed.

many off-with-their-heads tyrants have given absolutism a bad name. We understand, as we should, that any act of behavior is the sum total of a hundred parts, each part the sum total of a hundred influences; and if as a society we are no longer as committed as we once were to treating the act by curing the influence, we still hold that compassion and mitigation have a role in our daily doings. We are not a mean people, far from it; and there's a little larceny in the best of us. But if one shouldn't be surprised by the recommendation to do away with the single sanction that has always been the honor code's hallmark, I still reserve the right to be saddened by it.

I took part in an honor trial once, mostly as an innocent by- 8
stander. A dorm-mate from my first year, accused of cheating on a biology examination, had asked me to appear before the committee as a character witness; and so I found myself at 10 that night at the student union building. (Honor trials were always held as close to the lodging of the complaint as possible.) Shortly after 2 in the morning, after four hours of bridge with my fellow witnesses, I was called in to testify. There, I affirmed that I had never known my old dorm-mate to lie, cheat, or steal; and the hour being late and the occasion momentous, I settled back at the bridge table for the night. At 7 I wandered over to the cafeteria for breakfast; and there I saw my one-time dorm-mate, on recess from his own trial, a shadow of doom already crossing his face—a depth of sadness and despair that was awful to behold. A little over an hour later, he was found guilty. I never saw him again.

Under the proposed changes, my old dorm-mate needn't have 9
been so glum. He still would have been disgraced by a conviction, of course, but even in that last hour of his trial, when hope of establishing his innocence had long ago ebbed, there still would have been the possibility of rehabilitation, of a second chance. Mitigation will be on hand with the changes, and the concept of honor will no longer be so monolithic at the university, so secretly terrifying.

All that is kinder I suppose, and perhaps kindness should be the 10
issue here. But what's also at issue is the business of testing oneself, in a crucible where every deviation is fatal—not a Hemingway-esque test, not physical courage, not grace under pressure; but the kind of test where the matter being weighed runs straight through to the soul. That's what will be lost, and it will be a shame.

QUESTIONS

Understanding

1. According to Howard Means, why was the reign of honor under the old system at UVa also a "reign of terror" (par. 1)?
2. What big difference will the proposed system make in the way honor violations are handled?
3. Means is not actually arguing that the old, all-for-nothing honor system be retained at his *alma mater*. What is his position exactly? What does he feel will be lost with the passing of the old system?
4. Why is the author qualified to judge the new system of ethics?
5. Why is the University of Virginia (founded by Thomas Jefferson) an especially fitting place for Means to take his stand?

Strategies and Structure

1. Means sounds at first as if he is attacking the quaintness of the old honor system at the university. Where do you first learn that he is mourning its loss instead?
2. How does Means's account of his part in the honor trial increase our respect for his powers of ethical judgment?
3. Means uses three separate personal pronouns to refer to himself here: "we," "one," and "I." Distinguish among the persons represented by each pronoun. Which one does he use when speaking in the voice of a reasonable man of our times?
4. Which personal pronoun does Means use when he is being most "old-fashioned" and idiosyncratic?
5. The basis of Means's argument against the new system is personal preference. Is this a sufficient reason under the circumstances? Why or why not?
6. Why might personal preference count for more in an appeal to ethics as opposed to an appeal to reason?
7. Means's essay concludes by simply observing that the passing of an absolute system of honor will be a "shame" (par. 10). Should the author have thumped the table more strenuously at the end? Why do you think he concludes with this gentle tap instead?

Words and Figures of Speech

1. Why is "surgical" (par. 2) an apt description for justice under the old system as Means depicts it?

2. What is a "crucible" (par. 10)? What is tested or blended in one, and why is the METAPHOR fitting here?

3. *Draconian* (par. 4) means "severe." From the name of what ancient lawgiver does the word derive?

4. What are the CONNOTATIONS of *quaint* and *medieval* (par. 5)? Why does the author use these words despite their implied meanings?

5. How effective do you find the blocking-sled SIMILE in paragraph 3?

6. Why does the author speak of the "accused" (par. 2) rather than the "offender" or the "culprit"?

7. How acurate do you find "studied casualness" as a description of the attitude Means is recalling in paragraphs 3 and 4?

8. Turn to your dictionary for any assistance you might need with the following words: *specter* (par. 4), *troths* (par. 5), *antiquated* (par. 5), *absolutism* (pars. 5, 7), *larceny* (pars. 5, 7), *mitigating* (par. 5), *whit* (par. 5), *procedural* (par. 6), *discretion* (par. 6), *mean* (par. 7), *sanction* (par. 7), *hallmark* (par. 7), *momentous* (par. 8), *awful* (par. 8), *rehabilitation* (par. 9), *monolithic* (par. 9).

Topics for Discussion and Writing

1. As compared to an absolute standard of behavior, what is "situation ethics" (par. 4)? Do you agree or disagree that situation ethics is now the more realistic standard?

2. Under an ideal ethical system, should all offences be treated alike in your opinion? Is a lie always a lie, a grand theft as guilty as a "petty" one? Or can there be legitimate "mitigating circumstances"?

3. How are honor violations (for instance, plagiarism) handled at your school? Write an essay outlining the official system and then either attack or defend it. Refer to a specific case or cases if possible.

4. Have you ever witnessed or been the victim of a miscarriage of justice? Recount the event and argue the case as you see it.

Comparing

1. Does Means's account of changes on campus affirm or deny Colman McCarthy's analysis in "Phasing Out Campus Idealism" (Chapter 6)? Explain your answer.

2. Both Howard Means and Chief Seattle (in the preceding essay) are arguing about matters of ethics. The ethical appeal, however, depends less upon subject matter than upon the apparent character of the speaker. Which of these two men of honorable intent seems the more worthy of your trust and belief? Why?

Writers on the Writing Process:
Roger Verhulst

[*Editor's Note: The questions to which* Roger Verhultst *refers in the following notes on the composition of "On Being Prepared in Suburbia" were written inquiries from the editor about the process of writing the gun control essay and about his writing methods in general.*]

Let me take on your questions and see what happens.

Where did the idea come from? I suppose it came first from the opossum, which innocently served as a peg to hang my sermon on. My feelings against guns were already well formed, and the events of that cold night were just about as I described them. So when I sat back to reflect that I had actually picked up a weapon to use aggressively on a living thing, the thesis of the article was staring me in the face.

Therefore, I can't say that I set out to write an antigun essay, and then, while looking for a peg, remembered this incident. It was the other way around. At the same time, I look at many experiences—things I see, read, hear, argue about, trip over, feel, fantasize, remember—as potential sources for writing. Most of them never get written about, but it has become a habit for me to reflect upon experience in an embryonic, prewriting fashion, so that I formulate ideas and conclusions in my head the way that I *intend*, later, to put them on paper. And occasionally do. In other words, I try to be receptive to pretexts for writing, so that when one stumbles into my life I can recognize it.

How did I *develop* the idea for the gun control essay? Very slowly. I had a rough notion of where I wanted to go, but little clear sense of how to get there. Since I was aiming for the "My

Turn" section of *Newsweek*, I had to write from a first-person point of view. Besides, how I felt was pretty central to my thesis.

Yet I didn't want to sound abjectly confessional, or grandly narcissistic. So I kept trying to take out stuff about me and my kids and my neighbors and my preferences in music. Then I had to put some of this back in order to explain, for example, why I had the gun in the first place. The analysis itself tended to get even more out of hand than the personal details. It had to be trimmed and refined and some of it dropped altogether.   5

Which spills into your question about revising. Yes, I revised. At one point I had a pile of drafts and fragments about an inch thick on the floor. I wish I could write briskly and beautifully and never have to touch a word more than once, but that almost never happens to me. I am never entirely sure, while I'm working on it, just what feel or tone a finished article is going to have. So I can't tell along the way whether the words I'm using at the moment are going to fit. Once a piece is roughed out, the process becomes a little easier, but even then I do a lot of reworking.   6

For what it may be worth to your students, I console myself for having been denied the gift of inspiration by telling myself that this time-consuming process of reworking and refining distinguishes the professional writer from the nonprofessional. If everything that first tumbled from the ends of my fingertips were the best I could do, I would starve as a writer. I like to think that I have learned enough about writing to rcognize a problem when I see it, and to know a little how to fix it.   7

About the title. I didn't start with it. In fact, it was the last thing done. I wanted to arouse a little curiosity up front and also to give a clue to what followed. The "Being Prepared" of course plays off the boy scout motto, but I hoped it would serve as a snide commentary on what I regard as the foolish notion that guns are viable instruments of defense for average citizens. "Suburbia," I guess, was meant to sharpen the same point—who needs guns out here?   8

Problems? More with the beginning—which I'm still not crazy about, because it lunges rather gracelessly into the argument—than with the ending. By the time I got there, the ending had established itself pretty well in my mind. The basic problem was to discover for my self precisely what I wanted to say, and then to say it effectively in the space I had (1,200 words).   9

But of course that's always the problem. And the only way I know to solve it is to write a while longer before giving up for the   10 night. I try different words, different beginnings. It's an arduous process and it doesn't always work. But nothing else, including Scotch, works any better.

As for struggles with specific words and phrases: I remember having some doubts about the "holely terror" pun and then deciding, what-the-hell, leave it. That was self-indulgent, but I figured I was entitled. I had worked hard. [11]

Would I make any changes now? Yes, in fact. One line has always bothered me—after I saw it in print, of course. It's the first line of paragraph 13: "But he proved to be not only an unwelcome but also a recalcitrant guest." Those "buts" are one too many; they are intrusive. Maybe it would be better to say, "He proved, however, to be . . ." I suppose I could find other flaws, but this article has been good to me, and I rather like it as it is. [12]

Why do I write? For a number of reasons, not all of them known to me. Not least, I write because it's all I know how to do for which I can get paid. (Almost all the writing I do that earns any money is advertising copy.) [13]

Also, writing satisfied some urges: to save the world, to touch other people, to tinker with words for the sheer fun (and the challenge) of it, to indulge myself. I'm not sure why else. But I can't imagine not writing. [14]

Let me add just a couple of other notes that may be of interest to beginners. The response to the article when it appeared in *Newsweek* ran about 100-to-3 *against*—not only against the article, but against me. So the big ego trip of having it published in a national magazine quickly gave way to self-pity. There were now another 100 (at least) people in the world who didn't like me. Don't write because you want to be loved. [15]

This piece was the first I sent to *Newsweek*. It has not been the last, but it remains the only one accepted. So, second, don't learn to write in the expectation that you'll be able to coast then. It doesn' get easy—at least not for me. [16]

Finally, I'm not always sure why I make the decisions I do when I'm writing. I may use a particular word, for example, not because it is the best of all possible words for the immediate purpose but because it is the best word I know, or can think of. Or because I happen to like that word. [17]

If a decision I make during the writing process seems to work, I go with it. If not, I grope about for another. If all else fails, I yell at my kids. [18]

WRITING TOPICS for Chapter Ten
Essays That Appeal to Emotion and Ethics

Write an emotional or ethical appeal on one of the following subjects:

1. Marriage is (is not) a wretched institution

2. Doctors are (are not) technicians rather than healers

3. Lawyers are (are not) a dishonest breed

4. College athletics should (should not) be abolished

5. ROTC should (should not) be abolished on college campuses

6. Universities should (should not) allow radicals to speak in their facilities

7. Teachers should (should not) pass judgment on their students' work

8. Public schools are (are not) more responsive to the whole person than are private schools

9. Most college requirements are (are not) worthwhile

10. Seeking psychiatric help is (is not) a sign of weakness

11. The drug laws should (should not) be tightened up

12. Exercise: Analyze the appeal of several newspaper or magazine advertisements: For what audience are they intended? How do they attract that audience? What unstated assumptions do they make?

Essays for
Further Reading

Jonathan Swift

A Modest Proposal

The great satirist, Jonathan Swift (1667–1745), was born in Dublin, Ireland, and educated at Trinity College, Dublin, where he was censured for breaking the rules of discipline and graduated only by "special grace." He was ordained an Anglican clergyman in 1694 and became Dean of St. Patrick's, Dublin in 1713. His satires in prose and verse addressed three main issues: political relations between England and Ireland; Irish social questions; and matters of church doctrine. He is most famous for The Battle of the Books (1704); A Tale of a Tub (1704); and Gulliver's Travels (1726). His best-known essay was published in 1729 under the full title, "A Modest Proposal for Preventing the Children of Poor People from Being a Burden to Their Parents or the Country." Assuming a mask, or persona, Swift poured into the essay his contempt for human materialism and for logic without compassion.

It is a melancholy object to those who walk through this great town [1] or travel in the country, when they see the streets, the roads, and cabin doors, crowded with beggars of the female sex, followed by three, four, or six children, all in rags and importuning every passenger for an alms. These mothers, instead of being able to work for their honest livelihood, are forced to employ all their time in strolling to beg sustenance for their helpless infants, who, as they grow up, either turn thieves for want of work, or leave their dear native country to fight for the Pretender in Spain, or sell themselves to the Barbadoes.[2]

[1] Dublin, capital city of Ireland.
[2] The pretender to the throne of England was James Stuart (1688–1766), son of the deposed James II. Barbados is an island in the West Indies.

I think it is agreed by all parties that this prodigious number of children in the arms, or on the backs, or at the heels of their mothers, and frequently of their fathers, is in the present deplorable state of the kingdom a very great additional grievance; and therefore whoever could find out a fair, cheap, and easy method of making these children sound, useful members of the commonwealth would deserve so well of the public as to have his statue set up for a preserver of the nation.

But my intention is very far from being confined to provide only for the children of professed beggars; it is of a much greater extent, and shall take in the whole number of infants at a certain age who are born of parents in effect as little able to support them as those who demand our charity in the streets.

As to my own part, having turned my thoughts for many years upon this important subject, and maturely weighed the several schemes of other projectors,[3] I have always found them grossly mistaken in their computation. It is true, a child just dropped from its dam may be supported by her milk for a solar year, with little other nourishment; at most not above the value of two shillings,[4] which the mother may certainly get, or the value in scraps, by her lawful occupation of begging; and it is exactly at one year old that I propose to provide for them in such a manner as instead of being a charge upon their parents or the parish, or wanting food and raiment for the rest of their lives, they shall on the contrary contribute to the feeding, and partly to the clothing, of many thousands.

There is likewise another great advantage in my scheme, that it will prevent those voluntary abortions, and that horrid practice of women murdering their bastard children, alas, too frequent among us, sacrificing the poor innocent babes, I doubt, more to avoid the expense than the shame, which would move tears and pity in the most savage and inhuman breast.

The number of souls in this kingdom being usually reckoned one million and a half, of these I calculate there may be about two hundred thousand couple whose wives are breeders; from which number I subtract thirty thousand couples who are able to

---

[3] Men whose heads were full of foolish schemes or projects.
[4] The British pound sterling was made up of twenty shillings; five shillings made a crown.

maintain their own children, although I apprehend there cannot be so many under the present distress of the kingdom; but this being granted, there will remain an hundred and seventy thousand breeders. I again subtract fifty thousand for those women who miscarry, or whose children die by accident or disease within the year. There only remain an hundred and twenty thousand children of poor parents annually born. The question therefore is, how this number shall be reared and provided for, which, as I have already said, under the present situation of affairs, is utterly impossible by all the methods hitherto proposed. For we can neither employ them in handicraft or agriculture; we neither build houses (I mean in the country) nor cultivate land. They can very seldom pick up a livelihood by stealing till they arrive at six years old, except where they are of towardly parts;[5] although I confess they learn the rudiments much earlier, during which time they can however be looked upon only as probationers, as I have been informed by a principal gentleman in the county of Cavan, who protested to me that he never knew above one or two instances under the age of six, even in a part of the kingdom so renowned for the quickest proficiency in that art.

I am assured by our merchants that a boy or a girl before twelve   7
years old is no salable commodity; and even when they come to this age they will not yield above three pounds, or three pounds and half a crown at most on the Exchange; which cannot turn to account either to the parents or the kingdom, the charge of nutriment and rags having been at least four times that value.

I shall now therefore humbly propose my own thoughts, which   8
I hope will not be liable to the least objection.

I have been assured by a very knowing American of my ac-   9
quaintance in London, that a young healthy child well nursed is at a year old a most delicious, nourishing, and wholesome food, whether stewed, roasted, baked, or boiled; and I make no doubt that it will equally serve in a fricassee or a ragout.

I do therefore humbly offer it to public consideration that of   10
the hundred and twenty thousand children, already computed, twenty thousand may be reserved for breed, whereof only one fourth part to be males, which is more than we allow to sheep, black cattle, or swine; and my reason is that these children are

[5] Having natural ability.

seldom the fruits of marriage, a circumstance not much regarded by our savages, therefore one male will be sufficient to serve four females. That the remaining hundred thousand may at a year old be offered in sale to the persons of quality and fortune through the kingdom, always advising the mother to let them suck plentifully in the last month, so as to render them plump and fat for a good table. A child will make two dishes at an entertainment for friends; and when the family dines alone, the fore or hind quarter will make a reasonable dish, and seasoned with a little pepper or salt will be very good boiled on the fourth day, especially in winter.

I have reckoned upon a medium that a child just born will weigh twelve pounds, and in a solar year if tolerably nursed increaseth to twenty-eight pounds.   11

I grant this food will be somewhat dear, and therefore very proper for landlords, who, as they have already devoured most of the parents, seem to have the best title to the children.   12

Infant's flesh will be in season throughout the year, but more plentiful in March, and a little before and after. For we are told by a grave author, an eminent French physician,[6] that fish being a prolific diet, there are more children born in Roman Catholic countries about nine months after Lent than at any other season; therefore, reckoning a year after Lent, the markets will be more glutted than usual, because the number of popish infants is at least three to one in this kingdom; and therefore it will have one other collateral advantage, by lessening the number of Papists among us.   13

I have already computed the charge of nursing a beggar's child (in which list I reckon all cottagers, laborers, and four fifths of the farmers) to be about two shillings per annum, rags included; and I believe no gentleman would repine to give ten shillings for the carcass of a good fat child, which, as I have said, will make four dishes of excellent nutritive meat, when he hath only some particular friend or his own family to dine with him. Thus the squire will learn to be a good landlord, and grow popular among the tenants; the mother will have eight shillings net profit, and be fit for work till she produces another child.   14

Those who are more thrifty (as I must confess the times re-   15

[6] François Rabelais (1494?–1553), French satirist.

quire) may flay the carcass; the skin of which artificially [7] dressed
will make admirable gloves for ladies, and summer boots for fine
gentlemen.

As to our city of Dublin, shambles [8] may be appointed for this   16
purpose in the most convenient parts of it, and butchers we may
be assured will not be wanting; although I rather recommend buying the children alive, and dressing them hot from the knife as we
do roasting pigs.

A very worthy person, a true lover of his country, and whose   17
virtues I highly esteem, was lately pleased in discoursing on this
matter to offer a refinement upon my scheme. He said that many
gentlemen of this kingdom, having of late destroyed their deer, he
conceived that the want of venison might be well supplied by the
bodies of young lads and maidens, not exceeding fourteen years of
age nor under twelve, so great a number of both sexes in every
country being now ready to starve for want of work and service;
and these to be disposed of by their parents, if alive, or otherwise
by their nearest relations. But with due deference to so excellent
a friend and so deserving a patriot, I cannot be altogether in his
sentiments; for as to the males, my American acquaintance assured
me from frequent experience that their flesh was generally tough
and lean, like that of our schoolboys, by continual exercise, and
their taste disagreeable; and to fatten them would not answer the
charge. Then as to the females, it would, I think with humble sub-
mission, be a loss to the public, because they soon would become
breeders themselves: and besides, it is not improbable that some
scrupulous people might be apt to censure such a practice (although indeed very unjustly) as a little bordering upon cruelty;
which, I confess, hath always been with me the strongest objection
against any project, how well soever intended.

But in order to justify my friend, he confessed that this ex-   18
pedient was put into his head by the famous Psalmanazar, [9] a
native of the island Formosa, who came from thence to London
above twenty years ago, and in conversation told my friend that in
his country when any young person happened to be put to death,
the executioner sold the carcass to persons of quality as a prime

[7] Skillfully, artfully.
[8] Slaughterhouses.
[9] George Psalmanazar (1679?–1763), a Frenchman, fooled English society for
several years by masquerading as a pagan Formosan.

dainty; and that in his time the body of a plump girl of fifteen, who was crucified for an attempt to poison the emperor, was sold to his Imperial Majesty's prime minister of state, and other great mandarins of the court, in joints from the gibbet, at four hundred crowns. Neither indeed can I deny that if the same use were made of several plump young girls in this town, who without one single groat to their fortunes cannot stir abroad without a chair, and appear at the playhouse and assemblies in foreign fineries which they never will pay for, the kingdom would not be the worse.

Some persons of a desponding spirit are in great concern about [19] that vast number of poor people who are aged, diseased, or maimed, and I have been desired to employ my thoughts what course may be taken to ease the nation of so grievous an encumbrance. But I am not in the least pain upon that matter, because it is very well known that they are every day dying and rotting by cold and famine, and filth and vermin, as fast as can be reasonably expected. And as to the younger laborers, they are now in almost as hopeful a condition. They cannot get work, and consequently pine away for want of nourishment to a degree that if at any time they are accidentally hired to common labor, they have not strength to perform it; and thus the country and themselves are happily delivered from the evils to come.

I have too long digressed, and therefore shall return to my subject. [20] I think the advantages by the proposal which I have made are obvious and many, as well as of the highest importance.

For first, as I have already observed, it would greatly lessen the [21] number of Papists, with whom we are yearly overrun, being the principal breeders of the nation as well as our most dangerous enemies; and who stay at home on purpose to deliver the kingdom to the Pretender, hoping to take their advantage by the absence of so many good Protestants, who have chosen rather to leave their country than stay at home and pay tithes against their conscience to an Episcopal curate.[1]

Secondly, the poorer tenants will have something valuable of [22] their own, which by law may be made liable to distress, and help

---

[1] Swift blamed much of Ireland's poverty upon large landowners who avoided church tithes by living (and spending their money) abroad.

to pay their landlord's rent, their corn and cattle being already seized and money a thing unknown.

Thirdly, whereas the maintenance of an hundred thousand children, from two years old and upward, cannot be computed at less than ten shillings a piece per annum, the nation's stock will be thereby increased fifty thousand pounds per annum, besides the profit of a new dish introduced to the tables of all gentlemen of fortune in the kingdom who have any refinement in taste. And the money will circulate among ourselves, the goods being entirely of our own growth and manufacture. 23

Fourthly, the constant breeders, besides the gain of eight shillings sterling per annum by the sale of their children, will be rid of the charge of maintaining them after the first year. 24

Fifthly, this food would likewise bring great custom to taverns, where the vintners will certainly be so prudent as to procure the best receipts for dressing it to perfection, and consequently have their houses frequented by all the fine gentlemen, who justly value themselves upon their knowledge in good eating; and a skillful cook, who understands how to oblige his guests, will contrive to make it as expensive as they please. 25

Sixthly, this would be a great inducement to marriage, which all wise nations have either encouraged by rewards or enforced by laws and penalties. It would increase the care and tenderness of mothers toward their children, when they were sure of a settlement for life to the poor babes, provided in some sort by the public, to their annual profit instead of expense. We should see an honest emulation among the married women, which of them could bring the fattest child to the market. Men would become as fond of their wifes during the time of their pregnancy as they are now of their mares in foal, their cows in calf, or sows when they are ready to farrow; nor offer to beat or kick them (as is too frequent a practice) for fear of a miscarriage. 26

Many other advantages might be enumerated. For instance, the addition of some thousand carcasses in our exportation of barreled beef, the propagation of swine's flesh, and improvement in the art of making good bacon, so much wanted among us by the great destruction of pigs, too frequent at our tables, which are no way comparable in taste or magnificence to a well-grown, fat, yearling child, which roasted whole will make a considerable figure at a 27 lord mayor's feast or any other public entertainment. But this and many others I omit, being studious of brevity.

Supposing that one thousand families in this city would be con- 28 stant customers for infants' flesh, besides others who might have it at merry meetings, particularly weddings and christenings, I compute that Dublin would take off annually about twenty thousand carcasses, and the rest of the kingdom (where probably they will be sold somewhat cheaper) the remaining eighty thousand.

I can think of no one objection that will possibly be raised 29 against this proposal, unless it should be urged that the number of people will be thereby much lessened in the kingdom. This I freely own, and it was indeed one principal design in offering it to the world. I desire the reader will observe, that I calculate my remedy for this one individual kingdom of Ireland and for no other that ever was, is, or I think ever can be upon earth. Therefore let no man talk to me of other expedients [2]: of taxing our absentees at five shillings a pound: of using neither clothes nor household furniture except what is of our own growth and manufacture: of utterly rejecting the materials and instruments that promote foreign luxury: of curing the expensiveness of pride, vanity, idleness, and gaming in our women: of introducing a vein of parsimony, prudence, and temperance: of learning to love our country, in the want of which we differ even from Laplanders and the inhabitants of Topinamboo [3]: of quitting our animosities and factions, nor acting any longer like the Jews, who were murdering one another at the very moment their city [4] was taken: of being a little cautious not to sell our country and conscience for nothing: of teaching landlords to have at least one degree of mercy toward their tenants: lastly, of putting a spirit of honesty, industry, and skill into our shopkeepers; who, if a resolution could now be taken to buy only our native goods, would immediately unite to cheat and exact upon us in the price, the measure, and the goodness, nor could ever yet be brought to make one fair proposal of just dealing, though often and earnestly invited to it.

Therefore I repeat, let no man talk to me of these and the like 30

[2] The following are all measures that Swift himself proposed in various pamphlets.
[3] In Brazil.
[4] Jerusalem, sacked by the Romans in A.D. 70.

expedients, till he hath at least some glimpse of hope that there will ever be some hearty and sincere attempt to put them in practice.

But as to myself, having been wearied out for many years with offering vain, idle, visionary thoughts, and at length utterly despairing of success, I fortunately fell upon this proposal, which, as it is wholly new, so it hath something solid and real, of no expense and little trouble, full in our own power, and whereby we can incur no danger in disobliging England. For this kind of commodity will not bear exportation, the flesh being of too tender a consistence to admit a long continuance in salt, although perhaps I could name a country [5] which would be glad to eat up our whole nation without it.

After all, I am not so violently bent upon my own opinion as to reject any offer proposed by wise men, which shall be found equally innocent, cheap, easy, and effectual. But before something of that kind shall be advanced in contradiction to my scheme, and offering a better, I desire the author or authors will be pleased maturely to consider two points. First, as things now stand, how they will be able to find food and raiment for an hundred thousand useless mouths and backs. And secondly, there being a round million of creatures in human figure throughout this kingdom, whose sole subsistence put into a common stock would leave them in debt two millions of pounds sterling, adding those who are beggars by profession to the bulk of farmers, cottagers, and laborers, with their wives and children who are beggars in effect; I desire those politicians who dislike my overture, and may perhaps be so bold to attempt an answer, that they will first ask the parents of these mortals whether they would not at this day think it a great happiness to have been sold for food at a year old in the manner I prescribe, and thereby have avoided such a perpetual scene of misfortunes as they have since gone through by the oppression of landlords, the impossibility of paying rent without money or trade, the want of common sustenance, with neither house nor clothes to cover them from the inclemencies of the weather, and the most inevitable prospect of entailing the like or greater miseries upon their breed forever.

[5] England.

I profess, in the sincerity of my heart, that I have not the least   33
personal interest in endeavoring to promote this necessary work,
having no other motive than the public good of my country, by
advancing our trade, providing for infants, relieving the poor, and
giving some pleasure to the rich. I have no children by which I
can propose to get a single penny; the youngest being nine years
old, and my wife past childbearing.

E. B. White

Once More to the Lake

Elwyn Brooks White, the dean of American essayists, a story-
teller and a poet, was born in Mount Vernon, New York, in 1899.
After studying at Cornell University, he joined the staff of the
New Yorker in 1926. A gifted reporter of urban life, White was
to find the city too "seductive," and he gradually spent more and
more time on his farm in Maine, where he moved more or less
permanently in 1957. Widely praised for his prose style, White
wrote a regular column, "One Man's Meat" for Harper's and
editorials for the New Yorker. He has published numerous books,
including Charlotte's Web (1952, for children); The Second Tree
from the Corner (1954); The Elements of Style (1959, an en-
largement of William Strunk's handbook for writers); The Points
of My Compass (1967); and The Letters of E. B. White (1976).
"Once More to the Lake," a narrative about the generations, is
reprinted from Essays of E. B. White (1977); written in August
1941, it originally appeared in Harper's and later in One Man's
Meat (1942). Mr. White recalls the process of writing this
American classic in a letter to the editor reproduced at the end
of this chapter.

One summer, along about 1904, my father rented a camp   1
on a lake in Maine and took us all there for the month of
August. We all got ringworm from some kittens and had to
rub Pond's Extract on our arms and legs night and morning,
and my father rolled over in a canoe with all his clothes on;
but outside of that the vacation was a success and from then
on none of us ever thought there was any place in the world
like that lake in Maine. We returned summer after summer—
always on August 1 for one month. I have since become a
salt-water man, but sometimes in summer there are days

when the restlessness of the tides and the fearful cold of the sea water and the incessant wind that blows across the afternoon and into the evening make me wish for the placidity of a lake in the woods. A few weeks ago this feeling got so strong I bought myself a couple of bass hooks and a spinner and returned to the lake where we used to go, for a week's fishing and to revisit old haunts.

I took along my son, who had never had any fresh water up his nose and who had seen lily pads only from train windows. On the journey over to the lake I began to wonder what it would be like. I wondered how the time would have marred this unique, this holy spot—the coves and streams, the hills that the sun set behind, the camps and the paths behind the camps. I was sure that the tarred road would have found it out, and I wondered in what other ways it would be desolated. It is strange how much you can remember about places like that once you allow your mind to return into the grooves that lead back. You remember one thing, and that suddenly reminds you of another thing. I guess I remembered clearest of all the early mornings, when the lake was cool and motionless, remembered how the bedroom smelled of the lumber it was made of and of the wet woods whose scent entered through the screen. The partitions in the camp were thin and did not extend clear to the top of the rooms, and as I was always the first up I would dress softly so as not to wake the others, and sneak out into the sweet outdoors and start out in the canoe, keeping close along the shore in the long shadows of the pines. I remembered being very careful never to rub my paddle against the gunwale for fear of disturbing the stillness of the cathedral.

The lake had never been what you would call a wild lake. There were cottages sprinkled around the shores, and it was in farming country although the shores of the lake were quite heavily wooded. Some of the cottages were owned by nearby farmers, and you would live at the shore and eat your meals at the farmhouse. That's what our family did. But although it wasn't wild, it was a fairly large and undisturbed lake and there were places in it that, to a child at least, seemed infinitely remote and primeval.

I was right about the tar: it led to within half a mile of the shore. But when I got back there, with my boy, and we settled into a camp near a farmhouse and into the kind of summertime I had known, I could tell that it was going to be pretty much the same as it had been before—I knew it, lying in bed the first morning, smelling the bedroom and hearing the boy sneak quietly out and go off along the shore in a boat. I began to sustain the illusion that he was I, and therefore, by simple transposition, that I was my father. This sensation persisted, kept cropping up all the time we were there. It was not an entirely new feeling, but in this setting, it grew much stronger. I seemed to be living a dual existence. I would be in the middle of some simple act, I would be picking up a bait box or laying down a table fork, or I would be saying something, and suddenly it would be not I but my father who was saying the words or making the gesture. It gave me a creepy sensation.

We went fishing the first morning. I felt the same damp moss covering the worms in the bait can, and saw the dragonfly alight on the tip of my rod as it hovered a few inches from the surface of the water. It was the arrival of this fly that convinced me beyond any doubt that everything was as it always had been, that the years were a mirage and that there had been no years. The small waves were the same, chucking the rowboat under the chin as we fished at anchor, and the boat was the same boat, the same color green and the ribs broken in the same places, and under the floorboards the same fresh-water leavings and débris—the dead helgramite, the wisps of moss, the rusty discarded fishhook, the dried blood from yesterday's catch. We stared silently at the tips of our rods, at the dragonflies that came and went. I lowered the tip of mine into the water, tentatively, pensively dislodging the fly, which darted two feet away, poised, darted two feet back, and came to rest again a little farther up the rod. There had been no years between the ducking of this dragonfly and the other one— the one that was part of memory. I looked at the boy, who was silently watching his fly, and it was my hands that held his rod, my eyes watching. I felt dizzy and didn't know which rod I was at the end of.

We caught two bass, hauling them in briskly as though they were mackerel, pulling them over the side of the boat in a businesslike manner without any landing net, and stunning them with a blow on the back of the head. When we got back for a swim before lunch, the lake was exactly where we had left it, the same number of inches from the dock, and there was only the merest suggestion of a breeze. This seemed an utterly enchanted sea, this lake you could leave to its own devices for a few hours and come

back to, and find that it had not stirred, this constant and trustworthy body of water. In the shallows, the dark, water-soaked
sticks and twigs, smooth and old, were undulating in clusters on
the bottom against the clean ribbed sand, and the track of the
mussel was plain. A school of minnows swam by, each minnow
with its small individual shadow, doubling the attendance, so clear
and sharp in the sunlight. Some of the other campers were in
swimming, along the shore, one of them with a cake of soap, and
the water felt thin and clear and unsubstantial. Over the years
there had been this person with the cake of soap, this cultist, and
here he was. There had been no years.

Up to the farmhouse to dinner through the teeming, dusty field,   7
the road under our sneakers was only a two-track road. The middle
track was missing, the one with the marks of the hooves and the
splotches of dried, flaky manure. There had always been three
tracks to choose from in choosing which track to walk in; now the
choice was narrowed down to two. For a moment I missed terribly the middle alternative. But the way led past the tennis court,
and something about the way it lay there in the sun reassured me;
the tape had loosened along the backline, the alleys were green
with plantains and other weeds, and the net (installed in June and
removed in September) sagged in the dry noon, and the whole
place steamed with midday heat and hunger and emptiness. There
was a choice of pie for dessert, and one was blueberry and one was
apple, and the waitresses were the same country girls, there having
been no passage of time, only the illusion of it as in a dropped curtain—the waitresses were still fifteen; their hair had been washed,
that was the only difference—they had been to the movies and
seen the pretty girls with the clean hair.

Summertime, oh, summertime, pattern of life indelible, the   8
fade-proof lake, the woods unshatterable, the pasture with the
sweetfern and the juniper forever and ever, summer without end;
this was the background, and the life along the shore was the
design, the cottages with their innocent and tranquil design, their
tiny docks with the flagpole and the American flag floating against
the white clouds in the blue sky, the little paths over the roots of
the trees leading from camp to camp and the paths leading back
to the outhouses and the can of lime for sprinkling, and at the
souvenir counters at the store the miniature birch-bark canoes
and the postcards that showed things looking a little better than

they looked. This was the American family at play, escaping the city heat, wondering whether the newcomers in the camp at the head of the cove were "common" or "nice," wondering whether it was true that the people who drove up for Sunday dinner at the farmhouse were turned away because there wasn't enough chicken.

It seemed to me, as I kept remembering all this, that those 9 times and those summers had been infinitely precious and worth saving. There had been jollity and peace and goodness. The arriving (at the beginning of August) had been so big a business in itself, at the railway station the farm wagon drawn up, the first smell of the pine-laden air, the first glimpse of the smiling farmer, and the great importance of the trunks and your father's enormous authority in such matters, and the feel of the wagon under you for the long ten-mile haul, and at the top of the last long hill catching the first view of the lake after eleven months of not seeing this cherished body of water. The shouts and cries of the other campers when they saw you, and the trunks to be unpacked, to give up their rich burden. (Arriving was less exciting nowadays, when you sneaked up in your car and parked it under a tree near the camp and took out the bags and in five minutes it was all over, no fuss, no loud wonderful fuss about trunks.)

Peace and goodness and jollity. The only thing that was wrong 10 now, really, was the sound of the place, an unfamiliar nervous sound of the outboard motors. This was the note that jarred, the one thing that would sometimes break the illusion and set the years moving. In those other summertimes all motors were inboard; and when they were at a little distance, the noise they made was a sedative, an ingredient of summer sleep. They were one-cylinder and two-cylinder engines, and some were make-and-break and some were jump-spark, but they all made a sleepy sound across the lake. The one-lungers throbbed and fluttered, and the twin-cylinder ones purred and purred, and that was a quiet sound, too. But now the campers all had outboards. In the daytime, in the hot mornings, these motors made a petulant, irritable sound; at night, in the still evening when the afterglow lit the water, they whined about one's ears like mosquitoes. My boy loved our rented outboard, and his great desire was to achieve single-handed mastery over it, and authority, and he soon learned the trick of choking it a little (but not too much), and the adjustment of the needle valve. Watching him I would remember the things you could do with the old one-cylinder engine with the heavy flywheel, how you could have it eating out of your hand if you got really close to it spiritually. Motorboats in those days didn't have clutches, and you would make a landing by shutting off the motor at the proper time and coasting in with a dead rudder. But there was a way of reversing them, if you learned the trick, by cutting the switch and putting it on again exactly on the final dying revolution of the flywheel, so that it would kick back against compression and begin reversing. Approaching a dock in a strong following breeze, it was difficult to slow up sufficiently by the ordinary coasting method, and if a boy felt he had complete mastery over his motor, he was tempted to keep it running beyond its time and then reverse it a few feet from the dock. It took a cool nerve, because if you threw the switch a twentieth of a second too soon you would catch the flywheel when it still had speed enough to go up past center, and the boat would leap ahead, charging bull-fashion at the dock.

We had a good week at the camp. The bass were biting well   11
and the sun shone endlessly, day after day. We would be tired at night and lie down in the accumulated heat of the little bedrooms after the long hot day and the breeze would stir almost imperceptibly outside and the smell of the swamp drift in through the rusty screens. Sleep would come easily and in the morning the red squirrel would be on the roof, tapping out his gay routine. I kept remembering everything, lying in bed in the mornings—the small steamboat that had a long rounded stern like the lip of a Ubangi, and how quietly she ran on the moonlight sails, when the older boys played their mandolins and the girls sang and we ate doughnuts dipped in sugar, and how sweet the music was on the water in the shining night, and what it had felt like to think about girls then. After breakfast we would go up to the store and the things were in the same place—the minnows in a bottle, the plugs and spinners disarranged and pawed over by the youngsters from the boys' camp, the Fig Newtons and the Beeman's gum. Outside, the road was tarred and cars stood in front of the store. Inside, all was just as it had always been, except there was more Coca-Cola and not so much Moxie [1] and root beer and birch beer

1 Brand name of an old-fashioned soft drink.

and sarsaparilla. We would walk out with the bottle of pop apiece and sometimes the pop would backfire up our noses and hurt. We explored the streams, quietly, where the turtles slid off logs and dug their way into the soft bottom; and we lay on the town wharf and fed worms to the tame bass. Everywhere we went I had trouble making out which was I, the one walking at my side, the one walking in my pants.

One afternoon while we were there at that lake a thunderstorm   12
came up. It was like the revival of an old melodrama that I had seen long ago with childish awe. The second-act climax of the drama of the electrical disturbance over a lake in America has not changed in any important respect. This was the big scene, still the big scene. The whole thing was so familiar, the first feeling of oppression and heat and a general air around camp of not want-ing to go very far away. In midafternoon (it was all the same) a curious darkening of the sky, and a lull in everything that had made life tick; and then the way the boats suddenly swung the other way at their moorings with the coming of a breeze out of the new quarter, and the premonitory rumble. Then the kettle drum, then the snare, then the bass drum and cymbals, then crackling light against the dark, and the gods grinning and licking their chops in the hills. Afterward the calm, the rain steadily rustling in the calm lake, the return of light and hope and spirits, and the campers running out in joy and relief to go swimming in the rain, their bright cries perpetuating the deathless joke about how they were getting simply drenched, and the children scream-ing with delight at the new sensation of bathing in the rain, and the joke about getting drenched linking the generations in a strong indestructible chain. And the comedian who waded in carrying an umbrella.

When the others went swimming, my son said he was going in,   13
too. He pulled his dripping trunks from the line where they had hung all through the shower and wrung them out. Languidly, and with no thought of going in, I watched him, his hard little body, skinny and bare, saw him wince slightly as he pulled up around his vitals the small, soggy, icy garment. As he buckled the swollen belt, suddenly my groin felt the chill of death.

George Orwell
Politics and the English Language

Eric Arthur Blair (1903–1950, pseudonym George Orwell) was a
British novelist and essayist born in Bengal, India. He was educated
at Eton but, he said, "learned very little," returning to the East,
where he served with the Indian Imperial Police in Burma from
1922 to 1927 and ruined his health. A dishwasher, a poor tutor,
and an assistant in a London bookshop, Orwell finally began
earning enough money from his writing to move to the country
about 1935. He served briefly in the Spanish Civil War, was
wounded, and afterwards settled in Hertfordshire, England, to
raise hens and vegetables and write books. A brilliant political
satirist, Orwell is best known for Animal Farm (1945) and Nineteen
Eighty-Four (1949), an attack on political dictatorship. "Politics
and the English Language" is perhaps the best essay in English on
the social necessity of responsible writing.

Most people who bother with the matter at all would admit
that the English language is in a bad way, but it is generally
assumed that we cannot by conscious action do anything
about it. Our civilization is decadent and our language—so the
argument runs—must inevitably share in the general collapse.
It follows that any struggle against the abuse of language is a
sentimental archaism, like preferring candles to electric light
or hansom cabs to aeroplanes. Underneath this lies the half-
conscious belief that language is a natural growth and not an
instrument which we shape for our own purposes.

Now, it is clear that the decline of a language must ultimately have political and economic causes: it is not due simply
to the bad influence of this or that individual writer. But an
effect can become a cause, reinforcing the original cause and
producing the same effect in an intensified form, and so on

indefinitely. A man may take to drink because he feels himself to be a failure, and then fail all the more completely because he drinks. It is rather the same thing that is happening to the English language. It becomes ugly and inaccurate because our thoughts are foolish, but the slovenliness of our language makes it easier for us to have foolish thoughts. The point is that the process is reversible. Modern English, especially written English, is full of bad habits which spread by imitation and which can be avoided if one is willing to take the necessary trouble. If one gets rid of these habits one can think more clearly, and to think clearly is a necessary first step towards political regeneration: so that the fight against bad English is not frivolous and is not the exclusive concern of professional writers. I will come back to this presently, and I hope that by that time the meaning of what I have said here will have become clearer. Meanwhile, here are five specimens of the English language as it is now habitually written.

These five passages have not been picked out because they are 3 especially bad—I could have quoted far worse if I had chosen— but because they illustrate various of the mental vices from which we now suffer. They are a little below the average, but are fairly representative samples. I number them so that I can refer back to them when necessary:

(1) I am not, indeed, sure whether it is not true to say that the Milton who once seemed not unlike a seventeenth-century Shelley had not become, out of an experience ever more bitter in each year, more alien [sic] to the founder of that Jesuit sect which nothing could induce him to tolerate.

Professor Harold Laski (Essay in *Freedom of Expression*)

(2) Above all, we cannot play ducks and drakes with a native battery of idioms which prescribes such egregious collocations of vocables as the Basic *put up with* for *tolerate* or *put at a loss* for *bewilder*.

Professor Lancelot Hogben (*Interglossa*)

(3) On the one side we have the free personality: by definition it is not neurotic, for it has neither conflict nor dream. Its desires, such as they are, are transparent, for they are just what institutional approval keeps in the forefront of consciousness; another institutional pattern would alter their number and intensity; there is little in them that is natural, irreducible, or culturally dangerous. But *on the other side*, the social bond itself is nothing but the mutual

reflection of these self-secure integrities. Recall the definition of love. Is not this the very picture of a small academic? Where is there a place in this hall of mirrors for either personality or fraternity?

Essay on psychology in *Politics* (New York)

(4) All the 'best people' from the gentlemen's clubs, and all the frantic fascist captains, united in common hatred of Socialism and bestial horror of the rising tide of the mass revolutionary movement, have turned to acts of provocation, to foul incendiarism, to medieval legends of poisoned wells, to legalize their own destruction of proletarian organizations, and rouse the agitated petty-bourgeoisie to chauvinistic fervour on behalf of the fight against the revolutionary way out of the crisis.

Communist pamphlet

(5) If a new spirit *is* to be infused into this old country, there is one thorny and contentious reform which must be tackled, and that is the humanization and galvanization of the B.B.C. Timidity here will bespeak cancer and atrophy of the soul. The heart of Britain may be sound and of strong beat, for instance, but the British lion's roar at present is like that of Bottom in Shakespeare's *Midsummer Night's Dream*—as gentle as any sucking dove. A virile new Britain cannot continue indefinitely to be traduced in the eyes or rather ears, of the world by the effete languors of Langham Place, brazenly masquerading as 'standard English'. When the Voice of Britain is heard at nine o'clock, better far and infinitely less ludicrous to hear aitches honestly dropped than the present priggish, inflated, inhibited, school-ma'amish arch braying of blameless bashful mewing maidens!

Letter in *Tribune*

Each of these passages has faults of its own, but, quite apart from avoidable ugliness, two qualities are common to all of them. The first is staleness of imagery: the other is lack of precision. The writer either has a meaning and cannot express it, or he inadvertently says something else, or he is almost indifferent as to whether his words mean anything or not. This mixture of vagueness and sheer incompetence is the most marked characteristic of modern English prose, and especially of any kind of political writing. As soon as certain topics are raised, the concrete melts into the abstract and no one seems able to think of turns of speech that are not hackneyed: prose consists less and less of *words* chosen for the sake of their meaning, and more and more of *phrases* tacked together like the sections of a prefabricated hen-house. I list below, with notes and examples, various of the tricks by means of which the work of prose-construction is habitually dodged:

Dying Metaphors

A newly invented metaphor assists thought by evoking a visual [5] image, while on the other hand a metaphor which is technically "dead" (e.g. *iron resolution*) has in effect reverted to being an ordinary word and can generally be used without loss of vividness. But in between these two classes there is a huge dump of worn-out metaphors which have lost all evocative power and are merely used because they save people the trouble of inventing phrases for themselves. Examples are *Ring the changes on, take up the cudgels for, toe the line, ride roughshod over, stand shoulder to shoulder with, play into the hands of, no axe to grind, grist to the mill, fishing in troubled waters, on the order of the day, Achilles' heel, swan song, hotbed.* Many of these are used without knowledge of their meaning (what is a "rift", for instance?), and incompatible metaphors are frequently mixed, a sure sign that the writer is not interested in what he is saying. Some metaphors now current have been twisted out of their original meaning without those who use them even being aware of the fact. For example, *toe the line* is sometimes written *tow the line*. Another example is *the hammer and the anvil*, now always used with the implication that the anvil gets the worst of it. In real life it is always the anvil that breaks the hammer, never the other way about: a writer who stopped to think what he was saying would be aware of this, and would avoid perverting the original phrase.

Operators or Verbal False Limbs

These save the trouble of picking out appropriate verbs and [6] nouns, and at the same time pad each sentence with extra syllables which give it an appearance of symmetry. Characteristic phrases are: *render inoperative, militate against, make contact with, be subjected to, give rise to, give grounds for, have the effect of, play a leading part (role) in, make itself felt, take effect, exhibit a tendency to, serve the purpose of, etc., etc.* The keynote is the elimination of simple verbs. Instead of being a single word, such as *break, stop, spoil, mend, kill,* a verb becomes a *phrase,* made up of a noun or adjective tacked on to some general-purposes verb such as *prove, serve, form, play, render.* In addition, the passive voice is wherever possible used in preference to the active, and noun constructions are used instead of gerunds (*by examination of* instead of *by examining*). The range of verbs is further cut down by means of the *-ize* and *de-* formation, and the banal statements are given an appearance of profundity by means of the *not un-* formation. Simple conjunctions and prepositions are replaced by such phrases as *with respect to, having regard to, the fact that, by dint of, in view of, in the interests of, on the hypothesis that*; and the ends of sentences are saved from anticlimax by such, resounding commonplaces as *greatly to be desired, cannot be left out of account, a development to be expected in the near future, deserving of serious consideration, brought to a satisfactory conclusion,* and so on and so forth.

Pretentious Diction

Words like *phenomenon, element, individual* (as noun), *objective, categorical, effective, virtual, basic, primary, promote, constitute, exhibit, exploit, utilize, eliminate, liquidate,* are used to dress up simple statements and give an air of scientific impartiality to biased judgments. Adjectives like *epoch-making, epic, historic, unforgettable, triumphant, age-old, inevitable, inexorable, veritable,* are used to dignify the sordid processes of international politics, while writing that aims at glorifying war usually takes on an archaic colour, its characteristic words being: *realm, throne, chariot, mailed fist, trident, sword shield, buckler, banner, jackboot, clarion.* Foreign words and expressions such as *cul de sac, ancien régime, deus ex machina, mutatis mutandis, status quo, gleichschaltung, weltanschauung* are used to give an air of culture and elegance. Except for the useful abbreviations *i.e., e.g.,* and *etc.,* there is no real need for any of the hundreds of foreign phrases now current in English. Bad writers, and especially scientific, political and sociological writers, are nearly always haunted by the notion that Latin or Greek words are grander than Saxon ones, and unnecessary words like *expedite, ameliorate, predict, extraneous, deracinated, clandestine, subaqueous* and hundreds of others constantly gain ground from their Anglo-Saxon opposite numbers.[1] The jargon peculiar to Marxist writing (*hyena, hangman, cannibal, petty bourgeois, these gentry, lacquey, flunkey, mad dog, White Guard,* etc.) consists largely of words and phrases translated from Russian, German or French; but the normal way of coining a new word is to use a Latin or Greek root with the appropriate affix and, where necessary, the *-ize* formation. It is often easier to make up words of this kind (*deregionalize, impermissible, extramarital, nonfragmentatory* and so forth) than to think up the English words that will cover one's meaning. The result, in general, is an increase in slovenliness and vagueness.

Meaningless Words

In certain kinds of writing, particularly in art criticism and literary criticism, it is normal to come across long passages which are almost completely lacking in meaning.[2] Words like *romantic, plastic, values, human, dead, sentimental, natural, vitality,* as used in art criticism, are strictly meaningless in the sense that they not only do not point to any discoverable object, but are hardly ever expected to do so by the reader. When one critic writes, "The outstanding feature of Mr. X's work is its living quality", while another writes, "The immediately striking thing about Mr. X's work is its peculiar deadness", the reader accepts this as a simple difference of opinion. If words like *black* and *white* were involved, instead of the jargon words *dead* and *living,* he would see at once that language was being used in an improper way. Many political words are similarly abused. The word *Fascism* has now no meaning except in so far as it signifies "something not desirable". The

8

---

[1] An interesting illustration of this is the way in which the English flower names which were in use till very recently are being ousted by Greek ones, *snapdragon* becoming *antirrhinum, forget-me-not* becoming *myosotis,* etc. It is hard to see any practical reason for this change of fashion: it is probably due to an instinctive turning-away from the more homely word and a vague feeling that the Greek word is scientific [Orwell's note].

[2] Example: "Comfort's catholicity of perception and image, strangely Whitmanesque in range, almost the exact opposite in aesthetic compulsion, continues to evoke that trembling atmospheric accumulative hinting at a cruel, an inexorably serene timelessness . . . Wrey Gardiner scores by aiming at simple bull's-eyes with precision. Only they are not so simple, and through this contented sadness runs more than the surface bittersweet of resignation" (*Poetry Quarterly*) [Orwell's note].

words *democracy, socialism, freedom, patriotic, realistic, justice,* have each of them several different meanings which cannot be reconciled with one another. In the case of a word like *democracy,* not only is there no agreed definition, but the attempt to make one is resisted from all sides. It is almost universally felt that when we call a country democratic we are praising it: consequently the defenders of every kind of régime claim that it is a democracy, and fear that they might have to stop using the word if it were tied down to any one meaning. Words of this kind are often used in a consciously dishonest way. That is, the person who uses them has his own private definition, but allows his hearer to think he means something quite different. Statements like *Marshal Pétain was a true patriot, The Soviet Press is the freest in the world, The Catholic Church is opposed to persecution,* are almost always made with intent to deceive. Other words used in variable meanings, in most cases more or less dishonestly, are: *class, totalitarian, science, progressive, reactionary, bourgeois, equality.*

Now that I have made this catalogue of swindles and perversions, let me give another example of the kind of writing that they lead to. This time it must of its nature be an imaginary one. I am going to translate a passage of good English into modern English of the worst sort. Here is a well-known verse from *Ecclesiastes*:   9

> I returned and saw under the sun, that the race is not to the swift, nor the battle to the strong, neither yet bread to the wise, nor yet riches to men of understanding, nor yet favour to men of skill; but time and chance happeneth to them all.

Here it is in modern English: 10

> Objective consideration of contemporary phenomena compels the conclusion that success or failure in competitive activities exhibits no tendency to be commensurate with innate capacity, but that a considerable element of the unpredictable must invariably be taken into account.

This is a parody, but not a very gross one. Exhibit (3), above,   11 for instance, contains several patches of the same kind of English. It will be seen that I have not made a full translation. The beginning and ending of the sentence follow the original meaning fairly closely, but in the middle the concrete illustrations—race, battle, bread—dissolve into the vague phrase "success or failure in competitive activities". This had to be so, because no modern writer of the kind I am discussing—no one capable of using phrases like "objective consideration of contemporary phenomena"—would ever tabulate his thoughts in that precise and detailed way. The whole tendency of modern prose is away from concreteness. Now analyse these two sentences a little more closely. The first contains forty-nine words but only sixty syllables, and all its words are those of everyday life. The second contains thirty-eight words of ninety syllables: eighteen of its words are from Latin roots, and one from Greek. The first sentence contains six vivid images, and only one phrase ("time and chance") that could be called vague. The second contains not a single fresh, arresting phrase, and in spite of its ninety syllables it gives only a shortened version of the meaning contained in the first. Yet without a doubt it is the second kind of sentence that is gaining ground in modern English. I do not want to exaggerate. This kind of writing is not yet universal, and outcrops of simplicity will occur here and there in the worst-written page. Still, if you or I were told to write a few lines on the uncertainty of human fortunes, we should probably come much nearer to my imaginary sentence than to the one from *Ecclesiastes*.

As I have tried to show, modern writing at its worst does not   12
consist in picking out words for the sake of their meaning and inventing images in order to make the meaning clearer. It consists in gumming together long strips of words which have already been set in order by someone else, and making the results presentable by sheer humbug. The attraction of this way of writing is that it is easy. It is easier—even quicker, once you have the habit—to say *In my opinion it is a not unjustifiable assumption that* than to say *I think*. If you use ready-made phrases, you not only don't have to hunt about for words; you also don't have to bother with the rhythms of your sentences, since these phrases are generally so arranged as to be more or less euphonious. When you are composing in a hurry—when you are dictating to a stenographer, for instance, or making a public speech—it is natural to fall into a pretentious, Latinized style. Tags like *a consideration which we should do well to bear in mind* or *a conclusion to which all of us would readily assent* will save many a sentence from coming down with a bump. By using stale metaphors, similes and idioms, you save much mental effort, at the cost of leaving your meaning vague, not only for your reader but for yourself. This is the significance of mixed metaphors. The sole aim of a metaphor is to call up a visual image. When these images clash—as in *The Fascist*

octopus has sung its swan song, the jack-boot is thrown into the melting pot—it can be taken as certain that the writer is not seeing a mental image of the objects he is naming; in other words he is not really thinking. Look again at the examples I gave at the beginning of this essay. Professor Laski (1) uses five negatives in fifty-three words. One of these is superfluous, making nonsense of the whole passage, and in addition there is the slip *alien* for akin, making further nonsense, and several avoidable pieces of clumsiness which increase the general vagueness. Professor Hogben (2) plays ducks and drakes with a battery which is able to write prescriptions, and, while disapproving of the everyday phrase *put up with*, is unwilling to look *egregious* up in the dictionary and see what it means. (3), if one takes an uncharitable attitude towards it, is simply meaningless: probably one could work out its intended meaning by reading the whole of the article in which it occurs. In (4), the writer knows more or less what he wants to say, but an accumulation of stale phrases chokes him like tea leaves blocking a sink. In (5), words and meaning have almost parted company. People who write in this manner usually have a general emotional meaning—they dislike one thing and want to express solidarity with another—but they are not interested in the detail of what they are saying. A scrupulous writer, in every sentence that he writes, will ask himself at least four questions, thus: What am I trying to say? What words will express it? What image or idiom will make it clearer? Is this image fresh enough to have an effect? And he will probably ask himself two more: Could I put it more shortly? Have I said anything that is avoidably ugly? But you are not obliged to go to all this trouble. You can shirk it by simply throwing your mind open and letting the ready-made phrases come crowding in. They will construct your sentences for you—even think your thoughts for you, to a certain extent—and at need they will perform the important service of partially concealing your meaning even from yourself. It is at this point that the special connection between politics and the debasement of language becomes clear.

In our time it is broadly true that political writing is bad writing. 13 Where it is not true, it will generally be found that the writer is some kind of rebel, expressing his private opinions and not a "party line". Orthodoxy, of whatever colour, seems to demand a lifeless, imitative style. The political dialects to be found in pamphlets, leading articles, manifestos, White Papers and the speeches of under-secretaries do, of course, vary from party to party, but they are all alike in that one almost never finds in them a fresh, vivid, home-made turn of speech. When one watches some tired hack on the platform mechanically repeating the familiar phrases—*bestial atrocities, iron heel, bloodstained tyranny, free peoples of the world, stand shoulder to shoulder*—one often has a curious feeling that one is not watching a live human being but some kind of dummy: a feeling which suddenly becomes stronger at moments when the light catches the speaker's spectacles and turns them into blank discs which seem to have no eyes behind them. And this is not altogether fanciful. A speaker who uses that kind of phraseology has gone some distance towards turning himself into a machine. The appropriate noises are coming out of his larynx, but his brain is not involved as it would be if he were choosing his words for himself. If the speech he is making is one that he is accustomed to make over and over again, he may be almost unconscious of what he is saying, as one is when one utters the responses in church. And this reduced state of consciousness, if not indispensable, is at any rate favourable to political conformity.

In our time, political speech and writing are largely the defence   14
of the indefensible. Things like the continuance of British rule in India, the Russian purges and deportations, the dropping of the atom bombs on Japan, can indeed be defended, but only by arguments which are too brutal for most people to face, and which do not square with the professed aims of political parties. Thus political language has to consist largely of euphemism, question-begging and sheer cloudy vagueness. Defenceless villages are bombarded from the air, the inhabitants driven out into the countryside, the cattle machine-gunned, the huts set on fire with incendiary bullets: this is called *pacification*. Millions of peasants are robbed of their farms and sent trudging along the roads with no more than they can carry: this is called *transfer of population* or *rectification of frontiers*. People are imprisoned for years without trial, or shot in the back of the neck or sent to die of scurvy in Arctic lumber camps: this is called *elimination of unreliable elements*. Such phraseology is needed if one wants to name things without calling up mental pictures of them. Consider for instance some comfortable English professor defending Russian totalitarianism. He cannot say outright, "I believe in killing off your opponents when you can get good results by doing so". Probably, therefore, he will say something like this:

"While freely conceding that the Soviet régime exhibits certain   15 features which the humanitarian may be inclined to deplore, we must, I think, agree that a certain curtailment of the right to political opposition is an unavoidable concomitant of transitional periods, and that the rigours which the Russian people have been called upon to undergo have been amply justified in the sphere of concrete achievement."

The inflated style is itself a kind of euphemism. A mass of Latin 16 words falls upon the facts like soft snow, blurring the outlines and covering up all the details. The great enemy of clear language is insincerity. When there is a gap between one's real and one's declared aims, one turns as it were instinctively to long words and exhausted idioms, like a cuttlefish squirting out ink. In our age there is no such thing as "keeping out of politics". All issues are political issues, and politics itself is a mass of lies, evasions, folly, hatred and schizophrenia. When the general atmosphere is bad, language must suffer. I should expect to find—this is a guess which I have not sufficient knowledge to verify—that the German, Russian and Italian languages have all deteriorated in the last ten or fifteen years, as a result of dictatorship.

But if thought corrupts language, language can also corrupt 17 thought. A bad usage can spread by tradition and imitation, even among people who should and do know better. The debased language that I have been discussing is in some ways very convenient. Phrases like *a not unjustifiable assumption, leaves much to be desired, would serve no good purpose, a consideration which we should do well to bear in mind,* are a continuous temptation, a packet of aspirins always at one's elbow. Look back through this essay, and for certain you will find that I have again and again committed the very faults I am protesting against. By this morning's post I have received a pamphlet dealing with conditions in Germany. The author tells me that he "felt impelled" to write it. I open it at random, and here is almost the first sentence that I see: "(The Allies) have an opportunity not only of achieving a radical transformation of Germany's social and political structure in such a way as to avoid a nationalistic reaction in Germany itself, but at the same time of laying the foundations of a co-operative and unified Europe." You see, he "feels impelled" to write—feels, presumably, that he has something new to say—and yet his words, like cavalry horses answering the bugle, group themselves automatically into the familiar dreary pattern. This invasion of one's mind by ready-made phrases (*lay the foundations, achieve a radical transformation*) can only be prevented if one is constantly on guard against them, and every such phrase anaesthetizes a portion of one's brain.

I said earlier that the decadence of our language is probably curable. Those who deny this would argue, if they produced an argument at all, that language merely reflects existing social conditions, and that we cannot influence its development by any direct tinkering with words and constructions. So far as the general tone or spirit of a language goes, this may be true, but it is not true in detail. Silly words and expressions have often disappeared, not through any evolutionary process but owing to the conscious action of a minority. Two recent examples were *explore every avenue* and *leave no stone unturned*, which were killed by the jeers of a few journalists. There is a long list of flyblown metaphors which could similarly be got rid of if enough people would interest themselves in the job; and it should also be possible to laugh the *not un-* formation out of existence,[3] to reduce the amout of Latin and Greek in the average sentence, to drive out foreign phrases and strayed scientific words, and, in general, to make pretentiousness unfashionable. But all these are minor points. The defence of the English language implies more than this, and perhaps it is best to start by saying what it does *not* imply.

To begin with it has nothing to do with archaism, with the salvaging of obsolete words and turns of speech, or with the setting up of a "standard English" which must never be departed from. On the contrary, it is especially concerned with the scrapping of every word or idiom which has outworn its usefulness. It has nothing to do with correct grammar and syntax, which are of no importance so long as one makes one's meaning clear, or with the avoidance of Americanisms, or with having what is called a "good prose style". On the other hand it is not concerned with fake simplicity and the attempt to make written English colloquial. Nor does it even imply in every case preferring the Saxon word to the Latin one, though it does imply using the fewest and shortest words that will cover one's meaning. What is above all needed is to

[3] One can cure oneself of the *not un-* formation by memorizing this sentence: *A not unblack dog was chasing a not usmall rabbit across a not ungreen field* [Orwell's note].

let the meaning choose the word, and not the other way about. In prose, the worst thing one can do with words is to surrender to them. When you think of a concrete object, you think wordlessly, and then, if you want to describe the thing you have been visualizing you probably hunt about till you find the exact words that seem to fit. When you think of something abstract you are more inclined to use words from the start, and unless you make a conscious effort to prevent it, the existing dialect will come rushing in and do the job for you, at the expense of blurring or even changing your meaning. Probably it is better to put off using words as long as possible and get one's meaning as clear as one can through pictures or sensations. Afterwards one can choose—not simply *accept*—the phrases that will best cover the meaning, and then switch round and decide what impression one's words are likely to make on another person. This last effort of the mind cuts out all stale or mixed images, all prefabricated phrases, needless repetitions, and humbug and vagueness generally. But one can often be in doubt about the effect of a word or a phrase, and one needs rules that one can rely on when instinct fails. I think the following rules will cover most cases:

(i) Never use a metaphor, simile or other figure of speech which you are used to seeing in print.

(ii) Never use a long word where a short one will do.

(iii) If it is possible to cut a word out, always cut it out.

(iv) Never use the passive where you can use the active.

(v) Never use a foreign phrase, a scientific word or a jargon word if you can think of an everyday English equivalent.

(vi) Break any of these rules sooner than say anything outright barbarous.

These rules sound elementary, and so they are, but they demand a deep change of attitude in anyone who has grown used to writing in the style now fashionable. One could keep all of them and still write bad English, but one could not write the kind of stuff that I quoted in those five specimens at the beginning of this article.

I have not here been considering the literary use of language, but merely language as an instrument for expressing and not for concealing or preventing thought. Stuart Chase and others have come near to claiming that all abstract words are meaningless, and have used this as a pretext for advocating a kind of political quiet- 20 ism. Since you don't know what Fascism is, how can you struggle against Fascism? One need not swallow such absurdities as this, but one ought to recognize that the present political chaos is connected with the decay of language, and that one can probably bring about some improvement by starting at the verbal end. If you simplify your English, you are freed from the worst follies of orthodoxy. You cannot speak any of the necessary dialects, and when you make a stupid remark its stupidity will be obvious, even to yourself. Political language—and with variations this is true of all political parties, from Conservatives to Anarchists—is designed to make lies sound truthful and murder respectable, and to give an appearance of solidity to pure wind. One cannot change this all in a moment, but one can at least change one's own habits, and from time to time one can even, if one jeers loudly enough, send some worn-out and useless phrase—some *jackboot, Achilles' heel, hotbed, melting pot, acid test, veritable inferno* or other lump of verbal refuse—into the dustbin where it belongs.

Joan Didion
On Going Home

Novelist Joan Didion, author of Play It As It Lays (1970), A Book of Common Prayer (1977), and Democracy (1984), has emerged in recent years as one of America's leading essayists. In Slouching Towards Bethlehem (1968) and The White Album (1979), Didion probes our national life from the American family to the American freeway, recording its impressions upon her own jangled nerves. A native of California—she was born in Sacramento in 1934 and attended Berkeley—Didion was living in Los Angeles when she returned to her parents' house with a husband and a year-old daughter. "On Going Home" is her celebrated account of the tensions she met; its title is a distant echo of Thomas Wolfe's You Can't Go Home Again (1940).

I am home for my daughter's first birthday. By "home" I do not mean the house in Los Angeles where my husband and I and the baby live, but the place where my family is, in the Central Valley of California. It is a vital although troublesome distinction. My husband likes my family but is uneasy in their house, because once there I fall into their ways, which are difficult, oblique, deliberately inarticulate, not my husband's ways. We live in dusty houses ("D-U-S-T," he once wrote with his finger on surfaces all over the house, but no one noticed it) filled with mementos quite without value to him (what could the Canton dessert plates mean to him? how could he have known about the assay scales, why should he care if he did know?), and we appear to talk exclusively about people we know who have been committed to mental hospitals, about people we know who have been booked on drunk-driving charges, and about property, particularly about property, land, price per acre and C-2 zoning and assessments and freeway access. My brother does not understand my husband's inability to perceive the advantage in the rather common real-estate transaction known as "sale-leaseback," and my husband in turn does not understand why so many of the people he hears about in my father's house have recently been committed to mental hospitals or booked on drunk-driving charges. Nor does he understand that when we talk about sale-leasebacks and right-of-way condemnations we are talking in code about the things we like best, the yellow fields and the cottonwoods and the rivers rising and falling and the mountain roads closing when the heavy snow comes in. We miss each other's points, have another drink and regard the fire. My brother refers to my husband, in his presence, as "Joan's husband." Marriage is the classic betrayal.

Or perhaps it is not any more. Sometimes I think that those of us who are now in our thirties were born into the last generation to carry the burden of "home," to find in family life the source of all tension and drama. I had by all objective accounts a "normal" and a "happy" family situation, and yet I was almost thirty years old before I could talk to my family on the telephone without crying after I had hung up. We did not fight. Nothing was wrong. And yet some nameless anxiety colored the emotional charges between me and the place that I came from. The question of whether or not you could go home again was a very real part of the sentimental and largely literary baggage with which we left home in the fifties; I suspect that it is irrelevant to the children born of the fragmentation after World War II. A few weeks ago in a San Francisco bar I saw a pretty young girl on crystal take off her clothes and dance for the cash prize in an "amateur-topless" contest. There was no particular sense of moment about this, none of the effect of romantic degradation, of "dark journey," for which my generation strived so assidously. What sense could that girl possibly make of, say, *Long Day's Journey into Night*?[1] Who is beside the point?

That I am trapped in this particular irrelevancy is never more apparent to me than when I am home. Paralyzed by the neurotic lassitude engendered by meeting one's past at every turn, around

---

[1] Autobiographical play by Eugene O'Neill in which a young man, a would-be poet, agonizes over the dissipations and weaknesses of his family.

every corner, inside every cupboard, I go aimlessly from room to room. I decide to meet it head-on and clean out a drawer, and I spread the contents on the bed. A bathing suit I wore the summer I was seventeen. A letter of rejection from *The Nation*, an aerial photograph of the site for a shopping center my father did not build in 1954. Three teacups hand-painted with cabbage roses and signed "E.M.," my grandmother's initials. There is no final solution for letters of rejection from *The Nation* and teacups handpainted in 1900. Nor is there any answer to snapshots of one's grandfather as a young man on skis, surveying around Donner Pass in the year 1910. I smooth out the snapshot and look into his face, and do and do not see my own. I close the drawer, and have another cup of coffee with my mother. We get along very well, veterans of a guerrilla war we never understood.

Days pass. I see no one. I come to dread my husband's evening   4
call, not only because he is full of news of what by now seems to me our remote life in Los Angeles, people he has seen, letters which require attention, but because he asks what I have been doing, suggests uneasily that I get out, drive to San Francisco or Berkeley. Instead I drive across the river to a family graveyard. It has been vandalized since my last visit and the monuments are broken, overturned in the dry grass. Because I once saw a rattlesnake in the grass I stay in the car and listen to a country-and-Western station. Later I drive with my father to a ranch he has in the foothills. The man who runs his cattle on it asks us to the roundup, a week from Sunday, and although I know that I will be in Los Angeles I say, in the oblique way my family talks, that I will come. Once home I mention the broken monuments in the graveyard. My mother shrugs.

I go to visit my great-aunts. A few of them think now that I am   5
my cousin, or their daughter who died young. We recall an anecdote about a relative last seen in 1948, and they ask if I still like living in New York City. I have lived in Los Angeles for three years, but I say that I do. The baby is offered a horehound drop, and I am slipped a dollar bill "to buy a treat." Questions trail off, answers are abandoned, the baby plays with the dust motes in a shaft of afternoon sun.

It is time for the baby's birthday party: a white cake, strawberry-   6
marshmallow ice cream, a bottle of champagne saved from another party. In the evening, after she has gone to sleep, I kneel beside the

crib and touch her face, where it is pressed against the slats, with mine. She is an open and trusting child, unprepared for and unaccustomed to the ambushes of family life, and perhaps it is just as well that I can offer her little of that life. I would like to give her more. I would like to promise her that she will grow up with a sense of her cousins and of rivers and of her great-grandmother's teacups, would like to pledge her a picnic on a river with fried chicken and her hair uncombed, would like to give her *home* for her birthday, but we live differently now and I can promise her nothing like that. I give her a xylophone and a sundress from Madeira, and promise to tell her a funny story.

Writers on the Writing Process:
A Letter from E. B. White

In *a letter dated January 22, 1984, E. B. White responded as follows to questions from the editor about the composition of his "Once More to the Lake," an essay that has become a modern classic:*

I'm not an expert on what goes on under my hood, but I'll try to answer your questions.

When I wrote "Once More to the Lake," I was living year round in this place on the coast of Maine and contributing a monthly department to Harper's. I had spent many summers as a boy on Great Pond—one of the Belgrade Lakes. It's only about 75 miles from here and one day I felt an urge to revisit the lake and have a week of freshwater life, which is very different from saltwater. So I went over with my small son and we did some fishing. I simply started with a desire to see again and experience again what I had seen and experienced as a boy. During our stay over there, the "idea of time" naturally insinuated itself into my thoughts, because my son was the age *I* had been in the previous life at the lake, and so I felt a sort of mixed-up identity. I don't recall whether I had the title from the start. Probably not. I don't believe the title had anything to do with the composing process. The "process" is probably every bit as mysterious to me as it is to some of your students—if that will make them feel any better. As for the revising I did, it was probably quite a lot. I always revise the hell out of everything. It's the only way I know how to write. I came up with the "chilling ending" simply because I was describing a bodily sensation of my own. When my son drew on his wet bathing trunks, it was as though I were drawing them on myself. I was old enough to feel the chill of death. I guess.

Sorry I can't be more explicit. Writing, for me, is simply a matter of trying to find out and report what's going on in my head and get it down on paper. I haven't any devices, shortcuts, or tricks.

Glossary

ABSTRACT General, having to do with essences and ideas: Liberty, truth, and beauty are abstract concepts. Most writers depend upon abstractions to some degree; however, abstractions that are not fleshed out with vivid particulars are not likely to hold a reader's interest. See CONCRETE.

ALLUSION A passing reference, especially to a work of literature. When feminist Lindsy Van Gelder put forth the "modest proposal" that words of feminine gender be used whenever English traditionally uses masculine words, she had in mind Jonathan Swift's essay by that title (reprinted in "Essays for Further Reading"). This single brief reference carries the weight of Swift's entire essay behind it, humorously implying that the idea being advanced is about as modest as Swift's tongue-in-cheek proposal that Ireland eat its children as a ready food supply for a poor country. Allusions, therefore, are an efficient means of enlarging the scope and implications of a statement. They work best, of course, when they refer to works most readers are likely to know.

ANALOGY A comparison that reveals a primary object or event by likening it to a secondary one, often more familiar than the first. In expository writing, analogies are used as aids to explanation and as organizing devices. In a persuasive essay, the author may argue that what is true in one case is also true in the similar case that he is advancing. An argument "by analogy" is only as strong as the terms of the analogy are similar. For examples of analogies and a discussion of their kinship with metaphors, see the introduction to Chapter 7.

APPEAL TO EMOTION, TO ETHICS, and TO REASON See Modes of Persuasion.

ARGUMENTATION *See* Persuasion.

CAUSE AND EFFECT A strategy of exposition. Writing a cause and effect essay is much like constructing a persuasive argument; it is a form of reasoning that carries the reader step by step through a proof. Instead of "proving" the validity of the author's reasoning in order to move the reader to action, however, an essay in cause and effect is concerned with analyzing why an event occurred and with tracing its consequences. See the introduction to Chapter 4 for further discussion of this strategy.

CLASSIFICATION A strategy of exposition that places an object (or person) within a group of similar objects and then focuses on the characteristics distinguishing it from others in the group. Classification is a mode of organizing an essay as well as a means of obtaining knowledge. The introduction to Chapter 2 defines this strategy in detail.

CLICHÉ A tired expression that has lost its original power to surprise because of overuse: *We came in on a wing and a prayer; The quarterback turned the tables and saved the day.*

COMPARISON AND CONTRAST A strategy of expository writing that explores the similarities and differences between two persons, places, things, or ideas. It differs from description in that it makes statements or propositions about its subjects. The introduction to Chapter 6 defines this kind of expository essay in some detail.

CONCRETE Definite, particular, capable of being perceived directly. Opposed to *abstract. Rose, Mississippi, pinch* are more concrete words than *flower, river, touch.* Five-miles-per-hour is a more concrete idea than slowness. It is a good practice, as a rule, to make your essays as concrete as possible, even when you are writing on a general topic. For example, if you are defining an ideal wife or husband, cite specific wives or husbands you have known or heard about.

CONNOTATIONS The implied meanings of a word; its overtones and associations over and above its literal, dictionary meaning. The strict meaning of *home,* for example, is "the place where one lives"; but the word connotes comfort, security, and love. The first word in each of the following pairs is the more neutral word; the second carries richer connotations: *like/adore; clothes/garb; fast/fleet; shy/coy; stout/obese; move about/skulk; interested/obsessed.* See DENOTATION.

DEDUCTION A form of logical reasoning or explaining that proceeds from general premises to specific conclusions. For example, from the general premises that all men are mortal and that Socrates is a man, we can deduce that Socrates is mortal. See the introduction to Chapter 9 for more examples.

DEDUCTIVE *See* Deduction.

DEFINITION A basic strategy of expository writing. Definitions set forth the essential meaning or properties of a thing or idea. "Extended" definitions enlarge upon that basic meaning by analyzing the qualities, recalling the history, explaining the purpose, or giving synonyms of whatever is being defined. Extended definitions often draw upon such other strategies of exposition as classification, comparison and contrast, and process analysis. See the introduction to Chapter 5 for a full treatment of definition.

DENOTATION The basic dictionary meaning of a word without any of its associated meanings. The denotation of *home*, for example, is simply "the place where one lives." *See* Connotations.

DESCRIPTION One of the four traditional modes of discourse. Description appeals to the senses: it tells how a person, place, thing, or idea looks, feels, sounds, smells, or tastes. "Scientific" description reports these qualities; "evocative" description recreates them. See the introduction to Chapter 8 for an extended definition of the descriptive mode.

DICTION Word choice. Mark Twain was talking about diction when he said that the difference between the almost right word and the right word is the difference "between the lightning bug and the lightning." "Standard" diction is defined by dictionaries and other authorities as the language that educated native speakers of English use in their formal writing. Some other *Levels of Diction* are as follows; when you find one of these labels attached to words or phrases in your dictionary, avoid them in your own formal writing:

Nonstandard: Words like *ain't* that would never be used by an educated speaker who was trying to impress a stranger.

Informal (or *Colloquial*): The language of conversation among those who write standard edited English. *I am crazy about you, Virginia*, is informal rather than nonstandard.

Slang: Either the figurative language of a specialized group (*moll, gat, heist*) or fashionable coined words (*boondoggle, weirdo*) and extended meanings (*dead soldier* for an empty bottle; *garbage* for nonsense). Slang words often pass quickly into standard English or just as quickly fade away.

Obsolete: Terms like *pantaloons* and *palfrey* (saddle horse) that were once standard but are no longer used.

Regional (or *Dialectal*): For example, *remuda*, meaning a herd of riding horses, is used only in the Southwest.

ETYMOLOGY A word history or the practice of tracing such histories. The modern English word *march*, for example, is derived from the French *marcher* ("to walk"), which in turn is derived from the Latin word *marcus* ("a hammer"). The etymological definition of *march* is thus "to walk with a measured tread, like the rhythmic pounding of a hammer." In most dictionaries, the derivation, or etymology, of a word is explained in parentheses or brackets before the first definition is given.

EXPOSITION One of the four modes of discourse. Expository writing is informative writing. It explains or gives directions. All the items in this glossary are written in the expository mode; and most of the practical prose that you write in the coming years will be—e.g., papers and examinations, job applications, business reports, insurance claims, your last will and testament. See the Introduction for a discussion of how exposition is related to the other modes of discourse.

EXPOSITORY *See* Exposition.

FIGURES OF SPEECH Colorful words and phrases used in a nonliteral sense. Some of the most common figures of speech are:

Simile: A stated comparison, usually with *like* or *as:* He stood *like a rock.*

Metaphor: A comparison that equates two objects without the use of a stated connecting word: *Throughout the battle, Sergeant Phillips was a rock.*

Metonymy: The use of one word or name in place of another commonly associated with it. *The White House* [for the president] *awarded the sergeant a medal.*

Personification: Assigning human traits to nonhuman objects: *The very walls have ears.*

Hyperbole: Conscious exaggeration: *The mountain reached to the sky.*

Understatement: The opposite of hyperbole, a conscious playing down: *After forty days of climbing the mountain, we felt that we had made a start.*

Rhetorical Question: A question to which the author either expects no answer or answers himself: *Why climb the mountain? Because it is there.*

HYPERBOLE Exaggeration. *See* Figures of Speech.

INDUCTION A form of logical reasoning or explaining that proceeds from specific examples to general principles. As a rule, an inductive argument is only as valid as its examples are representative. See the introduction to Chapter 9.

INDUCTIVE *See* Induction.

IRONY An ironic statement implies a way of looking at the subject that is different (not necessarily opposite) from the stated way. For example, when Russell Baker writes in "A Nice Place to Visit" (Chapter 6) that Toronto "seems hopelessly bogged down in civilization," what he implies is that New Yorkers define "civilization" in an uncivilized way. His apparent attack on Canadian manners is really a swipe at American ill-manneredness. We should be bogged down in such crudity, he is saying. Irony of situation, as opposed to *verbal* irony, occurs when events in real life or in a narrative turn out differently than the characters or people had expected. It was ironic that Hitler, with his dream of world domination, committed suicide in the end.

METAPHOR A direct comparison that identifies one thing with another. *See* Figures of Speech.

MODES OF DISCOURSE Means or forms of writing or speaking. The four traditional modes of discourse are Narration, Exposition, Description, and Persuasion. This book is organized around these four modes. Chapter 1 gives examples of narration. Exposition is explained in Chapters 2–7; description, in Chapter 8; and persuasion (and argumentation), in Chapters 9 and 10.

MODES OF PERSUASION There are three traditional modes (or means) of persuading an audience to action or belief: the appeal to reason, the appeal to emotion, and the appeal to ethics. When applying the first of these, a writer convinces the reader by the force of logic; he or she constructs an argument which the reader finds to be correct or valid. When appealing to emotion, the writer tries to excite in the reader the same emotions the writer felt upon first considering the proposition he or she is advancing or some other emotion that will dispose the reader to accept that proposition. The appeal to ethics is an appeal to the reader's sense of what constitutes upright behavior. The writer convinces the reader that the writer is a good person who deserves to be heeded because of his or her admirable character. See the introductions to Chapters 9 and 10 for detailed discussions of these three modes.

NARRATION One of the four traditional modes of discourse. An accounting of actions and events that have befallen someone or something. Because narration is essentially story-telling, it is the mode most often used in fiction; however, it is also an important element in nonfictional writing and speaking. The opening of Lincoln's Gettysburg Address, for example, is in the narrative mode: "Fourscore and seven years ago our fathers brought forth on this continent a new nation. . . ."

PERSON The aspect of grammar that describes the person speaking, spoken to, or spoken about in a sentence or paragraph. There are three persons: first (I or we), second (you), and third (he, she, it, and they). *See also* Point of View.

PERSONIFICATION Attributing human characteristics to the nonhuman. *See* Figures of Speech.

PERSUASION The art of moving an audience to action or belief. According to traditional definitions, a writer can persuade a reader in one of three ways: by appealing to his or her reason, emotions, or sense of ethics. (*See* Modes of Persuasion.) *Argumentation*, as the term is understood in this book, is the form of persuasion that emphasizes the first of these appeals. An argument may be more concerned with pursuing a line of reasoning or stating the issued raised by a problem than with inciting someone to action. Nevertheless, an argument must persuade us that what it says is not only true but worthwhile; it must move us to believe if not to act. For a full explanation of persuasion and argumentation, see the introductions to Chapters 9 and 10.

PERSUASIVE ARGUMENT *See* Persuasion.

PLOT An aspect of narrative. Plot is the sequence of events in a story. It therefore has to do with actions rather than ideas.

POINT OF VIEW The vantage from which a story is told or an account given. Point of view is often described according to the grammatical person of a narrative. An "I" narrative, for example, is told from the "first person" point of view. A narrative that refers to "he" or "she" is told from the "third person" point of view. If the speaker of a third-person narrative seems to know everything about his or her subject, including their thoughts, the point of view is also "omniscient"; if the speaker's knowledge is incomplete, the point of view is third-person "limited." Sometimes point of view is described simply by characterizing the speaker of an essay. David E. Dubber's "Crossing the Bar on a Fiberglas Pole," for example, is told from the point of view of a dedicated college athlete as he arches over the horizontal bar in a pole-vaulting competition.

PROCESS ANALYSIS A form of expository writing that breaks a process into its component operations or that gives directions. Most "How To" essays are essays in process analysis: how to grow cotton; how to operate a fork lift; how to avoid shark bite. Process analyses are usually divided into stages or steps arranged in chronological order. They differ from narratives in that they tell *how* something functions rather than *what* happens to something or someone. See the introduction to Chapter 3 for further discussion of this expository technique.

RHETORIC The art of using language effectively in speech and in writing. The term originally belonged to oratory, and it implies the presence of both a speaker (or writer) and a listener (or reader). This book is a collection of the rhetorical techniques and strategies that some successful writers have found helpful for communicating effectively with an audience.

RHETORICAL QUESTION A question that is really a statement. *See* Figures of Speech.

SATIRE A form of writing that attacks a person or practice in hopes of improving either. For example, in "A Modest Proposal" ("Essays For Further Reading"), Jonathan Swift satirizes the materialism that had reduced his native Ireland to extreme poverty. His intent was to point out the greed of even his poorest countrymen and thereby shame them all into looking out for the public welfare instead of exploiting the country's last resources. This desire to correct vices and follies distinguishes *satire* from *sarcasm*, which is intended primarily to wound. *See also* Irony.

SATIRIZE *See* Satire.

SIMILE A comparison that likens one thing to another. *See* Figures of Speech.

SLANG Popular language that often originates in the speech of a particular group or subculture. *See* Diction.

SYNTAX The interrelationship among words. In the sentence, *The police chased the woman who had beaten her dog,* the phrase *the woman who had beaten her dog* is the "direct object." This term describes the syntax of the phrase because it defines the function of the phrase within the context of the entire sentence. In a larger sense, syntax refers to the total network of relationships, including meanings, among words in a discourse.

TENSE The time aspect of verbs. In the sentence, *He took the money and ran,* the past-tense forms indicate that the taking and running occurred at an earlier time than the writer's telling about those actions. There are six basic tenses in English: past, present, future, and the perfect forms of these three: past perfect, present perfect, and future perfect. (Here "perfect" means completed. An action in the future perfect—*He will have left,* for example— will be completed in the future before another stated future action: *He will have left before the police arrive.*) In writing, it is a good idea not to switch tenses unnecessarily. If you start an essay in the past tense, stick to that tense unless the sense of your remarks requires a change: *He took the money, but the police will catch him.*

TONE An author's revealed attitude toward his subject or audience: sympathy, longing, amusement, shock, sarcasm—the range is endless. When analyzing the tone of a passage, consider what quality of a voice you should assume for reading it aloud. William Allen's essay on broom-balancing ("How to Set a World Record," Chapter 3), for example, should be read with a suppressed snicker, as he says.

TOPIC SENTENCE The sentence in a paragraph that comes closest to stating the topic of the paragraph as a whole. The topic sentence is often the first sentence, but it may appear anywhere in the paragraph. Some paragraphs do not have clear-cut topic sentences, especially if they function chiefly to link preceding paragraphs with those to follow.

TRANSITION The act of passing from one topic (or aspect of a topic) to another; the word, phrase, sentence, or paragraph that accomplishes such a passage. For an excellent example, see paragraph 5 of Alexander Petrunkevitch's "The Spider and the Wasp" in Chapter 3. Polished transitions are necessary if an essay is to be carefully organized and developed.

UNDERSTATEMENT A verbal playing down or softening for humorous or ironic effect. *See* Figures of Speech.

Acknowledgements

Deairich Hunter: "Ducks vs. Hard Rocks," *Newsweek* August 18, 1980. Copyright 1980 by Newsweek, Inc. All rights reserved. Reprinted by permission.

Sam Keen: "The Faces of the Enemy" (as it appeared in *Esquire*, copyright © 1984 by Sam Keen) from *The Faces of the Enemy* by Sam Keen and Ann Page, published by Harper & Row, 1985. Reprinted by permission of Harper & Row, Publishers, Inc.

Garrison Keillor: "Attitude" from *Happy to Be Here*. Copyright © 1982 by Garrison Keillor. Reprinted with the permission of Atheneum Publishers.

Katie Kelly: "Garbage," *Saturday Review* September 9, 1972 © 1972. Saturday Review Magazine Co. Reprinted by permission.

William Least Heat Moon: Chapter 5 from *Blue Highways* (Boston, Little Brown & Company, 1982). Copyright © 1982 by William Least Heat Moon.

Barry Lopez: "My Horse." First appeared in *The North American Review*, Summer 1975. Copyright © 1975 University of Northern Iowa. "Writers on the Writing Process: Barry Lopez" Copyright © 1985 by Barry Lopez.

Colman McCarthy: "Phasing Out Campus Idealism," *The Washington Post*, December 4, 1983. © 1983, The Washington Post Company. Reprinted with permission.

Joyce Maynard: "Four Generations." Copyright © 1979 by Joyce Maynard. From *The New York Times*, April 12, 1979.

Howard Means: "The Terror and the Honor at University of Virginia," *The Washington Post* August 16, 1981. © The Washington Post.

Martha T. Mednick and Nancy Felipe Russo: "The Sexes Are Not Born with Different Brains" from *The Washington Post* August 5, 1979. Reprinted with permission of the authors.

Horace Miner: "Body Ritual among the Nacirema" reproduced by permission of the American Anthropological Association from *American Anthropologist* 58: 503–507, 1956.

Johnson C. Montgomery: "The Island of Plenty," copyright 1974 by Newsweek, Inc. All rights reserved. Reprinted by permission.

Desmond Morris: Excerpted from *Manwatching: A Field Guide to Human Behavior* by Desmond Morris. Text Copyright © 1977 by Desmond Morris. Compilation Copyright © 1977 by Elsevier Publishing Projects SA, Lausanne, and Jonathan Cape Ltd. London. Published by Harry N. Abrams, Inc., New York, N.Y. All rights reserved.

George Orwell: "Politics and the English Language" from *Shooting An Elephant and Other Essays* by George Orwell, copyright 1945, 1946, 1949, 1950 by Sonia Pitt-Rivers. Reprinted by permission of Harcourt Brace Jovanovich, Inc., the estate of the late Sonia Brownwell Orwell and Martin Secker & Warburg Ltd.

Charles Panati: "Nature's Building Blocks" from *Breakthroughs* by Charles Panati. Copyright © 1980 by Charles Panati. Reprinted by permission of Houghton Mifflin Company.

Alexander Petrunkevitch: "The Spider and the Wasp," *Scientific American* August 1952. Reprinted with permission. Copyright © 1952 by Scientific American, Inc. All rights reserved.

Fred Reed: "A Veteran Writes," copyright © 1980 by Harper's Magazine. All rights reserved. Reprinted from the December 1980 issue by special permission.

Richard M. Restak: excerpt from *The Brain: The Last Frontier* by Richard M. Restak. Copyright © 1979 by Richard M. Restak. Reprinted by permission of Doubleday & Company, Inc.

Jeremy Rifkin: excerpt from *Entropy: A New World View* by Jeremy Rifkin. Copyright © 1980 by the Foundation on Economic Trends. Reprinted by permission of Viking Penguin Inc.

Richard Selzer: "The Discus Thrower" from *Confessions of a Knife* by Richard Selzer. Copyright © 1979 by David Goodman and Janet Selzer, Trustees. Reprinted by permission of Simon & Schuster, Inc.

James Seilsopour: "I Forgot the Words to the National Anthem" by James M. Seilsopour was awarded a Bedford Prize in Student Writing in 1983. Reprinted from *Student Writers at Work: The Bedford Prizes*, edited by Nancy Sommers and Donald McQuade. Copyright © 1984 by St. Martin's Press, Inc. Reprinted with permission of the publisher.

Lewis Thomas: "On Societies as Organisms" from *The Lives of a Cell* by Lewis Thomas. Copyright © 1971 by the Massachusetts Medical Society. Originally published in *The New England Journal of Medicine*. Reprinted by permission of Viking Penguin Inc.

Susan Allen Toth: "Cinematypes," copyright © 1980 by Harper's Magazine. All rights reserved. Reprinted from the May 1980 issue by special permission

Calvin Trillin: "Literally." Copyright © 1982 by Calvin Trillin. From *Uncivil Liberties*, published by Ticknor & Fields. Originally appeared in *The Nation*.

Frank Trippett: "The Great American Cooling Machine." Copyright 1979 Time Inc. All rights reserved. Reprinted by permission from *Time*.

Roger Verhulst: "Being Prepared in Suburbia." Copyright 1976 by Newsweek, Inc. All rights reserved. Reprinted by permission.

E. B. White: "Once More to the Lake" from *Essays of E. B. White*. Copyright 1941, 1969 by E. B. White. Reprinted by permission of Harper and Row, Publishers, Inc.

George Will: "Why Not Use Food as Food?," *The Washington Post* September 25, 1983. © The Washington Post.

Ellen Willis: "Memoirs of a Non-Prom Queen," copyright © 1976 by Rolling Stone. Reprinted by permission of Ellen Willis.

Virginia Woolf: "The Death of the Moth," from *The Death of the Moth and Other Essays* by Virginia Woolf. Copyright © 1942 by Harcourt Brace Jovanovich, Inc.; copyright © 1970 by Marjorie T. Parsons, Executrix, the Author's Literary Estate and the Hogarth Press. Reprinted by permission of the publishers.

5. The realization that our enemies reside in a part of ourselves that we are forever seeking to hide may seem to hold faint promise for alleviating the constant warfare of the human race, but "Faces of the Enemy" nevertheless finds reason for optimism in our tendency to create "enemies" in our own buried images. What is that reason?

Strategies and Structure

1. DEFINITION (see Chapter 5) identifies the common distinguishing features of an entire class: *Wine is an intoxicating drink made from grapes.* Classification identifies the features that distinguish individual items in a class from others in the same class: *This is a glass of red wine; that is a glass of white.* Division separates a whole class into subclasses by identifying the distinguishing features of each subclass: *There are three kinds of wine: red, white, and pink.* Which of these closely related mental processes, would you say, is Keen predominantly engaged in here? Explain your answer.

2. In paragraph 4, which sentence flatly states the author's larger purpose for identifying the various faces we impose upon our "enemies"?

3. In which paragraph does Keen begin the actual business of classification and division? How does he signal that an extended treatment is coming?

4. In the last four paragraphs of "Faces of the Enemy," the author is no longer engaged in a form of classifying. What is his immediate purpose here?

5. Paragraph 4 of Keen's essay is a clear example of a writer's anticipating objections to his thesis. Why is this often a good strategy? How and how successfully do you think the author here defuses the argument that "there are real aggressors" (par. 3)?

6. Why do you think Keen ends his essay on an optimistic note? Is this a good strategy in your opinion?

Words and Figures of Speech

1. How effective do you find the "fire-and-ice" metaphor of paragraph 1? What is Keen comparing to fire? to ice?

2. In the language of psychology, what is the meaning of the term *neurosis* (par. 17)? To which particular neurosis does Keen ascribe humankind's tendency to invent enemies? In what paragraph does he name it?